A2-Level Economics

This book contains everything you'll need to score top marks in your A2 Economics exams (it covers every Unit for AQA, Edexcel and OCR).

There are clear, concise notes for each topic, plus plenty of warm-up and exam-style questions to test your knowledge and understanding.

It even includes a free Online Edition you can read on your computer or tablet!

How to get your free Online Edition

Go to **cgpbooks.co.uk/extras** and enter this code...

3083 0433 9471 0687

This code only works for one person. If somebody else has used this book before you, they might have already claimed the Online Edition.

A-Level revision? It has to be CGP!

Published by CGP

Editors:
David Broadbent, Chris Lindle, Kirstie McHale, Sarah Oxley, Andy Park.

Contributors:
John Grant, Alison Hazell, Samantha Uppal.

Proofreaders:
Glenn Rogers, Victoria Skelton.

ISBN: 978 1 78294 147 7

With thanks to Jane Hosking for the reviewing.

With thanks to Laura Jakubowski for the copyright research.

This book includes data adapted from the Office for National Statistics licensed under the Open Government Licence v.2.0.

Data on page 54 regarding the structure of employment from databank.worldbank.org International Labour Organization, Key Indicators of the Labour Market database

Gender Pay Gap data on page 54 from Tackling the gender pay gap in the European Union report © European Union, 2014

Data on pages 82, 84, 85 and 86 regarding transport use, prices and subsidies from the Department of Transport © Crown Copyright used under the terms of the Open Government Licence https://www.nationalarchives.gov.uk/doc/open-government-licence/version/2/

Clipart from Corel®

Printed by Elanders Ltd, Newcastle upon Tyne.

Based on the classic CGP style created by Richard Parsons.

Contents

Each topic's intro will tell you which units it's relevant to. This is where you'll find the relevant topics for each unit.

- *For **AQA Unit 3** see Sections 1, 2, 3 and 4*
- *For **AQA Unit 4** see Sections 7, 8 and 9*
- *For **Edexcel Unit 3** see Sections 1, 2 and 3*
- *For **Edexcel Unit 4** see Sections 3, 7, 8 and 9*
- *For **OCR Unit 3 (Work and Leisure)** see Sections 1, 2, 3, 4 and 5*
- *For **OCR Unit 4 (Transport)** see Sections 1, 2, 3, 5 and 6*
- *For **OCR Unit 5 (The Global Economy)** see Sections 7, 8 and 9*

The Costs of a Firm

These pages are for AQA Unit 3, Edexcel Unit 3 and OCR Unit 3 (Work and Leisure) and Unit 4 (Transport Economics).
A firm could be anything from a dog-walking business to a giant multinational like an oil or technology company. What all firms have in common is that they sell goods or services to try to make profit.

Firms combine **Factors of Production** to produce an **Output**

1) A firm is any sort of **business organisation**, like a family-run factory, a dental practice or a supermarket chain.
2) An **industry** is all the firms providing **similar** goods or services.
3) A **market** contains all the firms **supplying** a particular good or service **and** the firms or people **buying** it.
4) Firms generate **revenue** (money coming in) by **selling** their **output** (goods or services).
5) Producing this output uses **factors of production** (land, labour, capital and enterprise), and this has a **cost**.
6) The **profit** a firm makes is **its total revenue minus its total costs**.
7) In the **long run** firms need to make profit to **survive**.

Revenue and profit are explained properly later in the section.

Economists include **Opportunity Cost** in the **Cost** of **Production**

1) When economists talk about the **cost of production** they are referring to the **economic cost** of producing the output.
2) The economic cost includes the **money cost** of factors of production that have to be paid for, but it also includes the **opportunity cost** of the factors that aren't paid for (e.g. a home office that a business is run from).
3) The **opportunity cost** of a factor of production is the **money that you could have got** by putting it to its **next best use**. E.g. if you run your own business the money you **could earn** doing other work is the opportunity cost of your **labour**.
4) So, in economics, cost isn't just a calculation of money spent — it takes into account **all** of the effort and resources that have gone into production.

In the **Short Run** some **Costs** are **Fixed**

1) The **short run** is the period of time when **at least one** of a firm's factors of production is **fixed**.
2) The short run isn't a specific length of time — it **varies from firm to firm**. For example, the short run of a **cycle courier** service could be **a week** because it can hire new staff with their own bikes quickly, but a **steel manufacturer** might have a short run of **several years** because it takes lots of time and money to build a new steel-manufacturing plant.
3) The **long run** is the period of time when **all factors of production** can be **varied**.
4) Costs can be **fixed** or **variable** in the short run:

FIXED COSTS
- Fixed costs **don't vary with output** in the **short run** — they have to be paid whether or not anything is produced.
- For example, the **rent on a shop** is a fixed cost — it's **the same** no matter what the sales are.

VARIABLE COSTS
- Variable costs **do vary with output** — they increase as output increases.
- The cost of the **plastic bags** that a shop gives to customers is a variable cost — the **higher sales** are the **higher the overall cost** of the bags.

5) In the **long run all costs** are **variable**.

Total Cost and **Average Cost** include **Fixed Costs** and **Variable Costs**

Total cost (TC) is **all the costs** involved in producing a particular **level of output**.

The **total cost** for a particular output level is the **fixed costs** plus the **variable costs** for that **output level**.

Average cost (AC) is the **cost per unit produced**.

Average cost (AC) is calculated by **dividing** total costs by the **quantity** produced. It's also called average total cost (ATC).
Average fixed cost (AFC) = total fixed costs ÷ **quantity** produced.
Average variable cost (AVC) = total variable costs ÷ **quantity** produced.

The Costs of a Firm

Marginal Cost is the cost of **Increasing Output** by **One Unit**

Marginal cost (MC) is the **extra cost** incurred as a result of producing **the final** unit of output.

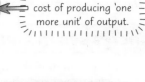

Or think of it as the cost of producing 'one more unit' of output.

Marginal cost is only affected by **variable costs** — fixed costs have to be paid even if **nothing** is produced. You can calculate it by finding the **difference** between total cost at the current output level and total cost at one unit **less**.

Output	Total Fixed Costs (£)	Total Variable Costs (£)	Total Cost (£)	Average Cost (£)	Average Fixed Cost (£)	Average Variable Cost (£)	Marginal Cost (£)
0	60	—	60	—	—	—	—
1	60	70	130	130	60	70	70
2	60	120	180	90	30	60	50
3	60	180	240	80	20	60	60
4	60	260	320	80	15	65	80
5	60	360	420	84	12	72	100
			60 + 360	420 ÷ 5	60 ÷ 5	360 ÷ 5	420 – 320

Rob had just broken it to Emma that they were going to have to cut back on dairy-free spread — margarinal cost was getting out of hand.

Lowest Average Cost occurs when **Marginal Cost** equals **Average Cost**

1) Marginal cost (MC) **decreases initially** as output increases, then begins to **increase** in the short run because of the **law of diminishing returns**. (This is explained on page 6.)
2) So the **MC curve** is always **u-shaped**.
3) Changes in marginal cost affect average cost:

- When the marginal cost is **lower** than the average cost (AC), the average cost will be **falling**. This is because each extra unit produced will **decrease** the average cost (adding something smaller than the average will decrease the average).
- When the marginal cost is **higher** than the average cost (AC), the average cost will be **rising** because each extra unit produced will **increase** the average cost.
- So the marginal cost curve meets the average cost curve at the lowest average cost, i.e. **average cost** will be **lowest** when **MC = AC** — this is the point of **productive efficiency** (covered at AS — and see p.22).

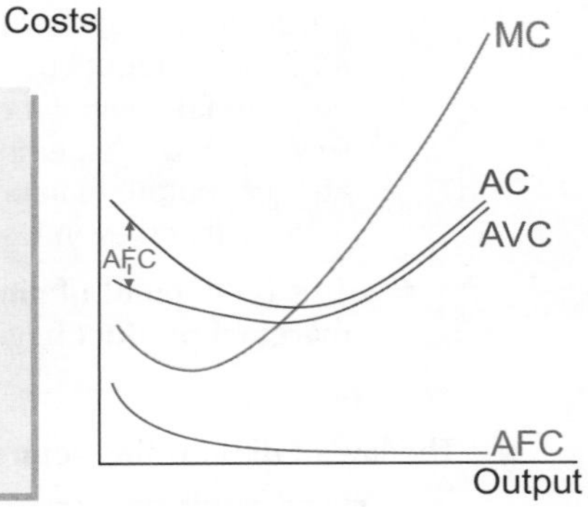

4) The MC curve also **meets** the AVC curve at the **minimum AVC**. (Marginal cost is made up of **variable costs**, so it increases and decreases AVC in the same way it does AC.)
5) This means AVC and AC curves also **always** form a **u-shape** in the **short run** — they both decrease until they reach a minimum, then begin to increase.
6) AFC (average fixed cost) **falls as output rises** because the total fixed cost is **spread** across the greater output.

Practice Questions

Q1 What are fixed costs?

Q2 Where does the marginal cost curve meet the average cost curve?

Exam Question

Q1 Firm X and Firm Y are producing the same product at the same output level and have the same variable costs. The fixed costs of Firm X are double the fixed costs of Firm Y. Firm X and Firm Y have the same:
A) average cost B) average fixed cost C) marginal cost D) fixed costs E) total costs
Explain your answer. [4 marks]

Chat-up lines for economists #23 — "I'm a big fan of you-shaped curves"...

There are loads of terms on these pages you need to know — make sure you've got the hang of the terminology first. It's also really important to understand the relationship between marginal cost and average cost — the average cost curve falls when marginal cost is below it, and rises when marginal cost is above it. The marginal cost doesn't have to be falling for the average cost to fall.

The Law of Diminishing Returns

***These pages are for** AQA Unit 3 **and** Edexcel Unit 3.*
Firms can increase their output by adding more of their factors of production (e.g. getting more staff). In the long run they can add more of all of their factors of production. But in the short run only some factors can be increased, while others stay fixed. The short run effect of changing only some factors is explained by the law of diminishing returns.

Increases in Output are Limited by Diminishing Returns in the Short Run

1) The **law of diminishing returns** explains what happens when a **variable factor** of production **increases** while other factors stay fixed. Because at least one factor stays **fixed**, the law of diminishing returns only applies in the **short run**.
2) When you increase **one factor** of production by **one unit**, but keep the others **fixed**, the **extra output** you get is called the **marginal product**. E.g. if you add one more unit of labour, the extra output is the **marginal product of labour**.

Marginal product (MP) is the **additional output** produced by adding **one more unit** of a **factor input** (i.e. by adding one more unit of any of the **factors of production** being used).

Another term for marginal product is marginal returns.

- Initially, as you **add more** of a factor of production the **marginal product** will increase — each unit of input added will **add more** output than the one before.
- This might happen because more **specialisation** is possible with more of a particular factor. As more **people** are employed, for example, they can specialise in carrying out particular tasks.
- Eventually, if you **keep adding** units of **one factor** of production, the other **fixed factors** will begin to **limit** the additional output you get, and the marginal product will begin to **fall**. E.g. if a clothes manufacturer only has 5 sewing machines, employing a 6th machinist will probably add less output than employing the 5th did, and employing a 7th will add even less.
- This is the **point of diminishing returns** — the point where **marginal product** begins to **decrease** as input increases.

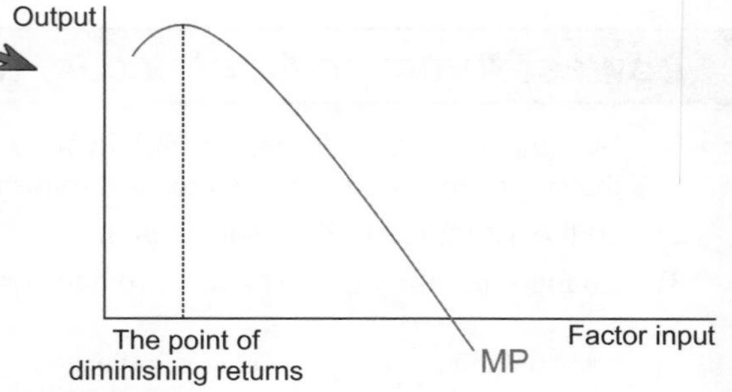

3) The **law of diminishing returns** says that there is always a point where marginal product begins to decrease.

THE LAW OF DIMINISHING RETURNS

If **one variable factor** of production is **increased** while **other factors** stay **fixed**, eventually the **marginal returns** from the variable factor will begin to **decrease**.

This is also called the law of diminishing marginal returns, or the law of variable proportions.

Andy's serves had really improved lately — he'd reached the point of diminishing returns.

Diminishing Marginal Returns increase Marginal Cost

1) **Marginal returns** (or marginal product, MP) are related to **marginal cost** (MC) — as shown in the diagram.
   - As marginal returns **rise**, marginal cost **falls**.
   - As marginal returns **fall**, marginal cost **rises**.

   The marginal cost curve is the mirror image of the marginal product curve.
2) Marginal cost will rise as marginal returns fall because, all other things being equal, if you're getting **less additional output** from each **unit of input** then the cost per unit of that output will be greater.

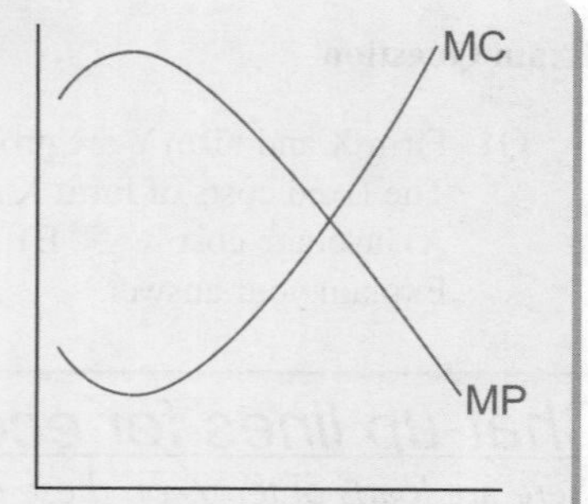

The Law of Diminishing Returns

AQA ONLY

Diminishing Marginal Returns eventually cause Productivity to Fall

1) The law of diminishing returns says that as the level of a variable factor input is increased, **marginal product** (or **marginal returns**) will eventually begin to diminish.
2) As the level of that factor input continues to be increased, the **average product** will eventually start to fall too, as shown on the right. The MP curve always meets the AP curve when the AP curve is at its **maximum**.

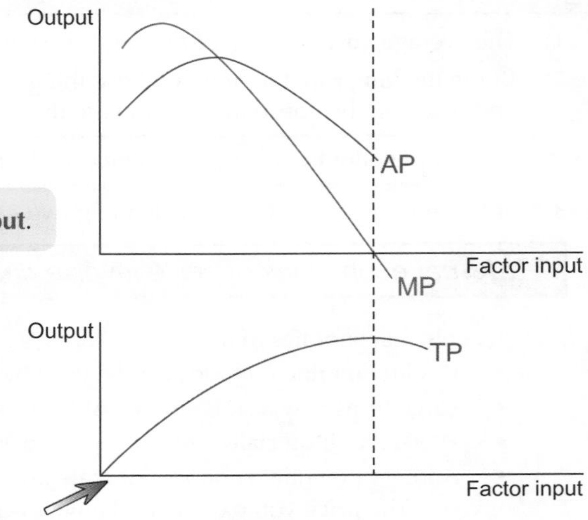

Average product (AP) is the **output** produced **per unit** of **factor input**.

3) The average product is also known as **productivity**. For example, if the variable factor is labour, the **labour productivity** would be the average output **per worker** (or **per worker-hour**).

You might have met productivity at AS level.

So if a firm employs more and more people, it will eventually find that the **productivity** of those employees falls.

4) If you then keep adding more of the variable factor, you can even reach a stage where **adding further input** results in a **fall** in the **total product** — e.g. because workers start getting in each other's way.

This happens when the marginal product becomes negative.

Total product (TP) is the **total output** produced using a particular combination of factor inputs.

See p.4-5 for more about marginal and average curves.

Productivity can be improved in various ways

1) There are various ways to increase **labour productivity** — for example, through **better training** or **better management**.
2) Improved **technology** can also help improve productivity — faster computers could allow employees to achieve more during their working day, for example.
3) Increasing productivity will allow a firm to **reduce** its **costs** of production.

Improved technology might also allow a firm to track its costs and productivity more accurately, meaning it can see when it's encountering the point of diminishing returns, for example.

Practice Questions

Q1 What is the marginal product?

Q2 Does the law of diminishing returns apply in the long run or the short run?

Q3 If a firm is experiencing diminishing returns, will its total output always be falling?

Exam Question

Q1 The marginal cost curve of a firm is shown on the right.

a) Explain the shape of the curve between A and B. [3 marks]

b) Explain the shape of the curve between B and C. [3 marks]

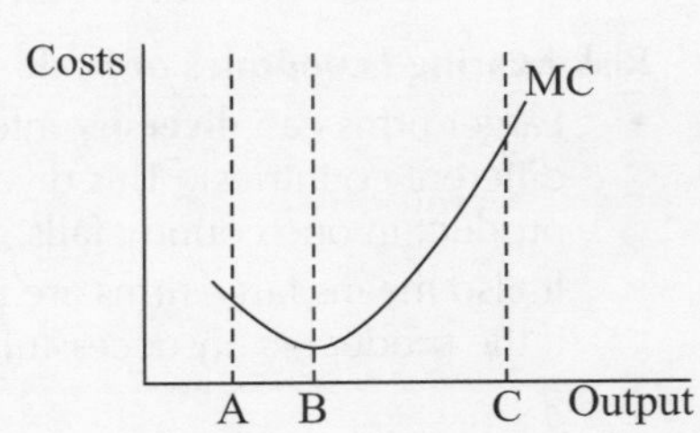

I fought the law of diminishing returns — and the law eventually won...

The key things to remember here are that diminishing returns only happen in the short run, and they don't have to mean decreasing output. It's pretty straightforward really — in the short run at least one factor of production stays fixed, so increasing input of other factors will eventually lead to diminishing returns, which will mean an increase in marginal cost.

Economies and Diseconomies of Scale

These pages are for AQA Unit 3, Edexcel Unit 3 and OCR Unit 3 (Work and Leisure) and Unit 4 (Transport Economics).
In the long run firms can increase their scale of production by increasing all of their factors of production.

Economies of Scale can be Internal or External

1) The **average cost** to a firm of making something is usually quite high if they **don't** make very many of them.
2) But in the **long run**, the more of those things the firm makes, the more the average cost of making each one **falls**. These falls in the cost of production are due to **economies of scale**.

See the long run average cost curve on p 10.

Economies of scale — the cost advantages of production on a large scale.

3) Economies of scale can be divided into two categories — **internal** and **external**.

Internal economies of scale involve changes Within a firm

Technical Economies of Scale
- **Production line** methods can be used by large firms to make a lot of things at a very low average cost.
- Large firms may also be more able to purchase other **specialised equipment** to help reduce average costs.
- Workers can **specialise**, becoming more efficient at the tasks they carry out, which might not be possible in a small firm.
- Another potential economy of scale arises from the **law of increased dimensions**. For example:
  - The **price** you pay to build a new warehouse might be closely related to the **total area of the walls and roof**, say.
  - If you make the dimensions of the walls and roof **twice as big**, the total **area** of the walls and roof will be **4 times greater** — so the warehouse will **cost about 4 times as much** to build.
  - But the **volume** of the warehouse will be **8 times greater**, meaning that you're getting more storage space for each pound you spend.
  - The same is true of things like **oil tankers** — e.g. bigger tankers reduce the cost of transporting each unit of oil.

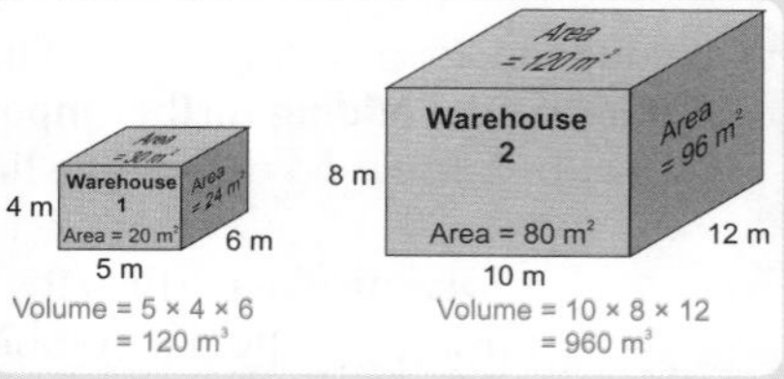

Purchasing Economies of Scale
- **Large firms** making lots of goods will need **larger quantities** of raw materials, and so can often **negotiate discounts** with suppliers.
- This isn't just the large firm driving a hard bargain — **suppliers' costs** are lower if they deliver **larger amounts** of goods.
- This table shows the general idea — the **cost per unit** to the supplier changes massively (since the **supplier's delivery costs** hardly increase when the order size **doubles**).

	Half load (50 units)	Full load (100 units)
Fuel	£50	£60
Driver costs	£100	£100
Tax / wear and tear	£20	£20
Total	£170	£180
Cost per unit	£3.40	£1.80

Managerial Economies of Scale
- **Large firms** will be able to employ **specialist** managers to take care of different areas of the business (e.g. finance, production, customer service). These specialist managers gain **expertise** and **experience** in a specific area of the business, which usually leads to better **decision-making** abilities in that area.
- And the number of managers a firm needs **doesn't** usually depend directly on the production scale — a firm probably won't need twice as many managers to produce twice as many goods. This **reduces** the management cost per unit.

Financial Economies of Scale
- Larger firms can often **borrow money** at a **lower** rate of **interest** — lending to them is seen by banks as less risky.

Risk-bearing Economies of Scale
- Larger firms can **diversify** into different **product areas** (e.g. make different things) and different **markets** (e.g. sell in different countries). This diversification leads to a **more predictable overall demand** — basically, if demand for one product in one country falls, there's likely to be a different product whose demand somewhere increases.
- It also means large firms are more able to take **risks** (e.g. by launching products that may or may not prove popular). If the product is unsuccessful, a large firm's other activities allow it to **absorb** the cost of **failure** more easily.

Marketing Economies of Scale
- **Advertising** is usually a **fixed cost** — this is spread over more units for large firms, so the cost **per unit** is lower.
- The **cost per product** of advertising several products may also be **lower** than the cost of advertising just one, e.g. a firm could advertise several products on a single flyer.
- Larger firms also benefit from **brand awareness** — products from a well-known brand will be **trusted** by consumers. This might mean a larger firm doesn't need to advertise as much to get sales.

Economies and Diseconomies of Scale

External economies of scale involve changes Outside a firm

- Local colleges may start to offer **qualifications** needed by **big local employers**, reducing the firms' training costs.
- Large companies locating in an area may lead to improvements in **road networks** or **local public transport**.
- If lots of firms doing **similar** or **related** things locate near each other, they may be able to **share resources** (e.g. research facilities). **Suppliers** may also decide to locate in the same area, reducing transport costs.

Extremely successful companies can gain Monopoly Power in a market

1) As a firm's **average cost** for making a product **falls**, it can sell that product at a **lower price**, undercutting its competition.
2) This can lead to a firm gaining a bigger and bigger **market share**, as it continually offers products at prices that are lower than the competition.
3) In this way, a firm can eventually force its competitors out of business and become the **only supplier** of the product — i.e. it will have a **monopoly**.

Undercutting means selling something at a lower price.

Diseconomies of Scale — Disadvantages of being big

1) Getting bigger and bigger isn't always good though — as a firm increases in size, it can encounter **diseconomies of scale**.
2) Diseconomies of scale cause average cost to **rise** as output rises. Diseconomies can be **internal** or **external**.

INTERNAL

- **Wastage** and **loss** can increase, as materials might seem in plentiful supply. Bigger warehouses might lead to more things getting **lost** or **mislaid**.
- **Communication** may become more difficult as a firm grows, affecting staff morale.
- Managers may be less able to **control** what goes on.
- It becomes more difficult to **coordinate** activities between different divisions and departments.
- A '**them and us**' attitude can develop between workers in different parts of a large firm — workers might put their department's interests before the company's, leading to less cooperation and lower efficiency.

EXTERNAL

- As a **whole industry** becomes bigger, the price of raw materials may **increase** (since demand will be greater).
- Buying large amounts of materials **may not** make them less expensive per unit. If local supplies aren't sufficient, more expensive goods from further afield may have to be bought.

High Fixed Costs create Large Economies of Scale

1) There are **huge economies of scale** in industries with **high fixed costs** but **low variable costs**. In some cases, the **structure** of whole industries can change to take advantage of this.
2) For example, **robot-based assembly lines** are hugely expensive to **set up**, but reduce the amount of **labour** required to produce each unit. This means **fixed costs** will **increase** (as the loans used to buy the equipment are repaid), while **variable costs** (e.g. labour costs) **fall**.
3) As a firm grows by taking advantage of its large **economies of scale**, other firms in the industry may be **forced** to follow the same strategy, or shut down. The result is an industry **dominated** by a few large firms (or even just a single firm).

This is an example of improved technology leading to changes in the structure of an industry.

Practice Questions

Q1 What's the difference between an internal economy of scale and an external one?

Q2 Give two examples of diseconomies of scale.

Exam Question

Q1 Explain why companies do not always reduce their average cost of production as their output increases. [5 marks]

Diseconomies of scale — when big isn't beautiful...

There are all sorts of economies of scale. But it's not all plain sailing for big firms — they can have their fair share of difficulties too. This is why someone, somewhere invented the term 'diseconomy of scale'. I know, 'diseconomy' doesn't sound like a real word, but the effects are very real indeed. You know the drill... learn the stuff, cover the page, try to recall it all, and then try the questions.

Long Run Average Cost

This page is for AQA Unit 3, Edexcel Unit 3 and OCR Unit 3 (Work and Leisure) and Unit 4 (Transport Economics).
The average cost curves on page 5 were short run average cost curves (SRAC curves), but to show economies and diseconomies of scale you need to use long run average cost curves (LRAC curves).

In the Long Run firms can Move onto New Short Run Average Cost Curves

1) In the **short run** a firm has at least one **fixed** factor of production.
2) This means that it operates on a particular **short run average cost curve** (SRAC curve), e.g. $SRAC_1$ on the diagram below.
3) As a firm increases **output** in the short run by increasing **variable factors** of production, it moves **along** its short run average cost curve.
4) But in the **long run** a firm can change **all factors** of production. When it does this it moves onto a **new SRAC curve**, e.g. $SRAC_2$.

The **MINIMUM POSSIBLE AVERAGE COST** at each level of output is shown by a **LONG RUN AVERAGE COST CURVE** (LRAC curve).

5) SRAC curves can **touch** the LRAC curve, but they can't go **below** it.
6) For a firm to operate on its LRAC curve at a particular level of output, it has to be using the **most appropriate mix** of all factors of production.
7) This means that it may **not** be able to reduce costs to this minimum level in the **short run** (since in the short run, some factors are fixed).
8) But in the long run a firm can vary **all factors** of production and bring costs down to the level of the LRAC curve.

There's an SRAC curve that touches the LRAC curve at the minimum of both (e.g. $SRAC_3$).

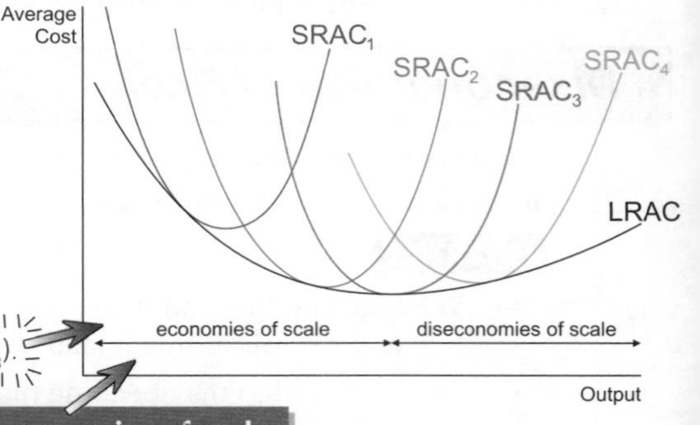

The shape of LRAC curves is determined by internal economies and diseconomies of scale

1) Average cost **falls** as output increases when a firm is experiencing **internal economies of scale**.
2) Average cost **rises** as output increases when a firm is experiencing **internal diseconomies of scale**.
3) Firms may face **specific** economies and diseconomies of scale at the **same** output level — whether the firm is experiencing economies or diseconomies overall will depend on which is having the **greater effect**.

External Changes can cause LRAC Curves to Shift

1) **External** economies of scale will cause the LRAC curve to **shift** downwards by reducing average costs at **all output levels**.
2) External **diseconomies** of scale will force the LRAC curve to shift **upwards**.
3) A change in **taxation** might cause the LRAC curve to shift up or down. For example, an increase in fuel duty would cause the LRAC curve of a bus company to shift up.
4) **New technology** could cause the LRAC curve to shift down if it means firms can use factors of production more efficiently at all levels, e.g. faster computers for workers.

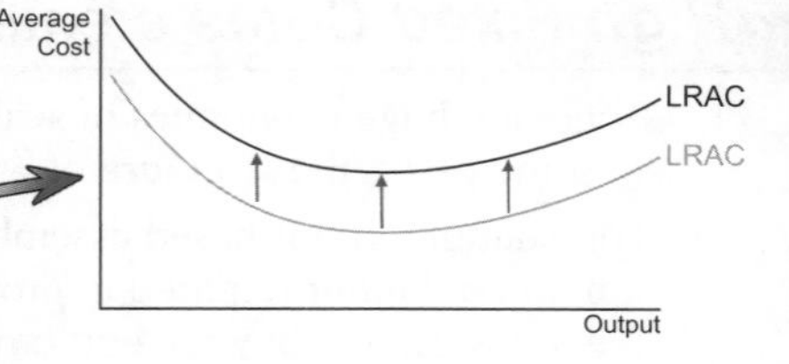

Practice Questions

Q1 Explain what's shown by an LRAC curve.

Q2 Explain why a short run average cost curve can't cross a long run average cost curve.

Exam Question

Q1 A firm is aiming for a particular level of output. Why might the firm **not** be able to reduce its costs to those shown on an LRAC curve for this level of output in the short run? [6 marks]

Long run average cost — very important for thrifty marathon participants...

Make sure you know which concepts apply to short run and to long run cost curves — mixing them up is a fairly common mistake.

Returns to Scale

This page is for AQA Unit 3, Edexcel Unit 3 and OCR Unit 3 (Work and Leisure) and Unit 4 (Transport Economics).
In the long run, the effect on output of increasing all of the factor inputs is described by returns to scale.

Returns to Scale describe the Effects of Increasing the Scale of Production

In the **long run** firms can increase **all** of their factor inputs.
Returns to scale describe the effect on **output** of increasing **all factor inputs** by the same proportion.

INCREASING RETURNS TO SCALE

There are **increasing returns to scale** when an increase in all factor inputs leads to a **more than proportional** increase in output. E.g. **doubling** all of the factor inputs results in a **tripling** of output.

CONSTANT RETURNS TO SCALE

There are **constant returns to scale** when an increase in all factor inputs leads to a **proportional** increase in output. E.g. **doubling** all the factor inputs results in a **doubling** of output.

DECREASING RETURNS TO SCALE

There are **decreasing returns to scale** when an increase in all factor inputs leads to a **less than proportional** increase in output. E.g. **tripling** all the factor inputs results in a **doubling** of output.

Rick was convinced that increasing his moustache size had led to a more than proportional increase in dating success.

Increasing Returns to Scale contribute to Economies of Scale

1) Returns to scale and economies of scale are **not** the same thing.
— **Returns to scale** describe how much **output** changes as input is increased,
— **Economies of scale** describe reductions in **average costs** as output is increased.
2) However, there is a link between the two ideas:
— **Increasing** returns to scale contribute to **economies of scale**,
— **Decreasing** returns to scale contribute to **diseconomies of scale**.
3) When returns to scale are **increasing**, long run average cost will **fall**. An increase in input leads to a **more than proportional** increase in output, so **more** output is being produced **per unit** of input.
4) When returns to scale are **constant**, long run average cost will stay the same — costs are increasing proportionally to output.
5) When returns to scale are **decreasing**, long run average cost will **rise**. **Less** output is being produced **per unit** of input.

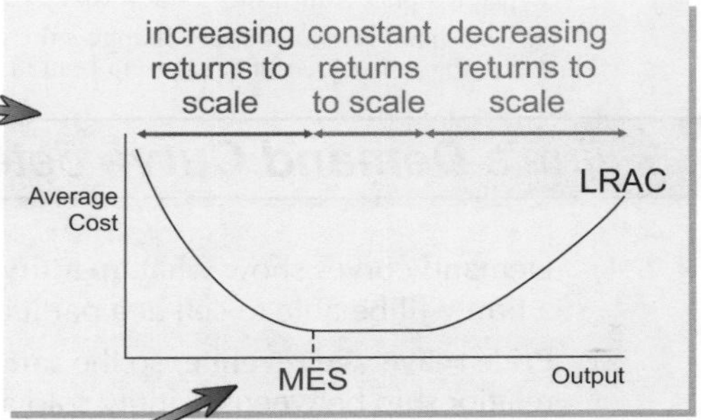

AQA ONLY

Long Run Average Costs are Minimised at the MES

1) The **minimum efficient scale of production** (MES) is the lowest level of output at which the **minimum possible** average cost can be achieved — it's the first point at which the LRAC curve reaches its minimum value.
2) There might be a **range** of production levels where LRAC is minimised, or the MES might be the **only** LRAC minimising level.
3) The MES **varies** between industries — industries with very high fixed costs (e.g. oil extraction) have a **very large MES**. This affects the whole **structure** of an industry — industries with a **large MES** will favour **large firms** more.

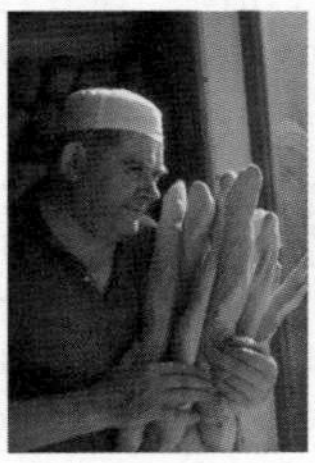

Matteo was wondering if he could cover up his secret bread habit by claiming his bakery had a high MES.

Practice Questions

Q1 What are decreasing returns to scale?

Exam Question

Q1 Explain how returns to scale affect average costs in the long run. [6 marks]

Increasing returns to scale — put a bit more in, get a lot more out...

You need to remember what increasing, constant and decreasing returns to scale are, and how they affect long run average costs.

The Revenue of a Firm

These pages are for AQA Unit 3, Edexcel Unit 3 and OCR Unit 3 (Work and Leisure) and Unit 4 (Transport Economics).
A firm's revenue is the money it receives from selling its production output. Revenue depends on the price a firm is able to get for the quantity of its product that it's selling. So revenue is affected by the demand curve the firm faces.

Revenue is the Money firms receive from Selling their Goods or Services

Total revenue (TR) is the **total amount** of money received, in a time period, **from a firm's sales.**

Total revenue is equal to the **total quantity** sold multiplied by the **price**. It's also called **turnover**.

Average revenue (AR) is the **revenue per unit sold.**

Average revenue is TR **divided** by quantity sold, so **average revenue = price**.

Marginal revenue (MR) is the **extra revenue** received as a result of selling **the final** unit of output.

Marginal revenue is the **difference** between TR at the new sales level and TR at one unit less.

Alicia wasn't sure why her accountant wanted to see her turn over...

Quantity sold	Price (£)	Total Revenue (£)	Marginal Revenue (£)
0	5	—	—
1	5	5	5
2	5	10	5
3	5	15	5
4	5	20	5

When the price is the same for any sales level, the marginal revenue doesn't change either.

Quantity sold	Price (£)	Total Revenue (£)	Marginal Revenue (£)
0	250	—	—
1	200	200	200
2	180	360	160
3	170	510	150
4	160	640	130
5	150	750	110
6	135	810	60

When the price has to change to increase sales, the marginal revenue will change depending on the quantity sold.

A firm's Demand Curve determines how Revenue relates to Output

1) Demand curves show what **quantity** of a product a firm will be able to sell at a particular **price**.
2) **Price = average revenue**, so the **same** curve shows the relationship between quantity sold and average revenue. (So the demand curve could be labelled **AR**.)
3) A firm's **total revenue** is given by **quantity × price**. TR at price P_1 is shown by the shaded area on the diagram.

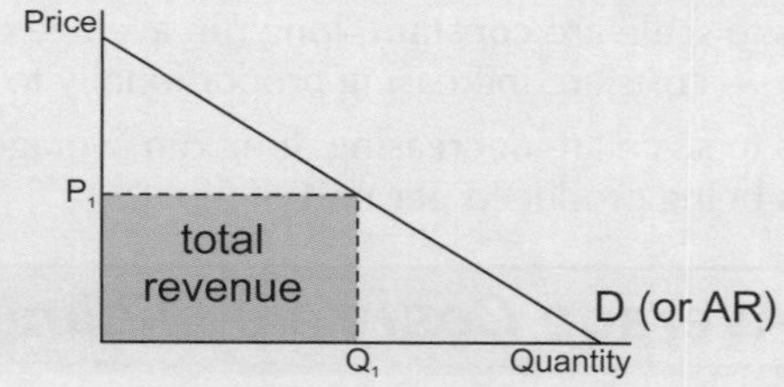

A Firm that's a Price Taker has a Perfectly Elastic Demand Curve

A firm that's a **price taker** has **no power** to control the price it sells at — price takers have to **accept** the price set by the **market**.

A price taker's demand curve will be completely flat — demand is **perfectly elastic**. If the firm **increases** the price then the quantity sold will drop to **zero**. And there's no reason to decrease the price because the **same quantity** would sell at the original **higher price**.

(There's more about price takers on p.20.)

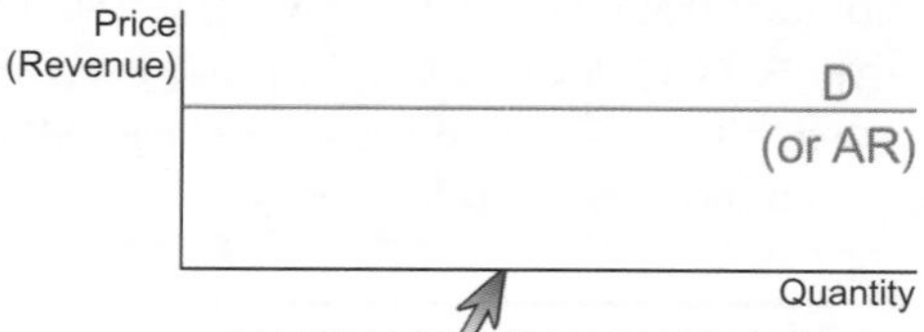

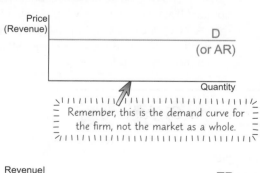

Remember, this is the demand curve for the firm, not the market as a whole.

With a Perfectly Elastic demand curve AR = MR

1) When demand is perfectly elastic the **price** is the **same**, no matter what the **output level**.
2) In this case **marginal revenue = average revenue**, because each extra unit sold brings in the same revenue as all the others.
3) When average revenue is **constant**, total revenue increases **proportionally** with sales, as in the diagram on the right.

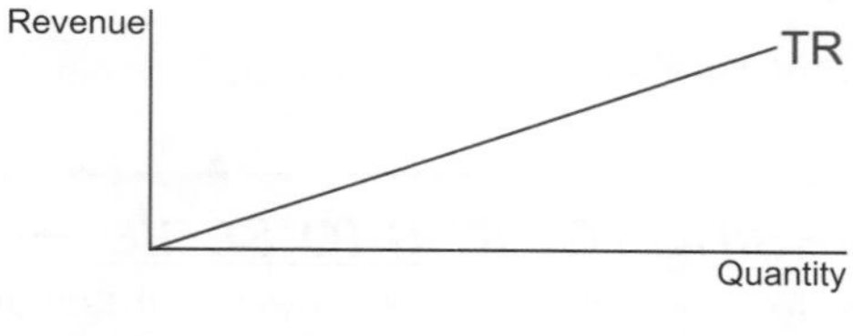

The Revenue of a Firm

A firm that's a **Price Maker** has a **Downward Sloping Demand Curve**

Price makers (e.g. monopolists — see p.26) have **some power** to set the price they sell at.

A price maker's demand curve will slope **downwards** — to increase sales the firm must reduce the price.

There's more about price makers on p.20.

With a **Downward Sloping** Demand Curve **TR is Maximised** when **PED = –1**

1) If a firm's demand curve is a **straight line sloping downwards** then price elasticity of demand (PED) will **change** depending on where the firm is operating on the curve.
2) At the **midpoint** of the demand curve **PED = –1**. This is covered in AS.
3) To the **left of the midpoint**, demand is **elastic**:
   - Decreasing a product's price **towards** the price at the midpoint will cause a **more than proportionate** increase in sales.
   - **Total revenue** will **increase** — the **gain** in revenue from increasing sales will **outweigh the loss** on each unit from decreasing the price.
4) To the **right of the midpoint**, demand is **inelastic**:
   - Decreasing a product's price **below** the price at the midpoint will cause a **less than proportionate** increase in sales.
   - **Total revenue** will **decrease** — the **loss** in revenue from decreasing the price of each unit will **outweigh the gain** from increasing sales.
5) This means that **total revenue is maximised** when the firm is operating **at the midpoint** of the demand curve — when **PED = –1**.

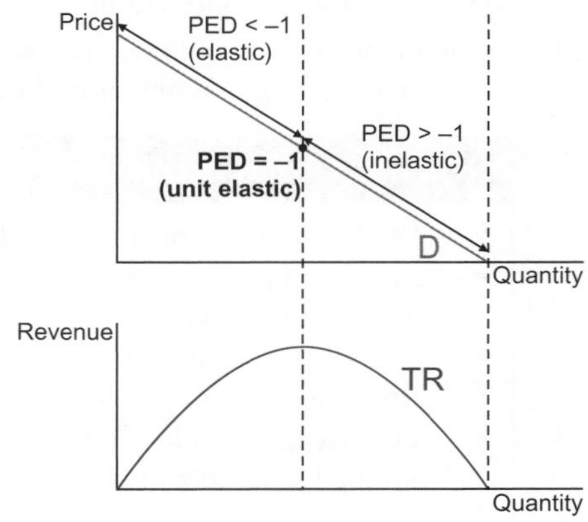

And **MR = 0** when **TR** is at its **Maximum**

1) The demand curve is also the **average revenue curve.**
2) So the **maximum total revenue** occurs at the **midpoint** of the average revenue curve.
3) The MR curve is always **twice as steep** as the AR curve.
4) When **total revenue** is at its maximum, **MR = 0**. (At the point where additional sales **reduce** total revenue, marginal revenue becomes **negative**.)

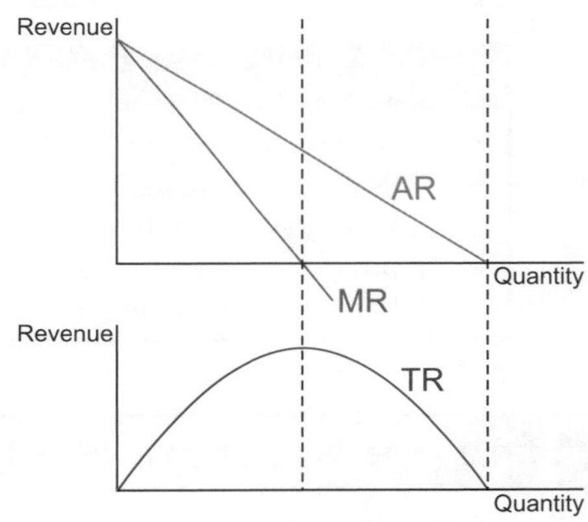

Practice Questions

Q1 What is turnover?

Q2 What is marginal revenue?

Q3 Is the price of a product the marginal revenue or the average revenue for that product?

Q4 How does price elasticity of demand change along a downward sloping demand curve?

Exam Question

Q1 Explain why the average and marginal revenue curves of a price-making firm slope down, while those of a price-taking firm are horizontal. [15 marks]

Downward sloping demand curve — an economist's favourite yoga pose...

Revenue is determined by the quantity a firm is able to sell at a given price, so the shape of a firm's revenue curves depends on the price elasticity of demand the firm faces. The price elasticity of demand, and how this changes at different output levels, will be different for different firms in different markets. There's a lot going on here — make sure you've got your head round all of it.

Profit

These pages are for AQA Unit 3, Edexcel Unit 3 and OCR Unit 3 (Work and Leisure) and Unit 4 (Transport Economics).
The basic idea here is that firms need to make a profit to survive. But be warned... some of this might seem a bit weird at first, because making a profit isn't quite as simple as bringing in more money than you pay out.

Economists distinguish between **Normal Profit** and **Supernormal Profit**

1) Here's the basic equation for working out **profit**:

Profit = Total Revenue (TR) – Total Costs (TC)

Remember... TC consists of the **money costs** of the things that have to be paid for **and** the **opportunity costs** of the things that aren't paid for.

2) There are actually two kinds of profit in economics — **normal profit** and **supernormal profit**.

Supernormal profit is also known as abnormal profit.

NORMAL PROFIT occurs when TR = TC

- A firm is making **normal profit** when its total revenue **equals** its total costs.
- So **normal profit** is an 'economic profit' of **zero** — i.e. a profit of zero if **all** costs are taken into account.
- This means normal profit occurs when the **extra revenue** left, on top of what's needed to cover the firm's money costs, is **equal** to the **opportunity costs** of the factors of production that aren't paid for.
- If the extra revenue is **less** than those **opportunity costs**, then the firm would have been **better off** putting the factors of production to a **different use**.
- In other words, **normal profit** is the **minimum** level of profit needed to keep resources in their **current use** in the long run.

A firm can make a 'money profit' (i.e. receive more money than it pays out), but an economic profit of zero.

SUPERNORMAL PROFIT occurs when TR > TC

- A firm is making **supernormal profit** when its total revenue is **greater** than its total costs.
- This means the **revenue** generated from using the factors of production in this way is **greater** than could have been generated by using them in any **other** way.
- If firms in an industry are making **supernormal profit**, this will create an **incentive** for other firms to try to **enter** that industry.

There's more about this in Section 2.

A firm needs to make **Normal Profit** to **Keep Operating** in the **Long Run**

1) If a firm can't make normal profit it will **close** in the **long run**, because its revenue is not covering all of its costs. Even if it is making a money profit, the factors of production it's using could be used to **better effect** elsewhere.
2) However, in the **short run**, a firm has **fixed costs** that it has to pay, whether or not it produces any output. So a loss-making firm may **not** close **immediately** — it all depends on how its revenue compares to its **variable costs**.

- If a firm's **total revenue** is **greater** than its **total variable costs**, then it will **continue to produce** in the short term.
- Any revenue generated above the firm's variable costs can **contribute** towards paying its **fixed costs**.
- If the firm **stops production** immediately, it will actually be **worse off**.

Or if its average revenue is greater than its average variable costs.

- If a firm's **total revenue** is **less** than its **total variable costs**, then it will close **immediately**.
- If it **continues** to produce, it will actually be **worse off**.

Or if its average revenue is less than its average variable costs.

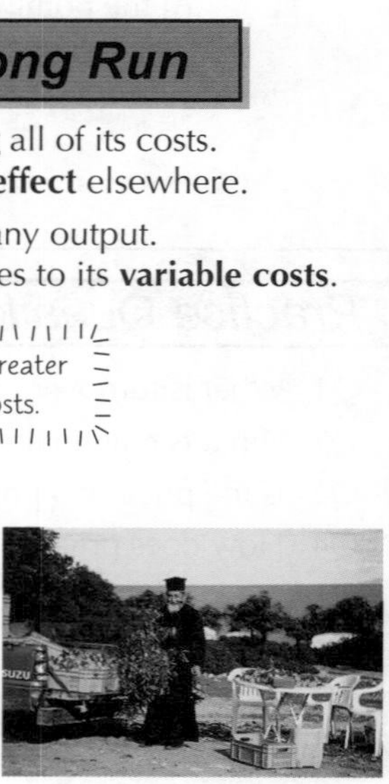

Alastor was only keeping his tangerine business open in the short run to minimise losses. If only he hadn't spent all that money on online marketing...

3) In the long run the firm can be **released** from its fixed costs (e.g. by no longer renting a factory) and it will shut down.

Profit

Profit is **Maximised** when **Marginal Cost = Marginal Revenue**

1) Economists generally **assume** that firms are aiming to **maximise** their **profits**. To do this, they need to find the optimum output level at which to operate.
   - If marginal revenue (MR) is **greater** than marginal cost (MC) at a particular level of output, the firm should **increase output**. This is because the revenue gained by increasing output is **greater** than the cost of producing it. So **increasing output adds to profit**.
   - If marginal revenue (MR) is **less** than marginal cost (MC) at a particular level of output, the firm should **decrease output**. This is because it's costing the firm more to produce its last unit of output than it receives in revenue. So **decreasing output adds to profit**.

See p.16 for more about this.

2) This means the **profit-maximising** output level occurs when **MC = MR**. This is known as the "MC = MR profit-maximising rule".

Profits are maximised when MC = MR.

Religious artists aim to maximise prophets.

3) You can use this rule to find a firm's **profit-maximising output level** from a diagram showing MR and MC, as in the two examples below.

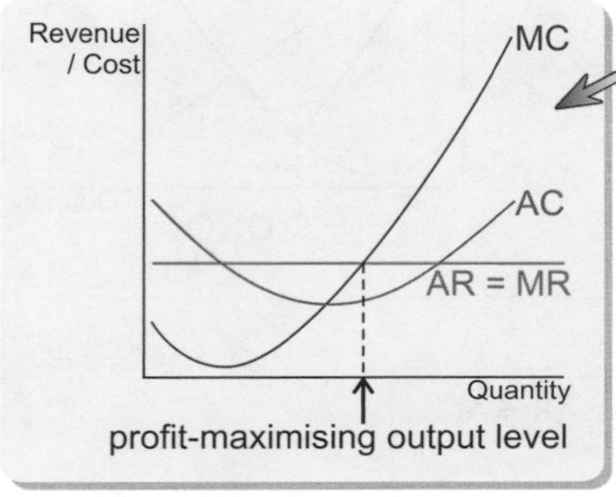

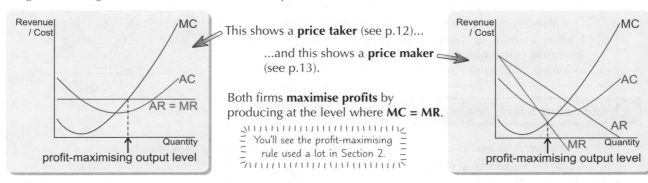

This shows a **price taker** (see p.12)...

...and this shows a **price maker** (see p.13).

Both firms **maximise profits** by producing at the level where **MC = MR**.

You'll see the profit-maximising rule used a lot in Section 2.

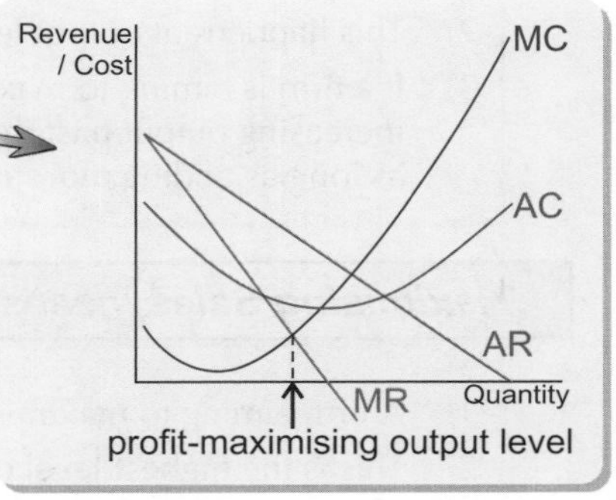

Practice Questions

Q1 What is supernormal profit?

Q2 State the condition for profit maximisation.

Exam Questions

Q1 Discuss when a firm whose average costs exceed its average revenue in the long run should close down. [4 marks]

Q2 The diagram shows the costs and revenues for a profit-maximising firm. The most suitable action for the firm, assuming no changes in costs or demand, would be to output at which of the levels shown?

Explain your answer. [4 marks]

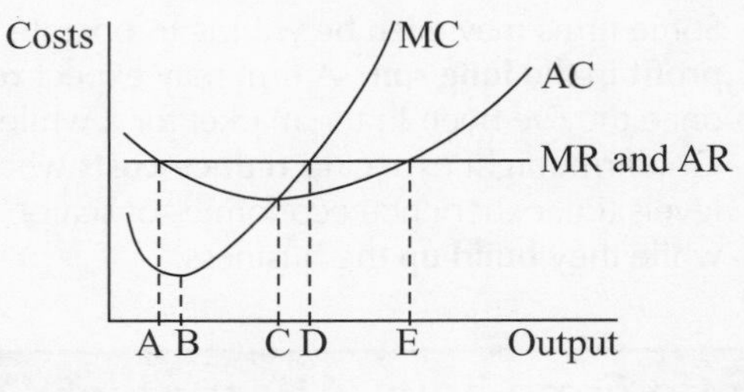

Supernormal profit — profit that wears its pants over its trousers...

Profit's a funny one — but the basic message here is that in the long run a firm needs to bring in enough revenue to cover all its costs. Sounds straightforward... but you have to remember that in economics, a firm's costs include the opportunity costs of things it's not had to pay for. So a business owner's time has to be included in a firm's costs, even if the owner doesn't take a wage from the business, for example. The upshot of this is that an 'economic profit' of zero is perfectly normal (no pun intended). I told you this was weird. Anyway, remember all that, plus all that stuff about why a loss-making firm might keep operating in the short run if it'll help it to pay its fixed costs. Also remember everything else in this book. Then you ought to do very well in your exam.

The Objectives of Firms

These pages are for AQA Unit 3, Edexcel Unit 3 and OCR Unit 3 (Work and Leisure) and Unit 4 (Transport Economics).
The objectives of firms vary — they will largely depend on who has control. Often, firms will accept some sort of compromise between different objectives in an attempt to 'keep everyone happy'.

Profit Maximisation is assumed to be the Objective of a firm

You wait 12 pages for the objective of a firm to come along...

1) The traditional **theory of the firm** is based on the **assumption** that firms are aiming to **maximise profit**.
2) But in reality, there are **other objectives** a firm might consider **more important**.
3) For example, **revenue maximisation** and **sales maximisation** are other common objectives.

Aiming for Other Objectives will Reduce Profit in the Short Run

A firm aiming to **maximise profit** will operate at output level Q, where **MR = MC**.
Firms that are aiming for **other objectives** will operate at **different** output levels.

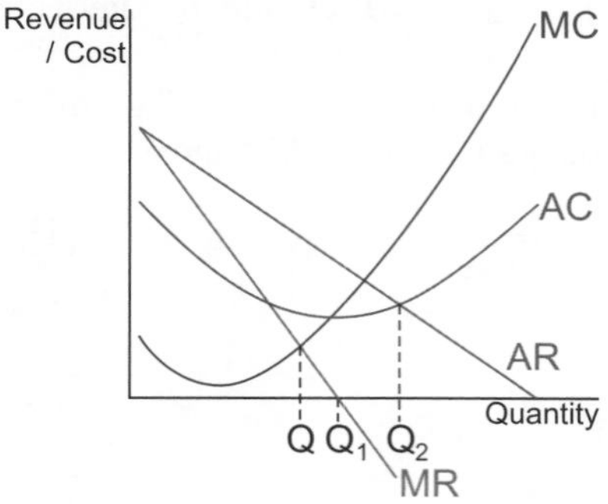

Maximising Revenue means producing where MR = 0

1) **Revenue** is maximised when MR = 0.
2) This happens at output level Q_1 — a higher output than Q.
3) If a firm is aiming to maximise revenue they will keep increasing output **past** the point where profit is maximised, as long as adding **more output** leads to **greater revenue**.

Maximising Sales means producing where AR = AC

1) A firm aiming to **maximise sales** will produce at an output level where **AR** = **AC**.
2) This is the **highest** level of output the firm can sustain in the **long run**.
3) Q_2 is the sales-maximising output level — it's **higher** than Q and Q_1.
4) If **sales increased further** the firm would be making a **loss**.

Maximising Profit might Only be an objective for the Long Run

1) **Maximising profit** in the **long run** sometimes means **sacrificing profit** in the **short run**.
2) Sometimes a firm will try to **maximise sales** or **revenue** in the **short run**.
For example, a firm might want to maximise revenue or sales to increase its **market share**, or to gain **monopoly** power so that it can make **supernormal profits** in the long run.
Or high sales might make it easier for the firm to **borrow money**.
3) Some firms may even be willing to operate at a **loss** in the **short run** in order to make a **profit** in the **long run**. A firm may expect **revenue to increase** in the future, for example, once they've been in the market for a while and their **brand recognition** increases.
Or a firm might expect to **reduce costs** when they're able to output at higher production levels (i.e. experience economies of scale), and so they may keep operating at a loss while they **build up** the business.

There's more about monopoly power in Section 2.

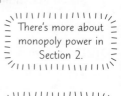

See pages 8-9 for more about economies of scale.

Some firms have Alternative Objectives

Some firms might aim for something not **directly** related to profit, revenue or sales.
But these objectives are usually pursued while **also** aiming to make at least **normal profit**.

1) For example, some organisations are **'not for profit'** — they don't pay out profit to their owners and their **main aim** is to 'do good' or provide some kind of benefit to the public.
2) Or a firm might aim to keep as many people in **jobs** as possible, or increase **pay** for its employees.

The Objectives of Firms

Divorce of Ownership from Control often happens as firms Grow

1) In **small** firms, the **owner** often **manages** the company on a day-to-day basis.
2) As firms **grow**, the owners often raise finance by **selling shares** — the new shareholders become **part owners** of the firm.
3) But the firm will actually be run by **directors**, who are appointed to **control** the business in the shareholders' interests.
4) This is known as the **divorce of ownership from control** — the owner(s) of the firm are **no longer** in day-to-day control.
5) **Directors** might have **different** objectives to the **owners**.
6) Employees and other **stakeholders** in firms may also have their own **objectives** and might have some level of **control**.

A firm's stakeholders includes everyone with an interest in or who is affected by the firm — e.g. employees, managers, suppliers, customers, etc.

- The **divorce of ownership from control** can result in firms pursuing objectives other than maximised profit.
- For example, if a manager's **pay** or **bonus** is linked to **revenue** or **sales**, then they may choose to maximise those (even though the owners would probably prefer the firm to pursue maximum **profits**).
- **Directors** might also be keen to grow some aspect of the firm (e.g. sales or market share) because they **enjoy** running a large organisation, or because being in charge of a large firm will further their **career**.
- **Employees** are likely to aim to increase their own **pay or benefits** (or just to keep themselves in a job), **ahead** of aiming to make profits for the firm.

The high street bank Richard worked for had serious problems with the divorce of ownership from control. The owners had no idea he'd turned one of their branches into a greengrocer's.

Owners can Retain Control with Accountability and Incentives

1) How much **control** the managers or directors running a firm have can depend on how **accountable** they are to the owners.
2) Shareholders can **remove** directors by vote if they're not happy with them, but they often **lack information** that might make them do this.
3) **Accountability** means managers and directors having to **justify** what they've done in the past and **explain** their future plans and intentions.
4) Owners might also try to **encourage** directors to aim for profit maximisation by offering **incentives** which make this an attractive objective for the directors to pursue — e.g. a **bonus** linked to profits, or free or discounted company **shares**.

Sometimes people Satisfice rather than Maximise to Make Life Easier

1) **Satisficing** means trying to do **just enough** to satisfy important stakeholders, instead of aiming to **maximise** a quantity such as profits (or **minimise** something like costs). It's sometimes described as 'aiming for an **easy life**'.
2) Satisficing often arises when different **stakeholders** have different objectives, which might be **conflicting**.
3) For example, rather than maximising profit, directors might aim to make '**enough profit**' to stop shareholders getting too concerned, and paying employees '**high enough wages**' that they don't look for work elsewhere or threaten to go on strike.

Practice Questions

Q1 Other than profit maximisation, give three other objectives firms might have.

Q2 What is satisficing?

Exam Question

Q1 Evaluate the view that all firms are aiming to maximise profit. [25 marks]

And I thought a stakeholder was a particularly robust fork...

Traditional economics assumes firms aim to maximise profit — but in reality this often isn't the case. Especially in larger firms, the people who control the business won't be the owners and will have their own objectives, such as revenue or sales maximisation. Remember, firms can only pursue other objectives while making at least normal profit in the long run, else they won't survive.

Why Firms Grow

These pages are for AQA Unit 3 and Edexcel Unit 3.
A firm grows by increasing its output. It can do this by increasing its own production scale or by taking over other firms. There are lots of reasons for a firm to grow, and also some reasons why a firm might want to stay small.

Growth can Increase Profit and bring Other Benefits

1) Firms usually grow to increase their **profit** — there are several ways that growth can achieve this:

> **Increasing economies of scale** — a firm might grow to reach the **minimum efficient scale** of production (MES), where long run average costs are minimised (see p.11 for more about MES).
>
> **Increasing market share** and **reducing competition** — if a firm controls a large part of the market they might gain some **monopoly power** that allows them to **set prices** and make **supernormal profits**.
>
> **Expanding into new markets** — a firm might try to sell its products in **different countries**, for example.

2) However, there are also **other reasons** why a firm might grow, such as to **achieve managerial objectives** — directors might seek the **status** of running a large firm, for example.

Internal Growth means Increasing Production Scale

1) **Internal growth** (also known as **organic growth**) is growth as a result of a firm increasing the levels of the **factors of production** it uses. For example, increasing output by building a larger factory, hiring more workers, and increasing the amount of raw materials used.
2) Firms expanding through internal growth have **control** over exactly how this growth occurs.
3) However, internal growth tends to be **slow**.

External Growth means Combining Firms

1) **External growth** (also known as **inorganic growth**) is growth as a result of **takeovers** and **mergers**.
— a **takeover** is when one firm **buys another firm**, which becomes part of the first firm,
— a **merger** is when two firms unite to form a **new company**.
2) External growth is **quicker** and may be **cheaper** than internal growth.
It might also be the easiest way to gain **experience** and **expertise** in a new area of business.
3) External growth can happen through **horizontal integration**, **vertical integration**, or **conglomerate integration**:

> The terms takeover and merger are often used interchangeably, but there are legal and technical differences between the two.

Horizontal and Vertical Integration happen between firms in the Same Market

1) **Horizontal integration** means combining firms that are at the **same stage** of the production process of **similar products** — for example, a **merger** between **two pharmaceutical companies** or between a **bookshop** and a **music shop**.
2) Firms can **increase economies of scale**, **reduce competition** and **increase market share** through horizontal integration.

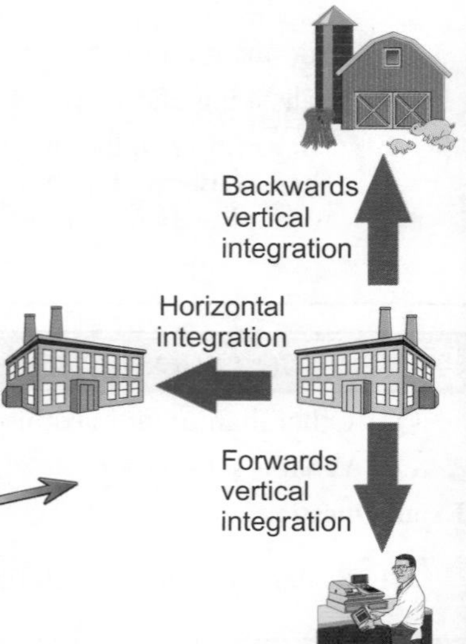

1) **Vertical integration** means combining firms at **different stages** of the production process of the **same product**.
   - **Forward vertical integration** happens when a firm takes over another firm that is **further forward** in the production process (closer to the end customer). E.g. a **leather manufacturer** buying a **shoe factory**.
   - **Backward vertical integration** happens when a firm takes over another firm that is **further back** in the production process (further away from the end customer). E.g. a **book printer** buying a **paper plant**.
2) By taking over suppliers or retailers, a firm can gain more **control** of the **production process**. This might be in order to maintain higher **quality standards**, or make the overall process more **efficient**.
3) This can create **barriers to entry** (see pages 24-25) by preventing competitors from accessing suppliers or retailers.

Why Firms Grow

Conglomerate Integration happens between firms in **Unrelated Markets**

1) **Conglomerate integration** means combining firms which operate in completely **different markets**. E.g. an **educational stationery supplier** merging with a **tractor manufacturer**.
2) Conglomerate mergers allow firms to **diversify**, which means they can **spread their risk** — if one part of the new firm does badly, this can be **compensated for** by profit from another part of the firm.
3) A conglomerate merger will also allow a firm to use **profits** generated by one product to **invest** in another.

A demerger is the breaking up of a firm into separate firms

1) If a firm is experiencing disadvantages as a result of expanding into different markets, it might sell off parts of its business to create **separate firms**. This is called a **demerger**.
2) The idea is to allow each new smaller firm to **focus** on a **specific market**, and make **more profit** than they did as part of the larger firm.
3) Sometimes a firm will sell off a particularly **weak** part of its business which is making little or no profit. It's likely to get a **low price** for this part of the firm, but it will hope that the sale will mean **profits are improved** for the remaining parts.

New Technology can (sometimes) help firms grow

1) The invention of new technology allows **new products** (e.g. tablet computers) to be produced, creating **new markets**.
2) Some new products sustain or increase demand for existing products — this is an example of **synergy demand**. For example, the invention of social media sites increased demand for computers.
3) But new products can also cause an **existing market** to **decline** or **disappear** — e.g. a lot of video rental shops closed once people could access films **online**, or through film packages on **cable** and **satellite TV** services.
4) And retailers selling via the **internet** had a disruptive effect on sales from high-street shops. Most high-street retailers have begun to sell **online** too now though.

There are lots of reasons why some firms **Stay Small**

1) Firms might be **forced** to remain small if they can't raise the necessary **finance** to expand.
2) If a firm supplies a **niche market**, it might only have a small **demand**, so may have no potential to expand its sales.
3) The **legal requirements** for small businesses can be **simpler** and **less expensive** to comply with.

   E.g. small firms may not need to have their accounts audited each year.
4) Firms may also be concerned about experiencing **diseconomies of scale** if they expand — they might then choose to remain small. Some possible concerns include:
   - Getting larger might mean their **relationships** with **customers** become more impersonal.
   - Large firms can become **complacent** about their operations and become less focused and efficient.
   - Larger firms also tend to be **less responsive** to change than smaller firms.
5) A firm's owners might not want the **extra work** and **risks** involved in expanding — they might prefer free time over profit.
6) Firms might want to remain small to **avoid being noticed** and taken over by larger firms.

Practice Questions

Q1 What is the difference between internal and external growth?

Q2 Give four reasons why a firm might prefer to remain small.

Exam Question

Q1 Discuss the potential benefits of horizontal integration in a market which is experiencing declining profits. [10 marks]

Horizontal integration? I suppose that's one way of bringing firms together...

Cover the book up and see how much of this stuff you can write down — if it hasn't sunk in, have another read through and try again...

Perfect Competition

These pages are for AQA Unit 3, Edexcel Unit 3 and OCR Unit 3 (Work and Leisure) and Unit 4 (Transport Economics).
Perfectly competitive markets don't happen in real life... but that doesn't mean they're not important.
They show the conditions needed to achieve some really useful outcomes.

Perfectly Competitive markets have certain Characteristics

1) The **model of perfect competition** is a description of how a market **would** work **if** certain conditions were satisfied.
2) It's a theoretical thing — there are **no** real markets that work quite like this. But understanding how perfect competition works makes it easier to understand what's going **wrong** with real-life markets when they have undesirable results.
3) In a **perfectly competitive** market, the following conditions are satisfied:

- There's an **infinite** number of **suppliers** and **consumers**.
  - Each of these suppliers is **small** enough that **no** single firm or consumer has any '**market power**' (i.e. no firm or consumer can affect the market on their own).
  - Each firm is a '**price taker**' (as opposed to a '**price maker**') — this means they have to buy or sell at the current **market price**.

So all firms have 0% concentration. See p.30 for more about concentration.

- **Consumers** have **perfect information** — i.e. perfect knowledge of all goods and prices in a market.
  - Every consumer decision is **well-informed** — consumers know how much **every** firm in the market charges for its products, as well as all the **details** about those products.
- **Producers** have **perfect information** — i.e. perfect knowledge of the market and production methods.
  - No firm has any 'secret' low-cost production methods, and **every** firm knows the prices charged by every **other** firm.
- **Products** are **identical** (**homogeneous**).
  - So consumers can always **switch** between products from different firms (i.e. all the products are perfect **substitutes** for each other).

This also means there's no branding, since branding makes some products seem different from others.

- There are **no barriers to entry** and **no barriers to exit**.
  - New entrants can **join** the industry very easily. Existing firms can **leave** equally easily.
- Firms are **profit maximisers**.
  - So all the **decisions** that a firm makes are geared towards maximising **profit**.
  - This means that all firms will choose to produce at a level of output where **MC = MR** (see p.15).

Perfect competition leads to Allocative Efficiency... usually

Here's the first good outcome from a perfectly competitive market.

See p.24-25 and 36-37 for more on barriers to entry and exit.

1) The conditions for a perfectly competitive market ensure that the **rationing**, **signalling** and **incentive** functions of the **price mechanism** work perfectly. In particular:
   - all firms are **price takers** ('the market' sets the price according to consumers' preferences, **rationing** resources and **signalling** priorities),
   - consumers and producers have **perfect knowledge** of the market, and there are **no barriers** to entry or exit (so firms can recognise and act on **incentives** to change their output level or enter/leave a market).
2) This means **producers** are **rewarded** for the goods and services they provide — at a level that reflects the **benefits** those goods and services bring to **consumers**.
3) In other words, in a **perfectly competitive** market, resources will be allocated **as efficiently as they can be** — i.e. perfect competition leads to **allocative efficiency**.
4) In fact, **without** perfect competition, a market **can't** achieve allocative efficiency.

Remember... in a market that achieves allocative efficiency: P = MC

Allocative efficiency and externalities
Perfectly competitive markets will achieve **allocative** efficiency, **assuming** that there are **no externalities.**
- Strictly speaking, allocative efficiency occurs when **P = MSC** (marginal social cost — i.e. including external costs to third parties).
- Perfect competition results in a long run equilibrium where **P = MPC** (marginal private cost — i.e. the cost to the firm of producing the product, **ignoring** external costs).
- But if there are **negative externalities**, say, then **MPC < MSC** — which means that **P < MSC**.
  This will mean that there's allocative inefficiency, and that will lead to **overproduction** and **overconsumption**.

Perfect Competition

Perfect Competition means Supernormal Profits are Competed Away

1) In perfect competition, **no firm** will make **supernormal profits** in the **long run**.
2) This is because any **short-term supernormal profits** attract new firms to the market (since there are **no barriers to entry**). This means supernormal profits are '**competed away**' in the long term — i.e. firms **undercut** each other until all firms make only normal profit.

Also, all firms are forced to become productively efficient (see next page for more information).

3) These diagrams show how this **equilibrium** is maintained in the **long run**.
   - Suppose there's **high demand** for a product across an **industry** as a whole, leading to a firm making **supernormal profits**, as shown in red in the diagram.

– The firm's **total revenue** is TR = Q × P (= the total area of the red and grey rectangles).
– The firm's **total costs** are TC = Q × c (= the area of the grey rectangle, since c is the firm's average cost (AC) at this level of output).
– **Subtract** TC from TR to find the firm's **profit**.
– Here, TR > TC, so this firm is currently making a **supernormal profit** of TR – TC (= the area of the red rectangle).

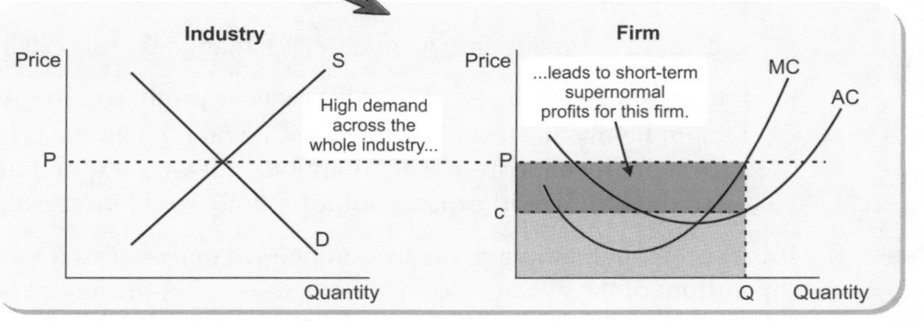

   - In a **perfectly competitive** market, those supernormal profits mean other firms will now have an **incentive** to enter the market. And since there are **no barriers to entry**, they can do this easily.
   - This results in a shift in the industry **supply curve** to the right...
   - ...meaning the **market price falls** until **all** excess profits have been **competed away**, and a new **long run equilibrium** is reached at price P_1 (with this firm supplying Q_1).

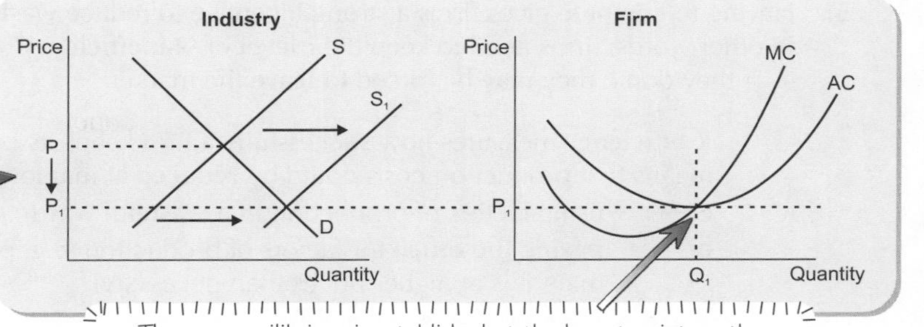

The new equilibrium is established at the lowest point on the firm's AC curve, so firms become productively efficient (see p.5).

A firm will Leave a market if it's Unable to make a profit in the Long Run

1) If the **market price** (AR) falls **below** a firm's average unit-cost (AC), the firm is making **less** than normal profit (i.e. a **loss**).
2) There are **no barriers to exit** in a perfectly competitive market (see p.20), so in the **long run** the firm will just **leave** the market.
3) However, in the short run, there are **two possibilities**:
   - If the selling price (AR) is still **above** the firm's **average variable costs** (AVC), then the firm may **continue to trade** temporarily.
   - If the selling price (AR) falls **below** the level of the firm's **average variable costs** (AVC), then it will leave the market **immediately**.

See p.14 for more about shut-down points.

Practice Questions

Q1 List the conditions needed for a perfectly competitive market.

Q2 Explain the link between perfect competition and allocative efficiency.

Q3 What would force a firm to leave a market immediately?

Exam Question

Q1 Describe, with diagrams, the long run equilibrium positions for a firm and its industry in a perfectly competitive market. [15 marks]

My perfect competition is a prize crossword in the Sunday papers...

In practice, no market completely satisfies the assumptions behind perfect competition. However, the closer a real-life market comes to satisfying them, the more likely it is to behave in the way predicted by the theoretical model. This is tricky stuff, but it's worth taking the time to really get your head round all those diagrams before you move on.

Perfect Competition

These pages are for AQA Unit 3, Edexcel Unit 3 and OCR Unit 3 (Work and Leisure) and Unit 4 (Transport Economics).
Perfect competition sounds pretty good... I mean... it's perfect, after all.
But for the exam, you need to know very specifically what's good about perfect competition.

Perfect competition leads to **Productive Efficiency**

1) **Productive efficiency** is about ensuring the **costs** of production are as **low** as they can be. This will mean that prices to **consumers** can be low as well.
2) In perfect competition, productive efficiency comes about as a **direct result** of all firms trying to **maximise** their **profits**.
3) At the long run equilibrium of perfect competition, a firm will produce a **quantity** of goods such that:

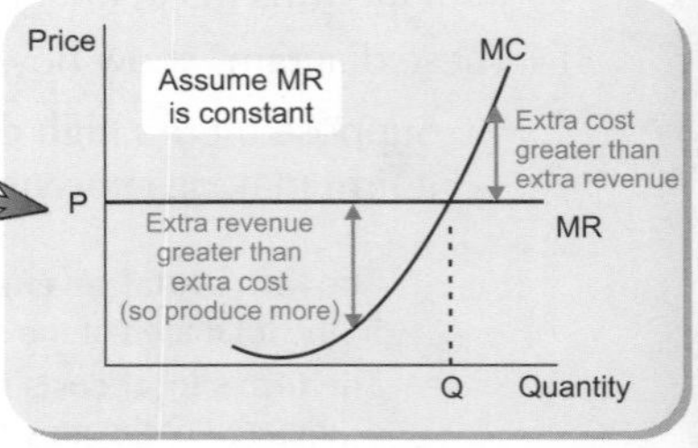

marginal revenue (MR) = marginal costs (MC)

- Output **above** this level (MC > MR) **reduces profit**, so firms wouldn't produce it.
- Output **below** this level (i.e. MR > MC) would mean the firm would **earn** more revenue from extra output than it would **spend** in costs — so the firm would **expand output** as this would **increase profit**.

4) It's no accident that in a perfectly competitive market, this long run output level is at the **bottom** of the average-cost (AC) curve — i.e. at the lowest possible cost level. In other words, firms in a perfectly competitive market will be **productively efficient**.
5) Having to **compete** gives firms a strong incentive to reduce **waste** and **inefficiency**. In other words, firms need to keep their level of '**x-inefficiency**' as low as possible — if they don't, they may be forced to **leave** the market.

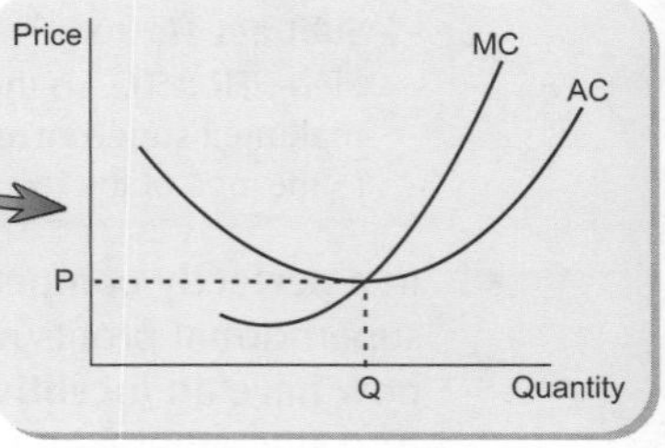

> **X-efficiency** measures how successfully a firm keeps its costs down. **X-inefficiency** (or '**organisational slack**') means that production costs could be **reduced** at that level of production. X-inefficiency can be caused by:
> **either** using factors of production in a **wasteful way** (e.g. by employing more people than necessary),
> **or** **paying too much** for factors of production (e.g. paying workers more than is needed or buying raw materials at higher prices than necessary).

6) But perfectly competitive markets only achieve **productive efficiency** if you assume that there are **no economies of scale** in the industry.
   - In a perfectly competitive market, there's an **infinite** number of firms.
   - This means that each firm is **very small**, and so **can't** take full advantage of **economies of scale**.
   - If there are economies of scale, then an industry made up of an **infinite number** of very **small** firms may be **less productively efficient** than if there was one very **big** firm (i.e. a monopoly — see p.26).

Perfect competition **Doesn't** lead to **Dynamic Efficiency**...

1) **Dynamic efficiency** is about **improving efficiency** in the **long term**, so it refers to the willingness and eagerness of firms:
   a) to carry out **research and development** to **improve** existing products or **develop** new ones.
   b) to **invest** in **new technology** or **training** to improve the production process and reduce production costs.
2) However, these strategies involve considerable **investment** and therefore **risk**, so they will only take place if there's adequate **reward**.
3) Firms in a **perfectly competitive** market earn only **normal profit**, so there's **no reward** for taking risks. This means dynamic efficiencies will **not** be achieved.
4) However, as long as a market is towards the 'perfect-competition end' of the spectrum shown on p.23, then firms can achieve a degree of **dynamic efficiency** without becoming too allocatively and productively **inefficient**. This is why firms do achieve some degree of **dynamic efficiency** — in real life, no market is perfectly competitive.

...but does lead to **Static Efficiency**

1) If **allocative** and **productive** efficiency are achieved at any particular point in time, this is called **static efficiency**. But static efficiency can't last forever, since **technology** and **consumer tastes** change. For example, the methods used to make cars in the 1920s might have been allocatively and productively **efficient** at the time, but they'd be hopelessly out of date now.
2) To remain allocatively and productively efficient, car makers would have needed to **invest** in new production technology and design new models at some point.

Perfect Competition

In *Real Life* there's a *'Spectrum'* of different market structures

1) In a **perfectly competitive** market, all the goods produced are **identical**, so the only way for firms to compete is on **price**.
2) In practice, firms usually compete in **other ways** than on price — for example, they might use:

This means the only way firms can compete with their rivals is by selling their products at a lower price.

Improved products	Better quality of service	Wider product ranges
Advertising and promotion	Nicer packaging	Products that are easier to use

3) In the real world, markets fall somewhere on a 'spectrum' of different **market structures**.

Perfect competition (Competition maximised) ⟷ **Pure monopoly** (No competition)

Every real-life market lies somewhere between these two extremes.

4) At one extreme are '**perfectly competitive** markets', and at the other are '**pure monopolies**' (where there's no competition at all — see p.26 for more info). **Real-life** markets lie somewhere between these extremes.
5) The **closer** an actual market **matches** the description of a perfectly competitive market, the more likely it is to **behave** in the same way.

Governments often try to *Encourage Competition* in markets

1) Perfectly competitive markets lead to **efficient** long run outcomes **in theory** (e.g. the long run equilibrium is allocatively and productively efficient, and firms are forced to become x-efficient).
2) By **encouraging competition**, governments hope to achieve these same kinds of efficiencies in **real life**. For example, governments want to make sure firms:
   (i) are forced to **produce efficiently**, reducing costs where possible,
   (ii) set **prices** at a level that's **fair** to consumers,

See p.46-47 for more about competition policy.

3) They also hope competition will encourage firms to **innovate**, leading firms to create both new **products** (giving **more choice** for consumers) and new **production processes** (allowing firms to reduce their costs further).
4) There are various **policies** a government can introduce to **increase competition** in the economy:

- Encourage **new enterprises** with **advice** and **start-up subsidies**.
- Increase **consumer knowledge** by ensuring that **comparison information** is available.
- Introduce more **consumer choice** and competition in the **public sector**. This might involve creating 'internal markets' in sectors such as health and schooling, for example.
- **Privatise** and **deregulate** large monopolistic nationalised industries.
- Discourage **mergers** and **takeovers** which might **reduce** the number of competing firms.
- Encourage more **international** competition — e.g. by joining the EU, countries enter into a multinational 'single market' (see page 136 for more information).

An internal market is where different parts of the same organisation compete against each other. For example, groups of hospitals in the NHS now compete for patients.

Practice Questions

Q1 What is meant by x-inefficiency?

Q2 What does it mean if a firm has static efficiency?

Q3 Describe three policies a government could introduce in order to increase the competitiveness of markets.

Exam Question

Q1 To what extent would you expect firms in a perfectly competitive market to be dynamically efficient? [5 marks]

Economics is all about real life — and perfectly competitive markets...

I think this is all quite interesting. I mean... perfect competition doesn't happen in real life. But understanding how it works in theory lets governments come up with all sorts of policies to try to get some of the benefits anyway. That's the benefit of an economic model — real life is hard to understand, so start by trying to understand something much simpler.

Barriers to Entry

These pages are for AQA Unit 3, Edexcel Unit 3 and OCR Unit 3 (Work and Leisure) and Unit 4 (Transport Economics).
Barriers to entry are 'obstacles' a firm might face if it tried to enter a new market — e.g. anything that makes entering a new market difficult or expensive.

Barriers to entry **Vary** between **Markets**

1) A **barrier to entry** is any **potential difficulty** or **expense** a firm might face if it wants to enter a market.
2) The '**height**' of these barriers determines:
   - **how long** it will take or **how expensive** it will be for a new entrant to establish itself in a market and increase the amount of competition,
   - **whether** new entrants can successfully join the market **at all**.

High barriers to entry mean entering a market will take longer or be more expensive.

3) Barriers to entry allow firms that are **already** in the market (called '**incumbent**' firms) to make **supernormal** profits, before new entrants enter the market and compete these profits away.
   How long **incumbent** firms can make supernormal profits for depends upon:
   - The **height** of the barriers to entry — i.e. how long the barriers can **prevent** new firms entering the market.
   - The **level** of supernormal profit being earned — this is because the **greater** the **profits** to be made, the more effort new entrants will be willing to make to **overcome** the barriers.
4) **Perfectly competitive** markets have **no barriers** to entry whatsoever.

They also don't have any barriers to exit — firms can leave a market whenever they choose (see p.36 for more about leaving a market).

5) In a **pure monopoly market** the barriers to entry are **total**.
   No new firms can enter, so the monopolist remains the **only** seller.

See page 26 for monopolies.

6) As usual, in **real life** the situation often lies somewhere between the extremes of perfect competition and a monopoly. There are normally **some** barriers to entry, but they're **not** usually **total**.

Barriers to entry can be created in **Various Ways**

1) Barriers to entry come about for **various** reasons. For example:
   a) The tendency (innocent or deliberate) of **incumbent** firms to **create** or **build** barriers.
   b) The **nature** of the industry leading to barriers over which incumbent firms and new entrants have **little control**.
   c) The extent of **government regulation** and **licensing**.
2) The **overall** barrier to entry into a market might be made up of a number of individual barriers:

Barriers to entry due to incumbent firms' actions

- An **innovative new product or service** can give a firm a head start over its rivals which can be difficult for a new entrant to overcome. If the new technology is also **patented** then other firms can't simply copy the new design — it's **legally protected**.
- Strong **branding** means that some products are very **well known** to consumers. The **familiarity** of the product often makes it a consumer's first choice, and puts new entrants to a market at a disadvantage.
- A strong brand can be the result of a firm making genuinely **better products** than the competition, or can be created by **effective advertising**. The barrier to entry is the **expense** and **difficulty** a new entrant to the market would have in attracting customers away from the market leaders.

Both create a barrier to entry.

- **Aggressive pricing tactics** by incumbent firms can **drive** new competition **out** of the market before it becomes established. Incumbent firms may be able to **lower prices** to a level that a new entrant cannot match (e.g. due to economies of scale) and drive them out of business. This is sometimes called '**predatory pricing**' (or '**destroyer pricing**' or '**limit pricing**').

It's often hard to distinguish between healthy price competition and predatory pricing.

- Just the **threat** of a '**price war**' may be enough to deter new firms from entering a market.

Barriers to Entry

Barriers to entry can be due to the nature of an industry

- Some '**capital-intensive**' industries require huge amounts of **capital expenditure** before a firm receives any revenue (e.g. steel production and airplane production require a massive investment in sophisticated manufacturing plants before any steel or airplanes can be sold). The **cost** of entering these markets is huge, so smaller enterprises may not be able to break through.
- If investments **can't** be **recovered** when a firm decides to leave a market, then that may make any attempt to break into a market very **risky** and **unappealing**. (See p.36 for more about these 'sunk costs'.)
- If there's a **minimum efficient scale of production** then any new firms entering the industry on a smaller scale will be operating at a **higher point** on the **average cost curve** than established firms. This means any new entrant has higher production costs per unit, so they'd have to sell the product to consumers at a higher **price**.

This barrier isn't the result of any deliberate obstruction by incumbent firms.

The barriers to exit can act as a barrier to entry.

Some economies of scale are only available to firms operating on a large scale — see p.11 for more about minimum efficient scale of production.

Barriers to entry can be due to government regulations

- If an activity requires a **licence**, then this restricts the **number** and **speed of entry** of new firms coming into a market. For example, pubs, pharmacists, food outlets, dentists and taxis all require licences before they can operate. Similarly, in a **regulated** industry (e.g. banking), firms have to be approved by a **regulator** before they can carry out certain activities.
- New factories may need **planning permission** before they can be built.
- There will also be regulations regarding **health and safety** and **working conditions** for employees that firms will need to keep to.

The reasons for needing a licence may be quite reasonable, but the process of getting one slows down (and can prevent) new entrants.

New entrants sometimes have their own **Advantages**

1) Not all new entrants to a market are **small firms** trying to compete against established 'giants'.
2) Sometimes the new entrants can be large successful companies that wish to **diversify** into new markets.
3) Their large size means they have greater **financial resources**, so they may be more successful in breaking into new markets.

When Virgin Money entered the banking sector, their large resources meant they could overcome the barriers to entry — but they had to invest heavily and advertise extensively.

Entering the pencil sharpener industry caused few worries for the directors of To the Edge of the Universe plc.

Practice Questions

Q1 Compare the barriers to entry in a perfectly competitive market and in a monopoly.

Q2 Describe the three main types of barrier to entry to a market.

Q3 How might the size of a potential new entrant influence its ability to break into a new market?

Exam Questions

Q1 Describe how branding can be used by incumbent firms to create barriers to entry to a market. [5 marks]

Q2 To what extent are barriers to entry always the result of anticompetitive behaviour by established firms? [15 marks]

A barrier to entry — what an economist calls a bouncer...

Barriers to entry change over time. For example, in the old days, if you couldn't find a publisher willing to print your new novel, there wasn't very much you could do about it — your masterpiece may have remained undiscovered forever. Nowadays though, you can easily get loads of copies printed using a self-publishing website. (There's more about this kind of thing on p.37.)

Monopolies

These pages are for AQA Unit 3, Edexcel Unit 3 and OCR Unit 3 (Work and Leisure) and Unit 4 (Transport Economics).
The word 'monopoly' is used by different people to mean slightly different things.
On the next couple of pages, it means an industry with only one firm in it.

A **Monopoly** is a market containing a **Single Seller**

1) In economics, a **monopoly** (or 'pure monopoly') is a market with only **one firm** in it (i.e. one firm **is** the industry). In other words, a single firm has **100% market share**.

In law, a monopoly is when a firm has a market share of 25% or more.

2) Even in markets with more than one seller, firms have **monopoly power** if they can influence the price of a particular good on their own — i.e. they can act as **price makers**.

In a monopoly, the price isn't determined by 'the market'.

3) Monopoly power may come about as a result of:
   - **Barriers to entry** preventing new competition entering a market to compete away large profits (see p.24).
   - **Advertising and product differentiation** — a firm may be able to act as a price maker if consumers think of its products as more desirable than those produced by other firms (e.g. because of a strong brand).
   - **Few competitors in the market** — if a market is dominated by a small number of firms, these are likely to have some price-making power. They'll also find it easier to differentiate their products.
4) Some industries lead to a **natural monopoly** — this can mean they have a great deal of monopoly power.
   - Industries where there are **high fixed costs** and/or there are **large economies of scale** lead to **natural monopolies**.
   - If there was **more than one** firm in the industry, then they would **all** have the same high fixed costs. This would lead to **higher costs** per customer than could be obtained by a single firm.
   - In this case, a monopoly might be **more efficient** than having lots of firms competing.
   - E.g. the supply of **water** is a **natural monopoly** — it makes no sense for competing firms to all lay **separate** pipes.
5) Even though firms with monopoly power are price makers, **consumers** can still **choose** whether or not to buy their products. So **demand** will still depend on the price — as always, the **higher** the price, the **lower** the demand will be.

A **Monopolist** makes **Supernormal** profits — even in the **Long Run**

This diagram shows how a firm behaves in a **monopoly market**.

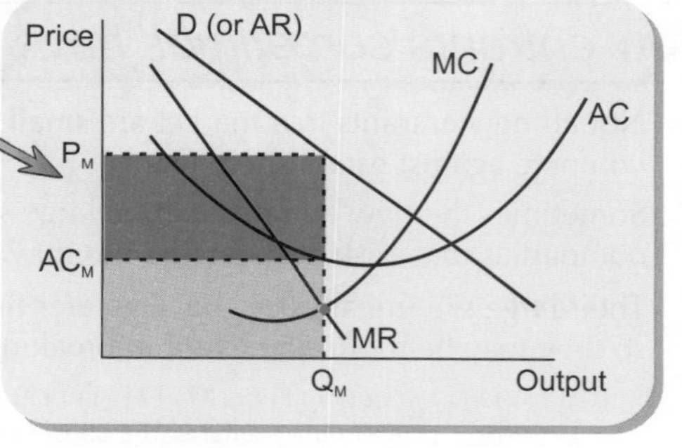

1) Assuming that the firm wants to **maximise profits**, its level of output will be where **MC = MR** (see p.15) — shown by the red dot.
2) If the firm produces a quantity Q_M, the **demand** (or AR) curve shows the **price** the firm can set — P_M.
3) At this output the **average cost** (AC) of producing **each unit** is AC_M.
4) The difference between AC_M and P_M is the **supernormal** (excess) profit **per unit**. So the **total supernormal profit** is shown by the **red** area.
5) In a monopoly market, the **barriers to entry** are **total**, so no new firms enter the market, and this supernormal profit is **not competed away**.
6) This means the situation remains as it is — this is the **long run equilibrium position** for a monopolist.

In perfect competition, a firm's marginal revenue and average revenue are the same — they both equal the equilibrium price (which is set by the market, not the firm — see p.21). In a monopoly market, this isn't true — see p.13.

Monopolies are **Productively** and **Allocatively Inefficient**

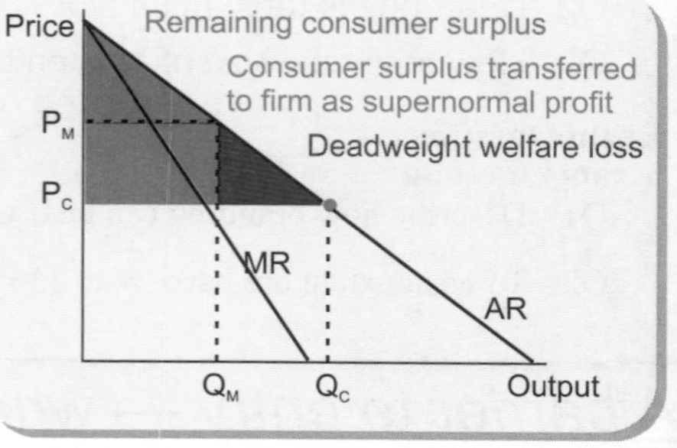

1) The above diagram shows that MC is **not** equal to AC at the **long run equilibrium position** for a monopoly (i.e. the firm is **not** operating at the **lowest** point on the AC curve). This means that a monopoly is **not productively efficient**.
2) The same diagram shows that the price charged by the firm is **greater** than MC. This means that a monopoly market is **not allocatively efficient**. Producers are being '**over-rewarded**' for the products they're providing.
3) Because of the restricted supply, the product will also be **underconsumed** — consumers aren't getting as much of the product as they want.
4) The red area shows how some of the **consumer surplus** (see p.28) that would have existed at the market equilibrium price P_C is transferred to the producer.
5) There's a **deadweight welfare loss** too. The grey area shows **potential** revenue that the **producer isn't** earning on the quantity Q_M to Q_C of the product that **consumers** would have been prepared to pay for (but which isn't produced).

Monopolies

Monopolies have further Drawbacks

There are other **potential disadvantages** in a monopoly market as well.

- There's no need for a monopoly to **innovate** or to respond to **changing consumer preferences** in order to make a profit, so they may become complacent.
- Similarly, there's no need to **increase efficiency**, so **x-inefficiency** can remain high.
- **Consumer choice** is restricted, since there are **no alternative** products.
- **Monopsonist** power (see below) may also be used to **exploit suppliers**.

Another drawback is that playing it ruins friendships — this fight is all over who gets to play with the racing car counter.

Monopolies have some Potential Benefits

Despite the disadvantages that a monopoly market causes, there can be **benefits**.

1) A monopolist's **large size** allows it to gain an advantage from **economies of scale**. If **diseconomies of scale** are avoided, this means it can keep **average costs** (and perhaps **prices**) low.

A monopolist will produce more than any of the individual producers in a perfectly competitive market would.

2) The **security** a monopolist has in the market (as well as the **supernormal profits**) means it can take a long-term view and **invest** in **developing** and **improving** products for the future — this can lead to **dynamic efficiency**.
3) Increased **financial security** also means that a monopolist can provide **stable** employment for its workers.
4) **Intellectual property rights** (**IPRs**) allow a form of legal **limited monopoly** that can actually be **in consumers' interests** because they'll benefit from better quality, innovative products.
    - There are various types of IPRs, such as **copyright** and **patents**. These allow a firm **exclusive** use of their **innovative ideas** (i.e. no one else is allowed to use them) for a **limited time**.
    - During this time, **supernormal profits** may be possible, but this is seen as the **reward** for **innovation** and **creativity**.
    - Without the **protection** of IPRs, firms would have **little incentive** to **risk** their resources investing in innovative products or processes — other firms would simply be able to **copy** those ideas (and immediately start to compete away any supernormal profits).

IPRs are particularly important in the 'creative industries' — e.g. music, television, video games, and so on.

A Monopsony is a market with a Single Buyer

1) A **monopsony** is a situation when a **single buyer** dominates a market.
2) A monopsonist can act as a **price maker**, and drive down prices.
3) For example, **supermarkets** are sometimes accused of acting as monopsonists when buying from their suppliers. Some people claim supermarkets unfairly use their market power to force **suppliers** to sell their products at a price that means those suppliers make a **loss**.
4) This could be seen as a monopsonist **exploiting** its suppliers. But it could be in the interests of **consumers** if the supermarkets **pass on** those low prices (by charging low prices to their **customers**).

Practice Questions

Q1 What are the characteristics of a monopoly?

Q2 What does it mean to say a monopoly is a 'price maker'?

Q3 Give two examples of arguments made in favour of monopolies.

Exam Question

Q1 Using a diagram, show how supernormal profit is earned in a monopoly, even in the long run. [10 marks]

Monopoly... monopsony... — it's all Greek to me...

Possibly the most important thing here is that a monopolist firm is a price maker, giving it a lot of 'market power'. Some economists actually say that monopolies aren't a big problem in reality, since monopoly profits inevitably lead to greater competition or the development of substitutes, and this then weakens the monopolist's market power. Overall, whether a monopoly is good or bad probably depends on the circumstances — the UK government's current view is that competition is generally preferable.

Price Discrimination

These pages are for AQA Unit 3, Edexcel Unit 3 and OCR Unit 3 (Work and Leisure) and Unit 4 (Transport Economics).
An example of price discrimination would be if you and a friend went into a restaurant and had exactly the same meal... but the restaurant charged you different prices.

Price Discrimination means charging Different Prices for the Same Product

1) **Price discrimination** occurs when a seller charges **different prices** to **different customers** for **exactly** the **same product**.
   - It's **not** price discrimination if the products **aren't exactly** the same.
   - So Business-class and Standard-class plane tickets are **not** an example of price discrimination, since it **costs more** to provide the comfier seats and extra legroom in Business class.

   Don't confuse price discrimination with price differentiation, where a producer charges different prices for similar but different products.

2) Several **conditions** need to be satisfied for a firm to make use of price discrimination:
   - The seller must have some **price-making** power (e.g. there might be barriers to entry preventing competition). So **monopolies** (and **oligopolies** — see p.30) can price discriminate.

     Price-taking firms in a perfectly competitive market cannot practise price discrimination.
   - The firm must be able to distinguish **separate groups** of customers who have **different** price elasticities of demand (**PED**). In fact, the **more groups** that the market can be subdivided into, the **greater** the gains for the seller.

     And the cost of finding out this information needs to be lower than any potential gains.
   - The firm must be able to prevent **seepage** — it must be able to prevent customers who have bought a product at a **low price** re-selling it **themselves** at a **higher price** to customers who could have been charged **more**.

Examples

- **Theatres** and **cinemas** offer 'concession' prices for certain groups (e.g. students and pensioners).
- **Window cleaners** could charge more in a smart neighbourhood than in a lower-income area.
- **Train tickets at rush hour** cost more than the same train ticket at other times of day.
- **Pharmaceutical drugs** may be sold at different prices in different countries.

Price discrimination transfers Consumer Surplus from Consumer to Producer

1) A **consumer surplus** is the difference between the **actual selling price** of a product and the price a consumer **would have been willing to pay**. For example, if the price of a cinema ticket was £8, but a consumer would have been willing to pay £10, then the consumer surplus is £2.
2) Price discrimination attempts to turn **consumer surplus** into **additional revenue** for the seller.

   i.e. turn consumer surplus into producer surplus.
3) There are different **degrees** of price discrimination.

First Degree price discrimination (or Perfect price discrimination)

- **First degree** price discrimination is where each **individual** customer is charged the **maximum** they would be willing to pay.
- This would turn **all** the consumer surplus into **extra revenue** for the seller. In the diagram, **total revenue** = **red** and **grey** shaded areas combined.
- However, the cost of **gathering** the required information to do this, and the difficulty in preventing **seepage**, makes this method unlikely to be used in practice.

All the **consumer surplus** that would have existed at price P is turned into **revenue**.

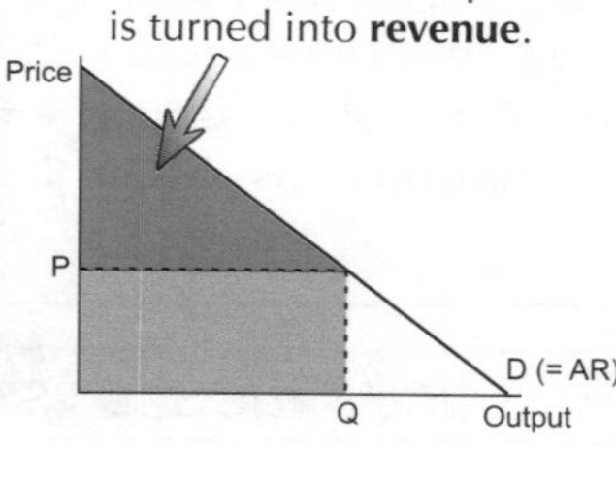

AQA ONLY

Second Degree price discrimination

- **Second degree** price discrimination is often used in **wholesale markets**, where **lower prices** are charged to people who purchase **large quantities** (i.e. price **varies** with quantity demanded).
- This turns **some** of the consumer surplus into revenue for the seller, and encourages **larger orders**.
- In the diagram, the seller charges P_1 per unit for the customer buying quantity Q_1, and P_2 per unit for the customer buying quantity Q_2.
- If **all** customers were charged P_1, then the firm's total revenue would be the **grey** area. By charging **some** customers P_2, the **red** area is turned into **additional revenue** for the firm.

Some of the **consumer surplus** that would exist at price P_1 is turned into **supernormal profit**.

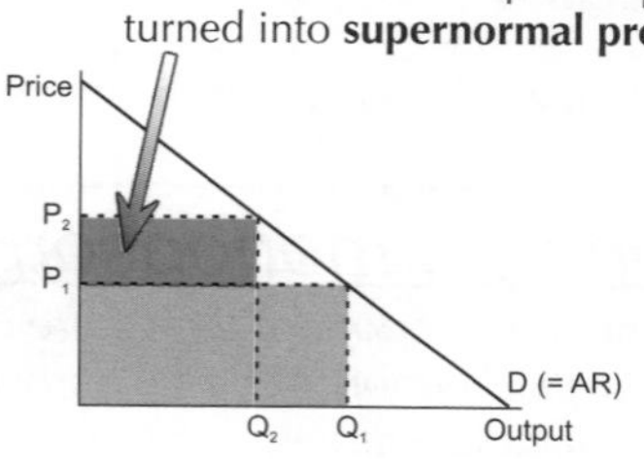

Price Discrimination

Third Degree price discrimination

- **Third degree** price discrimination is when a firm charges **different prices** for the **same product** to **different segments** of the market. These different segments could be:
  - customers of different **ages** — for example, a **leisure centre** might have different prices for adults, children and pensioners.
  - customers who buy at different **times** — for example, a **telephone company** might charge different amounts for phone calls made during **office hours** and phone calls made in the **evening**.
  - customers in different **places** — for example, a **pharmaceutical company** might sell its goods at different prices in different countries.
- For example, a seller can identify **two groups** of customers (Group A and Group B) with **different price elasticities** of demand (PED), as in these diagrams.

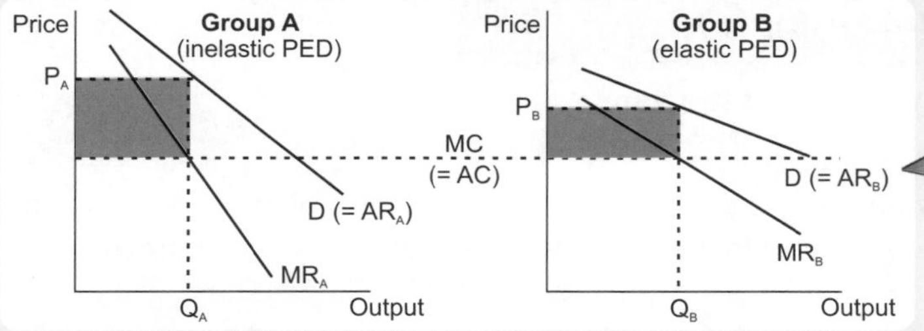

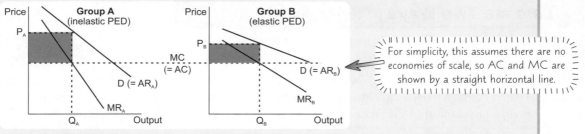

For simplicity, this assumes there are no economies of scale, so AC and MC are shown by a straight horizontal line.

- To **maximise profit**, the seller would set the price for each group at a level where **MC = MR**. This means:
  - it will charge a **higher price** to the group with a more **inelastic** PED (e.g. P_A for Group A).
  - It will charge a **lower price** to the group with a more **elastic** PED (e.g. P_B for Group B).
- The **red** areas represent the **supernormal profit** earned from each group. This **total** supernormal profit is **greater** than if the **same** price were charged to **everyone**.

*Price discrimination is **Good** for **Sellers** and **Possibly Bad** for **Others***

Price discrimination certainly results in **increased revenue** for the seller.
Whether this is seen as **fair** or **unfair** depends on what happens to that extra revenue.

1) The use of price discrimination means that **some** or **all** of the **consumer surplus** is **converted** into revenue for the **seller** — i.e. the seller increases revenue **at the expense of** the consumer. However, the extra revenue could be used to **improve products**, or **invested** in more efficient production methods which might lead to lower prices.
2) In all cases, the **average revenue** is greater than MC — so price discrimination does **not** lead to **allocative efficiency**.
3) Consumers are **not** treated equally, but often the people who end up paying **more** have **higher incomes**, so are more able to **afford** those higher prices. Some people see this as **fair**, especially if the greater profits made from some customers are used to **subsidise lower prices** paid by others (e.g. train passengers **commuting** to work pay **high fares**, and profits from these customers could be used to help support **daytime** services).

This is a form of income redistribution.

Practice Questions

Q1 Explain what is meant by the term 'price discrimination', and give two examples.

Q2 What conditions are needed for a firm to use price discrimination?

Q3 Explain with the use of graphs:
a) First degree price discrimination.
b) Second degree price discrimination.
c) Third degree price discrimination.

Exam Question

Q1 Discuss the extent to which price discrimination is beneficial to producers and consumers. [10 marks]

Perfect price discrimination — where everything costs what it's worth (to you)...

This is tricky stuff — no doubt about it. But if you can get your head round what those graphs are showing, then you've gone a long way towards understanding why firms make use of price discrimination. Whether it's a good or bad thing overall is basically a matter of opinion — for a lot of people it would depend on what firms actually do with their increased revenue.

Oligopolies

These pages are for AQA Unit 3, Edexcel Unit 3 and OCR Unit 3 (Work and Leisure) and Unit 4 (Transport Economics).
Before getting properly into oligopolies, it's useful to know about concentration ratios... so that's up first.
After that, it's oligopolies all the way, so enjoy.

Concentration Ratios show How Dominant the big firms in a market are

1) Some industries are **dominated** by just **a few** companies (even though there may be many firms in that industry overall). These are called **concentrated markets**.
2) The **level** of domination is measured by a **concentration ratio**.

- Suppose **three firms** control **90%** of the market, while another **40 firms** control the other **10%**.
- The **three-firm concentration** ratio would be **90%** (i.e. the three largest firms control 90% of the market).

There are Two Ways to define an Oligopoly

1) You can define an **oligopoly** in terms of **market structure**:

An **oligopoly** is a market:
- that's **dominated** by just a **few** firms (i.e. a small number of firms have a high concentration ratio),
- that has high **barriers to entry** (so new entrants can't easily **compete away** supernormal profits),
- in which firms offer **differentiated** products (i.e. products offered by different firms will be **similar** but **not identical**).

2) Or you can define an **oligopoly** in terms of the **conduct** of firms (i.e. how they **behave**):

An **oligopoly** is a market:
- in which the firms are **interdependent** — i.e. the actions of **each** firm will have some kind of **effect** on the **others**,
- in which firms use **competitive** or **collusive** strategies to make this interdependence work to their advantage.

Firms in an oligopoly can either Compete or Collude

1) Unlike with perfectly competitive markets and monopolies, there's **no single strategy** that firms in an oligopolistic market should adopt in order to **maximise profits**.
2) Firms in an oligopoly face a **choice** about what kind of **long-term strategy** they want to employ, and each company's decision will be affected by how the **other interdependent** firms in the market act.
3) This means that there are **different** possible scenarios in an oligopolistic market.

Competitive behaviour

This is when the various firms **don't cooperate**, but **compete** with each other (especially on **price**).

Collusive behaviour

- This is when the various firms **cooperate** with each other, especially over what **prices** are charged.
- **Formal collusion** involves an **agreement** between the firms — i.e. they form a **cartel**. This is usually **illegal**.
- **Informal collusion** is **tacit** — i.e. it happens **without** any kind of agreement. This happens when each firm knows it's in their best interests **not** to compete... as long as all the other firms do the **same**.
- Some firms in a collusive oligopoly might still be able to act as **price leaders**, setting the pattern for others to **follow** (i.e. if that firm changes its prices, other firms will do the same, so prices remain at **similar levels** to each other).

The model of the prisoners' dilemma illustrates why these agreements sometimes break down — see p.33.

So two different markets may both be oligopolies, but the behaviour of the firms involved in the two markets could be completely different.

4) The behaviour that occurs depends on the characteristics of a **particular market**.

Competitive behaviour is more likely when...
- One firm has **lower costs** than the others.
- There's a relatively **large number** of big firms in the market (making it harder to know what everyone else is doing).
- The firms produce products that are **very similar**.
- Barriers to entry are **relatively low**.

Collusive behaviour is more likely when...
- The firms all have **similar costs**.
- There are **relatively few firms** in the market (so it's easier to check what other firms are charging, etc).
- **'Brand loyalty'** means customers are less likely to buy from a different firm, even when their prices are lower.
- Barriers to entry are **relatively high**.

Oligopolies

Collusion can bring about similar outcomes to a **Monopoly**

1) **Collusive oligopolies** can produce results quite similar to those in a monopoly.
2) Collusive oligopolies generally lead to there being **higher prices** and **restricted output** (and **underconsumption**), as well as **allocative** and **productive inefficiency**. Firms in collusive oligopolies often have the **resources** to invest in more efficient production methods and achieve **dynamic efficiency**, but there's not always an **incentive** for them to do so. So collusive oligopolies can lead to **market failure**.
3) Because the firms in a collusive oligopoly **don't lower prices** even though they **could**, they make **supernormal** profits **at the expense of** consumers.
4) In the case where colluding firms have an **agreement** to restrict output to maintain high prices, the firms set a **price** (P_O) and a **level of output** (Q_O) that will **maximise profits** for the industry (i.e. where MC = MR for the industry). They then agree output **quotas** — the level of output each of the firms will produce. The resulting supernormal profits for one of these firms is shown in **red**.

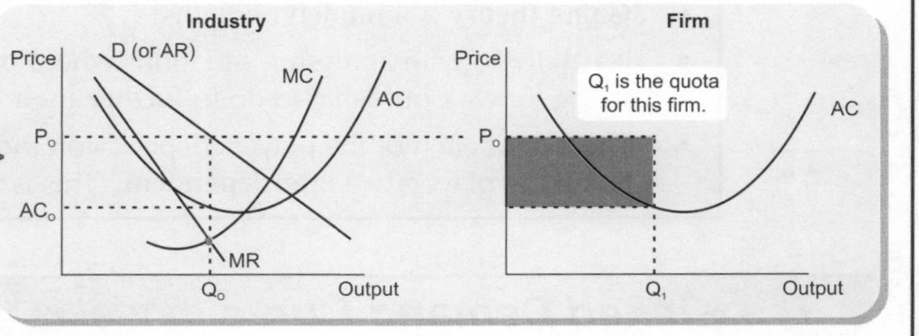

5) Firms that **collude** on **price** may still **compete** in other ways though, so the firms' **marketing policies** are very important.
   - For example, colluding firms may try to **differentiate** their products from their competitors' — either by **improving** them in some way or by trying to create a strong **brand** to attract and retain customers.
   - They could use **sales promotions** (e.g. 'loyalty' rewards for customers who make repeat purchases).
   - They may even try to find new **export markets**.
6) Other firms that try to break into the market may face **predatory pricing** tactics (see p.24 for more info). Even so, if the potential profits are large enough, they may **persevere** until they eventually establish themselves. However, they may then see that it's **not** in their interests to compete further — if so, **collusion** can re-emerge.

Oligopolies **Might Not** be as bad as they sound

1) Some economists argue that **collusive** oligopolies are either:
   a) **not as bad** as they're sometimes made to sound,
   b) **unstable** — i.e. they're unlikely to last for long,
   c) **both** of the above.

   There's more about this 'instability' on p.33.

2) They argue that **formal collusion** is quite unlikely to occur because it's usually **illegal**, and any **informal** collusion is likely to be **temporary**, because one firm will soon decide to '**cheat**', and lower its prices to gain an advantage (called **first-mover advantage** — see p.33). This kind of behaviour is likely to trigger a **price war** (and falling prices).
3) Even in a **collusive** oligopoly:
   - If firms aren't competing on **price**, then **non-price competition** might even be stronger, leading to some **dynamic efficiency**. This would be good for **consumers** if it led to product innovations and improvements.
   - Firms are **unlikely** to raise prices to **very high** levels. This is because **high prices** may provide a **strong incentive** for **new entrants** to join the market, even if the barriers to entry are high. (See p.35 for more info.)
4) **Competitive oligopolies** can achieve **high** levels of **efficiency** — these markets often work well in practice.

Practice Questions

Q1 Explain the two ways you can define an oligopoly.

Q2 What is meant by formal collusion? And informal collusion?

Q3 Explain why different oligopolistic markets can produce very different outcomes.

Exam Question

Q1 Discuss the extent to which the existence of oligopolistic markets is against the interests of consumers. [10 marks]

I reckon 'Oligopoly' would be an interesting game...

Oligopolies are quite different from perfectly competitive and monopolistic markets, because there's 'more than one way to play the game and win'. This means that it's much harder to predict what's likely to happen in an oligopoly. It could work out really badly for consumers, with firms making large monopoly-style profits... or it could all turn out very differently. It'll depend on how firms think they can best further their own interests. There's more about playing the 'oligopoly game' on the next couple of pages.

Interdependence in Oligopolistic Markets

These pages are for AQA Unit 3, Edexcel Unit 3 and OCR Unit 3 (Work and Leisure) and Unit 4 (Transport Economics).
Interdependence makes it tricky for a firm to decide how to act, since it'll then be affected by how competing firms decide to react. The 'models' on these pages can help you work out how firms are likely to behave.

Game Theory can be used to understand the results of *Interdependence*

1) In oligopolistic markets, each firm is affected by the behaviour of the others — the firms are **interdependent**.
2) This means that the behaviour of firms in oligopolistic markets can be looked at as a kind of '**mathematical game**'.

- **Game theory** is a branch of maths.
- It's all to do with analysing situations where **two or more 'players'** (e.g. people, firms, etc) are each trying to work out what to do to **further their own interests**.
- The fate of each of the players depends on their **own** decisions, and the decisions of **everyone else**. So all the players are **interdependent**. This is why it's often used to analyse situations in **economics**.

The *Kinked Demand Curve* model is used to explain *Price Stability*

1) You can understand some **outcomes** from certain oligopolistic markets by 'playing the game' from **each firm's perspective**.
2) For example, the model of the **kinked demand curve** illustrates why prices are often quite **stable**, even in some **competitive** oligopolies.
3) In the kinked demand curve model, there are **two assumptions**:

- If one firm **raises** its prices, then the other firms will **not raise** theirs.
- If one firm **lowers** its prices, then the other firms will **also lower** theirs.

4) The first assumption means that a firm which **raises** its prices will see quite a large **drop** in **demand**. This is because customers are likely to **switch** to buying their goods from **other** firms.
In other words:

When price is **increased**, demand is **price elastic**.

So it makes sense for the competing firms not to increase their prices.

This means any firm that **raises** prices will **lose out** — the **fall in demand** will more than **cancel out** the gains from charging a **higher price**.

5) The second assumption means that a firm which **lowers** its prices will **not gain** any **market share** (although the **overall size** of the market may **increase slightly**, given that **all** the firms will have lowered their prices).
In other words:

When price is **decreased**, demand is **price inelastic**.

Any competing firm not reducing its prices will lose revenue, since customers will buy elsewhere.

This means any firm that **reduces** prices will **lose out** — they **won't** gain market share but the average **price** for their products will have **fallen**.

6) The result of the above assumptions is a **kinked demand curve** — like this:

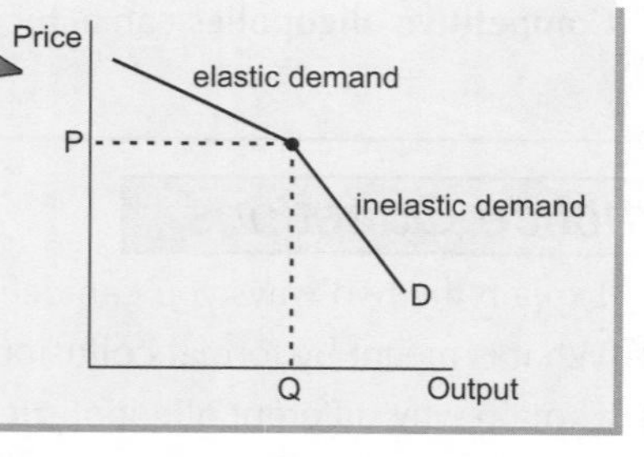

7) The outcome is that firms have **no incentive** to change prices. If they **either** raise **or** lower prices, they will **lose out** as a result.
8) The result is **price stability** for prolonged periods of time.

Note that the firms are competing here — not colluding. Each firm would reduce prices if that would help increase revenue... but it doesn't.

The *Kinked Demand Curve Model* describes just one possible outcome

1) The kinked demand curve model shows one type of **interdependence**.
2) This **doesn't** mean that it explains the behaviour of firms in **every** oligopoly.
3) The **assumptions** in the kinked demand curve model may **not** be appropriate for every oligopoly — and if they're **not**, the model **won't** predict firms' behaviour at all well. Other oligopolistic markets will be better described using **different** models.

Interdependence in Oligopolistic Markets

The **Prisoners' Dilemma** model can show **First-Mover Advantage**

1) The **prisoners' dilemma** model can be used to understand how **interdependent** firms might act in an oligopolistic market. In the version below there are actually **two firms** (instead of two prisoners).
   - Suppose there are just **two firms** in a market, Firm A and Firm B.
   - Each firm has to decide **what level of output** to produce in their oligopolistic market situation.
   - For simplicity, assume that each firm has **two options**:
     - produce a **high level** of output
     - produce a **low level** of output
   - Both firms **know** the **other** firm is also trying to decide what level of output to produce.
   - And both firms **know** that they're **interdependent** — i.e. **both firms** will be affected by **each other's decision**.
2) The results of the firms' different choices can be summarised using a **payoff matrix**. The **coloured** figures show the profit that each firm will make for different combinations of choices.

Firm A

Firm B	Low output	High output
Low output	200 / 200	300 / 100
High output	100 / 300	–100 / –100

For example, if Firm A outputs at a high level and Firm B outputs at a low level, then Firm A will make a profit of 300, while Firm B will make a profit of 100.

3) If the firms **cooperate** and agree to restrict output to **low levels**, then the outcome for **both** firms (a profit of 200) is **better** than if they **both** output at a **high level** (a loss of 100). This could work well for both firms... if they can **both** be **trusted**.
4) However, it's **in the interests** of each firm to stop cooperating and **raise output** — **as long as** they do this **before** the other firm decides to.
5) This is because if **one firm** decides to '**cheat**' and **increase output** (to get a profit of 300), then it's actually **in the interests** of the other firm to keep producing at a **low level** and take the **reduced profit** of 100 (instead of raising output and forcing both companies to make a **loss** of 100). This is an illustration of **first-mover advantage**.
6) The theory of first-mover advantage shows why **cartels** can be **unstable** — every firm knows they can get an advantage if they **break** the agreement **before** anyone else does.

If they both output at a high level, they'll 'flood the market' and drive down the price until it's below the cost of making it.

However, neither firm can be certain if (or when) the other will decide to raise output.

Being the first mover **Isn't** always an advantage

1) Being the **first mover** can give a firm an **advantage**... but it can also be a **disadvantage**.
2) **Different decisions** will make sense in **different situations** — it all depends on the numbers in the **payoff matrix** (i.e. the potential **profits** and **losses** that each firm could make in the various possible scenarios).
3) For example, suppose several firms are all deciding whether to launch a new type of product into a market.
   - The 'first mover' could make a **huge profit** by winning a large market share very early.
   - However, if they've **overestimated** the demand for the product, they may make **huge losses**.
   - Also, competitors may be able to use a lot of the technology that the first firm has **developed**, **reducing** their **costs**, and allowing them to charge a **lower price** than the first mover.

Practice Questions

Q1 Use the prisoners' dilemma to illustrate how a firm can obtain a first-mover advantage.

Exam Question

Q1 Explain how the kinked demand curve can explain price stability in some oligopolistic markets. [15 marks]

Unlike the prisoners, you face no dilemma — you really need to learn this...

The prisoners' dilemma gets its name because the same basic choices are usually described in terms of two prisoners who have jointly committed a serious crime. It's really cool... it looks so simple, but by changing the numbers in the payoff matrix you can show how all sorts of terrible outcomes (including ones that happen in real life) are actually the result of everybody acting 'sensibly'.

Monopolistic Competition

These pages are for Edexcel Unit 3 and OCR Unit 3 (Work and Leisure) and Unit 4 (Transport Economics).
Monopolistic competition is a market structure that sits somewhere between perfect competition and monopoly. As you might expect, it's got some of the characteristics of both structures.

Monopolistic Competition resembles a Lot of Real-life industries

1) **Monopolistic competition** (sometimes called **imperfect competition**) lies part-way along the range of market structures — between perfect competition and monopolies.

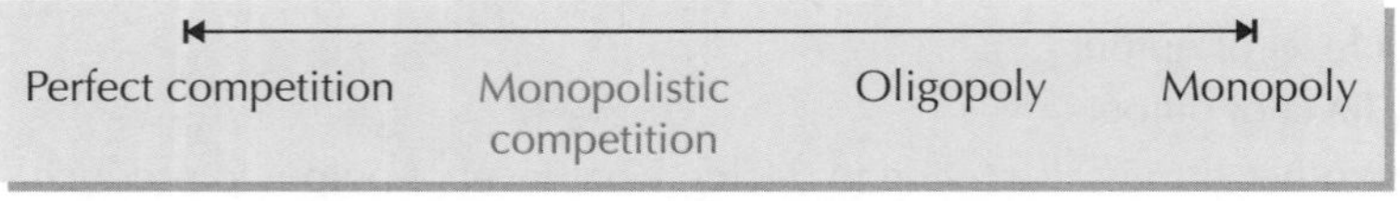

2) In **monopolistic competition**, the conditions of perfect competition are 'relaxed' slightly and instead become:
   - Some **product differentiation** — either due to **advertising** or because of **real differences between products**.
     - This means the seller has some degree of **price-making power**.
     - So each seller's demand curve **slopes downwards**.
     - But the **smaller** the product differences, the more **price elastic** the demand for each product will be.
   - There are **either** no barriers to entry **or** only very low barriers to entry.
     - This means that if very high supernormal profits are earned, new entrants can **join** the industry fairly easily.

Remember... if all the products were identical (as in perfect competition), a firm's demand curve would be horizontal.

3) These 'relaxed' conditions are actually **more typical** of firms in **real life**.
This means that the **behaviour** predicted in this model may also be more **realistic**.

The Short Run position is like a Monopoly...

In monopolistic competition, the **barriers to entry** and/or the **product differentiation** mean that **supernormal profits** can be made, but only in the **short run**.

- The **profit-maximising** level of output occurs where **MC = MR**.
- The diagram shows the **output** leading to the **profit-maximising** price (P).
- This means the firm earns **supernormal** profit.
  Here the supernormal profit is shown by the red rectangle.

This is basically the same as for a monopoly, although because there might be similar (i.e. substitute) products available, demand is likely to be more price elastic.

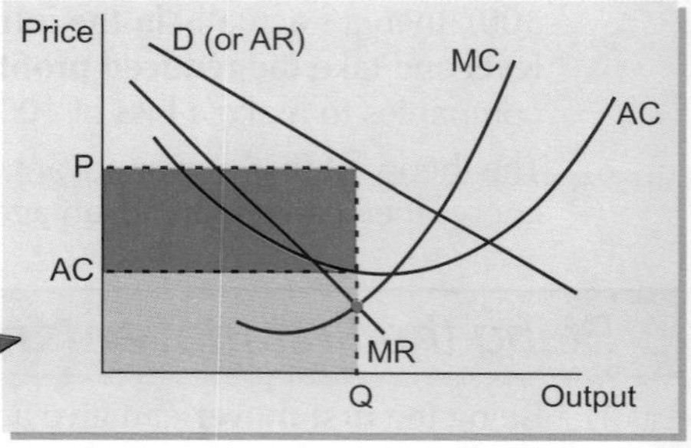

...but the Long Run position is more like Perfect Competition

1) But unlike in a monopoly, the situation shown by the above diagram **doesn't last** in the long run.
2) In monopolistic competition, the **barriers to entry** are **fairly low**, so new entrants will join the industry. These new entrants will cause the **established** firm's **demand curve** to shift to the **left** (since the overall demand is now **split** between **more** firms).
3) New entrants will **continue** to join (and the established firm's demand curve will **continue** to shift **left**) until:
   - **Only normal profit** can be earned — this is where **P = AR = AC**.
     At this point the slopes of the **AC curve** and the **demand** (or **AR**) **curve** touch **tangentially** (i.e. they meet, but they don't actually cross).
     This is shown by the **red** dot.
   - At this quantity, **MR = MC** (see the **blue** dot).

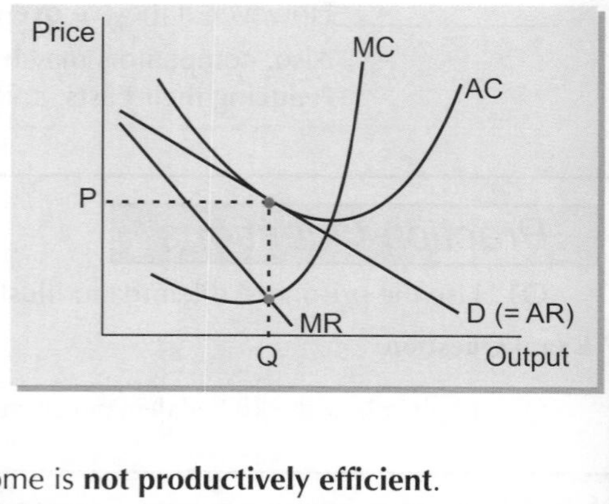

4) Since the firm is **not** producing at the **lowest point** on the AC curve, this outcome is **not productively efficient**.
5) And since the equilibrium price is **greater** than MC, this is **not allocatively efficient**.
6) But despite this, a monopolistically competitive market will generally achieve much **greater efficiency** levels than a monopoly market.

Monopolistic Competition

Prices in *Monopolistic Competition* are *Higher* than in *Perfect Competition*

1) The **short run** position of monopolistic competition is basically the same as in a **monopoly**. However, unlike in a monopoly, **new entrants** to the market will drive prices down until only **normal profit** is earned in the **long run**.

Remember... in a monopoly the high barriers to entry and lack of substitutes mean that supernormal profits continue to be made, even in the long run.

Exactly **how long** this process takes is important.
- If it takes a **very long** time, the market will resemble a **monopoly**.
- But if it all happens relatively **quickly**, then the market will be more like a **perfectly competitive** market.
- This is why firms are often willing to spend large amounts of money to try to **differentiate** their product (e.g. by **improving** it or by **advertising** to create a strong **brand**). The **longer** a firm can retain its **price-making power**, the longer it can make **supernormal** profit.

2) But unlike in **perfect competition**, in monopolistic competition the firm is **not** producing at the **lowest point** on the **AC curve**.
3) These different positions on the AC curve mean that **prices** in monopolistic competition tend to be **higher** than in **perfect competition**.
4) This is because firms in monopolistic competition need to spend money on **differentiating** their **product** (e.g by **advertising**) and creating **brand loyalty**.

There's no need for advertising in perfect competition because consumers already have perfect knowledge. And in perfect competition, all products are identical, so there's no price differentiation.

5) Firms in monopolistic competition have also **chosen** to **restrict output** in order to **maximise profits**. This means they **don't** benefit from all the **economies of scale** that they could.
6) Prices in monopolistic competition tend to be **lower** than those charged by a **monopoly** seller.
7) Generally, monopolistic competition is felt to work **reasonably well** in practice.

Monopolistic competition Doesn't usually lead to Dynamic Efficiency

1) The length of time it takes for new entrants to force **all** firms in monopolistic competition to only make **normal profit** is the length of time an **incumbent** firm can make **supernormal profits**.
2) These supernormal profits are reward for risky **production investment** or **product innovation**.
3) However, the **lack** of barriers to entry mean that firms are unlikely to invest huge amounts of money on new innovations — so there's likely to be less **dynamic efficiency** in a monopolistically competitive market.
4) In the **long run**, the **absence** of supernormal profit will mean there **won't** be much money available for investment.

Practice Questions

Q1 Describe the conditions that give rise to monopolistic competition.

Q2 Using a graph, explain:
a) the short run position for a firm in monopolistic competition.
b) the long run equilibrium position for a firm in monopolistic competition.

Q3 Compare price levels in monopolistic competition with price levels in:
a) a perfectly competitive market.
b) a monopoly.

Exam Question

Q1 Explain how the long run outcome in monopolistic competition differs from that in a monopoly market. [12 marks]

Monopolistic competition does what it says on the tin...

Monopolistic competition is what the name suggests... a sort of halfway house between a monopoly and perfect competition. You don't get all the drawbacks of a monopoly (drawbacks for a consumer, that is), but you don't get all the benefits of perfect competition either. It's actually a fairly good description of many real-life markets too, so you need to know all about it.

Contestability

These pages are for AQA Unit 3, Edexcel Unit 3 and OCR Unit 3 (Work and Leisure) and Unit 4 (Transport Economics).
To decide whether a market is contestable, you need to think about what the market could be like... not necessarily what it's like right now.

A Contestable market is Open to New Competitors

1) **Contestability** refers to **how open** a market is to **new competitors** (i.e. **potential** competition), even if currently there's little **actual** competition.

In a **contestable** market:
- The barriers to **entry** and **exit** are **low**. So if **excess profits** are made by **incumbent** firms, new firms will enter.
- **Supernormal** profits can **potentially** be made by new firms (at least in the short term).

It doesn't matter whether a market is currently a competitive market, an oligopoly or a monopoly — if new firms are able to enter it, it's contestable.

2) These two factors mean that incumbent firms always face the **threat** of increased competition. And increased competition is more likely if the incumbent firms make **large supernormal** profits.

Because new entrants will want to get some of the available profits.

3) This means incumbent firms have an **incentive** to set prices at a level that will **not** generate **vast** supernormal profits (see p.35).

High Barriers to Entry or Exit mean Low Contestability

It's the **low barriers to entry** that make potential competition a **genuine threat** to incumbent firms. So anything that makes barriers **higher** makes a market **less contestable**. Barriers to entry are **high** if:

1) There are **patents** on key products or production methods.
   - Patents give a firm **legal protection** against other firms **copying** its products or production methods.

Patents can protect products and processes.

2) **Advertising** by incumbent firms has already created **strong brand loyalty**.
3) There's a threat of **limit pricing** (i.e. **predatory pricing**) tactics by the incumbent firms.
   - If new entrants fear a **'price war'**, then they may decide not to enter the market.
   - This would be particularly difficult for new entrants if the incumbent firms had **lower costs** as a result of having been in the market for longer.
4) **Trade restrictions** are present (e.g. tariffs or quotas) — these don't allow new foreign entrants to compete in domestic markets on equal terms with the incumbent firms.
5) Incumbent firms are **vertically integrated** (see p.18).
   - This could mean that access to supplies of **raw materials** or **distribution networks** is difficult for new firms.
6) **Sunk costs** (a barrier to exit) are high.
   - Costs are 'sunk' if they **cannot be recovered** when a firm leaves an industry.
   - These costs might include **investment** in specialised equipment, or **expenditure** on advertising.
   - If these sunk costs are high then the **cost of failure** is high, and potential new entrants may be **deterred** from even entering the market.

High barriers were no problem for Dobbin, or his horse.

Hit-and-Run tactics can be used in contestable markets

1) The **low** barriers to **entry** and **exit** mean that new entrants can **'hit and run'**.

Hit-and-run tactics
- This means **entering** a market while **supernormal profits** can be made...
- ...and then **leaving** the market once prices have been driven down to **normal-profit** levels.

2) As long as the **profit** made while in the market is **greater** than the entry and exit costs, it's worthwhile for a firm to compete... even for a **short time**.

Firms can reduce the level of their sunk costs by leasing equipment rather than buying it.

Contestability

The contestability of a market affects the **Behaviour** of **Incumbent Firms**

1) In a **contestable** market, it's the **threat** of increased competition (as well as the **actual** competition from firms already in the market) that affects how incumbent firms **behave**.
2) For example, incumbent firms will know that high supernormal profits (which will maximise **short-term profits**) are likely to attract **new entrants**, and that these new entrants are likely to **drive down** prices.
3) So it might make more sense for the incumbent firms to sacrifice some short-term profits, and set **lower prices** to **avoid** attracting new entrants.

This may be the best way to maximise profit in the long run.

4) **Incumbent** firms have an interest in **creating** high barriers to entry if they can.
5) This could involve heavy spending on **advertising**, or making it clear they would be prepared to engage in **predatory pricing** if new firms enter the market.

Though firms have to be careful not to break any laws regarding predatory pricing.

6) But in the **long run**, firms in contestable markets will move towards **productive** and **allocative efficiency**, because supernormal profit is **competed away** and firms must settle for **normal profit**.

Barriers to entry can be '**Lowered**' or '**Raised**'

1) Barriers to entry to an industry are **not** fixed for all time.
2) New **technology** can help **lower** barriers to entry. For example, the **internet** allows small **retailers** to reach a huge number of potential buyers using **online marketplaces** — without the need for an actual shop or a market stall.
3) And because markets that are **not contestable** can lead to **higher prices** than necessary, governments will often try to **lower** high barriers to entry.
4) But barriers to entry can get **higher** too, especially in industries that come to be **dominated** by a few **very large** firms.

The airline industry

1) For many years the **airline industry** was dominated by a small number of 'national airlines' that enjoyed special privileges in their own country — this was an example of **protectionism** (see p.127).
2) More '**open skies**' policies (allowing airlines much greater freedom to choose where they fly from and to) mean airlines can now compete on a much more even basis.
3) This was made possible by a combination of **international treaties** and action by **individual governments** in their own country.
4) In recent decades, this has led to a **huge growth** in the number of airlines operating.

Petrol retailing

1) The retail petrol market is **less contestable** now than in the past.
2) There used to be thousands of **independent** petrol stations.

i.e. they weren't part of a national chain.

3) But petrol stations run by **major oil companies** became **larger**, and then **supermarkets** entered the market too. These firms could achieve **economies of scale** and cut **labour costs** (due to the growth of **self-service** petrol stations) in a way that made it increasingly difficult for the independent firms to compete.
4) Entering the industry and trying to compete on price nowadays would involve **tremendous costs**.

Practice Questions

Q1 What does contestability mean? What are the characteristics of a contestable market?

Q2 What are sunk costs? Why do high sunk costs make a market less contestable?

Q3 Describe one way in which incumbent firms can create barriers to entry in an industry.

Exam Question

Q1 Discuss the effect of high contestability on the behaviour of incumbent firms. [10 marks]

A contestable market is open for businesses...

Some people think that a market's contestability is more important than its actual structure. They say that just the threat of new competition is enough to make people act as though the competition already exists. This section has been full of complicated stuff — enough to make anyone's head hurt. So once you've learnt these pages, have a break — you've earned it.

Market Failure and Government Failure

These pages are for AQA Unit 3, Edexcel Unit 3 and OCR Unit 3 (Work and Leisure) and Unit 4 (Transport Economics).
You'll have learnt all about market and government failure at AS level. These three pages give you a quick reminder of the stuff you should already know, and a little taster of what's to come in the rest of this section. What a treat.

You need to know about **Different Types** of **Market Failure**

1) For A2 economics, you'll need to know about the following types of **market failure**:
   - Externalities
   - Merit and demerit goods (**AQA and OCR only**)
   - Public goods
   - Monopolies
   - Imperfect information
   - Immobile factors of production
   - Unstable commodity markets (**Edexcel and AQA only**)
   - Lack of equity
2) You'll have seen some of these at **AS** — so **look back** at your AS notes on market failure and make sure you know everything you needed to learn for your AS exam.
3) You'll need to know **a bit more** about some of these types of market failure for **A2**. But don't worry — these three pages give you a **brief recap** of what you should have learnt at **AS**, and tell you what **extra** stuff you'll need for **A2**.
4) Make sure you know about the methods of **government intervention** used to tackle these market failures too.

Externalities affect **Third Parties**

AS RECAP

1) **Externalities** are the effects that producing or consuming a good/service has on **third parties**. They can be both **positive** and **negative**.
2) Externalities cause **market failure** because in the free market only **private** costs and benefits are considered. Positive and negative externalities are **ignored** by the **price mechanism**.
3) The socially optimal level of output for a good is where **marginal social cost (MSC) = marginal social benefit (MSB)**.

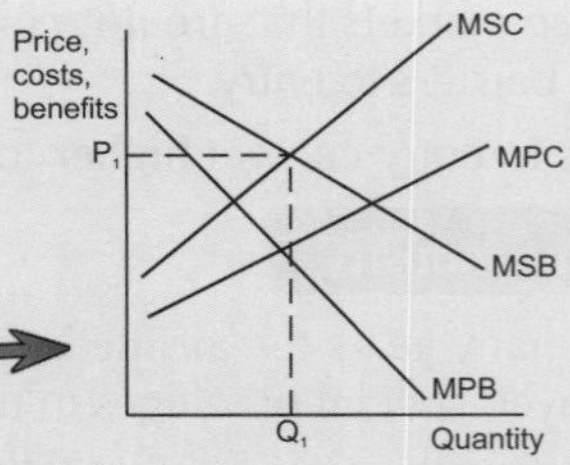

4) Governments use various **methods of intervention** when it comes to externalities, e.g. indirect taxation, subsidies and pollution permits. Make sure you're familiar with these methods.
5) If you're doing **AQA** or **OCR**, there's some **new stuff** on externalities later in this section:
   - You need to know about the impact of **externalities** on the **environment** — see p.41-43.
   - This will include **extending property rights** to try to **protect** the environment from negative externalities — see p.42.
   - Externalities are also **important** for **cost benefit analysis** — see p.48-49.

AQA & OCR ONLY

Merit Goods benefit society but **Demerit Goods** do the opposite

AS RECAP

1) **Merit** goods have **greater social benefits** than **private benefits** — their consumption has **positive externalities**. Merit goods are **underconsumed** because their positive externalities are **ignored** and consumers **don't realise** the **full benefits** they have.
2) **Demerit** goods have **greater social costs** than **private costs** — their consumption has **negative externalities**. Demerit goods are **overconsumed** because their negative externalities are **ignored** and consumers **don't realise** the **harm** that they can cause.
3) The **socially optimal** level of output for a good is where **MSC = MSB**.
4) In a free market, the **market equilibrium** for merit goods is **below** the socially optimal level of consumption. So, merit goods are underproduced/underconsumed, leading to a **loss** of the **potential welfare gain of ABC**.
5) In a free market, the **market equilibrium** for demerit goods is **above** the socially optimal level of consumption. So, demerit goods are overprovided/overconsumed, leading to a **welfare loss of DEF**.
6) **Short-term** decision making and **imperfect information** contribute to the misallocation of merit and demerit goods, causing **market failure**.

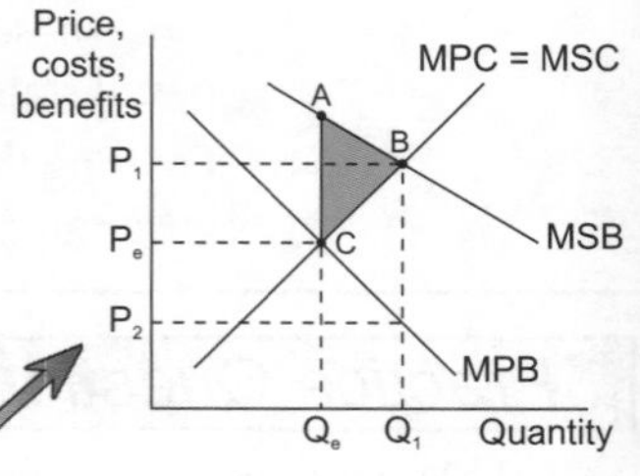

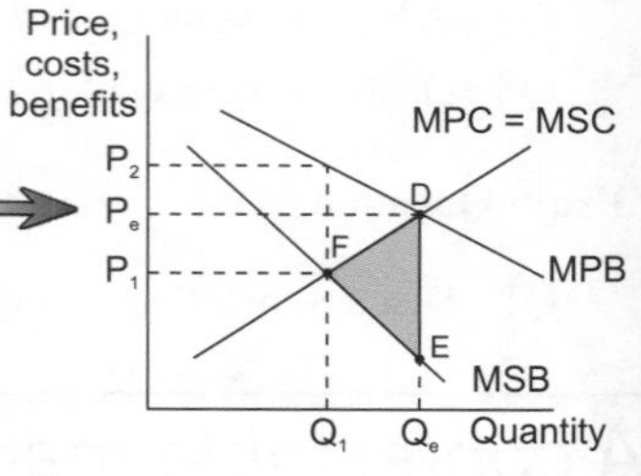

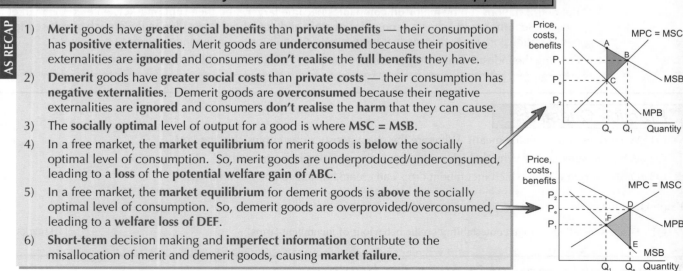

7) Government intervention to correct this market failure might include **subsidies** or **state provision** of merit goods, and **indirect taxation** or **regulation** of demerit goods.
8) Governments might also **provide information** on merit and demerit goods.

Market Failure and Government Failure

Public Goods have Two Main Characteristics

AS RECAP

1) **Public goods** have two main characteristics — **non-rivalry** (one person benefiting from the good doesn't stop someone else from benefiting from it) and **non-excludability** (people can't be stopped from consuming the good, even if they haven't paid for it).
2) Non-excludability leads to the **free rider problem**, which means the **price mechanism** doesn't work and public goods are **underprovided** in the free market, or **not provided at all**. This causes **market failure**.
3) **Private** goods are the **opposite** of **public** goods — they're **excludable** and **exhibit rivalry**.
4) Some goods exhibit the characteristics of a public good — but **not fully**. These are known as **non-pure** (or **quasi**) **public goods**.
5) For example, **roads** appear to have the characteristics of a public good — often they're **free** for everyone to use (non-excludable) and one person using a road **doesn't prevent** another person from using it too (non-rivalrous). However, **tolls** can make a road **excludable** and **congestion** will make a road exhibit **rivalry**.
6) Some aspects of the **environment**, such as the air, can be seen as **public goods** — see p.41.
7) **State provision** is the most obvious method of government intervention to correct market failure with public goods — the state must provide the public goods that the free market won't provide.
8) For public good aspects of the environment, governments can use methods such as **extending property rights** and **tradable pollution permits** (see p.42-43).

If there's One Firm in a market then it has a Monopoly

If you're doing AQA, you'll have learnt a bit about monopolies at AS.

1) A **pure monopoly** is a market with only **one supplier**. However, markets with **more than one** supplier will **also** be referred to as a **monopoly** if **one** supplier **dominates** the market (e.g. has 25% or more of the market share).
2) Monopolies often lead to **market failure** — for example, a monopoly might **restrict** the supply of a good, **raising** its price and causing a **misallocation of resources**. Because monopolies fail to reach P = MC (see p.26), they're also **allocatively inefficient** and they cause a **deadweight welfare loss**.
3) You'll need to know about **collusive oligopolies** (p.30-31) and **monopsonies** (p.27) too, and how they can misallocate resources.
4) Governments can intervene in various ways to **prevent** or **reduce** monopoly power — e.g. **privatisation**, **regulation**, **deregulation** (p.44-45) and **competition policy** (p.46-47).

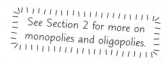

See Section 2 for more on monopolies and oligopolies.

Imperfect Information causes Market Failure

AS RECAP

1) **Symmetric** or **perfect information** means everyone has **equal** and **perfect** knowledge. It's assumed that in a **perfectly competitive market**, **everyone** has **perfect information**.
2) **Asymmetric** and **imperfect information** exists when there's a **lack** of perfect information in a market.
3) **Imperfect information** can mean that **merit** goods tend to be **underprovided** and **underconsumed**, and **demerit** goods tend to be **overprovided** and **overconsumed**.
4) Governments can use **regulations** (see p.44) to **protect** consumers and producers from **problems** arising from **asymmetric information** — e.g. the Sale of Goods Act **protects consumers** against firms supplying **substandard** goods.
5) Governments can also **intervene** to help consumers make well-informed decisions. They try to provide information on the **full costs** and **benefits** of goods and services — especially for merit and demerit goods. For example, in the UK, **cigarette** packets show **health warnings** and **schools** are ranked in **league tables** based on their performance.
6) The success of **privatisation**, **deregulation** and **competition policy** (see p.44-47) are all affected by **imperfect information**. Governments and regulators need the **best** information possible to help them to make **correct decisions**.

Market Failure and Government Failure

Immobile Factors of Production aren't just things which can't Physically move

AS RECAP

1) Factors of production, such as **land**, **labour** and **capital**, can be immobile.
2) For example, land **cannot** be **moved**, or it may only be good for **one type** of agriculture (e.g. land on which **rice** is grown may not be suitable for growing **wheat**).
3) Labour can be either **geographically** or **occupationally immobile** (see p.67).
4) Immobile factors of production cause **market failure** as there's an **inefficient** use of resources.

If you're doing OCR, this AS recap will probably be new to you — but as long as you learn what's here, you'll be fine.

5) **Structural unemployment** is made worse by occupational and geographical immobility.
6) Governments can intervene to help with labour immobility — for example, they might **provide education** and **training** to help occupationally immobile workers to learn **new skills** (see p.68).

AQA & EDEXCEL ONLY

Commodity Markets are often Unstable

If you're doing Edexcel, this is just a recap from AS — if you're doing AQA, this'll be new so you need to learn it.

1) Prices for **commodities** tend to be **unstable** because **demand** and **supply** are usually **price inelastic** — so, for example, even a **small** change in **supply** will cause a **big** change in **price**.
2) The **price instability** of commodity markets creates **uncertainty**, which leads to **inefficiency** and **market failure**. Uncertainty means that it's difficult for **producers** to **predict their income** from what they sell, which in turn can **discourage** investment. This means resources are used inefficiently.
3) Governments might use **buffer stocks** to correct this market failure. However, buffer stocks often aren't successful — they can be **expensive** to run, lead to overproduction and can cause resources to be **wasted** as some commodities are perishable. If there's a **run** of good or bad harvests, then stocks might become **excessively large** (potentially causing waste) or **run out**.

Income and Wealth are not distributed Equally in a market economy

1) Differences in **income** and **wealth** in an economy can be seen as **unfair**, and some see this as **market failure**.
2) You'll need to know about **poverty** and more on the **distribution of income and wealth** — see p.50-51.
3) You'll also need to know what **horizontal** and **vertical equity** are — see p.50.
4) Governments often try to distribute income and wealth **more equally**, through methods such as taxation, benefits, state provision of goods or services and a national minimum wage (see p.52-53).

Government Intervention can cause a Misallocation of Resources

1) **Government failure** occurs when government intervention results in a **misallocation** of **resources**. In general, this means the **costs** of the intervention **outweigh** its **benefits**.
2) Government failure can be caused by a **number of factors**. For example:
   - **High administration costs** — e.g. competition policy (see p.46-47) can have high administrative costs, which will sometimes **outweigh** the benefits.
   - **Imperfect information** doesn't just affect consumers and producers — if **regulators** have imperfect information, they might **misjudge** a situation and take the **wrong** action.
   - **Regulatory capture** — firms covered by **regulatory bodies**, such as utility companies, can sometimes **influence** the decisions of the regulator to ensure that the outcomes **favour** the **companies** and not the consumers.

You should look back at everything you learnt on government failure at AS.

Practice Questions

Q1 Explain two examples of market failure.

Exam Question

Q1 Analyse the likely effectiveness of one method of government intervention to reduce market failure in the market for a public good. [10 marks]

My uncle suffered from market failure — his fruit and veg stall fell down...

Don't go thinking that all you need to learn is what's written on these pages — some of this is just a recap of AS level stuff you should already know. Make sure you have a good understanding of what you learnt at AS before you tackle the rest of this section.

Environmental Market Failure

These pages are for AQA Unit 3 and some parts will be useful for OCR Unit 4 (Transport Economics).
Market failure (including environmental) occurs when there's an inefficient or inequitable allocation of resources. Governments might intervene to try to reduce market failure, but sometimes this will result in government failure.

***Environmental Market Failure** can occur in a **Number** of ways*

Resource Depletion** is the **Reduction** of **Available Natural Resources

1) The **reduction** of available **natural resources** is a **negative externality** of using some natural resources — the **third party** that's affected is the people who **can't use** these resources in the **future**.
2) The depletion of resources occurs with **non-renewable** resources, e.g. coal and gas, as once they're used they cannot be replaced.
3) **Renewable** resources, e.g. trees, can also be **depleted** if they're used up **more quickly** than they're replaced.

Make sure you know how to talk about externalities using MSC and MSB curves — look back at your AS notes if you're not sure.

Resource Degradation** is when a **Natural Resource** becomes **Less Productive

1) **Resource degradation** is when a natural resource becomes **less** productive over time. For example, if a river that's used for **fishing** is affected by **water pollution**, that river will become **less productive**. The fish may not **grow** as well, they may reproduce **less** and some fish may die.
2) Resource degradation can also be caused by **air pollution**, or **intensive** use of land, e.g. for farming.
3) This resource degradation is a **negative externality** — the **third party** that's affected is the people who will use the **less productive** resource in the **future**.

*Some **Parts** of the **Environment** are **Public Goods***

1) Parts of the environment are often considered to have the characteristics of **public goods**. For example, the air is a **public good** which **isn't** exchanged on a market — it's **non-excludable** and **non-rivalrous**.
2) As air has **no price** it can be used as much as people like. **Clean** air also has the **same value** as **polluted** air (i.e. no value), so even if clean air becomes **more scarce**, people will continue to use it as they always have.
3) The non-excludability of air leads to the **free rider problem**. The **benefits** of **not polluting** the air, or **cleaning** the air afterwards, **aren't restricted** to those who have 'paid' for the clean air by choosing **not** to pollute, or choosing to **clean** the air. Therefore, in the free market, it's **unlikely** that anyone will either choose not to pollute, or to clean up the pollution they make.
4) This relates to the economic theory known as the **tragedy of the commons** — the idea that everyone acts in their **own best interests**, so they'll overuse a **common resource** without considering that this will lead to the **depletion** or **degradation** of that resource.

*The **Free Market** can help to **Reduce Pollution***

1) **Government intervention** can also cause **environmental market failure**. In some cases, **government intervention** can actually cause **more** damage to the environment than if things were left to the free market.
2) For example, **buffer stocks** for farming can **harm** the environment. If farmers are guaranteed a **minimum price**, they may try to **increase** their output through **intensive farming** and **chemical fertilisers** — which both damage the environment. Without government intervention, farmers might **produce less output**, so there would be **less environmental damage**.
3) Another example is certain **government subsidies**, e.g. for **timber cutting**. Such subsidies encourage the **overuse** of **scarce** resources and therefore **resource depletion**. **Without** the subsidies, there would be **less resource depletion**.
4) Some economists argue that if everything that made up the **environment** was treated as a **scarce resource** that people had to **pay** to **use**, then the market forces of **supply** and **demand** would ensure that the environment would be **protected**.
5) This argument is put into practice with **property rights** (see the next page) — if someone **owns** the property rights for a **resource**, they can **charge** people for using it and use the revenue to **offset** any damage caused.

Environmental Market Failure

A lack of **Property Rights** can cause **Negative Externalities**

1) The idea behind extending **property rights** to environmental public goods, such as rivers or forests, is that someone will **own** the resource, so they'll have **control** over who's allowed to **use** (or pollute) that resource.
2) If **property rights** aren't extended over a **resource** (e.g. a river), **negative externalities** can arise (causing market failure) because **no one owns** the **resource** and takes **responsibility** for it. For example, a factory that emits waste water into a nearby river wouldn't be held accountable for this pollution if no one had property rights over the river.
3) Extending property rights over resources to organisations gives them **control** over the **usage** of a resource. For example, a water company with property rights over a river can allow, charge for, or refuse permission for others to pollute the river.
4) Government failure can occur if governments **don't extend** property rights, or if they **don't protect** existing property rights.

The **Extension** of **Property Rights** uses the **Market Mechanism**

1) **Negative externalities** are **internalised** by the extension of property rights. Owners of the rights can **charge** consumers and producers for using the property and **sue** if permission hasn't been granted. This puts a **value** on the resource, so its use will be determined by the forces of **supply** and **demand** — the **market mechanism**.
2) The **money raised** by using the market mechanism can be used to **reduce** the **effects** of any **negative externalities**.
3) An extension of property rights could **improve management** of **resources** so they'll **last longer** — the market mechanism will ensure resources **aren't overused**. It could also mean negative externalities are **more carefully monitored** and **regulated** because the **owner** has an interest in the **effect** of negative externalities on their resource.
4) Extending property rights also **reduces** the risk of **government failure**, as it **isn't** the government who has to put a **price** on the **externalities**.

There are several **Problems** associated with **Extending Property Rights**

1) It can be **difficult** for a **government** to **extend property rights**. For example, EU rules allow boats from other EU countries to fish in UK waters, stopping the allocation of property rights over these waters by the UK government.
2) **Externalities** can affect **more than one country**. For example, deforestation in Malaysia could have impacts for the whole world by contributing to climate change, but the UK can't extend property rights to Malaysia.
3) The **high costs** of **suing** an individual or company that infringes property rights can put off owners of these rights from taking action to uphold them.
4) It's **difficult** for the owner of a property to **put a value** on its use.
5) There are often difficulties in **tracing** the **source** of **environmental damage**. For example, a chemical leak into a river could kill fish in a fish farm a great distance from the source of the leak — but the property rights holder for the fish farm may not have the information available to demand compensation from the firm responsible.

Tradable Pollution Permits are used to try to **Control** pollution levels

You should have learnt about pollution permits at AS level — so it's a good idea to go back and refresh your memory.

1) Governments may try to **control** pollution by putting a **cap** on it. The government will set an **optimal level** of pollution and **allocate** permits that allow firms to emit a **certain amount** of **pollution** over a period of time (usually a year).
2) Firms may **trade** their permits with other firms, so if a firm can keep its emissions **low**, it can **sell** its permits to other firms who want to **buy** permits to allow them to **pollute more**.
3) Tradable pollution permits use the **market mechanism** — pollution is given a **value** and firms can **buy** and **sell** permits.
4) The **EU emissions trading system (ETS)** is a tradable pollution permit scheme, with permits called **emissions allowances**. These allowances (of greenhouse gas emissions) are **distributed** between the EU's **member** governments, who in turn **allocate** these allowances to **firms**.
5) Firms will be **fined** if they **exceed** their allowances, but they can **trade** allowances between themselves, so firms can buy **extra allowances** to cover any **extra emissions**.
6) Each year the number of allowances available is **reduced**. This gives firms an **incentive** to **lower their emissions** (e.g. by investing in technology to cut emissions) — if they don't then they might have to buy more allowances.
7) Firms in the ETS are allowed to invest in **emission-saving schemes** outside of the EU to **offset** their own emissions. For example, a UK firm could invest in **low-carbon power production** in India to offset some of its emissions in the UK.

Environmental Market Failure

There are Advantages and Disadvantage to Tradable Pollution Permit schemes

ADVANTAGES

- These schemes are a good way of trying to **reduce** pollution to an **acceptable** level, as they **encourage** firms to become **more efficient** and **pollute less**.
- Firms causing low levels of pollution will **benefit** from these schemes — they'll be able to **sell** permits, allowing them to **invest more** and **expand**.
- Governments can use any **revenue**, e.g. from fines, to **invest** in other **pollution reducing** schemes.
- These schemes **internalise** the externality of pollution.

DISADVANTAGES

- The **optimal pollution level** can be difficult to set. If the level is set too **high**, firms have **no incentive** to **lower** their emissions. If the level is set too **low**, new firms might not be able to **start up** at all, or existing firms might choose to **relocate** to somewhere they're **less restricted** (**harming** a country's **economic growth**). So, setting the optimal pollution level at the **wrong** level can lead to **government failure**.
- The pollution permit scheme creates a **new market** — there might be **market failure** within this new market.
- **High** levels of pollution in specific areas may still exist, and this would still be **harmful** to the environment.
- There are **administrative costs** involved in such schemes, to both **governments** and **firms**.

There are many other Methods governments can use to Intervene

1) Other methods of government intervention to try to **protect** the environment include:
   - **Road congestion schemes** (also called **road pricing**) which aim to **reduce** the externalities linked with traffic and road congestion (see p.90). The schemes work by **charging users** to travel on roads in areas where **congestion** is a **problem**. Ideally the charge needs to be set at a level that will result in the **socially optimal level of traffic**. However, working out what this charge should be can be very difficult.
   - Governments may provide **subsidies** for public transport (see p.91) — e.g. bus and train journeys may be **subsidised** to **reduce car usage** and **pollution levels**.
   - Fishing quotas set **limits** on the amount of fish that can be caught, aiming to keep stocks of fish **stable** and **prevent overfishing**.
2) As with any method of government intervention, there's always the possibility of **government failure**. For example:
   - Road congestion charges may be set at the **wrong level** — e.g. if the charge is too **low**, there may be little or no change in usage. So congestion **wouldn't** be reduced, and the **administrative cost** of the scheme might **exceed** revenue.
   - Public transport subsidies may **not** cause an increase in usage, as a bus journey is often viewed as an **inferior good**, so a **reduction** in the price won't always mean an **increase** in demand. Underused public transport services may actually contribute to higher overall emissions as people aren't using their cars less.
   - Fishing quotas may lead to fishing boats throwing dead fish **back** into the water because they don't want to **exceed** their quota — but the fish are **already** dead, so it's a **waste** of resources.

Practice Questions

Q1 Describe two examples of environmental market failure.

Q2 How might the free market reduce environmental pollution?

Q3 What are tradable pollution permits?

Exam Questions

Q1 Evaluate how extending property rights can help to protect natural resources. [10 marks]

Q2 Discuss the likely success of government intervention to reduce environmental market failure. [25 marks]

Extend your property rights — conquer your neighbour's garden...

There are a few parts to this environmental market failure stuff. You need to understand what environmental market failure is, how the free market might be able to reduce these problems itself, how governments might intervene to reduce environmental damage, and how the market might react to these interventions. Luckily, it's all on these three pages — all you need to do is learn it. Phew.

Privatisation, Regulation and Deregulation

These pages are for AQA Unit 3, Edexcel Unit 3 and OCR Unit 3 (Work and Leisure) and Unit 4 (Transport Economics).
Governments often try to increase efficiency or competition in markets. They can use methods of intervention to achieve this, e.g. regulation, or they can reduce their involvement in a market through methods such as privatisation and deregulation.

Privatisation aims to Improve Efficiency

1) A **publicly owned** firm/industry is owned by the **government**. The firm/industry will usually act in the **best interests** of consumers — so **prices** tend to be **low** and **output** tends to be **high**. This is possible as they **don't** have to make **profits**.
2) However, publicly owned firms/industries tend to be **inefficient** because they **lack competition**. Governments may decide to **increase** competition through **privatisation**.
3) **Privatisation** is the **transfer** of the **ownership** of a firm/industry from the **public** sector to the **private** sector.
4) Some economists believe this will lead to a **more efficient** firm/industry, because it'll be open to **free market competition**. Private firms have **shareholders**, so they'll usually need to **maximise** their **profits** to keep the shareholders happy.
5) Privatisation covers a number of different things, for example:

- The **sale** of public (nationalised) firms — e.g. the Royal Mail was owned by the government, but it was **privatised** through the **sale** of **shares**.
- **Contracting out** services — a government pays a **private firm** to carry out work on its behalf, e.g. **cleaning** government-owned buildings, such as **hospitals** or **schools**.
- **Competitive tendering** — private firms **bid** (or **compete**) to gain a **contract** to provide a service for the government. Firms will compete on **price** and the **quality** of the service offered.
- **Public Private Partnerships (PPPs)** — a private firm works **with** a government to build something or provide a service for the public. An example of a PPP is a **Private Finance Initiative (PFI)** — a private firm is **contracted** by the government to **run** a project. For example, in the UK, some hospitals or schools are **built** by a **private** firm, then the government **leases** the buildings from the firm (usually for a long period of time).

Advantages	Disadvantages
Increased competition **improves** efficiency and **reduces x-inefficiency** (see p.22).	A privatised **public** monopoly is likely to become a **private** monopoly — so extra measures, e.g. deregulation, need to be taken to avoid this (see p.45).
Improves resource allocation — privatised firms have to react to **market signals** of supply and demand.	Privatised firms may have **less focus** on **safety** and **quality** because they have **more focus** on reducing **costs** and increasing **profits**.
PFIs enable the building of **important facilities** that the government might not be able to **afford** to build.	The new private firm might need **regulating** (see below) to prevent it from being a **private monopoly** — this adds **cost** for **taxpayers**.
PFIs means **lower taxes** in the **short run** because the government won't pay for the new facility immediately.	A PFI will often **cost more** in the long run than it's worth — so it adds to **government debt** and may **not** represent value for money.
The government **gains revenue** from **selling** firms.	PFIs mean **higher taxes** for **future generations** to pay for the cost of the government leasing the facility.

Regulations are just enforced Rules

You'll have covered regulation at AS — here's a reminder of the main points.

1) Government **regulations** are **rules** enforced by the government.
2) Regulations are used to try to **reduce** market failure and its impacts. They can **help** with many areas of **market failure**:

- **Reducing** the use of **demerit** goods and services — e.g. by **banning** or **limiting** the sale of such products.
- **Reducing** the power of **monopolies** — e.g. using a regulating body to set rules such as **price caps** (see p.47).
- Providing some **protection** for consumers and producers — e.g. the Sale of Goods Act **protects consumers** against firms supplying **substandard** goods.

3) Firms or individuals who **don't** follow the regulations can be **punished**, e.g. with **fines**, **closure** of factories, etc.
4) Regulations can be **difficult** to **set** and **expensive** for the government to **enforce**. They can also act as a barrier to entry for some markets — reducing competition.

Privatisation, Regulation and Deregulation

Deregulation is basically the Opposite of Regulation

1) Deregulation means **removing** or **reducing** regulations. It removes some barriers to entry, so it can be used to **increase competition** in markets — particularly **monopolistic** markets.
2) Deregulation is often used **alongside/as part of** privatisation — privatising an industry effectively removes the legal barriers to entry that prevent other firms entering the market. **Additional** deregulation to reduce barriers to entry further can then be used to help prevent the privatised public monopoly from becoming a private monopoly.
3) Examples of deregulation in the UK include the deregulation of **directory enquiries**. BT, which was a **private** firm at the time, provided the directory enquiries service — it was deregulated to allow **other firms** to enter the market.

Advantages	Disadvantages
Improves resource allocation — removing regulations means the market becomes **more contestable**, so new firms are more likely to **enter** the market. The **threat** of **competition** from new firms, or the actual **entry** of new firms into the market, means prices **fall** closer to marginal cost (MC) and output **increases**.	It's difficult to deregulate some **natural monopolies**, e.g. utilities. These require **large infrastructures**, e.g. the water industry needs a **pipe network**. These infrastructures are **expensive** to build and maintain, and there's only a need for **one** of them.
It can be used alongside the **privatisation** of a public monopoly to prevent the privatised firm from becoming a **private** monopoly.	Deregulation can't fix other **market failures** such as negative externalities, consumer inertia or immobile factors of production.
Improves efficiency by **reducing** the amount of **'red tape'** and **bureaucracy**.	Deregulation might mean there's **less safety** and **protection** for consumers.

Consumer inertia is resistance to change by consumers — e.g. they might be reluctant to change energy suppliers because it's seen as too much effort.

Internal Markets can be created within Public Sector Services

The creation of **internal markets** in a public sector service means competition is created **within** that industry. For example:

1) **Schools** competing for **pupils** — in general, schools get **more** government funding for **each pupil**, so they'll **compete** with each other to get pupils to attend their school.
2) **GPs** competing for **patients** — if GPs' budgets are dependent on, for example, the **number** and **ages** of their registered patients, they'll **compete** with each other to get **more** patients — possibly from a particular age group.
3) **Hospitals** competing for **patients** — if hospitals receive funding based on the **number** of patients they **treat**, they'll want to **compete** with each other to get patients **referred** to their hospital.

Advantages	Disadvantages
Quality tends to **improve** if there's competition, because consumers have a **choice**.	The creation of new internal markets may lead to **market failure** within these new markets.
X-inefficiency is **reduced** by the increase in competition causing prices to **fall**.	Services which are performing **badly** will **struggle** to improve because they'll have **fewer** resources available.
Services which are performing **badly** are likely to **close**.	Good services can become **oversubscribed**, which might lead to a **reduction** in their **quality**.

Practice Questions

Q1 Explain two advantages of privatisation.

Q2 Give an example of an internal market which might be created in the public sector, and give one advantage and one disadvantage of that internal market.

Exam Question

Q1 Discuss possible methods to improve efficiency in an industry made up of a single public monopoly. [15 marks]

Competitive tendering — seeing who's best at pounding a steak...

Privatisation, deregulation and internal markets tend to increase competition and improve efficiency. Regulation can reduce market failures, such as the effects of demerit goods. Get to grips with these pages, then you'll be ready to move on to competition policy.

Competition Policy

These pages are for AQA Unit 3, Edexcel Unit 3 and OCR Unit 3 (Work and Leisure) and Unit 4 (Transport Economics). *Make sure you know all about monopolies and oligopolies (see Section 2) before you tackle these pages. Monopolies are often seen as a bad thing because they reduce the efficiency of a market, so governments often discourage their formation.*

Competition Policy aims to **Increase Competition** in a market

1) Governments often choose to **intervene** in **concentrated markets** where monopoly power is causing **market failure**.
2) For example, if a monopoly exists and prices are **above** the market equilibrium price, there's a **misallocation** of resources and a **deadweight welfare loss** (see p.26) — i.e. there's market failure.
3) The intention of the government is to **protect** the **interests** of **consumers** by **promoting competition** and **encouraging** the market to function more **efficiently**. The government can do this through the use of **competition policy**.

Governments often want to **Prevent Monopolies** from forming

The **European Commission** and the UK's **Competition and Markets Authority (CMA)** both monitor competition to look out for **unfair** monopolistic behaviour. Things they look out for include:

1) **Mergers** — they monitor mergers and takeovers so they can **prevent** those that aren't **beneficial** to the **efficiency** of the market or to **consumers**. They may choose to **stop** a merger that would give a firm **too high** a market share (e.g. over 25%) and make it a **monopoly**, or that would give a firm **too much** monopoly power.
2) **Agreements** between firms (e.g. **cartels**, **collusive oligopolies**) — these agreements can be open or not. Often, agreements involving **price fixing**, **splitting** markets or **limiting** production are **anti-competitive**, cause market **inefficiency** and are **unfair** to consumers.
3) The **opening** of markets to **competition** — this is when markets that were **controlled** by a government are **opened** up to competition. For example, if a **government-owned** transport service is **privatised**, the government might want to ensure the **existing** firm is open to free market competition and doesn't **dominate** the market as a private monopoly.
4) **Financial support** from governments (European Commission only) — if a government in **one EU country** gives financial support to firms in a certain market, this may give those firms an **unfair advantage** over firms in other EU countries in that same market.

Lisa had gained an unfair advantage by putting glue on her fellow athletes' starting blocks.

The European Commission and the CMA can **block mergers** and **impose fines** on firms **guilty** of anti-competitive behaviour.

Some Markets have their own **Regulating Bodies**

1) This is particularly common in **monopolistic** or **oligopolistic** markets.
2) These bodies have varying **responsibilities** — these might include regulating prices, monitoring safety and product standards, and encouraging competition.
3) Remember that regulating bodies can be at risk of **regulatory capture** (see p.40).

EXAMPLES OF UK REGULATING BODIES

- OFWAT — regulates the **water** industry.
- OFCOM — regulates the **communication** industries.
- OFGEM — regulates the **gas** and **electricity** markets.

Competition Policy is generally seen to be **Useful** and **Effective**

1) The **effectiveness** of competition policy is greatly affected by the **information** available to the European Commission or the CMA — they'll need to decide whether behaviour in different markets is **anti-competitive** or **unfair** to the **consumer** based on the information they have.
2) If the information available to the government is **reliable**, then it should be able to intervene in the market in a way that will **improve** efficiency, allocate resources **more effectively** and **improve** fairness to the consumer. If the information is **imperfect** then this could lead to **government failure**.
3) Competition policy and its implementation (e.g. through regulations) have **costs** — but in general, these costs are seen to be **outweighed** by the **benefits**. If the costs **outweigh** the benefits, this is an example of **government failure**.

Competition Policy

Governments can Intervene in various ways

There are many ways a government can **intervene** in a market to try to increase **competition**.

Privatisation can help to introduce Competition into a market where there's a Public Monopoly

1) A **publicly** owned monopoly can be **privatised** to open it up to competition and force it to respond to **market signals**.
2) However, privatisation alone **won't** increase competition, as the **public monopoly** may just become a **private monopoly**. There could also be an **increase** in **prices** and a **reduction** in **output**, as a **private** monopoly is **less likely** to act in the best interests of consumers. So, other steps need to be taken **alongside** privatisation, such as **deregulation** (see below), to **increase competition** and **protect consumers**.

Regulation can be used to Control or Prevent Monopoly Power

Price caps are common in the UK utility markets.

1) Governments might use **regulation** (see p.44) to **prevent** a firm from gaining **monopoly** power, or to **increase** competition by **reducing** the monopoly power a firm already has.
2) For example, a government or regulating body might introduce **price caps** (or **price ceilings**) to stop firms from charging prices that are considered to be **too high**. Price caps put a **maximum** on the **price increase** that firms can charge their customers. Here are **two types** of price cap:

- **RPI – X** means firms must make **real price cuts**. RPI is **inflation** (see p.102) and X is the **efficiency improvements** the government or regulating body **expects** firms to be able to make. So for example, if the **RPI** (inflation) was **3%** and **X** was **1%**, firms could only increase their prices by up to **2%**.
- **RPI – X + K** is commonly used in the **water industry**. **K** is the amount of **investment** firms will need to make in order to achieve efficiency improvements. In this case, the firm can charge **higher prices** to **offset** the cost of efficiency improvements.

Price caps **limit** price rises, making a market **fairer** to consumers. They also provide an **incentive** for firms to **increase efficiency** (the more efficient they are, the more profit they keep), and consumers **benefit** from **improved services**.

3) Alternatively, the government or a regulator could **monitor** prices to ensure they stay **reasonable** and **fair** to consumers.
4) Governments can impose **windfall taxes** on what it decides are **excessive profits** — this means the government will tax those profits at a **higher rate**. Windfall taxes can help to **prevent** firms from gaining too much **monopoly power**, but it **reduces** their **incentive** to **improve efficiency** (as the extra profits might be taxed).
5) Setting **performance targets** can also help to maintain competition, but they need to be combined with some sort of **penalty**, e.g. a **fine**, if a firm **doesn't** reach its target. Examples of performance targets include:
   - Firms might be given certain **standards** of **customer service** they need to achieve.
   - NHS departments might be given targets for the **number of patients** they should treat.

   There are **disadvantages** to performance targets. Health and safety, quality of service and any other areas of a business which aren't included in targets might be **overlooked** in order to reach performance targets.

Deregulation can also be used to Increase Competition

1) **Deregulation** can make a market more **contestable**, so it's easier for **new** firms to **enter** the market.
2) This **increases** competition, causing the **price** to **fall** closer to marginal cost, and **output** to **increase**.
3) It's usually used **alongside** privatisation to make sure that a **public** monopoly doesn't become a **private** one.

Practice Questions

Q1 Why might governments want to discourage monopolistic behaviour?

Q2 Briefly discuss the effectiveness of competition policy.

Exam Question

Q1 Explain what a body such as the Competition and Markets Authority (CMA) does to monitor competition. [10 marks]

Price cap — the latest economic fashion accessory...

Competition policy is all about encouraging competition and stopping behaviour that's likely to prevent a contestable market.

Cost Benefit Analysis

These pages are for AQA Unit 3 and OCR Unit 4 (Transport Economics).
Cost benefit analysis is used to decide whether projects that require major investment should go ahead. However, difficulties, such as calculating the value of costs and benefits, can lead to market or government failure.

Governments use **Cost Benefit Analysis** to **Evaluate** major investment projects

1) **Cost benefit analysis** (**CBA**) involves considering the **total costs** and **benefits** of a **major project**, such as building a new **motorway** or hosting an important **sporting event** (e.g. the London 2012 Olympics), over a fixed period of time.
2) When **politicians** (or other decision-makers) analyse the costs and benefits of a project, they have to look at the **impact** on **everyone** who's affected. For example, for a major sporting event, along with the **private** costs and benefits, the **external gains** to the **host nation**, such as **improved facilities** or **increased tourism**, need to be evaluated, as do the **external losses**, such as the **diversion** of **public funding** from other projects to pay for the event.
3) All of the **private** and **external** costs and benefits are given **monetary values** — then these values are used to calculate the **net social cost** or **benefit**.

There are **Various Stages in CBA**

1) Firstly, the **private** and **external costs** and **benefits** are **identified** as accurately as possible.
2) **Monetary values** are then given to the **costs** and **benefits**. Where these are assigned to something **without** a value, this is called **shadow pricing**. A shadow price can also be **assigned** to something that has a value, when that value isn't **truly reflective** of its real cost.
3) At the end, the **net social cost** or **benefit** is **calculated**:

net social benefit = social benefit – social cost

social benefit = private benefit + external benefit
social cost = private cost + external cost

4) There might be **uncertainty** about whether some of the costs and benefits in the CBA will **actually happen** — the **likelihood** (probability) of these things will be considered and **factored into** the final calculation.
5) In general, if there's a **net social cost**, then the project **won't** go ahead, but if there's a **net social benefit**, then it **will**.

It can be **Difficult** to put a **Value** on **Externalities**

Externalities (both positive and negative) need to be included in a CBA, but they're often **difficult** to put a **monetary value** on because they **don't** have a **price** decided by the market. For example:

1) **Tourism** — for example, a big sporting event is likely to **increase** tourism, which will **benefit** hotels, shops, restaurants, etc. It's very difficult to predict the **amount** of money this will bring to the economy.
2) **Multiplier effect** — an **injection** of money into the economy is likely to have a **multiplier effect**. However, it's very difficult to **predict** how much money will **leak** from the circular flow of income, and therefore what the size of the multiplier will be.
3) **Loss of human life** — this is one of the most **difficult** things to include. People may argue that human life is **priceless**, but for the purpose of a CBA it needs to be given a **value**. For example, a human life may be given a value in terms of **estimated earnings** for a person's **remaining** working life. However, this doesn't take into account the **effect** that person has on their family and friends, or anything else they might have **enjoyed** or **achieved** in their life.
4) **Pollution** — **air** and **noise** pollution can have many **negative** effects. For example, air pollution can affect people's **health**. It can also **damage** the **environment**, contributing to **global warming**. Noise pollution might affect people's **quality of life**, and **bring down** the value of their houses.
5) **Congestion** — congestion not only **increases pollution**, but it also **wastes** people's time. Some economists may calculate the value of **each hour** of wasted time as the amount of money that person would have **earned** if they were working instead. Other economists may count it as wasted **leisure** time, and therefore give it a different value.

Cost Benefit Analysis

Money will be worth **Less** in the **Future** than it is **Now**

1) **£10 of benefit** from a project in 10 years' time is likely to be worth **less than £10** today — i.e. due to **inflation**, £10 will buy **fewer** goods and services in the **future** than it'll buy **today**.
2) This means that for a CBA, **future** costs and benefits need to be **discounted** to find their **present values**.
3) The difficult part is trying to decide **what discount** to apply to future costs and benefits. Some people prefer to use **low** discount rates — for example, this might **encourage** investment **now**, and they see this as a **good** thing for economic growth. Others prefer to use **higher** discount rates, as this might **reduce** the amount of investment **now**, e.g. to help to **slow down** economic growth and **protect** the environment.
4) Most CBAs will only look at the **costs** and **benefits** over a **set** period of time, e.g. 25 years. This can have a **big** impact on the result of the CBA — if there are any **big** costs or benefits to come in the **future**, e.g. the cost of **decommissioning** a nuclear power plant, it can be argued that these **should always** be **included** in the CBA.

There are lots of **Advantages** and **Disadvantages** to consider

There are **advantages** to using a CBA to decide if a project should go ahead:

1) A CBA is a good way of thoroughly assessing the **various consequences** of a project before work begins, and of **assessing** and **considering** the **effects** of any **externalities**. The CBA will **provide** governments with the information they need to make a **decision**.
2) In general, using a CBA means that projects will only go ahead if the **benefits** to society **outweigh** the **costs**.

However, a CBA has certain **limitations** too:

1) Usually, some costs and benefits will be **missed**. Often these won't be big enough to **change** the overall outcome of a CBA, but sometimes they might have a more **significant** impact — e.g. they might make a project have a **net social cost** instead of a **net social benefit**.
2) It can be **difficult** to put monetary values on the costs and benefits (especially on externalities — see the previous page). This difficulty can also lead to **disagreements** between those who are in favour of a project and those who are against it, and **big variations** in the **estimated** value of any **costs** and **benefits** (causing **market failure**).
3) In the future, money will probably be worth less than it is now due to inflation (see above). This needs to be factored into a CBA, but it's difficult to accurately **predict** how money will change in value.
4) There's often a **significant** cost as a result of carrying out a CBA — this can cause **government failure** — especially if the CBA doesn't provide **useful** information.
5) CBAs often don't take **equity** into account — the costs and benefits might **affect different people**, so one group of people may **benefit** from a project, while another group has to **'pay'** for it.
6) A CBA needs to be **unbiased** to be effective, but **political factors** can affect a decision, causing **market failure**. For example, if a project is considered to be a **vote-winner** then the government might fund it, even if the costs outweigh the benefits. This is called **rent-seeking behaviour**.
7) Carrying out a CBA might mean decision makers have **too much information** — it can cause a decision to be **more confusing** and take **longer** to make (leading to **market** and **government failure**).

Practice Questions

Q1 Why might a government carry out a CBA?

Q2 Describe the difficulties involved in putting a monetary value on externalities in a CBA.

Q3 Why do future costs and benefits need to be discounted?

Exam Question

Q1 A country is considering making a bid to host a major sporting event. Evaluate the advantages and disadvantages to the country's government of using a CBA to decide whether to go ahead with the bid. [25 marks]

I'm surprised anything gets done with this CBA culture...

Carrying out a CBA is a useful way of taking the externalities of a project into account. It's important to remember some monetary values assigned to the costs and benefits are just people's best guesses, and might be influenced by their opinion of the project.

Equity and Poverty

These pages are for AQA Unit 3, Edexcel Unit 4 and OCR Unit 3 (Work and Leisure).
In most economies there's inequality and it can cause issues, but most people believe that some inequality is a good thing. However, when there's inequality to the extent that there's poverty, it becomes more of a problem.

Income *and* ***Wealth*** *are* ***Not*** *distributed* ***Equally*** *in a market economy*

1) An individual's **income** is the amount of money they receive over a **set** period of time, e.g. per week or per year.
2) Income comes from **many sources** — e.g. **wages**, **interest** on bank accounts, **dividends** from shares and **rent** from properties.
3) Wealth is the **value** in money of **assets** held — **assets** can **include** property, land, money and shares.
4) In the **UK**, and most other economies, income and wealth **aren't** equally distributed.
5) There are a number of factors affecting the **distribution** of **income**:
   - People earn **different wages** — different markets have different levels of **demand** and **supply**, which affect **wage rates** (see p.60). Certain skills are **more** in demand than others, so workers with those skills are likely to receive **higher** wages.
   - People who are **unwaged** (e.g. the unemployed or pensioners) often need to rely on **state benefits** such as Jobseeker's Allowance or state pensions, so their **incomes** tend to be **lower**.
   - **Tax** and **state benefits** — in the UK there's a **progressive** tax system (to some extent, see p.109-110 for more on taxation and taxes in the UK). Those with **higher** incomes are taxed a **higher percentage** of their earnings over certain levels. Some of this tax is then **redistributed** as benefits, e.g. to the unemployed, or to people with disabilities.
6) Wealth is **more unevenly** distributed than income:
   - Wealth often **earns** income — e.g. shares may **increase** in value and **generate** more income. Those who **earn income** from their **wealth** could **invest** that income again (e.g. by buying more shares), which in turn will generate **more income**, and this cycle will continue. This means the **wealthy** quickly become even wealthier, whereas those with **low** wealth don't have much (if anything) to invest, so their wealth will only grow by a **small** amount (if at all).
   - **Assets** tend to **increase** in **value** more quickly than **income rises**.
   - In the UK, income is **taxed**, but wealth isn't — so it's much **easier** to redistribute income than wealth.

Equity *and* ***Equality*** *are* ***Different*** *things*

1) **Equality** means that everyone is treated **completely equally** — they all get **exactly** the **same** things.
2) **Equity** is more about **fairness** — people have different **circumstances**, so it's more about people getting what they **need**.
3) Equality is **positive** (it's **objective** and deals with **facts**), whereas equity is **normative** (it's **subjective** and based on **opinion**).
4) There are **two** types of equity:
   - **Horizontal equity** — people with the **same circumstances** are treated **fairly** (i.e. they're treated the **same**).
   - **Vertical equity** — people with **different circumstances** are treated **fairly** but **differently**.

   Equity is normative, so decisions on how people are treated are based on **judgement**. People have **different** opinions on what's **fair**, so they'll have **different** opinions on what counts as **fair** treatment, and it's hard to come to an agreement.

EXAMPLE
1) People with the **same level of income** are taxed the **same amount** — this is **horizontal** equity.
2) People with **higher incomes** are taxed **more** — this is **vertical** equity.

The ***Distribution*** *of income and wealth has big* ***Impacts*** *on the* ***Economy***

There are both **positives** and **negatives** to an **unequal** distribution of income and wealth:

NEGATIVES
1) **Absolute** and **relative** poverty can remain **high** (see the next page).
2) It **restricts** economic growth and wastes people's talent, because the **poorest** people won't have the **funds** to start businesses.
3) As **income rises**, people generally **spend more** on **imports**, so this money would **leave** the circular flow.
4) **Crime** is likely to **increase** because people don't have what they **need**.

POSITIVES
1) Inequality provides **incentives** for people to work harder and earn more — so **rewarding** hard work **increases productivity**.
2) It encourages **enterprise** by those who have the funds available to start businesses.
3) It also **encourages** people to **work** instead of claiming benefits.
4) It may create a **trickle-down effect** — some economists argue that if there's **inequality** and **greater economic growth**, the **rich** will become even **richer** and **spend more** on goods and services, providing **more income** for the **poor**. This is known as the **trickle-down effect**. As a result, **relative poverty** may **increase**, but **absolutely poverty** will **decrease**.

Equity and Poverty

Big Differences in Income and Wealth often mean there's Poverty

1) There are **two** different types of poverty:
   - **Relative poverty** is when someone has a low income **relative to other incomes** in their country. So someone from a **rich county** might be classed as living in **relative poverty**, even though someone in a much **poorer** country with the **same income** might be considered **wealthy**.
   - **Absolute poverty** is when someone doesn't have the wealth or income to meet their **basic needs**, such as food, water and shelter.
2) There are many **causes** of poverty:
   - **Unemployment** — people who are unemployed are **most likely** to be in absolute or relative poverty. Even in a country where the state gives **unemployment benefits**, the unemployed are likely to be at the **bottom** level of income in that country.
   - **Low wages** — workers **most likely** to receive low wages are those with **few** skills or qualifications.
   - State benefits rising **more slowly** than wages — this means the **relative incomes** of people relying on state benefits **fall** over time.

The Poverty Trap

- The poverty trap can affect people who are in poverty — these may be people relying on **state benefits**, or those on **low wages** and **means-tested benefits** (these are just benefits based on a person's income).
- When these people earn **higher wages**, they may only **actually receive** a **small** percentage of their wage increase. This is because they'll need to pay income tax and National Insurance contributions (in the UK), and have their benefits **reduced** (because they're earning more money).
- In some cases, this could even cause a **drop** in their disposable income, and this means their **marginal tax rate** will be **high**.
- So the combination of income tax, National Insurance and the benefit system can result in a **disincentive** for these people to **find work**, or to **increase** the number of hours they work.

Marginal tax rate is just the percentage (tax) that'll be taken from the next pound you earn.

Lorenz Curves show the Extent of Income Inequality

1) The **Lorenz curve** can be used to represent the **distribution** of income graphically.
2) Along the **horizontal** axis is the cumulative percentage of the **population**, and up the **vertical** axis is the cumulative percentage of income.

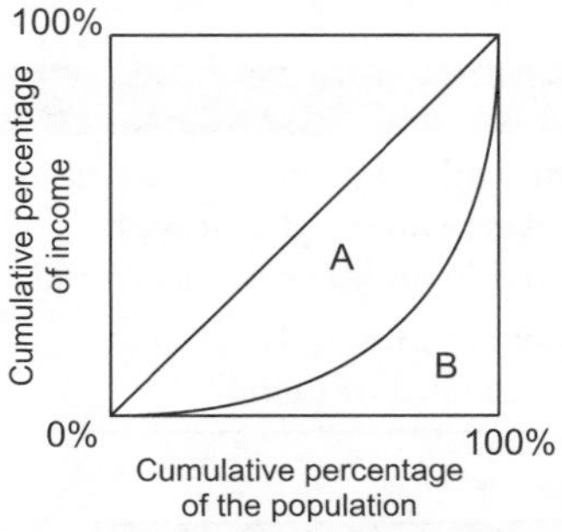

3) The **diagonal** curve represents **complete equality** — e.g. 10% of the population have 10% of the income.
4) The **further** the Lorenz curve is away from the diagonal, the greater the inequality in the country.
5) The **Gini coefficient**, a **measure** of **inequality**, can be found from the graph.
6) The Gini coefficient is calculated using the **formula**: $\text{Gini coefficient} = \frac{\text{area A}}{\text{area A + area B}}$
7) A coefficient of **0** represents **complete equality**. A coefficient of **1** represents **complete inequality**.
8) The Lorenz curve and Gini coefficient can also be used to represent the **distribution of wealth**.

Practice Questions

Q1 Explain the difference between equity and equality.

Q2 Define: a) horizontal and vertical equity b) absolute and relative poverty.

Exam Question

Q1 In the UK there's an unequal distribution of income and wealth. Discuss the possible reasons for this. [8 marks]

Only use the information from these two pages in your answer.

I caught nothing with my poverty trap — it was really poor...

There's an unequal distribution of income and wealth in most economies. Governments can use the idea of equity to help maintain or achieve an acceptable level of inequality — too much inequality will mean some people are in relative or even absolute poverty.

Government Policies to Tackle Poverty

These pages are for AQA Unit 3 and OCR Unit 3 (Work and Leisure).
Many governments want to reduce poverty, so they'll need to redistribute income and wealth. There are many ways in which they can do this — it's a case of weighing up the positive and negative effects of the available policies.

Governments often Intervene to try to Alleviate Poverty

Many governments **tackle poverty** by using policies that **redistribute** income and wealth. The first three policies below do this by **redistributing** income and wealth **after** it's been earned — the final two policies try to **change** the **amount** of income people receive instead.

Benefits

1) **Benefits** are used to **redistribute** income and **reduce** poverty — tax revenue (mostly from those with **higher** incomes) is used to **pay** for the benefits of those who **need** them.
2) However, as **means-tested state benefits** contribute to the **poverty trap** (see p.51), governments might take a **different** approach:
   - They could **remove** means-tested benefits completely — this would **greatly increase** the **incentive** to work, but is very unlikely to be effective (see the next page).
   - They could **change** means-tested benefits to universal benefits.
   - They could **reduce** means-tested benefits more gradually as income increases.

State provision

1) **State provided** services, such as **health care** and **education**, help to **reduce** inequalities caused by **differences** in income, e.g. someone on a **low income** can receive the **same** health care as someone on a **high income**.
2) State provided services also **redistribute income** because most of the money to **pay** for them comes from taxing people with **higher incomes**.

Progressive taxation

1) **Progressive taxation** means a **bigger** percentage of tax is taken from workers with **high incomes** than those with **low incomes**.
2) It helps to **reduce** the difference between people's **disposable incomes**, reducing **relative poverty**.

Jonny had good intentions — but when it came to tackling poverty, he was utterly clueless.

Economic growth

1) Perhaps the most **effective** way of reducing poverty is through **economic growth**.
2) Economic growth will mean **jobs** are created and therefore **unemployment** will be **reduced**.
3) It'll also tend to lead to **higher wages**.
4) The government will gain **more tax revenue**, which it can use to provide services.

National minimum wage (NMW)

1) A **national minimum wage**, if it's set at a sensible level, will **reduce poverty** among the lowest paid workers and provide an **incentive** to work.
2) It'll help those on **low incomes** to be able to afford a reasonable **standard of living**.

The Government has to Evaluate the Consequences of these Policies

1) These policies to **redistribute** income and **tackle** poverty have both **positive** and **negative** effects on the economy, so governments need to **evaluate** their effects to decide how best to approach the issues of inequality and poverty.
2) Governments are likely to consider:
   - Effects on **incentives to work** — in order to **reduce** poverty effectively, incentives to work need to **increase**. Incentives to work also play a big part in **removing** or **reducing** the **poverty trap**.
   - **Cost** — the government will need to consider the cost to **itself**, and to **society**.
   - The likely **effectiveness** — the government needs to consider if the policy will help those it's **aimed** at, and if it'll help to the **extent** that it's intended to. For example, will the **number** of people using certain support be a **high enough proportion** of those entitled to it?
3) **Different governments** have **different views** on **fairness** — so they may use **different ways** of tackling inequality and poverty.

Government Policies to Tackle Poverty

These **Policies** have **Varying** effects on the economy

Benefits

1) Although **means-tested benefits** can be used to **reduce** absolute and relative poverty, they may **reduce** the **incentive** to work too — they can **contribute** to the **poverty trap** (see p.51).
2) **Removing means-tested benefits** could **remove** the **poverty trap** and greatly **increase** the **incentive** to work. In the long term, this could mean a **reduction** in poverty. However, at least in the short term, it would cause **larger** differences in income, and **relative** and **absolute** poverty would **increase**.
3) **Replacing means-tested** benefits with **universal** benefits would help to **remove** the poverty trap, but the **cost** of these extra benefits might mean that those on low incomes are **taxed more**.

State provision

1) Those in poverty gain **access** to services they otherwise **wouldn't** be able to **afford**.
2) But, **free** access to these services **reduces** the incentive to work and is expensive to provide.

Progressive taxation

1) **Progressive taxation** helps to **reduce** relative poverty, but it can also **contribute** to the poverty trap.
2) Also, if high income earners are taxed **too much**, there's a risk that some of them will **move abroad** to an economy where they're **taxed less**. This will result in a **loss** of labour and money from the economy.

Economic growth

1) Economic growth can be **difficult** to achieve — for example, it requires **sufficient resources** to increase output and for **markets** to grow so that the increased output is always being bought.
2) Economic growth can actually result in **larger** inequalities in income — for example, economic growth might **mainly** benefit the rich so that they become even richer.
3) It can also cause other problems, such as **damage** to the environment, or the using up of **finite resources**. This will **limit** economic growth in the **future**, which might mean **more** poverty and inequality.

National minimum wage (NMW)

1) The NMW can **counteract** monopsony power (see p.27) — if a monopsony is **taking advantage** of its power by paying workers **low** wages (which result in the workers being in **relative** or **absolute** poverty), the NMW can **stop** the monopsony from doing this by **raising** the amount it pays.
2) However, the NMW might cause a **reduction** in the **demand** for labour because some employers would need to **raise** workers' wages, so they might want to employ **fewer** people. This would mean a **rise** in **unemployment**, and therefore a rise in **poverty**.
3) A NMW **doesn't** take into account that the cost of living **varies** depending on where someone lives, e.g. in the UK, the cost of living is **higher** in London than in Manchester. So the **standard of living** for people who are earning the NMW will **vary** depending on where they live.
4) A NMW **won't** benefit anyone who's **unemployed** and in **poverty**.

Practice Questions

Q1 Give two things a government might consider when looking at the effects of policies to redistribute income and wealth.

Exam Question

Q1 Comment on the likely effectiveness of using a national minimum wage and means-tested state benefits to alleviate poverty in a country where absolute and relative poverty are both quite high. [10 marks]

Disposable income — what a load of rubbish...

Bear in mind that these policies approach the issue in different ways — some redistribute income and wealth after it's been earned (benefits, state provision and progressive taxation), others try to tackle the amount of income paid (NMW and economic growth).

The Structure of Employment in the UK

These pages are for OCR Unit 3 (Work and Leisure) — but this information might be useful to students of all boards.
This spread will help you get an idea about the structure of employment in the UK and how it compares to some other countries.

The **Structure** of employment in the UK has **Changed Over Time**

1) Since the 1970s the **structure** of employment has **changed considerably** in the UK. A major change is that the proportion of workers employed in the **primary sector** (e.g. industries such as agriculture, fishing and mining) and **secondary sector** (e.g. construction and manufacturing) has **fallen** sharply, whereas the proportion employed in the **tertiary sector** (services) has **risen** considerably.
2) Today in the UK the **majority** of workers (about 80%) are employed in the **tertiary sector**. Workers employed in this sector work in a wide variety of service industries including education, health care, finance and leisure.
3) The leisure industry has grown in particular because people have become **wealthier**. As people become better off they can afford to have **more leisure time** — so **demand** for leisure services **grows**.
4) Other countries in the European Union (EU), such as **Germany** and **Belgium**, have a **similar employment structure**, with the majority of workers employed in the tertiary sector and much smaller numbers in the primary and secondary sectors.
5) However, there are **differences** within the EU. About 1% of the UK workforce is employed in agriculture, but in **Romania** the figure is about 30%. In addition, the tertiary sector employs only around 40% of the Romanian workforce.
6) In general, **developing countries** have a **large proportion** of the workforce employed in the **primary sector** and a relatively **small proportion** in the **tertiary sector**. For example, in **India** about 50% of the workforce works in agriculture, but less than 30% work in the tertiary sector.
7) The **age structure** of the workforce has also changed in the UK. The **baby boom** after the Second World War meant that in the 1990s/early 2000s a large proportion of the workforce were in their 50s. A lot of these workers are now at retirement age and this has had an impact on state pensions (see p.69).

The **Participation Rate** varies depending on **Gender**

1) The **participation rate** is the percentage of the working age population (aged 15 and above) that are **in work** or **actively seeking work** in an economy — in other words, the proportion of **economically active** people in the population.
2) In the UK the **male** participation rate has **fallen** (by about 20%) over the past couple of decades. In contrast the **female** participation rate has **increased** (by around 10%) during this time. These changes have meant that the male and female participation rates are now **roughly the same** (around 60%).
3) Participation rates for women in Europe vary from country to country. Denmark, Sweden and the Netherlands have **high** female participation rates whereas countries like Hungary, Greece and Malta have **much lower** female participation rates.
4) There are many possible reasons for the **decline** in the **male participation rate** in the UK.
   - There's been a major **decline** in **large manufacturing industries** where men dominated the workforce.
   - Many men aged 50-65 have taken **early retirement**, some due to ill health.
   - More men aged 16-24 have decided to **stay in education**. In fact the number of people aged 16-24 in full-time education has doubled over the last 30 years.

Participation rate can also be called activity rate.

5) Many things have changed for **women** too, which has led to an **increased participation rate**.
   - There's been a **change** in **social attitudes** and there's less pressure on women to stay at home and be homemakers.
   - **Anti-discrimination legislation** (see p.64) to ensure women are treated fairly in the workplace is encouraging more women to work.
   - Women now have the **same education opportunities** as men, which makes it easier for them to get jobs.
   - Women are having **fewer children** and having them **later**, which makes it easier for them to have a longer career.

In many economies there is a **Pay Difference** between **Men** and **Women**

1) The **difference** that exists between the **average hourly earnings** of **male** and **female** employees is known as the **gender pay gap**. This gap exists even though equal pay legislation has been in place for years.
2) The **average size** of the gap in the EU is around 16%, but there are big **variations** — e.g. in Italy it's around 7% and in Germany it's around 22%. In the UK the gap is 19%, but it's **decreasing** over time — in 1997 the gap was over 27%.
3) There are several related reasons for the gap, such as **direct discrimination** against women and the fact that **opportunities** for women to **progress** in their jobs can be negatively affected by having children. Another reason for the gap might be because many women choose to work part-time to fit their jobs around childcare responsibilities and **part-time jobs** are often **less well-paid** than full-time positions.

The Structure of Employment in the UK

Average Earnings vary considerably in the UK and the rest of the world

1) Since 1997 there have been several notable **trends** in **UK earnings**. Some of these include:

- Average weekly earnings for full-time workers (when adjusted for inflation) steadily **increased** between 1997 and 2008. Between 2008 and 2013 these earnings have **decreased** by around 8% in total — this decrease is likely to be linked to the economic downturn and they're likely to increase again as the economy recovers.
- Compared to the **private sector**, workers in the **public sector** (on average) **earn more** per week.
- Average weekly earnings for **men** are at their **highest** between the ages of **40 and 49**, whereas for **women** it's between **30 and 39**. Men and women aged 18-21 earn roughly half as much as men and women aged between 30 and 39.
- Average weekly full-time earnings also differ considerably between the **different regions** of the UK. The **highest** were in **London** and the **South East**, which is unsurprising given the large number of jobs available in the region and the proportion of those that are based in well-paid industries, such as finance. In 2013, the **North East** and **Northern Ireland** were the two **lowest** paid regions.
- In 2013, managers, directors and senior officials were paid the **highest** average full-time earnings. Workers in sales and customer services were paid the **lowest** average earnings.

2) The general increase in earnings in the UK **hasn't** been **evenly spread** — workers earning higher wages have received **bigger than average increases**. During the period 1986-2011 the top 10% of earners received real increases in wages of 81% while the bottom 10% received real increases of just 47%. This **wage inequality** is worst in London and the South East.
3) Other factors, such as **ethnicity**, can have an impact on earning. For example, it's claimed that almost half of Bangladeshi and Pakistani employees are paid a **low wage** (less than £7.00 per hour), which is a **much higher proportion** than employees from other ethnic groups. This difference may occur for several reasons, such as **discrimination** (see p.64), or because these people might live in poorer areas and they **don't** have access to **good schools**.
4) Regional differences in pay are partly due to the differences between the **regional labour markets**. As mentioned above, there are a large number of highly-paid jobs in London, whereas statistics suggest that average wages are, for example, lower in the North East. This is likely to be because there are more people employed in the North East in industries that offer lower pay, e.g. manufacturing.
5) Earnings in European countries **vary greatly** from country to country. **Denmark** has one of the highest average wages in Europe, whereas **Moldova** and **Ukraine** have the lowest average wages. The average wages in Moldova and Ukraine are **less than 10%** of the average wages in Denmark.
6) Elsewhere in the world increasing wages have come about due to economic success. A clear example of this is **China**, where wages have been **steadily increasing** for many years. Between 2004 and 2013 average wages have increased by **over 300%**.
7) Remember, an **increase** in **average wages** doesn't directly correspond to an **increase** in general **living standards**. In a majority of countries there's still a large gap between the rich and poor (see p.68) — even though statistics suggest average earnings are rising, this may be because the very rich are becoming richer.

Practice Questions

Q1 Briefly describe how the number of people employed in the primary, secondary and tertiary sectors has changed in the UK since the 1970s.

Q2 Give two reasons why the participation rate for women has increased.

Q3 What is the gender pay gap?

Exam Questions

Q1 Define the term 'participation rate'. [2 marks]

Q2 A recent government report found that the average wage was increasing in a country.
Explain why this might not mean that every person in the economy was receiving a higher wage per hour. [4 marks]

"You'll take the high wage, and I'll take the low wage..."

There's quite a lot of information thrown at you here. Make sure you get a grasp of some important trends in UK employment — a key one is how jobs have increasingly moved towards the service (tertiary) sector. Exam questions using the sort of information in this topic will often give you an extract to use in your answer, but it's very useful to have some background knowledge.

Labour Demand

These pages are for AQA Unit 3 and OCR Unit 3 (Work and Leisure).
Labour is important — without it firms can't produce goods and services. Although maybe in the future robots will run firms totally by themselves... imagine that. But for now they can't, so learn these pages.

The Demand for Labour is a Derived Demand

1) The **demand** for labour comes from **firms** and the **supply** of labour comes from economically active **people**.
2) When firms demand workers it's because they need them to make the goods that are being demanded by their customers. So the demand for labour is **driven** by the demand for the goods that this labour would produce — this is **derived demand**.
3) When demand for these goods **increases**, so does the demand for labour. When demand for goods **decreases**, the derived demand for labour also decreases, resulting in unemployment.

Firms will Only Demand Workers if they will Make Money by employing them

1) Firms demand labour in order to make **revenue** from selling the goods/services that the labour produces.
2) The **marginal productivity theory** says that the demand for any factor of production (e.g. labour or land) depends on its **marginal revenue product** (**MRP**).
3) The **marginal revenue product of labour** (**MRP_L**) is the **extra revenue gained** by the firm from **employing one more worker**.
4) **MRP_L** is calculated by multiplying the **marginal physical product of labour** (MPP_L, which is the output produced by the additional worker) by the **marginal revenue** (MR, price per unit).
5) Firms will **only hire workers** if they **add more** to a firm's **revenue** than they add to its **costs**. Here's an example:

> If an **extra worker** produced **10 units per hour** that were sold for **£12** each, the **MRP_L** would equal **£120** (10 × £12). As long as the worker costs less than this to employ (per hour), it's **profitable** to employ the extra worker.

6) The **cost** of hiring **one additional worker** is called the **marginal cost of labour** (**MC_L**). In a **perfectly competitive** labour market the **MC_L** is **equal to** the **wage** paid to the additional worker.
7) In a perfectly competitive market the firm cannot influence the wage — the wage (W) on the diagram is the **market equilibrium wage** (the wage where supply equals demand in that market). If you compare the wage to the MRP_L, this indicates the quantity of labour a firm needs to use to be most **cost-effective**.

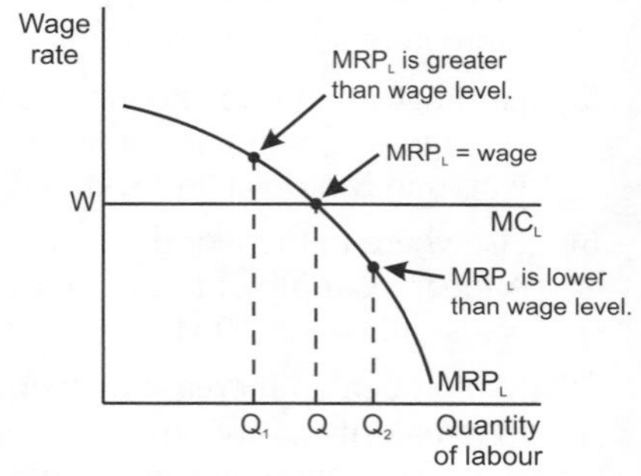

- When MRP_L is equal to the market equilibrium wage (MC_L), the firm has the **optimum number** of workers (Q) to maximise profits.
- When MRP_L is **greater than** the wage, a firm could increase its profits by employing more workers — the firm is employing too few workers (Q_1).
- When MRP_L is **less than** the wage, workers are adding more to costs than they are to revenue, so the firm is employing **too many workers** (Q_2).

The MRP_L curve is the Same Shape as the MPP_L curve

1) Remember, $MRP_L = MPP_L \times MR$ (marginal revenue). This means that the values that make up the **MRP_L** curve are the same as the ones that make up the **MPP_L** curve **multiplied** by the **MR** (which is assumed to be constant).
2) As the values on the MPP_L curve are multiplied by the **MR** to form the MRP_L curve, the curves are the **same shape**.
3) The MPP_L curve is **downward sloping** because of the **law of diminishing returns** (see p.6). In other words, as each new worker is employed the amount of **additional output** that's produced **falls**.

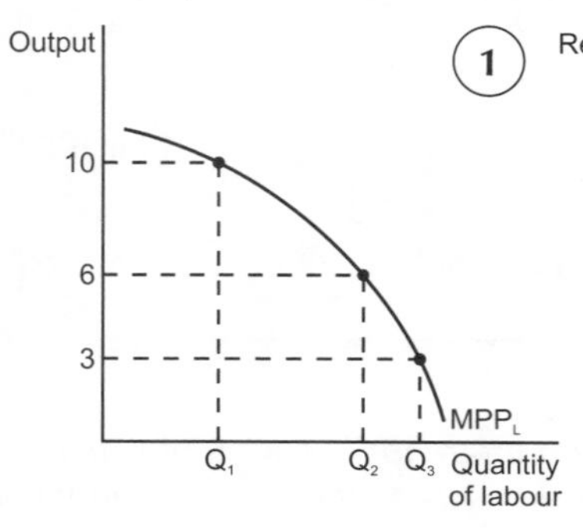

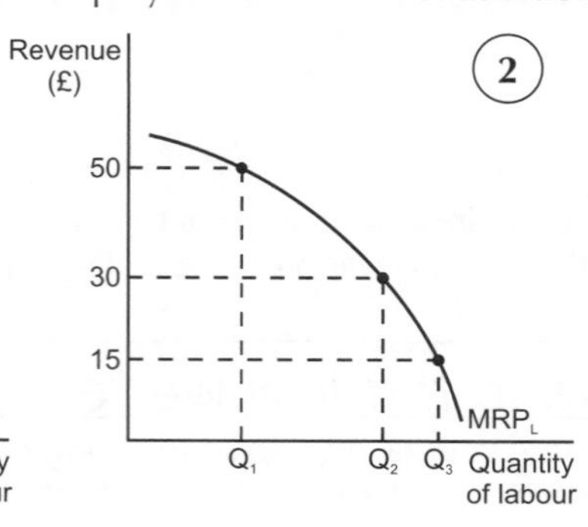

- The diagrams show the **MPP_L** and **MRP_L** curve of the same firm.
- By looking at these two diagrams it's possible to work out the **MR**. To get a revenue of **£50** at Q_1 on diagram 2, output at Q_1 on diagram 1 (**10**) must have been multiplied by **5** — so the MR is **£5**.

The MPP curve is sometimes shown with an initial upward slope because MPP (i.e. the average output per unit of labour) can increase at lower levels of employment.

Labour Demand

A firm's **Demand** for **Labour** is affected by **Productivity**

1) Generally, a firm's demand for labour will decrease if wages rise. However, this depends on whether the wage increase is accompanied by an increase in **productivity** (the output per worker per hour).
2) Higher levels of productivity reduce **unit labour costs**. Unit labour costs are the labour costs per unit of output.
3) So, if wages **increase** but are accompanied by an **equivalent increase** in worker **productivity**, this means that the **unit labour cost** stays the **same** and **demand** for labour is **unaffected**. For example:

> If a worker had a **wage** of **£10** per hour and iced **10** cakes per hour, the **wage cost per cake** would be **£1**. If the worker got a **10% wage rise** (wage would rise to £11) and this was matched with a **10% rise** in **productivity** (the worker would ice 11 cakes per hour), the wage cost per cake would still be **£1**.

4) High **unit labour costs** suggest there's low productivity and this would **reduce** a country's **international competitiveness**.

The MRP_L curve is also the **Demand** curve for **Labour**

This is because it shows the quantity of labour demanded at each wage rate.

Anything that affects the MRP (or MPP and MR) will **shift** the **demand (MRP_L) curve** for labour. Examples include:

- A change to the **price of goods** sold (**MR**) — if demand falls for a firm's product and its price falls, this would decrease the firm's demand for labour and the MRP_L curve would shift to the **left**.
- Factors that affect **labour productivity** — e.g. if **new technology** or **training** increases the productivity of workers, this would increase the demand for labour and cause the MRP_L curve to shift to the **right**.
- Increases to the **costs of labour** — the cost of labour doesn't only include wages. It also includes costs such as training, uniforms, safety equipment, and National Insurance contributions. If any of these labour costs increased, this would decrease the demand for labour and the MRP_L curve would shift to the **left**.

Demand for labour can be **Elastic** or **Inelastic**

1) **Elasticity of demand for labour** measures the **change in demand** for labour when the **wage level** changes. It's calculated by dividing the percentage change in the quantity of labour demanded by the percentage change in the wage rate.
2) When demand for labour is **elastic**, small wage changes can cause **large** changes in the quantity of labour demanded. When it's **inelastic** even large wage changes only cause **small** changes to the quantity of labour demanded.
3) There are several factors that can influence the elasticity of demand for labour:
   - The demand for labour is always **more elastic** in the **long run** as firms can make plans for the future to replace labour (or take on more). In the **short run**, changes are more difficult to make, so demand for labour is **more inelastic**.
   - If labour can be **substituted easily** by capital (e.g. machines), or other factors of production, then the demand for labour will be **elastic**. For example, if wage rates rise and a firm can easily replace workers with machines that do the same task equally well, but more cheaply, then it may choose to reduce its labour force.
   - If **wages** are a **small proportion** of a firm's **total costs** then the demand for labour will be **more inelastic** — this is because an increase in wages will have **little impact** on total costs. If wages are a **large proportion** of a firm's total costs then even small wage increases will have a **large impact** on total costs — these firms are very sensitive to wage increases and their demand for labour will be **more elastic**.
   - It's important to consider the **price elasticity of demand** (PED) of the **product** being made. The more **price elastic** the demand for the product is, the more elastic the **demand for labour** will be. In this situation, when **wages rise** firms **aren't able** to pass the increase in costs (higher wages) to consumers by **increasing prices**. If they did, their sales would decrease by a **greater proportion** than the increase in price — so overall their **sales revenue** would **fall**.

Practice Questions

Q1 Explain why the demand for labour is a derived demand.

Q2 Define MRP_L.

Exam Question

Q1 State and explain two factors that could increase the demand for labour. [6 marks]

They said my job could be done better by a machine — they were right...

For this topic it's important to learn the difference between MRP_L, MPP_L and MC_L. Remember that demand for labour is linked to the demand for the good or service the labour produces (it's a derived demand) and also the PED of the good or service.

Labour Supply

These pages are for AQA Unit 3 and OCR Unit 3 (Work and Leisure).
Unsurprisingly this topic is all about labour supply... more surprising is that it's not all about the wage that workers get paid. There's more to work than just getting paid — a well-stocked biscuit tin is a big perk...

Labour Supply can refer to an Individual or an Occupation

1) An **individual's labour supply** is the total number of **hours** that that person is willing to work at a given wage rate. For an **occupation** it's the number of **workers** willing to work in that occupation at a given wage rate.
2) As the **wage rate rises**, the quantity of labour supplied increases — usually, **individuals** are prepared to work **more hours**, and a **greater number of workers** are willing to work for higher wages. This means that the **supply curve** for labour **slopes upwards**.

An Individual's Supply Curve can be Backward Bending

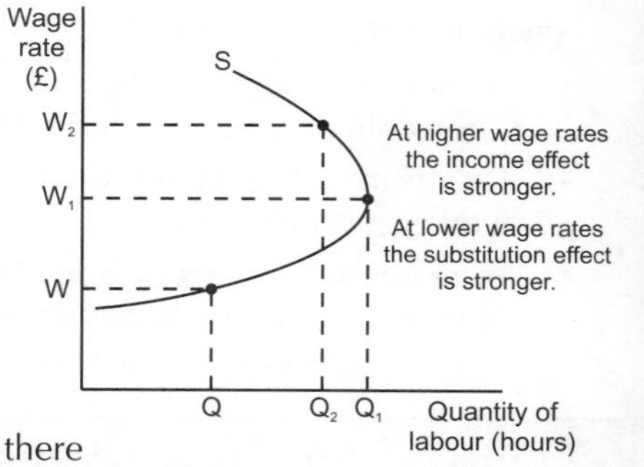

1) In the **short run** the **supply of labour** depends on an **individual's decision** to choose between **work** or **leisure** at a given wage rate.
2) Generally, **when wages rise** from a **low level** an individual's supply of labour **increases** because individuals are **more willing to work** for a **higher wage** to increase their standard of living. On the diagram, when the wage rate rises from W to W_1, the quantity of labour supplied increases from Q to Q_1.
3) **Leisure time** is time spent **not working**. People expect to be **compensated** (paid) to give up their leisure time for work. As wages rise the **opportunity cost** of **leisure time** becomes **greater**, which means that workers have an incentive to substitute more leisure time with work. This is called the **substitution effect**.
4) The **substitution effect** becomes **stronger** as the curve slopes upwards. However, there comes a point where this is no longer the case and people begin to choose to **work less** even though their **wage rate** continues to **increase** — this is called the **income effect**.
5) The backward bending supply curve (above W_1 on the diagram) shows that at higher wage rates workers generally **choose** to **work fewer hours** — when the wage rate rises from W_1 to W_2, the quantity of labour supplied decreases from Q_1 to Q_2. This is because they've reached a level of income that they're happy with (a **target income**). As their income **rises** they can afford to have more **leisure time** whilst **maintaining** their **target income** — the **income effect** is now **stronger**.

The Supply of Labour can be influenced by Job Satisfaction

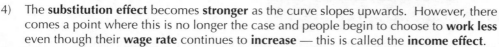

1) The supply of labour in the **long run** is determined by **pecuniary** (monetary) and **non-pecuniary** (non-monetary) factors. These factors determine the welfare gained by working, which is known as the **net advantage**.
2) The net advantage of a job can be divided into **two types** of benefits:

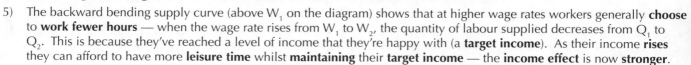

Pecuniary benefits: this is the welfare a worker gains from the **wage** they receive (or more specifically, what's bought with it).

Non-pecuniary benefits: this is the welfare a worker can gain from **non-wage benefits** of their job. Examples of these benefits include:

- flexible working hours
- employee discount
- a generous holiday allowance
- convenience of job location
- training available
- opportunities for promotion
- job security
- perks of the job (e.g. a company car)

Firms offering non-pecuniary benefits can **encourage workers** to **supply more labour** at a given wage rate. So they can effectively cause the position of the labour supply curve to shift.

3) When a worker enjoys their job (has high job satisfaction) they're **more willing** to accept a **lower wage** (low pecuniary benefits) because they gain **high non-pecuniary benefits** from their job.
4) Unpleasant or boring jobs with low job satisfaction have **low non-pecuniary benefits**. Workers doing these jobs will want a **higher wage** to **compensate** for the low non-pecuniary benefits they receive.

Labour Supply

Other factors can affect the Supply of Labour to a Particular Job or Industry

Factors that affect the supply of labour include:

- The size of the **working population** in an area or the country as a whole. For example, if there's an ageing population with a large proportion of people in retirement then there may be insufficient workers to meet demand for labour.
- The **competitiveness of wages** — workers may pick the job that will pay them the highest wage. Firms/industries that pay poor wages may struggle to attract enough labour.
- The **publicising of job opportunities** — it may be difficult to attract sufficient workers to a particular job/industry if jobs are not advertised effectively.

The quantity of labour supplied depends on the Elasticity of the labour supply

1) The main determinant of the elasticity of labour supply is the level of **skills and qualifications** needed for a job.

Low-skilled jobs

1) In **low-skilled jobs** the supply of labour tends to be **elastic**. This means that a small rise in the wage rate causes a proportionately larger rise in the quantity of labour supplied. This is because there's a **large pool** of low-skilled workers and many may be unemployed and looking for work (i.e. very willing to work).
2) It's also important to remember that most low-skilled jobs tend to have **similar wage rates**. If one low-skilled job increases its wage rate, even by a small amount, low-skilled workers from other occupations will be attracted quickly.

Skilled jobs

1) The supply curves for **skilled jobs** such as doctors, pilots and lawyers tend to be **inelastic**, particularly in the short run. This can be explained by looking at the following example.
2) If there was a **shortage** of doctors in the UK, a rise in the wage rate would not be enough to increase the supply in the **short run** as it takes several years to train to become a doctor. Increasing wage rates would have the effect of persuading more people to choose medicine at university (in order to become doctors), but this would only have an effect in the **long term**.

Net migration of doctors from other countries into the UK could increase supply in the short run — see below.

2) The **mobility of labour** is also another important factor that affects the elasticity of labour supply.
   - If workers are **occupationally mobile** (they can move from one occupation to another quickly), labour supply will be more **elastic**.
   - If workers are **geographically mobile** (they can move locations to where the jobs are), then labour supply will also be more **elastic**.

Net Migration of Labour can Increase the supply of labour

1) The UK is part of the EU, which supports the **free movement of labour** between its member states (see p.71).
2) **Net migration of workers** to the UK can **increase** the **supply of labour** and help alleviate shortages of skilled workers. For example, a lack of certain medical staff in the NHS.
3) It can also help with the increased demand for **seasonal workers**, for example in agriculture and construction.

Practice Questions

Q1 What is the opportunity cost of work?

Q2 List four non-pecuniary factors that may determine the supply of labour.

Q3 Why is the supply of low-skilled workers elastic?

Exam Question

Q1 Analyse how rising wage rates affect whether an individual chooses work over leisure in the short run. [15 marks]

Gymnasts — always willing to bend over backwards to supply labour...

Labour supply is all about the number of hours people are willing to work. If you have a job that you love then you might want to spend loads of time at work. Then again, you might change jobs if you see one advertised that offers better pay.

Wages

These pages are for AQA Unit 3 and OCR Unit 3 (Work and Leisure).
Right, there are a few diagrams to learn here (I know, sorry). A key thing to notice is that things are different depending on whether the labour market is perfectly or imperfectly competitive.

Market Forces can determine wages in a **Labour Market**

1) **Wage differentials** are the differences in wages between different groups of workers, or between workers in the same occupation. There are many reasons why these differentials exist, for example:
   - Workers that are **highly skilled** tend to be paid more, e.g. if they're highly trained or have high-level qualifications.
   - Wages vary in **different regions** and between **industries** — in some locations/industries workers will earn more.
   - A **trade union** can influence the wage rate paid to a group of workers (see p.62-63).
2) Wages will probably be **higher** if demand is high and inelastic, and supply is low and inelastic. Wages tend to be **low** when demand is low and elastic, and supply is high and elastic. This can be seen in the examples below:

Lawyers
- **Lawyers** are paid **high wages**.
- Demand for lawyers is **high** because they have a high MRP (marginal revenue product, see p.56) — in other words they're able to make lots of revenue for their firm.
- Demand is also **inelastic** because lawyers are **not easily replaced** — few people have the right skills and experience.
- Supply will be **low**, especially in the short run, as it takes a long time to train to become a lawyer, and not everyone has the abilities to become one.

Office cleaners
- **Office cleaners** are paid fairly **low wages**.
- Demand for cleaners is relatively **low** compared to the supply. The MRP for cleaners is low — this means demand for them is low as cleaners don't contribute greatly to the revenue of their employer.
- Supply will also be **high** and **elastic** as there are no long training periods involved. Many people can do the job as no specific skills or qualifications are needed.

Wages are made up of **Transfer Earnings** and **Economic Rent**

1) In a labour market, **transfer earnings** can be seen as the **minimum payment** that's required to keep labour in its **current occupation** — i.e. the minimum pay that will stop a worker from switching to their next best paid job. The **size** of this transfer payment **differs** between workers.
2) Workers are often paid in **excess** of their transfer earnings — the excess above transfer earnings is called **economic rent**.
3) So a worker's **wages** can be **divided** into **two parts**: transfer earnings and economic rent. For example, a worker earns £400 per week. In his next best job he'd earn £350 per week. So his weekly wage is made up of £350 transfer earnings and £50 economic rent.
4) Transfer earnings and economic rent can be shown using a diagram like the one below:

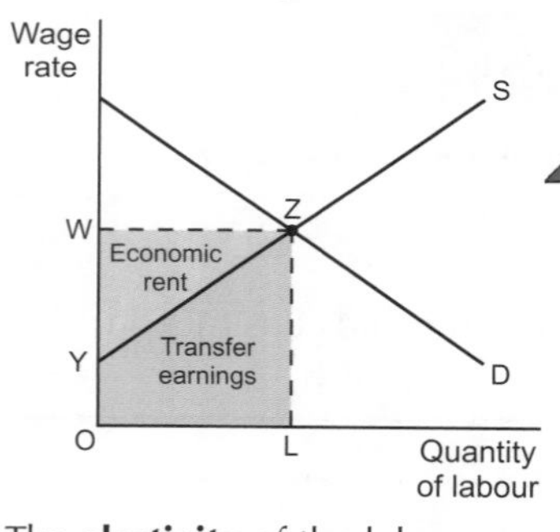

- In this market the **equilibrium wage rate** is **W**. A worker who's paid this wage supplies their labour at the margin because if the wage was **reduced**, the worker would **leave** this labour market and look for **alternative employment**. For the marginal worker the **wage** rate is **equal to** their **transfer earnings**.
- The area under the supply curve below the equilibrium point (OYZL) is equal to the **transfer earnings** of workers in this market.
- The total earnings of all the workers in the market is equal to OWZL. **Economic rent** is equal to the part of this area which isn't accredited to transfer earnings — the triangle above the supply curve (YWZ).

5) The **elasticity** of the labour supply curve has a significant impact on the **proportion** of the total earnings that makes up **transfer earnings** and **economic rent**. This is shown on the diagram to the right.
   - As the **supply curve** becomes more **elastic**, the proportion of the total earnings that's economic rent **decreases** and the proportion that's transfer earnings **increases**.
   - The **opposite** occurs if the **supply curve** becomes more **inelastic**.

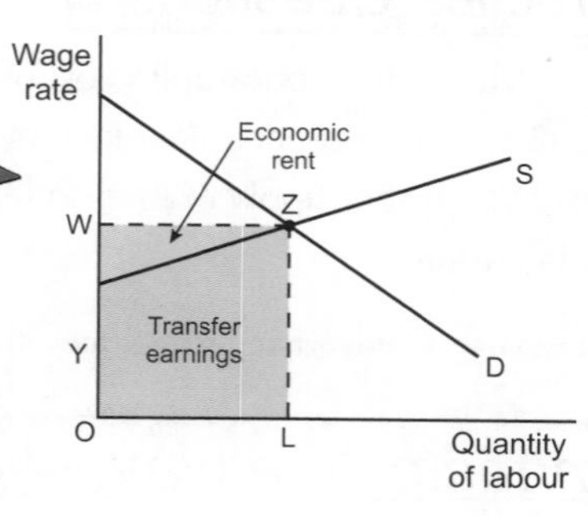

6) For occupations where the supply of labour is **elastic**, the earnings of each worker will be **mainly transfer earnings**. The opposite is true for occupations that have an **inelastic** supply of workers (their earnings will be mainly **economic rent**).

Wages

In a Perfectly Competitive Labour Market *firms are* Price Takers

The diagrams show the equilibrium wage rate and level of employment for a perfectly competitive **labour market** and an **individual firm** within it:

- In diagram 1 the **ruling market wage** (W) is determined by the forces of demand and supply.
- Individual firms have no power to influence the wage level so they're forced to accept the ruling market wage, i.e. firms are **price takers** — see diagram 2.

You might also see price takers called wage takers.

1 The whole labour market

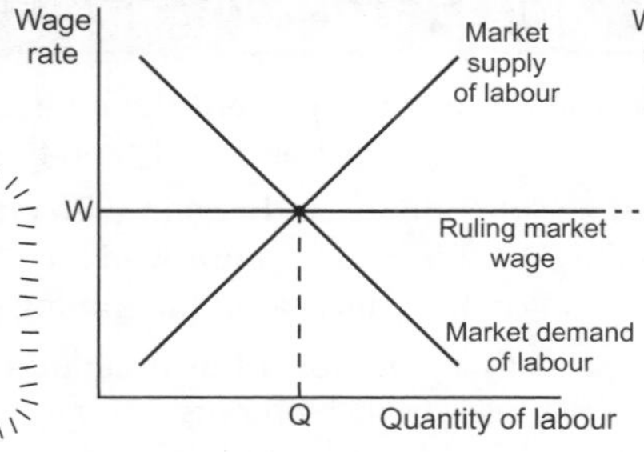

2 An individual firm in the labour market

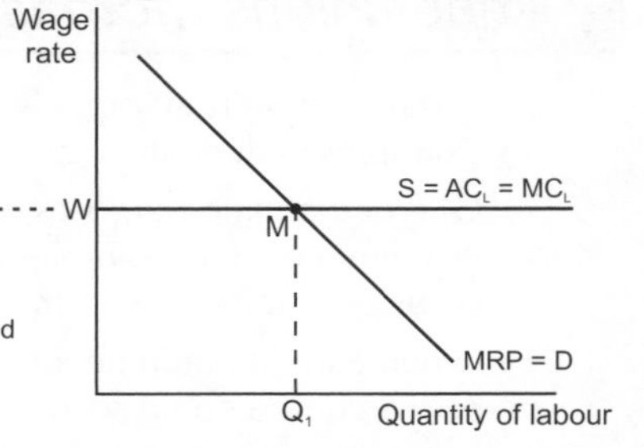

- The ruling market wage is also the **individual firm's labour supply curve**. This curve is **perfectly elastic** because the wage rate is **set by the market** and the firm can **hire as many workers as it wants** at this wage rate (W). Notice that the supply curve is also the **average cost of labour** (AC_L) curve (total wages divided by number of workers is equal to the wage rate) and the **marginal cost of labour** (MC_L) curve (the cost of employing one more worker is equal to the wage rate).
- In diagram 2, the firm decides to use the quantity of labour Q_1 because at Q_1 it **maximises profits** (MRP = MC_L at point M, which is where a firm has the optimum number of workers — see p.56). (In a perfectly competitive market the MC_L is **equal** to the **ruling wage**, so a firm will take on labour up to the point at which **MRP** is **equal to the wage rate** (W).)
- Remember, this is only a **theoretical model** as perfectly competitive labour markets don't exist in the real world. However, it's still useful to compare this model with real markets, which are all **imperfectly competitive** to some extent (see below).

AQA ONLY

A Monopsony Labour Market *is an example of an* Imperfect Market

1) This example shows the difference that **imperfections** can make to a labour market.
2) A **monopsony** means there's only **one buyer** in a market. In a **monopsony labour market** there's a **single employer**, so workers have only one choice of employer to work for.
3) A monopsonist employer can pay a wage that's **less than** a **worker's MRP** and **less than** what would've been paid in a **perfectly competitive labour market**. Monopsonist employers can also **drive down** the **level of employment** below the level that would exist in a perfectly competitive labour market.
4) The wages and employment levels in a monopsony labour market can be shown using the diagram below:
   - The **marginal cost of labour** (MC_L) curve is **above** the average cost of labour (AC_L) curve, so the cost of employing one more worker is more than the average cost.
   - The **average cost of labour** (AC_L) curve shows the number of workers that are prepared to work for the monopsonist at different wage levels — so the AC_L curve is also the **supply curve**.
   - Firms will hire the number of workers that **maximise their profits** (where MRP = MC_L). This is at **T**, and the number of workers hired is $\mathbf{Q_1}$. The **wage paid** is $\mathbf{W_1}$ — the supply curve clearly shows that Q_1 workers will accept W_1 wage.
   - Unlike in a perfectly competitive market, this wage is **lower** than the **MRP** of these workers. The monopsonist could pay a wage **higher** than W_1, but it doesn't need to as Q_1 workers are happy to work for W_1. So, monopsonists are **price makers** — unlike firms in a perfectly competitive market, who are price takers.

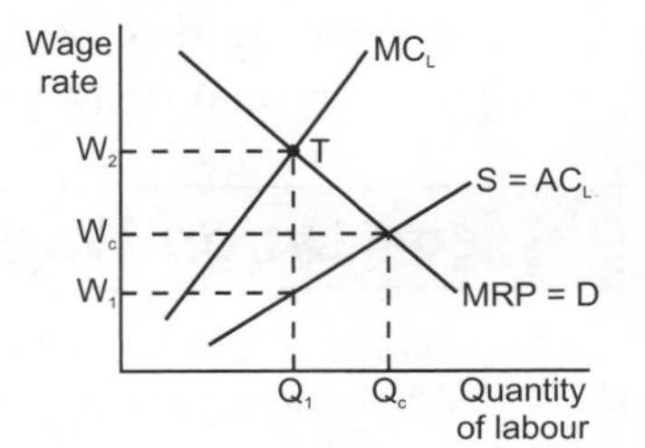

Practice Questions

Q1 Describe briefly what is meant by the term 'price taker'.

Q2 Draw a diagram to show how a monopsonist employer can pay a wage that is less than a worker's MRP.

Exam Question

Q1 Using a diagram, explain the difference between transfer earnings and economic rent in the labour market. [15 marks]

If you've got big skills it probably means you can pay big bills...

Blimey, there are a fair few diagrams to learn here. It's important to understand the difference between transfer earnings and economic rent, and to learn about how wages are determined in perfect markets (and imperfect markets too if you're doing AQA).

Labour Market Failure: Trade Unions

These pages are for AQA Unit 3 and OCR Unit 3 (Work and Leisure).
Trade unions are formed when workers come together and try to get a better deal from their employers. They can mean that workers get a higher wage, but it's not all good news and Margaret Thatcher wasn't a big fan.

Trade unions **Increase** the **Bargaining Power** of **Workers**

1) A **trade union** is an organisation formed to **represent the interests** of a **group of workers**. Examples include the National Union of Teachers (NUT) and the Professional Footballers Association (PFA).
2) One of the main purposes of a trade union is to **bargain with employers** and get the best outcome for its members. For example, they can bargain for **improved pay**, **better working conditions** and **job security**. Members of a trade union have **increased bargaining power** compared to **individual workers**.
3) When a trade union negotiates with an employer this is called **collective bargaining**. A trade union could secure a pay rise for its members through collective bargaining.
4) Collective bargaining can be done on a **national level** (e.g. to secure a pay rise for all workers in a particular industry) or at **plant level** (e.g. negotiating improved working conditions for employees at an individual workplace).
5) Trade unions might also negotiate **performance-related pay agreements**. This is when workers get pay increases that are linked to the quality of their work and their productivity.
6) Trade unions can also have a role in making sure workers are safe at work by making sure any laws about working conditions are adhered to. For example, they will make sure workers have **sufficient breaks** and their place of work meets **health and safety requirements**.
7) Trade unions can also help to protect their members from **discrimination** (see p.64-65).

When looking at the effects of trade unions you should assume a **'closed shop'**, i.e. every worker is a trade union member. This limits the available labour supply and means that firms can only pay the wage rate agreed by the trade union.

Trade union **Membership** in the UK was at its **Peak** in the **Late 1970s**

1) Trade unions are **most powerful** when they have **huge membership** — the more members a union has, the more influence it can have. At their peak in 1979, the trade unions in the UK were **very powerful** and had around 13 million members.
2) During the **1980s**, when Margaret Thatcher was the Prime Minister, the Conservative government acted to **reduce the power of trade unions** — e.g. by making it more difficult for trade unions to go on strike. The government at the time saw **weakening** the **trade unions** as a supply-side policy that would help make UK industry **more flexible** and **competitive**.
3) In addition, there was a big decline in the **large manufacturing industries** (e.g. shipbuilding) in the 1980s and 90s, which had huge trade union membership. This **de-industrialisation** meant that there was a shift in employment towards jobs in the **service sector** where unions tend not to exist — so union membership **fell sharply**.
4) Modern trends in the economy have also **reduced** union membership further. Workers on **flexible contracts** and **part-time workers** (both of which are becoming more common in the economy) are **less likely** to **join a union**.
5) Since the **mid 1990s** trade union membership has remained **fairly stable** at around 7 million members.

Trade Union Wage Negotiations may result in **Unemployment**

1) Market failure occurs when the market forces of demand and supply fail to allocate resources efficiently. When the supply of labour **exceeds demand** it causes **unemployment**.
2) Trade unions can **cause labour market failure** by **forcing wages up** to a level **higher** than the **market equilibrium wage** — causing a **surplus of labour** (i.e. **unemployment**). Some of a firm's income is redistributed to the workers and its **costs of production increase**.
3) The effect of **trade union wage negotiations** in a **perfectly competitive labour market** can be seen on the diagram below:

- **Without trade union action** firms would pay the **equilibrium wage rate** (W_e) and the level of employment would be L_e.
- When the trade union forces the wage rate up to W_t this means firms can't employ workers for less than this wage. This results in a **kinked supply curve** (shown in red). At W_t the quantity of labour employed **falls** to L_1.
- At this higher wage rate (W_t) there's an **oversupply of workers** — there's **insufficient demand** for the number of workers willing to work, so there's **unemployment** (L_1 to L_2), and this is labour market failure.
- The **level of unemployment** caused by the wage increase depends on the **elasticity** of the labour demand curve.

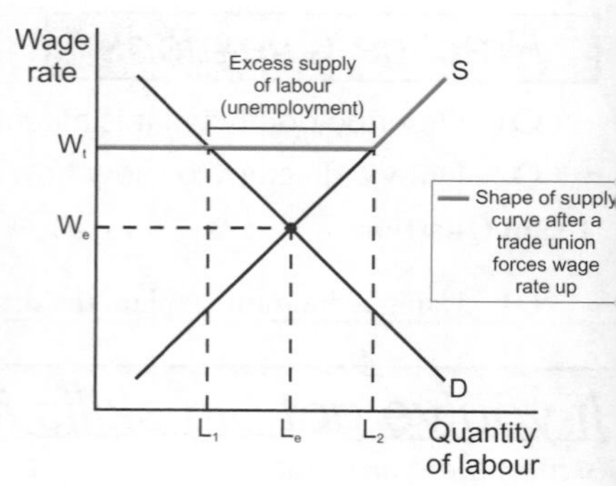

Labour Market Failure: Trade Unions

Pay Rises negotiated by trade unions *May Not* lead to *Unemployment*

1) Trade unions can help to increase the wages of their members without causing unemployment. To do this the **productivity** of trade union members must **increase** — this would **increase demand** for workers from firms and help **prevent** the situation of an **excess supply** of labour described on the previous page.
2) Trade unions can help persuade their members to agree to **more efficient working practices** which **increase worker productivity**. This is good for firms as a **more productive workforce** may **increase** their **profits**. Workers will benefit from higher wages and trade union membership won't be reduced by unemployment.
3) When workers become **more productive** a firm's **MRP** (demand) curve **shifts** to the **right**. Firms can afford to pay wages that are equal to a worker's MRP (see p.56), so if a trade union can help raise the MRP of workers, then an increased wage can be justified.

In *Monopsonistic Labour Markets* trade unions can *Increase Wages* and *Jobs*

1) A monopsonistic employer pays workers a wage that's lower than their MRP (see p.61). If a trade union was involved it could **increase** the **wage rate** whilst maintaining the same level of employment, or even increasing it.
2) When a trade union enters a monopsonistic labour market this is an example of a **bilateral monopoly**. This is when there's a **single buyer** and a **single seller** — so in this case there's a single buyer of labour (the monopsonist) and a single seller (the trade union).

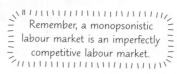

Remember, a monopsonistic labour market is an imperfectly competitive labour market.

- W_1 is the wage that the monopsonist would have paid its workers **without a union** (check p.61 to recap why).
- The presence of a union may increase wages to W_2. In doing this it will change the shape of the **supply/average cost of labour (AC_L) curve**, and that'll then change the shape of the marginal cost of labour (MC_L) curve.
- The **profit maximising** level of workers is still where the MC_L curve crosses the marginal revenue product (MRP) curve. This is now at **point U**, giving a **new increased level of employment** of L_2.
- The union has managed to **increase wages** from W_1 to W_2, and **increase employment** from L_1 to L_2.

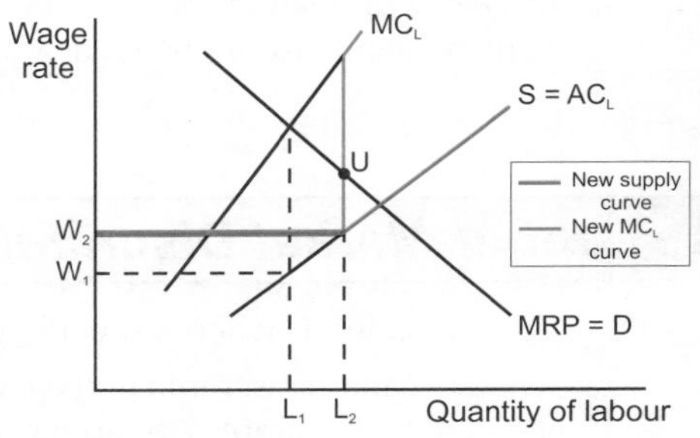

3) The presence of the trade union in the market means that the **wage rate** and **level of employment** have been brought **closer** to the levels that they would be in a **free market**. The trade union has had a positive impact on the labour market.

Trade Unions are *Less Likely* to cause *Market Failure Today*

1) Government legislation has **reduced** the **power** of **trade unions**. They're **less likely** to cause **market failure** (e.g. by increasing unemployment) because they have **less influence**.
2) Trade unions have made big changes in the workplace though. In return for **higher pay** and **better working conditions** firms have benefited from a **more productive** and **flexible workforce**. Don't forget that the increased productivity of workers may drive an **increased demand** for workers and lead to a **reduction** in the level of **unemployment**.

Practice Questions

Q1 Describe what a trade union is.

Q2 Describe the trend in trade union membership in the UK since the 1970s.

Q3 Draw a diagram to show how a trade union can increase wages and the level of employment in a monopsonistic labour market.

Exam Question

Q1 Discuss the extent to which trade unions cause labour market failure. [20 marks]

"We want better pay! When do we want it? NOOOOOOOOOOOOOOW..."

Ah, trade unions — makes me think of disgruntled miners going on strike, but that's not the only thing they do. Of course they're linked to some strike action in the UK, particularly in the 1970s, but they also have an important role in protecting workers' rights and negotiating for a fair wage. Learn the theory about how trade union action might create jobs or increase unemployment.

Labour Market Failure: Discrimination

These pages are for AQA Unit 3 and OCR Unit 3 (Work and Leisure).
Workers can be discriminated against for reasons that aren't related to their ability to do a particular job — this is pretty unfair. Wage discrimination is also covered on this spread, which is a bit different.

Wage Discrimination can result in Lower Wage Costs for firms

1) **Wage discrimination** is **similar** to **price discrimination**.
2) Wage discrimination takes place when **employers** with **monopsony power** pay **different wage rates** based on different workers' **willingness to supply labour**. This can be shown by the diagram below:

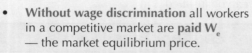

Price discrimination occurs when a seller charges different prices to different customers for the same product — see p.28-29.

- **Without wage discrimination** all workers in a competitive market are **paid W_e** — the market equilibrium price.
- The **total wage cost** for firms is OW_eAL_e.
- When employers start to pay the **minimum** each worker is prepared to work for (i.e. their transfer earnings), the total wage cost is **reduced** to $OBAL_e$ (the green area shown on the diagram).
- **Employers gain** while **workers lose out**.

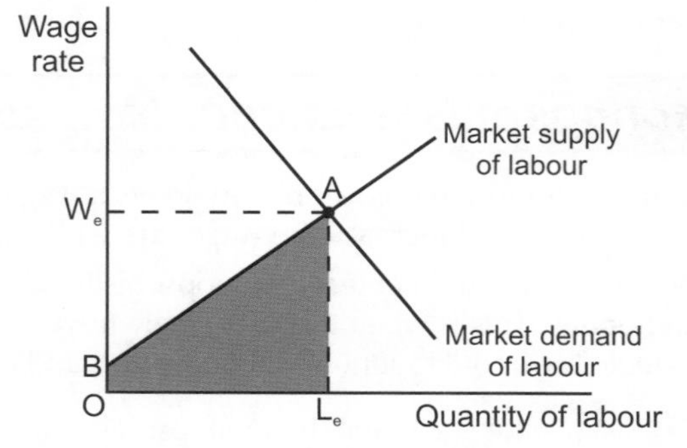

3) Wage discrimination shouldn't be confused with **labour market discrimination**. This is a different concept based on workers being discriminated against depending on differences between them, such as **gender** and **race** — see below.

Labour Market Discrimination is a Cause of Labour Market Failure

1) Discrimination is when a **specific group of workers** is **treated differently** to other workers in the same job.
2) Workers can be discriminated against because of their **race**, **gender**, **sexuality**, **religion**, **disability**, **age**, etc. Here are two examples of labour market discrimination:

Racial discrimination can occur when employers only want to work with and employ people from a **particular ethnic background**. They're prepared to pay a price for this — the **loss in productivity** from not employing a worker that's perhaps the most suited for the job.

The **gender pay gap** (see p.54) is where average pay rates are lower for women than for men. Part of this pay gap is thought to be due to **discrimination by employers** that are prepared to pay male employees more than female employees for doing the **same job**.

3) In the UK this sort of discrimination is **against the law**. The Equality Act of 2010 replaced all previous anti-discrimination laws and made discrimination **illegal** in the UK.
4) Discrimination can be one cause of the **unequal distribution of wealth and income** (see p.50) and lead to a **misallocation of resources**, **reduced efficiency** and **increased costs**.

Workers suffering from Discrimination tend to Earn Less

1) Workers who suffer from discrimination are generally forced to accept **lower wages**.
2) Discrimination can also mean that some workers find it more difficult to find a job. They may resort to accepting a **lower-paid job** that they're **overqualified for**. This is unfair to them and is also a **misallocation of resources**.
3) In addition, workers who are the victims of discrimination may be **put off** from going for **promotions**, which can leave them in low-paying jobs with **limited career prospects**.

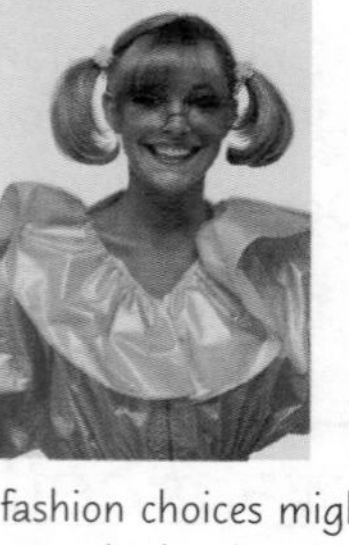

Marie's fashion choices might be the reason why her boss never gave her a 'customer-facing' role.

Labour Market Failure: Discrimination

Employers who Discriminate can incur Increased Costs

1) Employers who are influenced by their own prejudices believe that the **marginal revenue product** (MRP) of the discriminated group of workers is **lower** than it really is. This means that they demand **fewer** of these workers.
2) When demand falls the MRP/demand curve **shifts left**, which means that **wages go down** for the discriminated group.
3) By discriminating like this, firms have **fewer workers to choose from**. By ignoring workers who may have been more suited to a job and more efficient, they **increase** their **costs of production**. Increased costs may lead to **increased prices**.
4) This discrimination can be shown by the diagrams on the right.
   - For discriminated workers, **MRP** is **lower** than the level in the free market and this results in a **lower wage rate** (W_d).
   - For favoured workers employers believe their **MRP** to be **greater** than it really is. This shifts the MRP curve to the right, **increasing** the **wage rate** for these workers (to W_f).

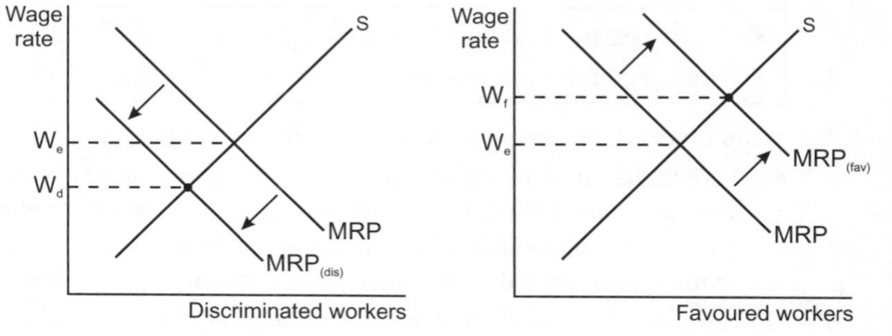

5) Employers that **don't discriminate** have access to a **greater supply** of labour.
   - As the **demand** for discriminated workers is **reduced** in firms that **discriminate**, there are **more workers** available to supply their labour to firms that **don't discriminate**.
   - The **supply curve** for these firms **shifts right** and the **wage rate decreases**. This means discriminated workers could lose out again, but it's worth remembering that this doesn't take into account the **national minimum wage** — wages can't fall below a certain level (see p.70).

Discrimination leads to Increased Costs for the Government and Economy

1) The government may need to increase **welfare payments** to support **discriminated workers**.
2) Discriminated workers working for **unfairly low wages** will also reduce the government's **tax revenues**, which would be higher if these workers were paid fairly.
3) If discriminated workers aren't in a job that's well suited to them (e.g. if they're overqualified), their levels of **productivity** can **fall**. When **output** and **efficiency** (both allocative and productive) **fall**, a country may **lose international competitiveness**. This could negatively affect the country's **balance of payments**, reducing the **sale of exports**, and this in turn may cause **unemployment**.

Practice Questions

Q1 Define wage discrimination.

Q2 Workers can be discriminated against because of their age. List three other forms of worker discrimination.

Q3 What effect does labour market discrimination have on worker earnings?

Q4 Explain how discrimination can lead to increased costs for governments.

Exam Questions

Q1 Explain the impact of labour market discrimination on workers' wages and productivity. [8 marks]

Q2 Use a diagram to explain how firms that discriminate against workers can experience increased costs. [8 marks]

"Yes Sir, sorry, I mean, Miss" — darn my poor gender discrimination...

Discrimination is another type of labour market failure. There are two types of discrimination you need to know about. Wage discrimination is where workers are paid different wages depending on their willingness to supply labour. Discrimination in the labour market is when workers are discriminated against because of something like their age or ethnicity — this is illegal in the UK.

Labour Market Failure: Imperfections

These pages are for OCR Unit 3 (Work and Leisure).
There are several different causes of labour market failure — this topic explains a selection of them.

Not all Economic Inactivity is Labour Market Failure

1) People are classed as **economically inactive** if they're **not working** and also **not looking for work**.
2) Economically inactive people are considered by economists as a **waste** of a **scarce resource** (labour).
3) People are economically inactive for several reasons:
   - They **care** for sick, elderly or young people (unpaid).
   - They're in **full-time education**.
   - They have a **long-term illness** or **disability**.
   - They're **choosing not to find a job** or have **given up**.
4) It can be **good** for some people to be economically inactive. For example:
   - People that are looking after family members may actually save the government money. For example, the benefits paid to people caring for an elderly relative may be **less expensive** than the cost of providing a professional carer.
   - Those in **full-time education** are also going to **add value** to the economy in the future when they will **increase** the **quality** of the **labour force**.
5) However, people who are inactive due to **long-term illness** or **disability**, but are still **able** to work, represent **market failure**. Labour is a scarce resource and these people could still add to an **economy's output** if work can be found for them.
6) **Discouraged workers** who have tried to look for work but have **given up** are also a waste of scarce labour in exactly the same way. Discouraged workers are also more likely to suffer from depression, which can add to **health care costs**.

All labour markets suffer from Imperfect Information

1) **Imperfect information** is another source of labour market failure.
2) Perfect information would exist if **workers knew everything** about every **job** and **employers knew everything** about every potential **worker**. Using this information workers and employers would find their **ideal job** and **employees**.
3) Of course, the **real world isn't perfect**:
   - Many **workers** end up in jobs that **aren't the best fit** for them (e.g. that don't utilise their skills fully and keep them motivated) and/or **don't pay enough**. Or, they might end up with **no job** at all.
   - **Employers** end up with workers that aren't as **productive** as they could be, which increases their **costs of production** and makes their goods **less competitive**.
4) Imperfect information increases **frictional unemployment**. When people are between jobs they need to **spend time researching** to find the **right job**. If they had the benefit of **perfect information** their task would be **simpler**.

Skill Shortages increase the Costs Of Production for firms

1) A shortage of anything **drives up** its **price**. Therefore shortages of skilled labour drive up the **wage costs** for **firms**, which in turn **increases** their **costs of production**.
2) A shortage also means that firms may be forced to **employ workers** who **don't** have the **desired level** of **qualification/experience** for the job, and this will **reduce productivity** and **quality** levels.
3) **Training** can increase employee skills and make them **more productive**, but employers can be **reluctant** to **provide it** as they worry about other firms **poaching** their **newly-trained employees** without incurring the costs of this training.

Unemployment exists when the Supply of labour is More Than the Demand for it

1) Unemployed workers are a **waste of scarce resources** — unemployment means an economy isn't making use of all its resources effectively. However, in an economy there's always some level of unemployment, and unemployment actually helps to **keep wages down**.
2) For example, if everyone in an economy had a job and an employer wanted to hire a worker, they would have to offer them a **higher wage** than their current job. A firm could offer better **non-pecuniary benefits** (e.g. a health care package, greater career progression opportunities — see p.58) instead, but this would still **increase** the firm's **costs**.
3) Unemployment only becomes a **serious market failure** if it's at a **high level** and persists for a **long period** of time.
4) Unemployment can also be caused by the level of **unemployment benefit** being **too high**. This means that people can be better off by **choosing not to work** (**voluntary unemployment**) and claiming unemployment benefit rather than **working** for a **low wage** — this is called the **unemployment trap**.

The unemployment trap is different to the poverty trap — see p.51

Labour Market Failure: Imperfections

Barriers *that stop people* ***Changing Job*** *create* ***Segmented Labour Markets***

1) In theory, if there were **no barriers** to entry and exit, workers would move from low wage jobs to high wage jobs until **everyone** had the **same wage**. However, in reality there would still be **some wage differentials** because **not everyone** has the motivation and talent to do a **high-paying job** (such as a surgeon).
2) In fact some people in **vocational jobs**, like **nursing**, aren't motivated by money (e.g. they choose to do their job mainly because they love doing it), so they wouldn't get a job in a **different profession** to earn **higher wages**. They might, however, move to a **different nursing job** with **higher pay**.
3) In reality **barriers** to entry and exit **do exist** and they prevent the free movement of workers between all of the different jobs that are available — this is what causes **segmented labour markets** to exist. Rather than one labour market there are **many** distinct labour markets.
4) The **main barrier** to entry in segmented labour markets is **qualifications/skill levels** — this **limits supply** and **increases wages** of particular groups of workers. The existence of these barriers might lead to **market failure** because the forces of demand and supply can't act to equalise wages — i.e. the market equilibrium wage can't be the same across a segmented labour market.
5) Barriers aren't all bad though. Making sure workers in **highly-skilled occupations** have the **necessary skills** is crucial to **keep people safe** — no one wants an unqualified dentist. So, **minimum qualifications** make sure the **right people** are doing the right job — making the market **more efficient**.

Some people are ***More Geographically Mobile*** *than others*

1) **Geographical immobility** of labour is when workers aren't able to (or are reluctant to) **move to different locations** to find the best jobs for themselves. When this happens they end up either **unemployed** or in jobs that **aren't suited to them** — there's a misallocation of resources and market failure occurs.
2) There are a number of reasons behind geographical immobility. They include:
   - People make **friends** and have **family** that they don't want to move away from.
   - It's **expensive** to **move house**. Not only does it cost to buy a house, but it costs to sell your house too.
3) Geographical labour immobility can lead to labour **shortages** in one area and labour **surpluses** in another. This can then be followed by **regional wage differences** — **high** wages in the areas with **shortages** and **low** wages in the areas with **surpluses**.

Occupational immobility *is when it's* ***Difficult*** *to* ***Switch Jobs***

1) **Occupational immobility** is when workers **aren't able** to **move** from **one occupation to another** with ease.
2) In an ideal world workers would be able to **transfer their skills** from one job to another or **retrain** with ease, but in reality this **often isn't the case**. When workers have **specific skills** they aren't always able to use them in another job.
3) Occupational immobility can be affected by age. **Younger workers** are **more likely to retrain**, but older workers may lack the confidence or motivation to do so.
4) Some occupations also require **high-level qualifications** and particular **personality traits**. For example, not everyone is cut out for the years of academic study required to become a vet and not everyone can cope with the sight of blood.

Practice Questions

Q1 Describe three reasons why people can be economically inactive.

Q2 Explain how a shortage of skilled labour can increase a firm's costs of production.

Q3 Describe two types of labour immobility.

Exam Question

Q1 Explain how barriers to entry and exit can result in segmented labour markets. [8 marks]

Keep economically active — revise economics whilst jogging...

I don't know about you, but I always take a revision guide on a jog... OK, that's a lie, but seriously getting a grip of labour market imperfections is important — they're the reasons why perfectly competitive labour markets don't really exist. Mind-blowing stuff.

Government Intervention in the Labour Market

***This page is for** OCR Unit 3 (Work and Leisure).*
This topic gives you an introduction to why governments intervene in the labour market.

Governments Intervene** in the labour market to **Correct Market Failure

1) Governments intervene to **correct labour market failure** because it causes several problems.
2) For example, labour market failure will mean that firms become allocatively and productively **inefficient**, which would cause **costs of production** to **increase** and is likely to lead to **higher prices**. In turn, this might make **exports less competitive**, **worsening** the current account of the **balance of payments** and possibly increasing **unemployment**.

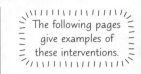

The following pages give examples of these interventions.

***Labour Force Flexibility** is **Good** for the economy*

1) A **flexible labour force** is one where workers can **transfer between activities** quickly in response to changes in the economy. For example, a worker in a flexible labour force would be able to retrain or transfer their skills to another job easily if something badly affected the industry they were employed in.
2) Governments can act to increase the flexibility of the workforce:
   - To **increase** the **flexibility** of workers, governments can **promote** or **subsidise training** and **education schemes** that help workers gain **skills and knowledge** that are attractive to employers. They can also **provide training** directly, e.g. skills training to the unemployed.
   - The UK government has also increased flexibility by **reducing** the **power** of **trade unions**, which can cause inflexibility in the labour market (e.g. by negotiating for longer working contracts).
3) For **employers**, a flexible workforce is one that can be hired and fired easily. Laws that make it **easy** to hire and fire workers encourage employers to **take on more workers**. This is because firms know they can change the size of their workforce quickly (and therefore cheaply) in response to changes in the market.
4) Different types of **contract** (such as short-term and zero-hour) can also make workers more flexible for employers:
   - **Short-term** contracts allow firms to hire a worker for a **certain length of time** (e.g. six months) — if the firm still needs the worker towards the end of the contract they can extend the contract for a longer period (or not) to suit their needs. **Zero-hour** contracts are where firms can hire workers without guaranteeing them a definite number of hours of work per week — the employer can offer these employees a number of hours that suits their needs.
   - The cost of employing staff on short-term and zero-hour contracts is **less** than **full-time** contracts (e.g. employees on zero-hour contracts don't need to be given sick pay).
   - An increasing number of part-time workers and increasingly flexible working times in the UK also increases the **temporal flexibility** of labour (the ability to change the number of hours worked).
5) Zero-hour contracts are **popular** with **governments** because they **reduce unemployment figures**, but they can **cause problems** — workers on these contracts **don't** have a **guaranteed income**, so it's hard for them to manage their finances.

*Market failures that **Increase** the gap between the **Rich** and **Poor** are inequitable*

1) The gap between the very rich and the very poor is **widening** in most developed economies.
2) Free market economists would say the gap between the rich and poor is **necessary** — they believe that the gap gives an **incentive** for entrepreneurs to start businesses. They also believe in the **trickle-down theory** (see p.50) that suggests that the poor benefit from the jobs and income that are created by entrepreneurs and the spending of the rich.
3) The UK government does intervene to help close the gap, which they believe is inequitable. **Welfare payments** (**benefits**), the use of a **progressive taxation system** (to some extent — see p.109) and having a **national minimum wage** (see p.70) are ways the government has tried to **reduce inequality**.

Wage Flexibility** is an important characteristic of a **Flexible Labour Force

1) **Wage flexibility** refers to the ability of real wages to **change** in response to changes in **demand for and supply of labour**.
2) **Performance-related pay** and **regional pay awards** are examples of uses of flexible wages.
(Regional pay awards are used to account for variations in living costs in different regions, e.g. workers in London are usually paid higher wages than workers elsewhere in the UK because it's more expensive to live there.)
3) Wage flexibility can be an important feature during a **recession** — **wage cuts** and **pay freezes** can be accepted by workers as an alternative to losing jobs.

Government Intervention: Taxes and Benefits

***This page is for** OCR Unit 3 (Work and Leisure).*
Governments receive a lot of income from taxes and pay out money in the form of benefits.

Taxes and Benefits can affect the Level of Employment and Wage Rates

Governments can **increase** the **incentive to work** to address the market failure that's caused by economic inactivity in the labour force. They can do that by **lowering income taxes** and **benefit payments**.

Income Tax

1) **Lowering marginal tax rates** (see p.51) means workers get to **keep more** of their earnings. This acts as an **incentive** to **work more** and can **increase** the **labour supply** in the economy.
2) At the moment, workers in the UK have a **tax-free allowance** — this means they pay **no tax** on the first part of their earnings (in 2014/15, workers didn't pay tax on the first £10 000 they earned). Recent government policy has seen the size of the tax-free allowance **increase**. This increases people's **incentive to work** and increases **equity**.

Benefits

1) Lowering benefits **increases the gap** between **income** earned in **work** and income **without work** (from benefit payments). This gives people a **greater incentive** to work, **increasing** the **participation rate** and **labour supply**.
2) Lowering benefits will also reduce the effect of the **unemployment trap** and cut **voluntary unemployment**.

An Ageing Population puts a Strain on an economy

1) The UK government pays a **state pension** (a certain amount of money per week) to workers once they reach the **state pension age** and have made a minimum number of years of **National Insurance contributions**.
2) The UK's **ageing** population is putting a strain on the economy — there are an **increasing number** of people claiming a **state pension**, and their use of the **NHS** is likely to **increase** with age.
3) Providing increased pension payments and health care treatments involves **increased government spending**. Much of the government's revenue comes from **income taxes**, but there's concern that the **cost of pensions** and **increased NHS health care** will become **too great** for workers as the number of **pensioners increases**.

Governments might be forced to make Changes to Pensions

1) As **more people** are **living longer**, governments may need to **change** the way that state pensions work to ensure that they can continue to afford to pay pensions to an **increasing number of people** for an **increasingly long time**.
2) There are a number of methods governments can use, which include:
   - **Raising** the **state pension age** — this will mean that on average pensioners will have fewer years claiming the state pension. The justification behind this is that because people are **living longer**, they should **work longer** before starting to claim a pension. In the UK the **state pension age** for men and women will **increase** to **66** by **2020** and it's predicted to rise further in future years.
   - **Increasing** the **contributions** necessary to **qualify** for a state pension. In the UK to **qualify** to receive state pension you need to have paid **National Insurance contributions** for a **certain number of years** — this is paid by workers when they earn a certain amount. Pension reforms may see the **number of years** of necessary contributions **increase**.
   - **Decreasing** the amount **paid out**. However, to make sure people have **enough money to live on** when they retire, people would need to **plan** and **save** for retirement while they're **working**. This is why the UK government has made it **compulsory** for **employers** to enrol workers on a **workplace pension** (although workers can opt out), which would give retirees extra income in addition to the amount they will receive from their state pension.

Practice Questions

Q1 Briefly explain how income tax and benefits can affect the level of employment in an economy.

Q2 List two ways that a government could reform pensions as the population ages.

Exam Question

Q1 Analyse the different methods that governments can use to increase labour force flexibility. [8 marks]

As a contortionist, the flexibility of my labour is considerable...

It's a government's dream to have a highly flexible workforce that can do all sorts of different jobs, although it doesn't seem easy to switch from being a builder to a surgeon. Then again, there's plenty of time to retrain before you can start to claim your pension...

Government Intervention: Minimum Wage

This page is for AQA Unit 3 and OCR Unit 3 (Work and Leisure).
In the UK the government sets a minimum wage that workers are to be paid per hour.

The **National Minimum Wage (NMW)** aims to make wages fairer

1) The NMW sets a legal **minimum hourly rate of pay** for different age groups. It was introduced in the UK in 1999 to stop firms setting wages so low that their employees couldn't afford a decent standard of living. It aims to prevent the exploitation of workers due to the **payment** of **unfairly low wages**.
2) By increasing the pay of the poorest workers the NMW leads to a **more equitable distribution** of **income**.
3) The NMW helps to **encourage people to work**. For example, having a minimum wage might encourage workers to **get a job** instead of **claiming benefits**.
4) In addition, increasing the number of people in work **increases** the **participation rate**, which is good for the economy and **increases** the **labour supply**.

Humphrey absolutely refused to move until he was paid the NMW.

It can be argued that introducing a **NMW** leads to **Unemployment**

1) Using supply and demand diagrams it could be argued that **increasing the wage rate** would lead to a **contraction** in **demand** for **labour**. This can be seen in the diagrams below:

This is similar to when trade unions negotiate a pay rise — see the diagram on p.62.

- Introducing a minimum wage that's higher than an industry's equilibrium wage (W_e) would **raise** the **wage rate** from W_e to **NMW**. This would cause the supply of labour to increase from Q_e to Q_2 and demand to fall from Q_e to Q_1.
- This could cause **unemployment** of Q_1 to Q_2 because there's an **excess supply of labour**.
- Introducing a minimum wage when the demand and supply of labour is fairly **elastic** (diagram 1) results in **greater unemployment** than when the demand and supply of labour is more **inelastic** (diagram 2) — the **difference** between Q_1 and Q_2 is **larger** in diagram 1.

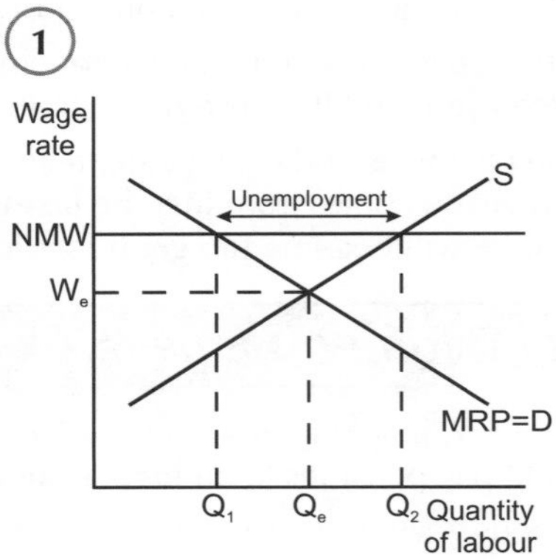

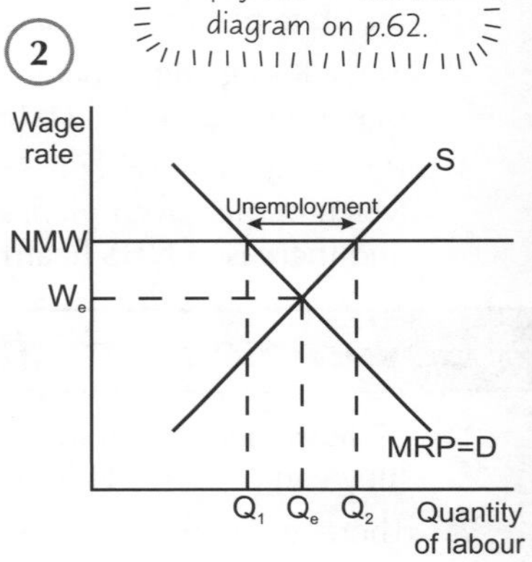

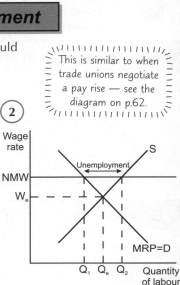

2) Unemployment caused by the introduction of a NMW would be an example of government failure. However, there's evidence to suggest that the NMW **hasn't caused** a significant **negative impact** on the **level of employment** in the UK.

Introducing a NMW can have a number of **Advantages** and **Disadvantages**

Advantages

- Introducing a NMW may help those on **very low incomes** and **reduce** the level of **poverty** in a country.
- A NMW may also **boost** the **morale** of workers as they'll receive better wages. Happier workers tend to be **more productive**, so output may increase as a result.
- A NMW means there's **greater reward** for doing a job that pays the NMW. It gives people more **incentive** to get a job rather than be unemployed.
- The government's **tax revenue** is likely to be **greater** if a NMW is introduced.

Disadvantages

- A NMW can **increase wage costs** for firms. This might mean they have to **cut jobs**, resulting in increased **unemployment**.
- A NMW could decrease the **competitiveness** of **UK firms** compared to firms in other countries that have lower wage costs.
- UK firms may have to **pass on** increased wage costs to consumers by **increasing** their **prices**, and this could contribute to **inflation**.
- There are **doubts** about whether introducing a NMW really **decreases poverty**. This is because many of the poorest members of society, such as the elderly and disabled, are **not in work** (so aren't able to benefit from an increased wage rate).

If you got an exam question about what would happen if the NMW was increased, then you could use these advantages and disadvantages too.

European Union Intervention and Migration

***This page is for** OCR Unit 3 (Work and Leisure).*
One way that the European Union (EU) can affect the law in the member states is by issuing directives.

EU Directives set Requirements for EU Member States to achieve

1) EU directives are **sets of instructions** issued to EU member states. They describe **particular objectives** that need to be achieved within these states. A directive could affect **all member states**, or it could affect a **single member**.
2) Authorities within member states covered by the directive must act to deliver the objectives by a **certain date**.
3) **How** each member state accomplishes this (i.e. how they make changes to their laws to deliver the objectives of the directive) is **up to them**. This gives member states some **flexibility** over this process.

The Working Time Directive sets rules for Working Hours in the EU

1) The Working Time Directive is an example of an EU directive. It sets out **rights for workers** such as:
   - A **limit** to average **weekly working hours** of 48 hours.
   - Employers must give a minimum of **4 weeks paid leave** per year.
   - A **minimum daily rest period** of 11 consecutive hours in every 24 hours.
   - Average **working hours** for **night workers** shouldn't exceed 8 hours per 24-hour period.
2) The UK was allowed an **opt-out** clause for the limit to weekly working hours. This means that employees could formally agree to work **more than 48 hours per week**. Employers can ask this of their employees but not force them to do this.
3) This directive has **advantages** and **disadvantages** for employees and firms.
   - **Advantages** for employees include that they're entitled to a minimum amount of **paid leave** which is standard across all jobs, and that workers **aren't overworked**.
   - However, a **disadvantage** for employers is that implementing the directive can **increase their costs**.

Migrant Workers increase the Labour Supply of a country

1) Migrant workers that are young, skilled and flexible will generally have a **positive effect** on the economy — these workers will **earn** and **spend** money, which **increases aggregate demand** and grows the economy.
2) Migrant workers can **fill skills gaps** in the economy. For example, the NHS has many nurses and doctors from foreign countries who have helped to do this.
3) **Free movement of workers** between the EU member states has allowed workers to migrate to different EU countries. For example, there was an influx of workers into the UK from Eastern European countries that became members of the EU (such as Poland) — part of the reason for this was the higher wages in the UK.
4) As migrant workers increase the supply of labour available, it's possible that migrant workers entering a labour market could **depress** the **market wage rate**. This is thought to be especially true of low-skilled workers, such as farm labourers:

- **Before immigration** the wage rate of farm workers was W_1.
- When migrant workers expand the labour supply it **shifts** the **supply curve** to the right (from S to S_1).
- At this level of supply (S_1), there is an **excess supply** of farm labourers at W_1. The **wage rate falls** until it clears the market, which it does at W_2.
- The increased supply of farm labourers has resulted in the **wage rate falling** from W_1 to W_2.

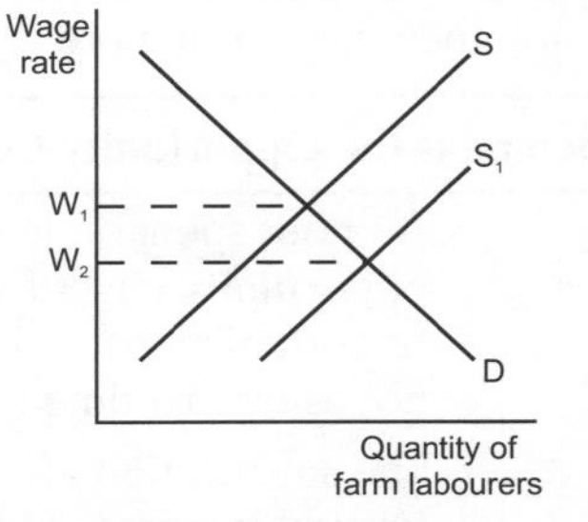

Practice Questions

Q1 Give two benefits of a National Minimum Wage.

Q2 What is an EU directive?

Exam Question

Q1 Discuss the implications for an economy of introducing a national minimum wage. [15 marks]

Wearing pink on a Friday — an unlikely objective of an EU directive...

The minimum wage is a classic example of an intervention in the labour market, but it's worth remembering that it's not all positive — there are some potential drawbacks. EU interventions sound a bit dull, but they can have an important impact on the labour market.

Leisure

These pages are for OCR Unit 3 (Work and Leisure).
Leisure is free time. These pages cover what affects people's decisions on how much free time to have, and how to spend it.

Leisure Time is time left to Do What You Want after Work and Chores

1) Lots of people spend part of their time **working** — work usually means doing something to **earn money**, though some people do **voluntary** work which they're not paid for.
2) People spend a lot of the rest of their time sleeping, doing chores, and getting to and from places (like work). These sorts of things are known as **maintenance activities** — they're tasks that are **necessary** to daily life, but aren't paid work.
3) The time that people have left to **spend how they like**, after work and maintenance activities are done, is **leisure**.
4) There isn't a precise definition of which activities are leisure — generally it's used to mean any activity that you **enjoy** doing and you **don't** earn **money** from.
5) Some things are only leisure for **some people**, e.g. some people enjoy cooking but other people consider it a chore.

There are only So Many Hours in a Day...

1) People have to **choose** how to spend the **limited** time they have each day.
2) The pie chart shows the results of an Office of National Statistics (ONS) study in 2005, which asked people to **record** how they spent their time.
3) **Men and women** spent **similar** amounts of time on most types of activity.
4) The main **difference** was that **women** spent 10% of their time on paid work and 16% on domestic work (things like cleaning) on average, whereas **men** spent 16% on paid work and 9% on domestic work.

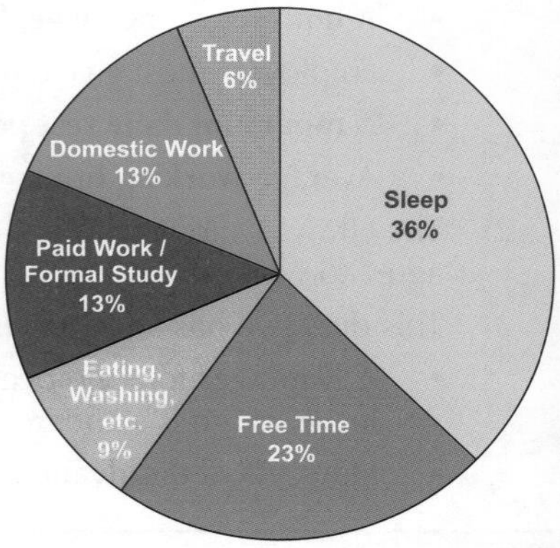

These are average figures — they include unemployed and retired people, and people who work full- and part-time.

People have to Choose how to Split Their Time between Work and Leisure

1) People decide how to split their time between work and leisure based on the relative **costs** and **benefits** of each, as well as their own **personal circumstances**.
2) Working for money means **giving up** time for leisure, but most people **need** to earn money to live or support a family. Or they may **want** to earn more money because they're saving up for something, say.
3) **Wages**, **taxation** and **benefit** levels affect how much **difference** working more or less will make to people's income.
4) Income isn't the only benefit of work — **job satisfaction** is also important for some people. If somebody enjoys their job they may work more — they'll have less leisure time, but they may not want as much if they're **happy** at work.

Income is the Opportunity Cost of Leisure

1) An hour spent on leisure can't be spent working, so a person's hourly wage rate is the **opportunity cost** of an hour's leisure — the higher a person's wage the higher their opportunity cost of leisure. That means the cost of leisure is the opportunity cost of not using that time to work, plus the cost of the activity itself.
2) The **substitution effect** (see p.58) suggests that as **wages** (and the opportunity cost of leisure) **increase**, people will choose to work more. However, there eventually comes a point when people will reach a **target income** where they'll be prepared to 'spend' **more** on 'consuming' leisure by choosing to **work less** — this is the **income effect**.
3) An individual's target income will **vary** from **person to person**.

In practice people often can't choose exactly how many hours to work — lots of jobs have fixed hours.

Income also Pays for Leisure Activities

1) Working also brings in money to **pay** for leisure.
2) People might choose to **work more** to pay for **expensive** leisure activities. E.g. somebody might prefer to work more and go on a luxury holiday, rather than have more free time for cheaper leisure activities.

It doesn't matter what income you're on — leisure time is always fun.

Leisure

People divide their time between **Different Types of Leisure**

1) Leisure activities can be **classified** into different types:

> **Home-based** — e.g. entertaining friends, craft, DIY and watching TV.
> **Passive** — activities that **don't** involve much mental or physical effort, e.g. going to the cinema.
> **Active** — activities that **do** involve mental or physical effort, e.g. playing sport or going to a language class.

2) An ONS survey in 2010 asked people aged 16 or over whether they'd taken part in a list of **activities** in the last year. The **most popular** activities are shown on the chart.
3) Watching **television** had the **highest** number of participants.
4) People spend an average of about **4 hours a day** watching television — this hasn't changed much over the last 10 years.
5) The **popularity** of **passive activities** (e.g. watching television) has been linked to some **negative externalities**, such as **obesity** and **diabetes**.

Percentage of adults participating in activities in 2009/10

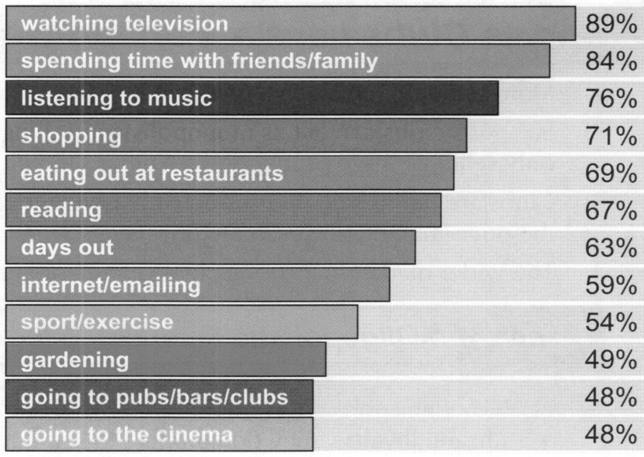

Demand for **Leisure Activities** can be **Income Elastic**

1) Demand for leisure activities is mainly **income elastic**, though this is less true for the cheapest leisure activities.
2) Many leisure products are **luxury goods**, for example theme park tickets and high-end sporting goods.
3) There's **cross elasticity of demand** between leisure activities — some leisure activities are **substitutes** for one another, e.g. an increase in the price of exercise classes might increase demand for swimming pool admissions.
4) The price of **complementary goods** can also affect the demand for a leisure activity, e.g. demand for holidays could be affected by the price of travel insurance.

Lower Working Hours and **Higher Real Incomes** mean **More Leisure Spending**

1) As people **earn more** they **spend more on leisure**. This creates **leisure jobs**, so more people have money to spend, and so on. The leisure industry is a **big part** of the **UK economy** — it provides a significant proportion of **jobs**.
2) But people will only spend on leisure if they have enough **free time** to do so.
3) This is used as an argument for **increasing pay** and **reducing working hours** — leisure firms need **consumers** who have **time and money**.
4) There is a long-term trend of **decreasing working hours** and **increasing real incomes** in the UK, which has been accompanied by a **real increase in leisure spending**.
5) **Technological advances** have also contributed to an increase in free time by decreasing the time spent on **domestic work** — there are lots of **machines** available that make domestic tasks much **quicker**, e.g. washing machines.

> Although real incomes have fallen in the last few years, they're still well above where they were 25 years ago.

Practice Questions

Q1 What's the difference between active and passive leisure?

Q2 List two reasons why people have more leisure time.

Exam Question

Q1 Explain what is meant by 'leisure'. [2 marks]

Deciding how to spend your leisure time can be hard work...

How much time people have for leisure depends on what they're paid, how much they need to live on, and the time they spend on chores or childcare. The type of leisure activities that people want to do can affect how much they choose to work — some people would rather have lots of leisure time to enjoy cheaply, whereas others prefer to work more to enjoy more expensive leisure.

The Spectator Sports Market

These pages are for OCR Unit 3 (Work and Leisure). Pages 74-79 give you some information about different leisure markets. You need to think about how closely these markets match the market models you read about in Section 2, and what's been done in the markets to increase competition for the benefit of consumers. Let's kick off with the market for spectator sports.

Sports Clubs have a Monopoly on selling to Supporters

1) Many people **support one team** and don't see other teams' products (e.g. match tickets) as a **substitute** for their team's products.
2) So sports clubs can act as **monopolists** in selling tickets and merchandise to **supporters** — for supporters their club is the **only seller** of these products. This means the clubs are **price makers**.
3) Clubs are **unlikely** to be **productively efficient** as they're monopolies. **Allocative efficiency** may also be poor — the price-making power that clubs have may allow them to make **supernormal profits** (if they have enough fans).
4) The wider market that sports clubs operate in, including other revenue sources, has features of **other market structures**:

There are Oligopolistic Features to the market that Sports Clubs operate in

1) Though sports clubs might not have to compete when selling things like tickets and merchandise (because of **brand loyalty**), they do **compete** to sell **advertising space** and **sponsorship rights**.
2) Clubs can **differentiate** their 'product' through their **on-field success**. The more successful they are on the pitch, the more **price-making power** they have with sponsors, who want to be **associated** with a strong, successful brand.
3) Large sponsorship and advertising **revenues** help big clubs become even **more successful** — the **best players** command **high wages** and **only** big clubs can afford to pay them. As a result, these clubs have even **more price-making power** — creating a **barrier to entry** that **stops** small clubs competing for revenue from big sponsors.

Premier League Clubs get Large Amounts of Broadcasting Revenue

1) The top football league in England is called the Premier League. The Premier League sells the rights to broadcast games **collectively** (i.e. it sells the rights to all Premier League games), then shares out the revenue between the clubs.
2) This means broadcasting revenue is spread **more equally** than if each club were to sell the broadcasting rights to its own games, as they do in some other European leagues. When clubs sell their own rights the top clubs tend to get a **large share**.
3) Sharing the revenue in this way reduces the **advantage** of teams who have previously done well.
4) The amount of money the Premier League gets by selling **broadcasting rights** has **risen sharply**:
   - The broadcasting deal for **1992-97** brought in about **£630 000 per game** of revenue.
   - The deal for **2013-16** brings in **£6.6 million per game**.
   - Around **half of the total revenue** of Premier League clubs in 2012/13 came from selling **broadcasting rights**.
5) This **monopsony situation** means income from broadcasting rights is fairly **evenly** distributed. However, there's still **massive inequality** between larger and smaller clubs due to the huge differences in their revenues from **sponsorship** and from selling **merchandise**, **advertising rights**, **tickets** and **food and drink**.

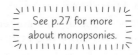

See p.27 for more about monopsonies.

Regulators have intervened in the Football Broadcasting Rights Market

1) From 1992 (when the Premier League was set up) until 2004 the **UK broadcasting rights** for live Premier League football were sold as a single exclusive package — only one broadcaster could buy the rights.
2) The satellite TV broadcaster **BSkyB** bought the rights in **every deal** negotiated over this period, so it had a **monopoly** over broadcasting live Premier League football.
3) The European Commission ruled that selling broadcasting rights **exclusively** to one broadcaster **damaged competition**, so it forced the Premier League to split the rights up into **bundles**. BSkyB bought **all** of the bundles in the 2004-2007 deal, **maintaining** its **monopoly**, but the Commission then ruled that from 2007 onwards **no single broadcaster** could own all of the rights on offer.
4) Initially, smaller broadcasters bought a **small proportion** of the rights. But with only a few matches to broadcast they were **unable** to attract customers away from BSkyB, so **couldn't** make a **profit**.
5) However, attracted by BSkyB's **supernormal profits**, BT entered the market. For the deal from 2013 onwards, BT bought a **larger proportion** of the broadcasting rights, which may mean it'll be able to more successfully compete with BSkyB — possibly competing away its supernormal profits.
6) BT's move into the market for live Premier League broadcasting rights has **changed** it from a **monopoly** to a **duopoly** (an **oligopolistic market** dominated by **two firms**).

Mike was gutted that regulators had blocked his club's merger with an airline — he'd been practising for weeks.

The Cinema Admissions Market

And here's the market for cinema admissions — get your 3D glasses ready.

The Cinema Market has Oligopolistic Features

Concentration ratios are on page 30.

1) The cinema market is **dominated** by a small number of large firms — it has a **high concentration ratio**.
2) Cinema firms are highly **interdependent**, and there may be **tacit collusion** on pricing. There's almost **no competition** on price — most firms charge very similar prices for all films.
3) Rather than competing on price, cinema firms try to **gain market share** by **differentiating** their product. For example, they vary the films they show and when they show them, the comfort of their cinemas, and the food and drinks they sell.
4) This cinema market is **not contestable** — the advantages **large firms** have in the market create high **barriers to entry**:
   - Large firms have more **negotiating power** with distributors (the firms that manage the release of films in cinemas) — they can get **better deals** and are more likely to get the right to show films close to their **release date**.
   - There are also **economies of scale** available for large firms, e.g. from booking systems shared across a large chain.
   - Larger chains have access to the **finance** needed to build **multiplexes** (cinemas with several screens), so they can attract a wider range of customers by offering more films at once, and **reduce** their **risks** if one of the films they pick to show **isn't very popular** (they'll have other films on other screens).
5) Generally **smaller firms** are only able to compete by serving **niche markets** — e.g. by showing foreign or classic films.

Cinema-Chain Mergers are Common and have been Investigated by Regulators

1) The benefits of **economies of scale** have led to **mergers** of cinema firms — some have been **investigated** by UK **regulators**.
2) The regulators consider the **negotiating strength** that the merged firm would have (with distributors and other suppliers), and the effect on the level of **competition** in an **area**. For example:
   - The merger between **Cineworld** and **Picturehouse** in 2013 was referred to **regulators**. The regulators decided their merger had **reduced competition**, despite Cineworld's argument that they had always been **different kinds** of cinemas with **different customers** — i.e. they sold a different product to different consumers.
   - The regulator ruled that Cineworld had to **sell one cinema** in three places where it owned **both** a Picturehouse and a Cineworld cinema to stop Cineworld having a **monopoly** in these places.

There are Lots of Substitutes for Going to the Cinema

1) There are lots of forms of entertainment that are **substitutes** for going to the cinema — other activities outside the home like watching a **sports game** or going to the **theatre**, as well as home-based activities like **watching TV**.
2) Substitutes **reduce demand** for cinema tickets. For example, watching films at home is a **close substitute** for going to the cinema, and this has had a big impact on the cinema industry:
   - Cinema admissions in the UK **peaked** in the **1940s**, then began to fall as **television** became available.
   - By the **mid 1980s** admissions had **dropped** to about **3% of their peak level**.
   - Admissions then began to **rise** again as **multiplex cinemas** developed — the first one in the UK opened in 1985. In 2013 admissions were **three times as high** as in the mid 1980s, but still only about **10% of their peak level**.
3) The availability of good substitutes limits the **price-making power** that large cinema firms would otherwise have in the oligopolistic market — consumers might switch to watching films at home if cinema prices were increased.
4) Watching films at home has become easier as **technology** has developed, e.g. on-demand film streaming from the internet.

Practice Questions

Q1 Briefly explain how a sports club can have the character of a monopolist.

Q2 Is the cinema market contestable?

Exam Questions

Q1 Discuss the level of competition in the market for live Premier League broadcasting rights in the UK. [15 marks]

Q2 Explain two economies of scale which are available in the cinema industry. [8 marks]

Hoping this page is all over? It is now...

These pages, and the four that follow, will provide you with useful examples for your exam answers. Memorise as much as you can.

The Holiday Market

These pages are for OCR Unit 3 (Work and Leisure).
Foreign holidays have got much more popular over the years, partly because falling prices have meant that more people can afford them. There's a range of holiday types, and each part of the holiday market has its own market structure.

The Market for Holidays Abroad has Grown Dramatically

1) The number of **foreign holidays** taken by UK residents more than **tripled** from **1980 to 2013**.
2) Even taking account of population growth, this is a dramatic increase — the number of **trips per person** more than **doubled** from **1981 to 2011**.
3) There have been some **drops** in the overall increasing trend — particularly from **2008 to 2010**, during and after the **recession**.

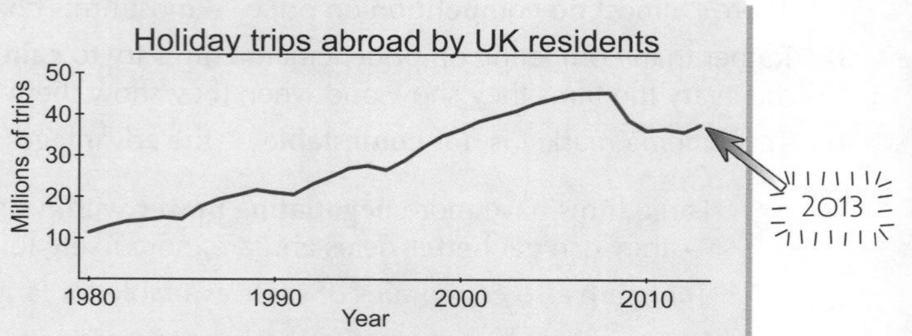

Different Types of holiday have Different Income Elasticities of Demand

1) Holidays were traditionally considered a **luxury** good, with a high **income elasticity of demand**.
2) However, as prices have fallen, **more people** can afford holidays — so they're beginning to be considered a **necessity**.
3) Some holidays have become **so cheap** that they could be considered an **inferior good** — people choose cheap trips rather than **no holiday** if their income falls, but switch to **more expensive** options if their income rises.

The Package-Holiday Market is Oligopolistic

1) About **half** of foreign holidays booked in the UK are **package holidays** — where accommodation, transport and sometimes meals are sold as a package.
2) UK residents spent nearly **£23 billion** on package holidays abroad in 2012.
3) The package-holiday market structure has the features of an **oligopoly**:

The market is **dominated** by a few large tour operators — there's a high **concentration ratio**.

Holidays can be **differentiated** — for example, they differ on type of destination and quality.

There are high **barriers to entry**:
- Firms aim to **differentiate** their product further by advertising to create a **strong brand**, but the **advertising cost** of attracting customers away from other firms is high.
- The large tour operators are **vertically integrated** and own both travel agents and airlines. This makes it harder for new entrants to **access customers** and **suppliers**.
- Large firms achieve **economies of scale** by providing the same package to large numbers of people — for example, they often block book hotels at discounted rates.

Arthur couldn't wait for his first package holiday to start.

Travel agents help customers to book flights, hotels, activities etc. before they go to their holiday destination.

Price Wars are common in the Package-Holiday Market

1) The package-holiday market fits the **kinked demand curve model** for oligopolies (see p.32) — rivals will follow price falls, but not price rises.
2) You would expect this to lead to price stability, but in fact **price wars** are common in the package-holiday market.

A **price war** happens when **one firm lowers prices** and **other firms follow suit** to retain their market share. This may trigger a **series of price cuts** as firms continually try to **undercut** one another.

3) These package-holiday price wars happen because the market is **mature** — further growth and innovation is unlikely, so for firms to gain sales they need to increase their market share at the **expense** of their competitors.
4) Because rivals follow price falls but not price rises, these price wars have led to **prices falling** over time. This has meant **decreased profit** for firms, but has led to greater **productive efficiency**, as they strive to **reduce costs**.

The Holiday Market

The *Specialist Holiday Market* is *Monopolistically Competitive*

1) The **specialist holiday market** provides holidays to more unusual destinations, or holidays based around certain activities (e.g. horse riding). Each firm operates in a **niche market** for their particular holiday type, so firms are usually quite small.
2) **Barriers to entry** are low:
   - **Advertising costs** are relatively **low** — brand is less important as holidays are **more obviously differentiated** by their destination or activity.
   - Specialist holiday firms **aren't** usually **vertically integrated**, as firms aren't large enough to have their own airline etc.
   - **Economies of scale** are not usually significant in **niche markets**.
3) Because specialist holidays are **more differentiated** than package holidays, **demand** for them is **less price elastic** — specialist holidays have few direct **substitutes**, e.g. a sailing holiday is not a direct substitute for a skiing holiday, whereas a package holiday in Corfu is a good substitute for a package holiday in Malta.

The *Internet* has *Changed* the *Holiday Market*

1) People can now book holidays **online**, either **directly with providers** (for example a hotel) or through an **online travel agent**. This only began to become possible in the mid 1990s.
2) Online travel agents have **lower costs** than traditional high street travel agents. This has **removed** a barrier to entry to the holiday market, making it **more contestable**. Traditional travel agents have **reacted** by setting up their own online services.
3) Firms offering specialist holidays tend to **lose less business** as a result of people booking independently online. This is because they offer advice on their particular **area of expertise**, which people are willing to pay for.
4) Some package-holiday firms are trying to protect their market share from loss to independent booking by **specialising** in **all-inclusive holidays**. The idea is that people are more **budget-conscious** since the recession, so they'll appreciate the certainty of the **fixed price** that all-inclusive holidays offer. This is something that independent booking can't always provide.

On an all-inclusive holiday, everything (including food and drink) is included in the price of the holiday.

The *Package-Holiday Market* has been *Investigated* by *Regulators*

1) Because of the **economies of scale** available, there have been lots of **mergers** in the package-holiday industry. These mergers have **increased concentration ratios** and **reduced competition**.
2) A merger between two package-holiday firms (Airtours and First Choice) was **blocked** by the **European Commission** in 1999 — they ruled that it'd **damage competition** by creating a level of **market concentration** that made **collusion** likely.
3) But this decision was **revoked** after a court found that collusion was unlikely **in practice**. There were several reasons for this:
   - The market wasn't sufficiently **transparent** for firms to be sure of what their competitors were doing.
   - There was no way for firms to **retaliate** against a firm who **deviated** from any agreed collusion.
   - The behaviour of **customers** and **smaller competitors** was likely to limit the success of collusive behaviour for firms.
4) Other similar mergers have since been **allowed** — in 2007 two mergers of large firms were **passed** by the European Commission in quick succession (between MyTravel and Thomas Cook and between TUI Travel PLC and First Choice). This may reflect a change in the regulator's **approach**, but it could reflect **increasing competition** from independent booking.

Practice Questions

Q1 List three characteristics that suggest the market for package holidays is oligopolistic.

Q2 How has the internet affected the contestability of the holiday market?

Exam Question

Q1 To what extent could the holiday market be classed as monopolistically competitive? [20 marks]

The holiday market — not just a source of regrettable souvenir purchases...

People want different things from holidays, and this affects the structure of the market. Some people want minimum fuss and are happy to buy a package which meets their needs for a fixed price. Other people are looking for a more unique holiday — firms providing these niche products are likely to be smaller. Right, all this talk of holidays has tired me out — I'm off to put my feet up.

The Air Travel Market

These pages are for OCR Unit 3 (Work and Leisure). This first page is also useful for OCR Unit 4 (Transport).
Air travel hasn't been around for that long, so the market has changed quite a lot in the last few decades.

Deregulation has made the Air Travel Market more Contestable

1) The air travel market used to be **dominated** by large state-run or state-subsidised **national airlines** that **cooperated** with each other (e.g. British Airways). **Regulation** regarding which airlines could fly between different countries was also **very strict**.
2) Since the late 1970s governments have generally tried to **encourage competition** in air travel.
3) One strategy has been to privatise many of the national airlines — e.g. British Airways was privatised in 1987.
4) Another strategy has been to make **broad agreements** (known as **open skies agreements**) that give airlines far more **freedom** to choose which countries they fly from and to.
   - In the late 1980s rules on **competition** in the EEC (the forerunner of the European Union) meant that routes had to be **opened** to more airlines. There's now an **open skies** agreement within the EU.
   - An **open skies** agreement between the **EU and the United States** came into force in 2008. It allowed US and EU airlines to operate on any route between the EU and the US. It also allowed US airlines to operate routes **between** EU countries.
5) The opening up of routes to more airlines has removed a **barrier to entry**, making the air travel market more **contestable**.

The Air Travel Market has some Characteristics of an Oligopoly

1) A **few** large firms **dominate** the market (e.g. British Airways and Lufthansa) — so there's a high **concentration ratio**.
2) There are high **barriers to entry**:

- Buying **aeroplanes** is expensive, though leasing can lower this barrier.
- Many national airlines are still **state owned**, and governments often support them with **subsidies**.
- Large **economies of scale** are available (e.g. **purchasing** economies for fuel, **technical** economies from larger planes).
- Airports only have a limited number of **takeoff and landing slots**, which are often subject to 'grandfather rights' (i.e. airlines are entitled to keep the slots they've traditionally had), so new entrants can only access new slots.
- To avoid congestion the number of **licences** available for any route is limited.

The Market also has some Characteristics of Monopolistic Competition

1) The airline industry is actually quite **competitive** — it has some features of **monopolistic** (and even **perfect**) **competition**.
2) **Information** on schedules, prices and what each airline offers is **readily available** to customers.
3) Though **barriers to entry** to the industry are high, improved access to routes means **existing airlines** can often enter the market for individual routes fairly **easily**.
4) This **contestability** means **supernormal profits** on particular routes are likely to be **competed away** reasonably quickly.
5) This should improve **productive efficiency** as airlines **reduce costs** to compete on price.

The Low-Cost Air Travel Market is More Competitive than the Traditional Air Travel Market

1) Because **low-cost** airlines offer a very **basic service**, their products are good **substitutes** for each other and their **cross elasticity of demand** is high.
2) This is less true for **traditional airlines**, which aim to **differentiate** their products on quality by providing better in-flight meals, more legroom and so on. This **reduces** cross elasticity of demand **between** airlines.
3) **Branding** provides some differentiation for all airlines, but it's particularly important for traditional airlines, which attempt to build a **strong reputation** and earn consumer loyalty based on the **quality of service** they provide.

The Air Travel Market is becoming More Concentrated

But regulators try to control this.

1) **Mergers** are common in the airline industry (e.g. between British Airways and Iberia). This increases market **concentration**.
2) In theory this should **cut costs**. But in practice traditional airlines usually **retain their brand** to keep their price-making power, which means there's lots of duplication in merged firms, e.g. they might have separate marketing departments.
3) The UK **regulatory authorities** have put **conditions** on particular mergers taking place. For example, the British Airways and Iberia merger was only allowed to go ahead if the merged firm **gave up** some of its takeoff and landing **slots**.
4) Rather than merging, airlines often **collude** by joining **alliances** — where airlines offer integrated booking and loyalty schemes, but remain separate firms. This is most common among **traditional airlines**.

The Television Broadcasting Market

Right, let's switch over to the television broadcasting market.

The TV Broadcasting Market is subject to Government Regulation

Because of the nature of the industry, the **UK government** has always **intervened** in the TV broadcasting market.

- The BBC originally had a **monopoly** on TV broadcasts, but in 1954 the government granted broadcast licences to **commercial TV** firms. However, the original '**analogue**' technology allowed **few channels** to be broadcast — creating a barrier to entry and a lack of **competition**.
- Television can be seen as a **merit good** (e.g. it can be used to provide information and to educate). All the broadcasters that were licensed before 1998 (the BBC, ITV, Channel 4 and Channel 5) are **public service broadcasters** — i.e. as a **condition** of their broadcasting licence they must provide a certain amount of **some types of programme**, e.g. news programmes and programmes made in the UK.
- Analogue television broadcasting has some characteristics of a **public good** — if you own a TV and an aerial then TV broadcasts are **non-rivalrous** and **non-excludable**. This means that if it's left to the free market, analogue TV broadcasts would be **underprovided** because of the **free rider** effect.

The Television Broadcasting Market has Oligopolistic Features

1) The market for television broadcasting is **highly concentrated** — it's dominated by a small number of large firms, such as the BBC, ITV, Channel 4 and BSkyB. TV channels are also **differentiated** by their content and schedule.
2) The cost of producing programmes is **fixed**, and the **marginal cost** of an extra viewer is minimal (if anything). So channels with large audiences get big **economies of scale**. This forms a **barrier to entry**.
3) The market for **subscription** and **pay-per-view** television services is also **oligopolistic**:
    - The market is **highly concentrated** — one firm (BSkyB) has an extremely high market share.
    - There are **high barriers to entry**:
      — Firms are **vertically integrated** — they make lots of their own programmes and transmit them over their own network to sell to customers. This prevents **new entrants** from accessing programmes or networks.
      — Maintaining a **transmitter network** (e.g. satellites) is very **expensive**. In the case of satellites this is a fixed cost, so huge **economies of scale** are available if firms can attract a large number of customers.
4) The **high capital costs** in the industry encourage **mergers**. For example, in the early days of satellite television in the UK there were two competing firms (British Satellite Broadcasting and Sky) who merged to form BSkyB in 1990.

The TV Broadcasting Market also has features of Monopolistic Competition

1) There are some areas of the TV broadcasting market that are **more competitive**.
2) There are a **large number** of **small firms** competing in **niche markets** (e.g. for religious or home-improvement programmes).
3) There are **low barriers to entry**:
    - The switch from analogue to digital TV signals has made it easier to set up more channels.
    - Many channels concentrate on **cheap programming**, e.g. quiz shows or repeats from other channels. Because their costs are low they don't need to attract huge audiences, so they can operate on a **different model** to the big channels.
    - Channels often enter and leave the market, so the **barriers to exit** are low too — the market is **contestable**.
4) **Internet-based television services** can now compete for pay TV customers. The ability to provide TV over the internet has **removed a barrier to entry** to the market — new firms can avoid the huge **set-up costs** of building a transmission network.

Practice Questions

Q1 What is an open skies agreement?

Q2 Give two examples of barriers to entry that exist in the pay-per-view television market.

Exam Questions

Q1 Comment on whether the air travel market can be considered to be oligopolistic. [8 marks]

Q2 Discuss the extent to which the television broadcasting market is contestable. [8 marks]

Come fly with me, let's fly, let's fly away, if you could use some economics clues...

Pay attention to the changes in both markets and how the changes affected their structure — that kind of thing is exam answer gold.

Transport

***These pages are for** OCR Unit 4 (Transport Economics).*
People need to get places and goods need to be moved around — the transport market provides these services.

Transport is the Movement of Goods and People

1) Transport is the **movement** of freight (goods) and passengers (people) from one place to another.
2) Without transport most production and trade would be very difficult — transport is **vital** to the functioning of the economy.
3) Transport is almost always a **derived demand** — it usually results from demand for other goods and services:
   - People want to **get to places** for work, leisure activities and holidays, and shopping and other chores.
   - Firms want to bring **factors of production together**, and bring **goods to customers**.
4) There are various **modes of transport**, most of which require some kind of **infrastructure**.

MODES OF TRANSPORT

A **mode of transport** is a **means** of moving goods or people:
- **Bus**
- **Car**
- **Pipeline**
- **Barge**
- **Train**
- **Lorry**
- **Airliner**
- **Ship**

TRANSPORT INFRASTRUCTURE

Transport infrastructure refers to the **structures** that need to be in place for transport modes to operate:
- **Roads**
- **Cycle paths**
- **Railway tracks**
- **Ports**
- **Canals**
- **Stations**

The Transport Mode that Passengers Choose is influenced by Lots of Factors

There are **positives** and **negatives** of each transport mode for passengers — these affect people's travel choices.

1) The **cheapest** mode of transport for a journey will depend on what kind of route it is — for example, the cheapest option **within a city** is usually bus travel, but air travel is often the cheapest for **very long-distance** routes.
2) Most people don't choose which mode of transport to use **purely** on price — they **weigh up** the cost against other factors like speed, convenience and comfort.
3) The **availability** of transport modes is limited by the **infrastructure** that's in place. Often the only transport modes available are road-based ones — most places have roads but many places don't have other infrastructure like railways.
4) Bus services aren't available everywhere, so sometimes travelling by **car** is the **only option**.
5) Using a **car** you can travel **door to door** on a single transport mode, at any time. You can also **cycle** or **walk** door to door whenever you like, but this isn't an option for everybody, especially for **longer journeys**.
6) On the other hand, **congestion** can make road transport **slow**, and cause **unpredictable journey times**. This affects cars and buses, but some cities have **bus lanes** so that buses are less affected than cars.
7) Many transport modes have **fixed routes and timetables**, which might not be convenient. You might also have to get to a **station**, **port** or **airport** to use them — so you might have to use **more than one mode** of transport on a single journey.
8) **Trains** are often **faster** than road transport, but **air travel** is usually the fastest mode over **long distances**.
9) **Comfort** can also affect people's choice of transport mode (e.g. some people find **trains** more comfortable than **buses**), and there are various other things that may influence people's choice, such as **environmental concerns** (see p.89), or **safety**.

Cost is the Main Consideration for Freight Transport

1) Generally firms will aim to transport freight at **minimum cost**, but this has to be balanced with **speed** — there's an **opportunity** cost to the time that goods spend in transit.
2) **Ship** transport is usually the **slowest** and the **cheapest** option, and **air** transport the **fastest** and the **most expensive**. The difference in cost is particularly large for **bulk goods** like coal — this is covered more on the next page.
3) If goods are **perishable** or needed quickly for a **fixed deadline** then the need for speed will almost always outweigh cost — **air transport** is often used for these goods.
4) As with passenger transport, the **availability** of modes of transport for freight is limited by the **infrastructure** that's in place. Firms can sometimes **build their own** infrastructure (individuals usually can't) — for example, a slate-mining firm could build a railway to transport the slate from their mine to the nearest sea-port. However, this is often prohibitively **expensive**.
5) Road transport is often used by firms at the **start and end** of journeys — most firms don't have a railway or port **on site**.
6) However, loading and unloading goods **adds cost**. So it's sometimes cheapest to use road transport for the **entire journey**, rather than, say, a combination of road and rail (even if for a portion of the journey, rail would be cheaper).
7) **Congestion** is a problem with road transport for freight as well as passengers — journeys can be **slow** and **unpredictable**.

Transport

There are Large Economies of Scale in Transporting Goods by Rail, Ship or Pipeline

1) **Rail and ship** are usually the cheapest options for **bulk transport** — moving **large amounts** of stuff at once.
2) This is because of the technical **economies of scale** available — you'd have to use lots of lorries or planes to transport bulk goods by road or air, but a single train or ship can have a very **high capacity**.
3) **Sea transport** is usually cheapest for **very long distance** bulk transport.
4) **Pipelines** have **huge economies of scale**. Once a pipeline is built the cost of transporting goods is low, so the more goods that are transported the **lower** the average cost (as the **fixed cost** of construction is spread out).
5) However, **pipelines** are only suitable for a **limited range** of goods — they're mostly used for oil and gas.

Demand for Transport is Income Elastic and Price Elastic

1) Transport as a **whole** has a **positive income elasticity of demand** (YED) — as incomes increase the demand for transport increases (i.e. it's a normal good). However, each transport mode also has its **own** income elasticity of demand.
2) **Car** and **air travel** are generally considered to have a **positive YED**, but **bus travel** is thought to have a **negative YED** — bus travel is considered an **inferior good** (i.e. as incomes **rise**, demand for bus travel **falls**).
3) Demand for transport is also **price elastic** to some extent. People might cut back on **leisure travel** if prices rise, but **commuter travel** is less likely to be affected.
4) There is **cross elasticity of demand** between transport modes that are suitable **substitutes** for one another.

In the long term, transport prices can affect where people choose to live or locate factories and shops, which will affect all types of transport demand.

5) Most passenger transport modes just have a **price per journey**, but the price of car travel includes the **fixed costs** of buying a car, paying road tax and getting insurance, as well as **variable costs** — mostly fuel.
6) **Demand** for car travel is affected by the **cost of fuel** and levels of **car ownership** in the short term.
7) In the long term the **cost of car ownership** will affect demand too — more people will own a car if it becomes cheaper, and this will **in turn** affect demand for travelling by car.
8) Long-term **transport use patterns** are affected by **investment in infrastructure** — for example, building more roads is likely to increase car usage.
9) **Transport demand** is also affected by changes in the **economy**:
   - **Rising GDP** means **demand** for **goods and services** is increasing, so **derived demand** for transport will also be increasing.
   - **Population growth** increases **demand** for **goods and services**, which increases **derived demand** for transport.
   - Rising **employment levels** increase transport demand — people often use transport to get to work, or as part of their job.

Demand for roller skate transport had shot up after government investment in 'park and glide' services.

Practice Questions

Q1 What is a mode of transport?

Q2 Give two reasons why passengers might choose to use bus transport.

Q3 Give a disadvantage of rail transport for freight.

Exam Question

Q1 Why is the demand for transport usually a derived demand? [5 marks]

Transport is a derived demand, except for Sunday drivers...

The transport options available are determined by what transport infrastructure is in place, so trends in transport use over time are affected by investment in infrastructure as well as what's going on in the economy. There are lots of factors that influence which transport mode an individual or a firm chooses to use — the best option will vary from journey to journey. Moving on...

Trends in Transport

These pages are for OCR Unit 4 (Transport Economics).
The demand for transport changes over time. Transport forecasts predict future demand to help plan infrastructure and policy.

Demand for Passenger Transport in the UK has Increased Over Time

1) How much transport people in the UK are using can be measured by the **total distance** travelled by passengers each year.
2) The total distance travelled has generally **increased** from year to year, but it **fell** every year from 2008 to 2011 — **real incomes fell** in the UK during this period, and the economy was in **recession** during 2008 and 2009.
3) **Population growth** only explains a small part of this increase — the average distance travelled **per person** was about 50% **higher** in 2013 than 1973.
4) The graph shows how the distance travelled and the **split** between transport modes has **changed**.

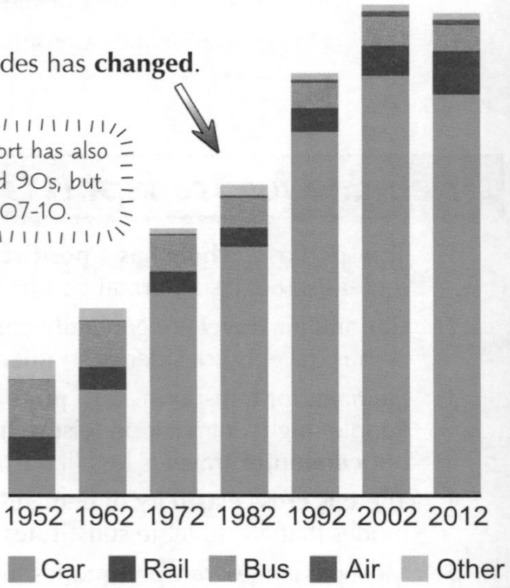

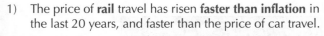

Rail freight transport has also risen since the mid 90s, but it fell from 2007-10.

RAIL

1) The price of **rail** travel has risen **faster than inflation** in the last 20 years, and faster than the price of car travel.
2) But the distance travelled by **rail** stayed fairly **steady** from 1950 to 1995, and since 1995 it's been **increasing**.
3) This could be because the effects of **rising incomes**, **population** and **GDP** (see p.81) have outweighed the effect of price rises.
4) Another possible factor is that the **speed** and **quality** of the service may have increased along with the price since passenger rail services were **privatised** in 1995 (see p.84).
5) **Environmental concerns** may have encouraged people to **switch** some travel to rail from air or car transport.

BUS

1) The price of **bus** travel has risen at about the same rate as rail travel in the last 20 years (faster than inflation).
2) The distance travelled by **bus** was falling until about 1990. Overall it's been fairly **stable** since then, but it's been rising in London and falling outside of London.
3) This may be due to **negative income elasticity** of demand for **bus travel** — bus travel has generally **decreased** as income has risen, and it **increased** from 2007 to 2010 as incomes fell.

AIR

1) The price of **air travel** has **fallen dramatically** in the last 50 years. Even in the last 20 years the **real price** of air travel has **fallen**.
2) The total distance travelled by **air** has **risen dramatically** as prices have fallen and incomes have risen, but it still only makes up a **small proportion** of the total distance people travel.

CAR

1) The total distance travelled by car **increased rapidly** in the 1950s and 1960s, then continued to increase at a slower rate. After 2000 it **levelled off**, and then **fell** every year from 2008 to 2011 (despite the population increasing).
2) Over the last 20 years the overall cost of car travel has stayed about the same in **real terms**, but it's got **cheaper** relative to bus and rail travel.
3) Generally, demand for transport by **car** has **increased** with **rising incomes**. In the last few years the **distance travelled by car** has fallen as **real incomes** have fallen.
4) The recent decrease in car travel might also have other causes:
   - **Fuel prices** have **increased** in real terms.
   - More people are living in **cities**, where they travel shorter distances for work and leisure, and **public transport** is **cheaper** and more **available** than in rural areas.
   - Increasing **congestion** and concerns over the **environmental impact** of cars may have discouraged driving.

Road transport of freight has followed a similar trend.

There are Similar Patterns for transport across the European Union

1) The **patterns** and **trends** in transport use are generally fairly similar **across the EU**.
2) As countries get **richer**, car use tends to increase. In most EU countries the level of car use has **risen** in a similar way to in the UK and has now **flattened out**, but in some countries car use is **still rising**.
3) Each country has different **infrastructure** available depending on its **geography** and on levels of **investment**.
4) The infrastructure **available** in a country will affect the **usage** of each transport mode. For example, transport on inland waterways makes up a much higher proportion of freight transport in the Netherlands than in the UK.

Trends in Transport

Transport Forecasts are a useful tool for **Governments** and **Planners**

1) Forecasts of **future demand** for transport are made to try to work out whether the **current infrastructure** has enough **capacity** for future demands, and how much **new infrastructure** might be needed.
2) Transport forecasts are also used to calculate the **effects** of future demand (e.g. pollution) so that governments can attempt to control these effects. This may mean trying to **influence demand**, or just trying to control its impact (see pages 90-91).
3) Forecasts are based on **historic data** and estimates of how the factors that **influence demand** might change in the **future**. There are **loads** of factors that might be considered — some of the most important ones are:

- **GDP** / economic growth.
- **Population growth** and **demographics**.
- Changes in **employment** levels.
- Changes in **disposable incomes**.
- **PED** and **YED** of each mode.
- The **price** of a particular mode and the price of **substitutes**.
- Future **government policy** (like changes to tax).
- **Car ownership** levels and the number of **licence holders**.
- The future **quality** and **availability** of each mode and of **substitutes** (taking predicted changes in investment into account).

PED = Price elasticity of demand.
YED = Income elasticity of demand.

People's future plans for vehicle ownership affect transport forecasts.

Problems with **Forecasting** mean **Transport Forecasts** are often **Inaccurate**

Models are used to help forecast future transport use, but these (and the forecasts they produce) can turn out to be **inaccurate**.

1) Forecasts are based on **estimates**, for example of future GDP. If these estimates are wrong then the forecast probably will be too.
2) A **causal relationship** that's assumed in the model may be **wrong** — for example, a forecast could rely on the assumption that rising incomes **cause** motorbike use to fall, but this might not actually happen.
3) There may be **unforeseen events** like a terrorist attack or economic shock. These may not be factored into the forecast.
4) **Experts** who are consulted to provide forecasters with information may be **biased** towards a particular outcome (e.g. more road building). If forecasters **aren't aware** of this then it could lead to an inaccurate prediction.
5) **Government policy** that was factored into the forecast may **change**.
6) Collecting data is expensive and time-consuming, so if **funding** or **time** is limited this may mean there **isn't enough** data available to make an accurate forecast, or the data used may be **unrepresentative** of the population as a whole. This isn't generally a problem for the UK government, but it may be for firms or governments with less resources.
7) In practice forecasters often factor some uncertainty into their model and come up with a **range** of estimates of future demand — such as '**high**', '**low**' and '**most likely**' versions.

Practice Questions

Q1 List three trends in passenger transport usage over recent years.

Q2 Give a way in which British transport-usage trends match trends across the EU.

Q3 Why are transport forecasts made?

Exam Question

Q1 Explain why air travel by UK residents has increased over the last two decades. [4 marks]

Cycling with your trousers tucked into your socks is a classic transport trend...

The main trend in transport use in the last 50 years has been rising demand for transport overall, and for car and air transport in particular. This has mostly been caused by rising real incomes, but falling air travel prices have contributed too. Bus travel has fallen as car travel has risen, but rail travel has stayed fairly steady. Transport forecasts try to predict what future trends will be.

Privatisation

***These pages are for** OCR Unit 4 (Transport Economics).*
The government used to provide lots of transport services, but now most transport markets have been opened up to private firms.

Most **Transport Provision** in the UK has been **Privatised**

1) A **nationalised** industry is owned by the **government**. In the past lots of transport services were nationalised because transport was seen as a **natural monopoly**, where costs would be lowest if there was a single provider (see page 26).
2) Transport also has **external costs and benefits** (see pages 88-89), which may be ignored by private providers.
3) However, publicly owned industries tend to be **inefficient** because they **lack competition**. Governments may decide to **increase** competition through **privatisation**.
4) **Privatisation** is the **transfer** of the **ownership** of a firm from the **public** sector to the **private** sector.
5) Various **nationalised** transport services in the UK were **privatised** in the 1980s and 1990s. Before privatisation lots of transport services were being **subsidised** by the government. It was hoped that private firms competing for passengers could provide the services more **efficiently**, which would reduce the need for government funding.
6) The idea is that private firms have to make a profit to survive, and the **incentive of profit** should motivate them to:
   - Reduce **x-inefficiency** — profit acts as an incentive for firms to **reduce costs**.
   - Improve **dynamic efficiency** through **investment** and **innovation** — this should improve **quality** and **choice**.
   - Reduce **prices** to compete with other firms in the market (where competition exists).
   - Improve the **allocation of resources** by responding to **market forces**.
7) Selling publicly owned transport operators also brought in **revenue** for the government, reducing **government borrowing**.

Rail Privatisation separated **Infrastructure**, **Passenger** transport and **Freight**

When the railway industry was **privatised** in the mid 1990s it was **split up** into several markets:

1) **Infrastructure**
   - Rail infrastructure provision (i.e. railway lines, signals and stations) is a **natural monopoly**.
   - After privatisation, the **private company** Railtrack was the only provider of infrastructure — it was a **private monopoly**.
   - There were concerns that Railtrack was risking safety by **under-investing** in infrastructure and coordinating maintenance poorly. Railtrack had also struggled to be profitable and needed **subsidies** to continue to operate, so in 2002 it was replaced by Network Rail, a **not-for-profit** company which has **no shareholders**.
   - Network Rail **charges** for the use of its infrastructure, but it also receives **government funding**, and in 2014 it was effectively **re-nationalised** when it became a **government body**.

2) **Passenger Services**
   - Passenger services are run by **train-operating companies**. Generally these firms are awarded franchises by the government — a franchise permits the operator to run passenger train services in a particular area for a fixed period of time.
   - Usually only **one franchise** is available for an area, so operators often have **regional monopolies**. They only **compete** on routes that **overlap** another franchise area (and on routes with Open Access services — see below).
   - However, operators do compete to **win franchises** — generally they **pay** the government for these, but for some franchises they're **paid** by the government. As a condition of the franchise, operators are required to offer a **specified set of services** and to meet certain **standards**. The government **awards** the franchise based on how much firms are willing to pay (or how little they're willing to be paid), and on the service and quality **commitments** they're offering.
   - Operators get **revenue** from **ticket sales**, and most franchisees (operators with franchises) get **government subsidies** for running **socially beneficial** services that wouldn't otherwise be profitable. All operators also get an **indirect subsidy** through the **reduced fees** they pay for using infrastructure, as a result of the government partially funding Network Rail.
   - Almost all **franchisees** are subsidised by the government **overall** — they're either paid to run the franchise, or the direct and indirect subsidies they receive **exceed** what they paid for the franchise.
   - Some operators run **Open Access** services instead of getting a franchise — these operators pay Network Rail for the right to run the **specific services** that they want to provide, and they **don't** receive subsidies. This is fairly rare though — it's only possible when there's enough **capacity** for these services to run (usually in addition to franchise services).

3) **Freight**
   - Freight companies don't have to bid for a franchise — they just pay **track charges** for using the infrastructure.

Privatisation

Bus Privatisation meant many **Cross-Subsidies** between routes **Stopped**

1) Before 1986 the market for **local bus services** was controlled by **local authorities**, who had to give approval for operators to run services. **Inter-city** bus travel was provided by a single **nationalised** operator.
2) Bus travel was **privatised** in the mid 1980s — the nationalised operator was **broken up** into separate regional companies and these were **sold off**, along with local bus companies.
3) Previously the government had run services on unprofitable routes by **cross-subsidising** them with profit from other routes.
4) A completely free market would only provide **profitable services**. To avoid a situation where **less popular routes** (which are unprofitable) aren't provided, the government now **intervenes** by offering **subsidies** to private firms. Firms bid to provide these services at the **lowest** subsidy.
5) In the last 20 years the **total subsidy** that the government pays to bus operators has **increased**, despite **bus fares increasing**. This may be partly because buses are running with **fewer people** on them — people are using buses less, but the distance travelled by buses each year hasn't gone down.

Transport Privatisation has some **Downsides**

There are some **drawbacks** to privatisation, and some of the benefits it was **expected** to deliver may not have appeared.

1) Private firms can ignore the **externalities** of transport. This creates **allocative inefficiency**, so government intervention will still be needed to prevent this (see pages 90-91).
2) Profit objectives could conflict with **safety standards** — cost reductions might be made at the expense of safety.
3) Lots of transport industries are **natural monopolies** because there are large **economies of scale**.
   - Replacing a public monopoly with a **private monopoly** will not necessarily improve **productive** or **allocative efficiency**, and may lead to **higher prices**.
   - But **splitting up** a natural monopoly between several private firms may also **reduce productive efficiency** — smaller firms won't be able to maximise economies of scale.
4) Breaking up transport networks between multiple firms also makes transport **less integrated** — there's no **central planning**, so services might not **link together** conveniently for customers.
5) There may actually be **less investment**, as some profits are paid to **shareholders** rather than reinvested.
6) Privatisation has resulted in some **unprofitable routes closing**, for example in **rural areas** where there are fewer people. This can be damaging to **local economies** and is seen by many as **inequitable**, since people who can't afford a car may not be able to access jobs, shops or leisure activities. It's also likely that those who can afford a car will drive more, which creates negative externalities (see page 88).

Practice Questions

Q1 How can privatisation of transport services reduce government spending?

Q2 What are cross-subsidies?

Q3 Explain how franchising is used in the UK rail industry.

Exam Question

Q1 Discuss whether or not transport privatisation will always improve economic efficiency. [8 marks]

Transport privatisation — getting two bus seats to yourself...

Rail, bus and air transport have all been privatised in the UK. Privatisation should improve quality and lower prices for customers, and save money for the government through improved efficiency. There are some problems with privatisation though — firms tend to ignore the wider effect of their decisions on society, and the need for firms to make profit might mean a worse service for users in some cases. So it's not a case of privatisation definitely being better or worse than nationalisation — there are pros and cons to both approaches. How beneficial privatisation is depends partly on how the government intervenes in the market, and how successful this is. Read on...

Deregulation and Market Structure

These pages are for OCR Unit 4 (Transport Economics).
Privatisation is often accompanied by deregulation — the rules on firms entering the market are relaxed to encourage competition.

Deregulation can make *Markets* more *Contestable*

Contestable markets tend to be more competitive because it's easier for firms to enter the market.

1) Deregulation means **removing** or **reducing** regulations. It removes some **barriers to entry** (making the market more **contestable**), so it can be used to **increase competition** in markets.
2) Deregulation is often used **alongside/as part of** privatisation.
3) In a **nationalised industry**, private firms are prevented from entering the market and competing with the government provision, usually by **legal barriers to entry**.
4) When an industry is privatised, as well as government-owned operations being sold off, these legal barriers are often **removed** so that the market doesn't become a **private monopoly** — **competition** is introduced to the market.

Outside London the *Bus Travel Market* has been *Deregulated*

1) Outside London the bus market was **deregulated** when it was privatised — **price controls** have been removed, and any firm can now **enter the market** as long as they meet safety standards.
2) This made the bus market more open to **competition**, which should have resulted in better **efficiency** and **lower prices**, but this may not have happened in practice — there's more about this on page 87.
3) In London the market **wasn't** deregulated — it's controlled by the local government body **Transport for London** (TfL). TfL is responsible for most aspects of transport in London, including the Underground and the Congestion Charge.
4) Private companies compete by **bidding** to provide services, but TfL sets prices, routes, timetables and quality standards.
5) Once the rights to run services have been won, the market **isn't contestable**, and firms don't compete for **passengers**.
6) Full deregulation wasn't allowed in London because it was thought firms would focus on the most **profitable routes**, which would increase **congestion** and mean **higher fares** and a **reduced service** on less popular routes.
7) Bus usage in London has **increased** since the 1980s, whereas it has **decreased** in the rest of the country — this is used to support the argument that deregulating the bus market outside of London has not been beneficial (although bus usage was already in decline **before deregulation**).

Air Transport has been *Deregulated*

There's more about the air transport market on page 78.

1) Originally air travel was very **tightly regulated** — governments had to come to a **specific agreement** to allow an airline to fly on a given route. **Prices** were often set by government and only a few airlines could operate on each route.
2) The industry was gradually **deregulated** as **open skies policies** were adopted, which allowed more airlines to fly on various routes. This made the market much more **contestable**.
3) **Low-cost airlines** began to enter the market as it was deregulated, so **competition** increased.
4) This has meant **prices have fallen** and customers have **more choice** of airlines and routes.
5) However, greater supply and lower prices have resulted in an **increase in flying**, and in the **negative externalities** of flying. For example, emissions of greenhouse gases have risen, contributing to **climate change**. There's more about this on page 89.

There are still *Barriers to Entry* in *Deregulated Transport Markets*

Though **deregulation** makes transport markets **more contestable**, high **barriers to entry** often still exist:

- **High set-up costs** and **sunk costs** exist in **rail** and **ship** transport — vehicles are expensive to buy and these costs may not be recoverable if a firm leaves the market. **Leasing** has lowered this barrier, but it's still expensive to get started.
- **Regulatory barriers** — **licences** are needed for most transport provision (e.g. lorry drivers need a heavy goods vehicle driving licence), and firms have to keep to **working hours directives**, and follow **health and safety** and **public safety** laws.
- **Franchising** is a barrier to entry to the **passenger rail market** — franchises last for **several years**, and new firms have to wait until a franchise is available to enter the market. Often only **one firm** at a time can hold a franchise for a route. However, firms can also enter the market through **Open Access** if there's enough **capacity** on the railway (see page 84).
- **Predatory pricing** — there's evidence of this happening on some **bus routes** (this is explained on the next page).
- **Economies of scale** may give large firms an **advantage** — for example, firms with one **passenger rail franchise** might be more likely to win another one, as they'll be able to take advantage of large economies of scale.
- **Brand loyalty** is a barrier to entry to the **passenger air travel** market — there's more about this on page 24.

Deregulation and Market Structure

Privatisation and Deregulation might not result in a Competitive Market

1) The aim of privatising and deregulating transport is to allow **market forces** to allocate resources in the **most efficient way**.
2) For this to **work well** there needs to be **competition** in the market, but not all transport markets are competitive.
3) Generally markets with **higher barriers to entry** and **greater economies of scale** have less competition — these markets are less **contestable** and large firms have an advantage, so **mergers** are common.

EXAMPLE

1) The **minicab** market is highly **competitive** in many areas — low set-up costs and limited regulatory barriers to entry mean the market is **contestable**, so the market is made up of **lots of small firms**.
2) There's not much **differentiation** between firms' services — one firm's service is a good **substitute** for another's.

EXAMPLE

1) The Channel Tunnel is a **natural monopoly** because the high **sunk cost** of building a tunnel creates a huge **economy of scale**. This sunk cost also creates a very high **barrier to entry**.
2) But **ferry services** do compete with the **train service**.
3) The cross-Channel ferry market is **oligopolistic**, mostly due to mergers — large economies of scale are available in ferry transport too.

The Bus Travel Market has become Oligopolistic

1) When the bus travel market was deregulated it became **contestable**, because the set-up costs for bus transport are fairly low.
2) Soon after deregulation lots of firms **entered the market** and it became **much more competitive**.
3) The market then began to get more **concentrated** as some firms grew, often through **mergers**.
4) Small firms couldn't **compete** and many went out of business. There are a few reasons for this:
   - Larger operators have **lower average costs** because there are economies of scale in purchasing, running and maintaining larger fleets of buses. This allows larger firms to offer **lower prices**, forcing smaller firms out of business.
   - There have also been accusations of bus companies engaging in **predatory pricing**. On routes where they face competition, large firms can afford to offer **very low prices** that don't cover the cost of running the service, because they're making profit on other routes. Small firms can't do this so they're **forced out of the market**.
   - Larger firms can offer a network of services that **link together** conveniently (e.g. with timetables and stations that allow quick and easy connections). Some large bus companies even run **train services** as well. This improves the **quality** of the service for customers, but it makes it difficult for smaller firms to **compete**.
5) The market has now become **oligopolistic** — a few large firms dominate the market.
6) In some places the market is a **local monopoly** — firms tend to concentrate on certain areas rather than providing a nationwide service, so though there are several firms in the market as a whole they're often not in **direct competition**.
7) This is a **market failure** — lack of competition in the market is likely to result in **higher fares** and **poorer quality**.

Practice Questions

Q1 Explain three barriers to entry to the air travel market.

Q2 Explain how the privatisation of the London bus travel market was different to the privatisation of the market elsewhere.

Exam Question

Q1 Discuss the extent to which the deregulation of bus transport has been successful in bringing competition to the market. [20 marks]

The submarine transport market isn't contestable — it has high sunk costs...

Privatisation and deregulation generally make markets more competitive by removing barriers to entry, but in some transport markets there are high sunk costs and economies of scale that limit how contestable the market can be. In these cases privatisation might result in a market structure that isn't fully competitive, and so is less likely to provide the benefits that are expected.

Transport Market Failure

These pages are for OCR Unit 4 (Transport Economics).
Transport creates costs for society, like pollution. This causes market failure because the market doesn't take these costs into account.

Transport has Negative Externalities which cause Market Failure

1) Transport use has **negative externalities**:

Pollution — **air** and **water** pollution can harm wildlife and people's health. **Noise pollution** can also be a problem, for example next to a busy motorway or under a flight path.

Climate change — carbon dioxide and other **greenhouse gas emissions** from transport are contributing to climate change (there's more about this on page 89).

Greenhouse gas emissions are another form of pollution.

Accidents — these have external costs such as **lost work**, as well as the cost to the people involved.

Blight (this means some sort of 'deterioration' to an area) — transport **infrastructure** can negatively affect **communities**. For example, a new motorway might divide a community, cause people to **leave the area** and decrease the **value** of people's homes. Blight can also be caused by plans for new infrastructure, even if it's never actually built — **suggested plans** may put people off living in an area.

Stress — this can affect those **around transport routes**, e.g. people living next to a busy road.

Congestion — this is a big problem on roads, and also happens at busy airports and stations.

There's more on congestion below.

2) These negative externalities cause **market failure** — the **private cost** of some modes of transport doesn't reflect the negative externalities, so these modes are **underpriced**, which leads to **overconsumption**:
   - **Negative externalities** mean that marginal social cost (MSC) is **higher** than marginal private cost (MPC).
   - So the **market equilibrium** is at price P_e and output Q_e.
   - The equilibrium **price** is **lower** than the **socially optimal price** (P_1), and **output** is **higher** than the **socially optimal level** (Q_1).
   - This means the **allocation of resources** is not optimal.

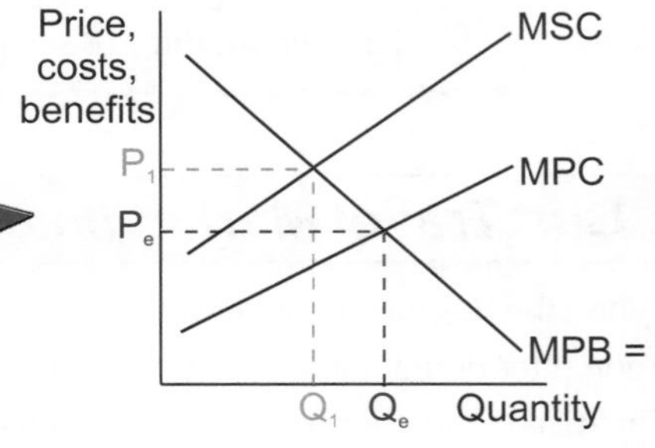

Traffic Congestion is a case of Market Failure

1) **Traffic congestion** occurs when **demand** for road space **exceeds capacity**. There are several **costs** of congestion:
   - **Slower journeys** have an opportunity cost, including **lost working time**.
   - **Delays** and **uncertainty** about when deliveries will arrive at firms may **reduce productivity** if production is held up.
   - **More fuel** is used when traffic is congested — fuel is wasted stopping and starting, and while sitting in traffic. This increases cost as well as **pollution** and **greenhouse gas emissions**.
   - Congestion can cause **accidents** — for example, if cars meet a stationary queue unexpectedly.
   - People travelling through congestion and people who work or live near **busy roads** may feel extra **stress**.
2) Some of these costs are imposed on the **individual** or **firm** that chooses to make a journey — these are included in their **private cost** of making the journey.
3) But lots of these costs affect other drivers, or society as a whole — they're **negative externalities**, which cause **market failure**.

Transport Infrastructure is Underprovided by the Market

1) Another type of **market failure** that happens in transport markets is the **underprovision of public goods**. This is caused by the **free rider problem** — people benefiting from things they haven't paid for (see page 39).
2) Some types of **transport infrastructure** are considered public goods, for example lighthouses and street lights.
3) Road space can be considered a **quasi-public good** because it appears to be **non-rivalrous** and **non-excludable**, but in practice it doesn't quite have these characteristics:
   - There are some **exclusions**. For example, there are some **toll roads** in the UK (such as the M6 Toll), which you have to **pay** to access — see page 90.
   - Road space can also display **rivalry** because roads have limited **capacity**, so at peak times **congestion** means that one person's decision to use road space may **limit** somebody else's ability to do so.

Transport Market Failure

Sustainable Transport Use has a Lower External Cost

1) Some transport modes have **fewer negative externalities** and **greater positive externalities** than others, i.e. overall it's better for society if people use some modes rather than others where possible. A **sustainable** transport system balances the use of the various modes in a way that works well for society **now** and in the **future**:

> A **sustainable transport system** meets people's needs in the present, without **depleting resources** or causing damage which will prevent **future generations** from meeting their needs.

2) There are lots of things that contribute to the sustainability of transport use, such as the effect it has on people's **health** and the **environment**, its use of **scarce resources**, and its contribution to an **equitable** society. How sustainable transport use is will depend on how efficiently the **transport network** as a whole functions (see page 95).
3) **Greenhouse gas emissions** are generally felt to be the **biggest sustainability concern**. Greenhouse gas emissions from transport contribute to **climate change** — this is a **negative externality** of transport use which will impact on **future generations**, not just on people in the present. Emissions of greenhouse gases **vary** between modes:
   - **Passenger trains** and **buses** usually have relatively **low emissions** per passenger.
   - **Cars** and **lorries** usually have **high emissions** compared to most other modes.
   - **Electric vehicles** can have lower emissions than petrol or diesel vehicles, but this depends on **where** the electricity they're charged with comes from. In the UK electricity mostly comes from burning **coal and gas**.
   - **Air transport** generally produces the **highest emissions** for passengers and freight.
   - Using **sea transport** for freight produces very low emissions.
   - **Canal** and **rail transport** also have fairly low emissions for freight.
4) Comparing emissions between transport modes can be **tricky** — there's lots of **variation** in emissions, for example depending on how **efficient** vehicles are.
5) It's not always **clear** which modes are actually being used in a **more sustainable** way — for example, a bus with hardly any passengers might produce higher emissions per passenger than if they'd all made the same trip in small efficient cars.

Otto was chuffed with his new low-emission vehicle. He was less chuffed with his new co-driver, especially his taste in hats.

Bus and Rail Transport are Underconsumed

1) The **negative externalities** of transport use will be reduced if people and firms **switch** from transport modes with **high emissions per passenger** (like car and air) to transport modes with **lower emissions per passenger** (like rail and bus).
2) Switching **away from car use** will also reduce other negative externalities — **congestion** is mainly associated with car use, and many more people are **killed** or **injured** travelling by car than by bus or rail (taking into account distance travelled).
3) This difference in external cost isn't reflected in the **relative prices** of modes of transport, so at market equilibrium the level of bus and rail use is **lower** than the **socially optimal** level, while car use is **higher** than is socially optimal.
4) This causes **market failure** — transport modes with fewer negative externalities are **underconsumed**.

> If the government can intervene to get consumption of each transport mode to the socially optimal level (see pages 90-91), this will improve sustainability.

Practice Questions

Q1 Give four negative externalities of transport.

Q2 Why can road space be classed as a quasi-public good?

Exam Question

Q1 Explain how the negative externalities produced by the use of transport lead to market failure. [4 marks]

The negative externalities of transport are a serious problem. No joke.

Transport produces things like pollution which have a negative effect on society. Many of these things are ignored by the market, so the transport modes that have the biggest negative impact are used too much and the modes with the smallest negative impact are used too little. This is one type of market failure. Another market failure in transport comes from the fact that some bits of transport infrastructure are public goods (anybody can access them), so nobody wants to pay for them — this is the free rider problem.

Government Intervention in Transport

***These pages are for** OCR Unit 4 (Transport Economics).*
The government intervenes in transport markets to correct market failure. There are a few methods governments can use for this...

Taxes and *Charges* increase the *Price* of transport that has an *External Cost*

1) Governments can use **taxation** and **charges** to **increase the price** of using transport modes that have greater negative externalities, like car and air travel.
2) Fuel duty and air passenger duty are examples of UK **taxes** that do this, and **road charges** also exist in the UK — there's more about this below.
3) The higher price (P_1 on the diagram) should **deter** people from using that mode of transport, so the quantity consumed will fall (from Q to Q_1).
4) This **internalises** the negative externality by making the private cost **equal** to the social cost (i.e. the **external cost** is now **included** in the private cost).
5) If the tax/charge is set at the **right amount** (equal to external cost) then the **socially optimal** level of output can be achieved.

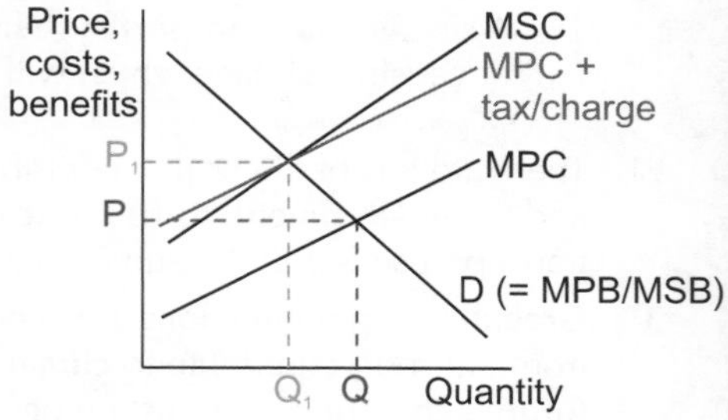

6) The **revenue** brought in from taxation and charging can also be used to help provide **alternative** modes of transport — this is important because demand will generally only fall if there are **alternatives** available.

DRAWBACKS

1) It's hard to set the tax/charge at the **right level** — measuring the **external cost** of transport use is difficult.
2) Higher prices won't reduce transport use by much if demand is **price inelastic** — this may be the case, especially where there's no **alternative** mode of transport available for people to **switch** to.
3) Taxes and charges increase the cost of using transport for firms, which will increase their **cost of production** and may mean they can't **compete internationally**.

Road Pricing can be the most effective *Intervention* for *Reducing Congestion*

1) The government can intervene to reduce road congestion by building new roads to increase **capacity**.
2) However, some people argue that this doesn't help because the extra road space just **increases demand**. There are also lots of places where there isn't **space** to do this easily — especially in central London.

Roads can be widened too.

3) **Taxation** can also be used to reduce congestion, but this has problems too — it's not a very **targeted** method:
   - A **vehicle tax** (e.g. vehicle excise duty in the UK) increases the price of **running a car**, not the price of a journey.
   - A **fuel tax** increases the price of all journeys — it doesn't **target** journeys on congested roads.

See also p.43.

4) **Road pricing** (charging to use roads) can be **targeted** on congested areas, so it may be **more effective**.
5) Road pricing can also be used to **reduce car use** generally, but because it's likely to be targeted on particular roads it might just **displace** traffic onto roads that don't have a charge, rather than reducing car use overall.
6) There are two common types of road pricing — **congestion charges** and **toll roads**.

You could price all roads, but this would probably be very unpopular.

Congestion Charges apply to *Everybody Driving* in a *Congested Area*

1) In 2003 a **congestion charge** was introduced for driving in an area of central London (the Congestion Charge zone). A **fixed daily charge** applies on **weekdays** between 7 am and 6 pm (but people living in the zone get a big discount).
2) You pay the charge in advance or on the day (usually online), and **cameras** are used to enforce **fines** for not paying.
3) By law, the **revenue** raised from the Congestion Charge has to be used to **improve public transport** in London.
4) Congestion has **reduced** in the Congestion Charge zone since the charge was introduced — this has also happened in **other cities** where a congestion charge has been brought in (e.g. Stockholm).

Toll Roads put a *Price* on using a *Particular Road*

1) **Toll roads** are stretches of road that you pay to drive along. Usually there's a **fixed price** for each type of vehicle. You pay at a **toll station** on the road — barriers often stop people from using the road without paying.
2) Charging people to use a road can help **cover the cost of building** it — road bridges often have a toll for this reason (e.g. the Humber Bridge). Most toll roads in the UK are **bridges** or **tunnels**.
3) The **M6 Toll** is a motorway that was built in the early 2000s to **reduce congestion** on the M6 around Birmingham.
4) A **private company** built the road under an agreement that allows them to receive the **revenue** from the tolls for the first 50 years that the road is open — after this the road will become **publicly owned**.

Government Intervention in Transport

DRAWBACKS

1) A **flat rate** congestion charge doesn't impose a **higher cost** on journeys made at **more congested** times. The Stockholm congestion charge **varies** by time of day, which reduces this problem.
2) The technology and administration needed to **enforce** tolls and congestion charges can be **expensive**.
3) Congestion might increase in the area **around the toll or charge zone** if people just change routes to avoid it.
4) On toll roads congestion can be caused by vehicles **stopping** to pay the toll. Some toll roads use an **automated system** that allows people to buy passes in advance and go through tolls more quickly.

Subsidies aim to *Increase Supply* of transport with *Lower External Costs*

1) Governments can use **subsidies** to encourage people to use some types of **public transport** more — rail and bus transport are both subsidised in the UK.
2) If people **switch** from car travel to these modes it will reduce **negative externalities** (there's more about this on page 89).
3) A subsidy **lowers the cost of production** of public transport, which will cause the supply curve to shift right (from S to S_1 on the diagram) — **supply will increase**.
4) Equilibrium will then be at a **lower price** (P_1) and a **higher quantity** (Q_1) — lower prices will encourage more people to use public transport.
5) If the subsidy is set at the **right amount** (equal to the reduction in external cost), then the new equilibrium will be at the **socially optimal** level of output.

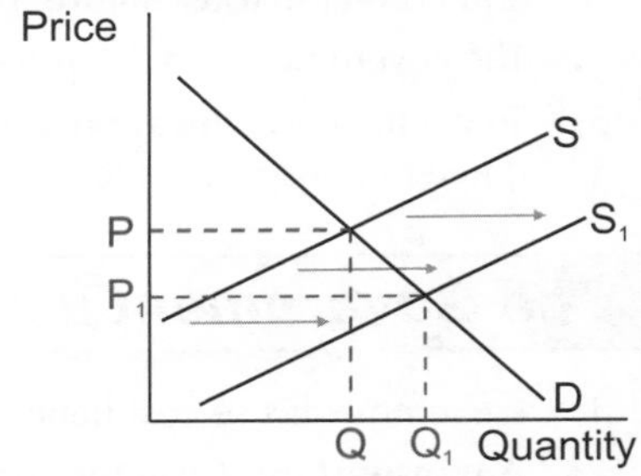

DRAWBACKS

1) Working out the **right level** to set the subsidy at is difficult — it's hard to calculate what the reduction in **external cost** is likely to be if people switch mode.
2) Subsidies might not decrease prices — firms could use them to **increase profits** instead.
3) If demand is **price inelastic** then falling prices won't increase the use of public transport by much — people often choose car or air travel for **reasons other than price**, so cheaper public transport might not make people switch.
4) Subsidising public transport **costs the government money**, which could be put to other uses.

See also p.43.

Regulation aims to *Limit Supply* of transport with an *External Cost*

1) Governments can use regulation to **limit the use of transport** with greater negative externalities, and to **reduce the negative externalities** that firms create.
2) Some forms of regulation aim to limit the external cost of transport use by setting **legal standards** which firms must meet in order to operate. For example, in the UK airlines are legally required to use planes which meet **noise regulations**.
3) Regulation will decrease usage of the modes of transport it applies to — complying with regulation **increases the cost of production** for transport providers, which shifts the supply curve to the left, increasing price and **reducing consumption**.

DRAWBACKS

1) It's difficult to decide **how much** regulation is needed to reduce output to the **socially optimal** level — **excessive regulation** can make the market **operate inefficiently**.
2) Regulation can be difficult to **enforce** — firms might find ways to **avoid** having to comply fully with regulations, or might be willing to **ignore** them if the cost of doing this (e.g. fines) is too low.
3) Regulating transport **costs the government money**.
4) Some of the cost of complying with regulations is passed on to transport users, including other firms. This increases the **cost of production** for firms and could mean they can't **compete internationally**.

Practice Questions

Q1 How can taxation help solve market failure in transport markets?

Exam Question

Q1 Discuss the effectiveness of public transport subsidies as a method for reducing road congestion. [8 marks]

I'm campaigning for a congestion charge to stop people sneezing on trains...

Make sure you can explain how each type of government intervention works, and what the disadvantages of each method are.

Resource Allocation

***These pages are for** OCR Unit 4 (Transport Economics).*
Private firms sometimes provide transport infrastructure, if they think it'll be profitable.
But it's quite often the government that builds the UK transport infrastructure.

The Public and Private Sectors are both involved in Providing Transport

1) In the UK most freight and passenger transport is provided by the **private sector**.
2) The **public sector** provides quite a lot of **transport infrastructure** — most of the **road network** is government provided, and the **rail network** is publicly owned and partially funded by government (though private firms contribute too).
3) Providing transport infrastructure through the **public sector** is one way that the government can **intervene** to try and correct **market failure** in the transport market — e.g. the underprovision of public goods (see p.88-89).
4) The government can use **private funding** to get transport infrastructure built by using a **private finance initiative** (see page 44).
5) To get the best **allocation of resources** in transport there needs to be **long-term planning** which **coordinates** decisions about different transport modes (see p.94) — public-sector provision allows this (it's unlikely to be provided by the private sector).

The Government uses Cost Benefit Analysis (CBA) to Allocate Resources

1) Governments use **cost benefit analysis** (CBA) to evaluate **major investment projects**.
2) A **transport infrastructure project** will have lots of different costs and benefits, including **externalities**. For example, for a new motorway:

CBA isn't the only method — nowadays it's usually part of a wider assessment.

Costs
- Capital costs of **land**, **design** and **construction**.
- **Maintenance** costs.
- **Lost revenue**, e.g. if fuel tax revenue decreases because less fuel is used.
- **Blight** (see page 88).

Benefits
- Faster travel — users **save time**.
- **Cheaper** travel for users, e.g. from using less fuel.
- **Safety** improvements — a reduction in **accidents**.
- Reduced **congestion**.

3) Cost benefit analysis is one way for the government to **weigh up** all of these costs and benefits to work out which infrastructure projects will be the **most beneficial** — this should ensure the **best allocation of scarce resources**.
4) CBA gives a **monetary value** to the costs and benefits of a project over a **fixed time period** (often 50 years or more).
5) The costs and benefits are all given **current values**, but they're **discounted** (reduced) based on how far in the **future** the cost or benefit will appear. For example, a cost of £1000 for road maintenance that will be needed in 50 years might be given the value of £200, whereas if it were needed in 5 years it might be valued at £850.
6) A scheme's total costs are **deducted** from the total benefits to give a **net social cost** or **benefit**. Infrastructure projects will only **go ahead** if they're expected to deliver a net benefit.
7) CBA allows different projects to be assessed in a **consistent** way, so projects can be **ranked**. This means the **limited resources** available can go to the projects which deliver the **most benefit**.
8) However, CBA is unlikely to give a **completely accurate** net cost/benefit for new infrastructure (see pages 48-49). This is a problem because **resources will be misallocated** if decisions are made based on inaccurate costs and benefits.

Cost benefit analysis is covered in more detail on p.48-49.

In the Private Sector Resources are Allocated to the Most Profitable Projects

Private firms also **appraise** (i.e. evaluate) new projects by weighing up costs and benefits, but their **approach** is slightly different:

1) Some parts of UK **transport infrastructure**, like airports, are built by **private firms**.
2) Unlike governments, private firms generally don't consider **externalities** when they decide whether or not to build infrastructure — their decisions are based on **profit**.
3) Costs and benefits to **users** may be ignored too if they won't affect profit. (This might be the case if the users aren't fully aware of the cost or benefit — e.g. health benefits.)
4) The profit **expected** from a scheme can be calculated by **deducting** the expected costs of building and maintenance from the revenue it's expected to generate.
5) Firms will expect a certain level of profit to **compensate** them for the **risk** of investing in the project.
6) The projects that are expected to produce the **highest profit** will go ahead.

"And you're sure you don't want to go with the waterslide option?"

Resource Allocation

To Include Externalities in a CBA you need to give them a Monetary Value

A **monetary value** can be put on **negative externalities**, so they can be included in a **cost benefit analysis**. There are several ways of **deciding** this monetary value:

1) **Shadow Pricing**
   - When no actual market price for something exists, a shadow price can be calculated by working out the **opportunity cost** of lost output.
   - For example, the shadow price of an **accident** could be calculated by multiplying the **working hours lost** by the average **hourly wage rate**.
2) **Cost of Compensation**
   - The cost of **compensating people** who are affected by the negative externality.
   - For example, the cost of providing **double glazed** windows to all the people who are affected by **noise pollution**.
3) **Revealed Preference**
   - The amount that people are actually **willing to pay** to **avoid** the negative externality.
   - For example, this could be worked out by looking at the average amount that has **actually been spent** on measures to reduce noise pollution (e.g. double glazing) by people on affected streets.
   - Working out what people are **actually spending** to remove a negative externality is tricky because there isn't usually a product that does this exactly. For example, double glazing reduces noise pollution in homes, but it doesn't get rid of it **entirely**, and it has **other benefits** that you're paying for too (e.g. it keeps the heat in better than single glazing).
4) **Increased User Costs**
   - The **extra cost** that the negative externality imposes on **other transport users**.
   - For example, the cost of **congestion** could be calculated using the extra fuel costs of slower journeys.
   - The **average extra cost** would be **multiplied** by the **number of drivers** affected.

The Government has changed its approach to Evaluating Road Schemes

1) The way the government **evaluates** road building and improvement projects has changed over the years.
2) In the past they mainly used a method of CBA that balanced the **cost** of a scheme with its **benefit to users** — the main concern was whether a new scheme would **reduce journey times** and the number of **accidents**.
3) This approach was criticised for ignoring the **wider impact** of schemes on society, so other types of appraisal began to be used in addition to CBA, such as methods considering **environmental impact**.
4) In 1998 the government adopted the New Approach to Appraisal (NATA), which aimed to consider the effect of a new scheme on the **environment**, **safety**, the **economy**, **accessibility** (e.g. if a road blocks a pedestrian route), and the **integration** of the transport network (see page 94).
5) This approach was also criticised for not considering a **wide enough range** of factors, as well as for reducing factors to a **monetary value** in cases when this wasn't felt to be the most appropriate method.
6) Road appraisal now uses a **variety of methods**, including CBA. Some of these express costs and benefits with **numbers** (including monetary values), and others make '**quality judgements**'.

Practice Questions

Q1 Explain four ways in which a monetary value can be attached to a negative externality.

Q2 Give two criticisms that have been made over the years of the government's approach to road appraisal.

Exam Question

Q1 Analyse the effectiveness of cost benefit analysis (CBA) as a method of assessing the overall worth of transport infrastructure projects. [15 marks]

It's hard to put a price on the joy of learning transport economics...

There are limited resources available to provide transport infrastructure — land is in short supply and there's only so much public funding available. The government tries to take all of the costs and benefits of a new infrastructure project into account so they can decide what the best use is for these limited resources. In the private sector resources will go to the most profitable projects.

Transport Policy

***These pages are for** OCR Unit 4 (Transport Economics). It's important to have policies in place to make sure transport effectively meets current requirements. It's also vital that there are plans set out to make necessary changes for future transport needs.*

The UK has a number of different **Transport Policies**

1) The government has **transport policies** which cover all modes of transport and which are intended to address various transport-related issues, such as the need to reduce **emissions**, increase **efficiency**, **capacity** and **safety**, and achieve the **best allocation of resources** possible.
2) Specific government policies currently exist to **improve road and rail networks**, **reduce emissions** from transport, and make **aviation more sustainable** (see page 95).
3) The government can use various methods to **implement** its policies, for example **taxation**, **investment**, **regulation**, and **government provision** of services. Pages 84-85 and 90-93 cover government involvement in transport in more detail.

EXAMPLE

Reducing car use for short journeys by making other transport modes **more attractive** is one current government policy. The methods the government is using to achieve this include **subsidising** bus services, funding **cycle parking** and **cycle safety schemes**, and helping local authorities to **design infrastructure** that encourages walking and cycling.

4) Governments use **forecasts** to **estimate future demand** for transport (see page 83). They can then make policies that either aim to **meet future demand** (e.g. for road space), or to **influence** that demand (e.g. to reduce road traffic).
5) Transport policy has to consider transport needs in the **long term** — **infrastructure** can take a **long time** to plan and build.

EXAMPLE

HS2 (High Speed 2) is a new rail link that's designed to **increase the capacity** of the rail network (which is getting busier) and **reduce travel times** between the north and south of the UK. The initial plans were put forward in 2010, but the first trains aren't expected to run until **2026**, and the project won't be fully finished until well after that.

Integrated Transport Policy can reduce **Government Failure**

1) **Government failure** can occur when attempts to implement one policy **conflict** with the objectives of another policy.
2) For example, the government's current policy of **improving** the quality of the **road network** may **increase road usage**, which will **conflict** with another current government policy to **reduce greenhouse gas emissions** from transport.
3) An **integrated transport policy** considers the **transport network** as a **whole**, rather than looking at each mode in **isolation** — this should mean that individual policies 'fit together' **neatly**.
4) This involves considering the **knock-on effects** of decisions about one mode of transport on **other modes** — e.g. the effect of new cycle lanes on the level and flow of road traffic.
5) The **wider implications** of transport plans are also taken into account — for example, **environmental impacts** and the interaction of transport policy with policy in other areas, like **land-use** and **health**.
6) A properly integrated **transport system** makes it easy for passengers or freight to **move between transport modes**. To achieve this, **inter-modal policies** are needed:

Local and central government often have to work together to achieve integrated policy.

INTER-MODAL POLICIES

Policies which aim to **coordinate** transport modes and improve **links** between them (i.e. make the transport system more integrated) are known as **inter-modal policies**. Examples of this type of policy include:

- Building **transport interchanges** that combine bus and train stations (e.g. Bradford Interchange).
- Setting up **park and ride schemes** which offer out-of-town car parking served by public transport to take people into more congested areas.
- Enabling '**through ticketing**' — where passengers can buy a single ticket for a journey that uses more than one mode of public transport (e.g. bus and train).
- Constructing **rail freight interchanges** which connect the rail network to the road network (so freight can be transferred easily from one to the other).
- Improving or creating **road and rail links** to **ports**.

Transport Policy

Sustainability is an important consideration of *Transport Policy*

1) **Sustainable transport policies** meet current transport needs without reducing the ability of **future generations** to meet their needs — there's more about **sustainability** in transport on page 89.
2) These policies aim to make transport use sustainable by encouraging people, where possible, to use transport modes which have fewer **negative externalities** (see page 89). They also attempt to influence the **demand for transport** (e.g. by supporting **remote working** to reduce the overall demand, or **'staggered' office hours** to reduce congestion at peak times).

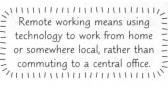

Remote working means using technology to work from home or somewhere local, rather than commuting to a central office.

3) Policies that create **integrated transport systems** are important for sustainability because they aim to reduce some of the **problems** that currently lead to such a heavy reliance on private road vehicles. For example, they can make public transport more **convenient** for passengers, and make **loading freight** from one mode to another **cheaper** for firms.
4) Other policies that can be used to **encourage** sustainable transport use include:
   - **Road pricing** (see page 90).
   - Increasing the **price of fuel** through **taxation** (see page 90).
   - Investment in infrastructure that supports **sustainable transport networks** (e.g. cycle paths).
   - Increasing the **maximum weight** permitted for vehicles carrying freight — this may reduce the number of vehicles needed.

The new bike route meant Jack finally had an excuse to wear his favourite vest to work.

Sustainability is a focus of *EU Transport Policies*

1) **Greenhouse gas emissions** are a major sustainability concern — their impact is **global** (see page 89). Governments need to **work together** to reduce these emissions — if one country **alone** introduced measures to reduce emissions this might:
   - **Reduce** the **competitiveness** of that country in world trade.
   - Encourage polluters to simply **move their operations** elsewhere.
   - Create pressure on that government to **reverse** their policies (e.g. from businesses).
   - Have a **limited impact** on global emission levels.
2) **EU transport policy** can **coordinate** efforts to reduce emissions across the EU, which should help reduce these problems. E.g. **legal limits** have recently been set on the **carbon dioxide emissions per kilometre** allowed for all new cars in the EU.
3) **Sustainable freight transport** has been a particular focus of EU transport policy recently. This is considered important because there are **high levels of congestion** on major routes in the EU, and there's lots of potential to **reduce emissions** by shifting freight transport to less polluting modes (e.g. rail).

EXAMPLE

In 2011 EU rules on road charging for **heavy goods vehicles** (HGVs) were updated to allow charges to **vary** depending on the **emissions** of vehicles, and the **time of day**. Member states can now **target** higher charges on firms using **inefficient** HGVs, or using HGVs at **congested times** (to internalise these negative externalities).

Practice Questions

Q1 Give two current aims of UK transport policies.

Q2 What is an integrated transport policy?

Q3 Give an example of a way in which policy can be used to increase the sustainability of freight transport.

Exam Question

Q1 Analyse what is meant by a sustainable transport policy. Include examples in your answer. [15 marks]

Integrated transport — not just for triathletes...

Transport policy covers all the different aspects of transport. Imagine having to coordinate government policy for all the different modes of transport in a country — that's lots of policies. The main things to take away from this topic are the major themes of transport policy (e.g. minimising emissions), understanding what integrated transport policy is, and the fact that future considerations shape this policy.

Economic Growth

These pages are for AQA Unit 4, Edexcel Unit 4 and OCR Unit 5 (The Global Economy).
This section builds on your knowledge from AS. It might be worth having a look back at your AS Economics notes on economic growth, aggregate demand, aggregate supply, and all the other topics in this section before tackling these pages. We've provided a bit of a recap of a few things, but you'll need to be very familiar with the AS material.

GDP is used to Measure Economic Growth

1) Economic growth is measured by the changes in national output over a period of time — this is usually calculated as changes to **Gross Domestic Product** (**GDP**).
2) To measure the **standard of living** in a country, economists sometimes use **GDP per capita** figures. GDP per capita is calculated by dividing the total GDP by the country's population.
3) Sometimes, **Gross National Income** (**GNI**) or **GNI per capita** is used to measure **economic growth** and the **standard of living** in a country. GNI is GDP plus **net income** from abroad (the total income earned on investments and other assets **minus** the income earned by foreigners on investments domestically).

You need to know about Short Run and Long Run Economic Growth

1) Economic growth can be defined as an **increase** in the **productive potential** of an economy.
2) In the **short run** it's measured by the **percentage change** in real national output (real GDP) — this is known as **actual growth**. Increases in short run growth are usually due to **increases** in **aggregate demand** or short run **aggregate supply** (see next page). Actual growth **doesn't** always increase — it tends to **fluctuate up** and **down**.

Remember, aggregate demand is made up of C + I + G + (X - M).

3) **Long run** growth is caused by an **increase** in the **capacity** (or **productive potential**) of the economy. This happens when there's a **rise** in the **quality** or **quantity** of the **factors of production**. **Increases** in long run growth are caused by increases in **aggregate supply** (or **long run aggregate supply**).
4) Long run growth is shown by an **increase** in the **trend rate** of growth. The trend rate of growth is the **average rate** of economic growth over a period of both economic **booms** and **slumps**.
5) On a **production possibility frontier** (**PPF**) diagram a movement from a point **within** the PPF curve **to** the PPF curve is an example of **short run growth** (e.g. the movement from point A to point B). A **shift outwards** of a PPF curve will be an example of **long run growth** (e.g. the movement from point B to point C).

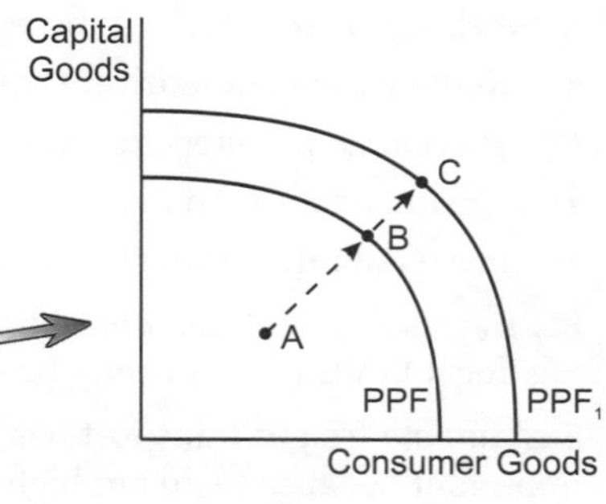

The Economic Cycle has Different Phases

1) The actual growth of an economy **fluctuates** over time. These **fluctuations** are known as the **economic cycle**.
2) A **boom** is when the economy is **growing quickly**. Aggregate demand will be **rising**, leading to a **fall** in **unemployment** and a **rise** in **inflation**.
3) A **recession** is when there's **negative economic growth** for at least **two consecutive quarters**. Aggregate demand will be **falling**, causing **unemployment** to **rise** and a **fall** in **price levels**.

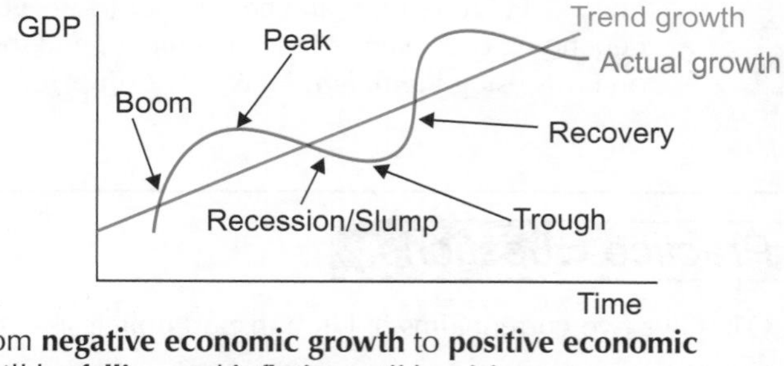

4) During a **recovery** the economy begins to **grow again**, going from **negative economic growth** to **positive economic growth**. Aggregate demand will be **rising**, so **unemployment** will be **falling** and **inflation** will be **rising**.
5) **Fluctuations** in economic growth can be caused by **demand-side shocks**, which can cause aggregate demand to **rise** or **fall**, or by **supply-side shocks**, which can cause aggregate supply to **rise** or **fall**.

Examples of demand-side shocks:
- If a country's **major trading partners** go into a **recession**, this may significantly reduce demand for the country's **exports**.
- If consumer confidence is **boosted**, e.g. due to **house prices rising**, this will **increase consumer spending**.

Examples of supply-side shocks:
- The discovery of a major **new source** of a raw material will greatly reduce its price and increase its supply — **increasing** the **capacity** of the economy.
- A **poor harvest** reduces the supply of food, increases its price, and **reduces** the economy's **capacity**.

Economic Growth

Output Gaps can occur during periods of Boom or Recession

1) A **negative output** gap is the **difference** between the level of **actual output** and **trend output** when actual output is **below** trend output. A negative output gap will occur during a **recession** when the economy is **under-performing**, as some resources will be **unused** or **underused**.
2) A **positive output gap** is the **difference** between the level of **actual output** and **trend output** when actual output is **above** trend output. A positive output gap will occur during a **boom** when the economy is **overheating**, as resources are being fully **used** or **overused**.
3) During a **recovery** an economy will go from having a negative output gap to having a positive output gap as actual output **rises above** trend output.

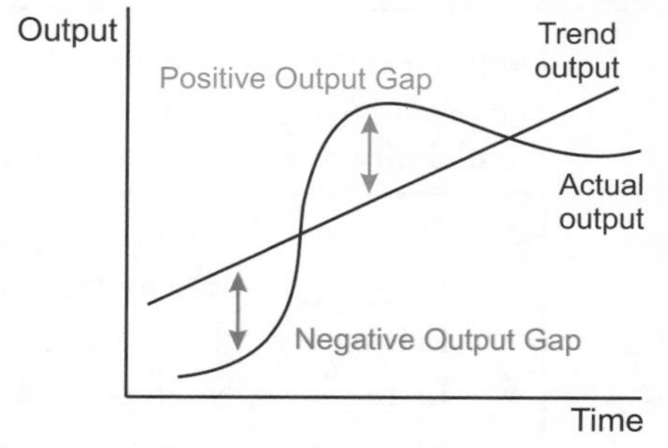

Short Run economic growth can be created by Increasing Aggregate Demand

1) A rise in **aggregate demand** (**AD**) will create **short run** economic growth. When **AD** rises the **AD** curve **shifts** to the **right**.
2) An increase in AD will be caused by **demand-side factors** — here are some examples:
   - **Lowering** interest rates **encourages** investment and **increases** consumption.
   - **Increasing** welfare benefits **increases** government spending and consumption.
3) How much the AD curve shifts depends on how big the **multiplier effect** is — the **process** by which an **injection** into the **circular flow of income** creates a **change** in the size of **national income** that's **greater** than the size of the **initial injection**.
4) The size of the multiplier is determined by how big the **leakages** from the circular flow of income are and the **marginal propensity to consume** (**MPC**) — the **proportion** of an **increase** in income that people will **spend** instead of saving.
5) The **bigger** the size of the **multiplier** (and the higher the MPC) the **greater** the shift to the right of the AD curve.

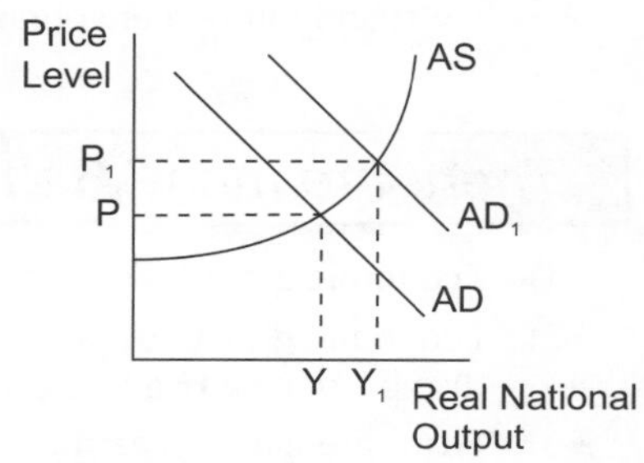

In AD and AS diagrams, you could label the horizontal axis 'Real GDP' instead of 'Real National Output'.

The accelerator process

- If firms expect that there will be a **long period** of **demand** for certain products, then they're likely to **invest** in **new capital** (e.g. machinery) to **increase** their **ability** to meet this demand.
- For any **given change** in demand for goods/services beyond capacity, there will be a **greater percentage increase** in demand for **new capital goods** that firms need to produce those extra goods/services — this is called the **accelerator process** (or the **accelerator effect**). Firms will make 'accelerated' investment in **capital goods**, expecting to make **profit** in the future.
- This process is likely to occur when the economy is going through a **recovery**, or at the start of a **boom**. These are the times when **demand** will be rapidly increasing and firms will need to invest in order to meet this demand.
- If firms **increase** investment, this will **increase AD**, and any increase in investment will have a **multiplier effect**.
- The accelerator process and multiplier effect can both also happen **in reverse** — for example, during a recession, there's likely to be a **fall** in **demand** and a **fall** in **investment**, which will then have a **reverse multiplier effect**.

Short Run Aggregate Supply Increases also create Short Run economic growth

1) A **rise** in **short run aggregate supply** (**SRAS**) will also create short run economic growth. When SRAS **rises** the SRAS curve **shifts** to the **right**.
2) Any factor which **reduces production costs** will cause an **increase** in SRAS. Here are some examples:
   - A **fall** in the price of oil will **reduce** production costs and increase SRAS.
   - A **fall** in wages will **reduce** production costs and increase SRAS.
3) An **increase** in **productivity** will also **increase** SRAS. If firms can produce more by using the factors of production that they have **more efficiently**, then they can **increase** their **output** — causing the SRAS curve to **shift** to the **right**.

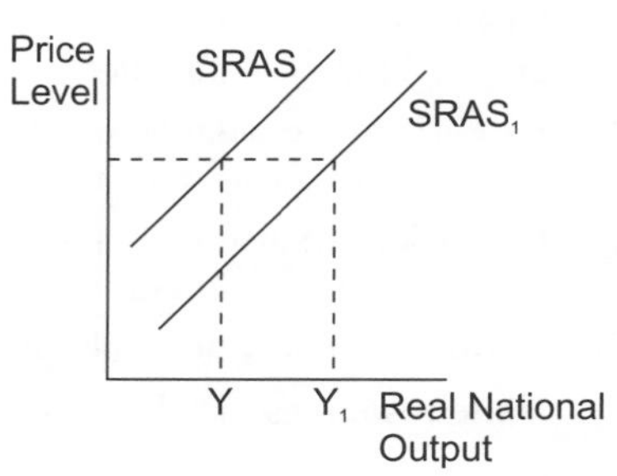

Economic Growth

We're not done yet with economic growth...

There are several ways to create Long Run Economic Growth

1) **Long run** economic growth is the result of **supply-side factors** that increase the **potential** for **economic growth**.
2) The **productive potential** of a country can be **increased** by **raising** the **quantity** or **quality** of the **factors of production**, for example:

- Through **innovation** — e.g. new technology.
- **Investing** in more **modern** machinery (i.e. improving **capital stock**).
- **Raising** agricultural **output** by using genetically modified (GM) crops.
- **Increasing** spending on **education** and **training** to improve **human capital**.
- **Increasing** the **population size**, e.g. by encouraging immigration, to increase the size of a country's **workforce**.

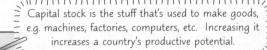

Capital stock is the stuff that's used to make goods, e.g. machines, factories, computers, etc. Increasing it increases a country's productive potential.

3) An **increase** in a country's productive potential **shifts** the LRAS (or AS) curve to the right.

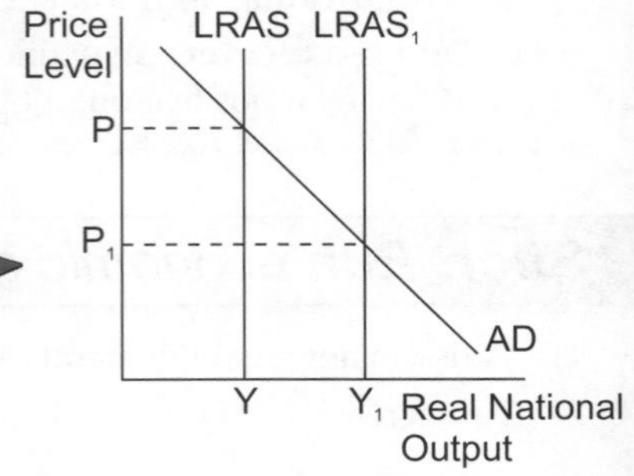

4) A **government** can also help to create long run economic growth by **creating** stability in a country (e.g. by enforcing laws) and through encouraging **economic stability**.

There are many Benefits of Economic Growth

1) **Economic growth** will **increase demand** for labour, leading to a **fall** in **unemployment** and **higher incomes** for individuals.
2) Economic growth usually means that firms are **succeeding**, so employees may get **higher wages**. This will also produce a **rise** in the **standard** of **living**, as long as prices **don't** rise more than the increase in wages.
3) **Firms** are likely to earn **greater profits** when there's economic growth as consumers usually have **higher incomes** and **spend more**. Firms can use these profits to **invest** in better machinery, make **technological advances** and **hire** more employees — causing an **increase** in the **economy's productive potential**.
4) As firms are likely to **produce more** when there's economic growth then this can **improve** a country's **balance of payments** because it will sell **more exports**.
5) **Economic growth** causes wages and employment to **rise**, which will **increase** the **government's tax revenue** and **reduce** the amount it pays in **unemployment benefits**. The government can use this **extra revenue** to **improve** public services or the country's infrastructure **without** having to **raise taxes**, which is good for individuals.
6) Economic growth will **improve** a government's **fiscal position** because if it receives greater tax revenues and spends less on things like unemployment benefits then this will **reduce** the government's need to **borrow money**.
7) There might be some **benefits** to the **environment** brought about by economic growth, e.g. firms may have the resources to **invest** in **cleaner** and **more efficient** production processes.

Unfortunately, there are some Costs of Economic Growth

1) Economic growth can create **income inequality** — **low-skilled workers** may find it hard to get the **higher wages** that other workers are benefiting from.
2) **Higher wages** for employees are often linked to an **increase** in their **responsibilities** at work (e.g. if they've been promoted). This can **increase stress** and **reduce productivity**.
3) Economic growth can cause demand-pull inflation (see p.102) because it causes **demand** to **increase faster** than **supply**. It can also cause cost-push inflation (see p.103) as economic growth **increases** the **demand** for **resources**, pushing up their prices. However, the effects of inflation will be **reduced** if **aggregate supply** (or long run aggregate supply) also **increases**.
4) A **deficit** in the **balance of payments** can be created because people on **higher incomes** buy **more imports**. Furthermore, **firms** may **import more resources** to increase their production to meet the higher levels of demand.
5) **Industrial expansion** created by economic growth may bring **negative externalities**, such as pollution or increased congestion on the roads, which **harm** the **environment** and **reduce** people's quality of life.
6) **Beautiful scenery** and **habitats** can be **destroyed** when **resources** are **overexploited**.
7) **Finite resources** may be **used up** in the creation of economic growth, which may **constrain** growth in the **future**.

Economic Growth

Sustainable Growth is Difficult to Achieve

1) **Sustainable economic growth** means making sure the economy **keeps growing** in the future, **without** causing **problems** for future generations (there's more on sustainability on p.150). Sustainable growth relies on a country's ability to:

- **Expand output** every year.
- Find a **continuous supply** of raw materials, land, labour and so on, to continue production.
- Find **growing markets** for the increased output, so it's always being bought.
- **Reduce negative externalities**, e.g. pollution, to an acceptable level so they don't hamper production.
- Do all of the above things at the **same time** as many **other** countries who are pursuing the **same objectives**.

2) It's **very difficult** for a country to do all of these things at the same time, so sustainable growth is **hard** to achieve.
3) To be able to achieve sustainable growth, countries will need to **develop renewable** resources. Non-renewable resources will **run out** and, for growth to be sustainable, a **continuous supply** of raw materials is **necessary**.
4) Countries will also need to **innovate** to create **new technologies** that **reduce negative externalities**, such as pollution, and the **degradation** of resources, such as land or rivers, **without** stopping output from expanding.
5) A country that achieves **sustainable** growth will gain **long-term** benefits to society — it can more easily **plan ahead**, since it can be more confident about its long-term economic prospects.

You need to know about the UK's Recent Macroeconomic Performance

1) It's **important** for the exam that you've got some idea of the **UK's recent macroeconomic performance**. You can really improve what you write if you can put **relevant** information about the UK economy into your **answers**.
2) You should keep an eye on the **news** and look for any **important developments** about the **UK's economy** — e.g. there might be a rise in interest rates or a large fall in unemployment. Here are a few **general points** to get you started:
   - From **2000** until **2008** the UK enjoyed **continuous GDP growth** of, on average, **just under 3%** each year. However, in 2008 the UK went into a **recession** that lasted for **several months** and was followed by a long period of **slow recovery**.
   - During the recovery the UK economy went through **short bursts** of growth followed by **slow-downs** — it almost went **back** into a **recession** in **2012**. From **2013 onwards**, the UK has had much more **consistent GDP growth** and, by **2014**, **GDP returned** to the level it was **just before** the recession — suggesting that the **recovery** is **complete**.
   - Between **2000** and **2014** the rate of **inflation** in the UK, as measured by the **Consumer Price Index** (**CPI**), has been quite **steady** — generally inflation has been **between 0.5** and **3%**.
   - There have been **some exceptions** to this steady level of inflation. On a **couple** of occasions, inflation rose to about **5%**, **well above** the government's target of **2%**. This happened just at the **start** of the **recession** in **2008** and **again** in **2011**. Since then, inflation has **dropped** back down to a **steady rate** between 0.5 and 3%.
   - **Unemployment** in the UK remained **quite low** between **2000** and **2008** — **between** about **1.4** and **1.7 million**.
   - Between **2008** and **2011** unemployment **rapidly rose**, reaching a **high** of about **2.7 million** (an **unemployment rate** of **8%**). Since then unemployment has **fallen**, but, by August 2014, it was still **higher** than it was at the start of 2008.
   - The UK has had a **current account deficit** in its **balance of payments** for the **whole period** between **2000** and **2014**. The deficit reached its **all-time low** during this period at the **end of 2013**.
   - Although the UK **massively increased** its **exports** between 2000 and 2014, it also **increased** its **imports** at **roughly** the **same rate**. **Imports continued** to be **higher** than **exports**, so the **deficit steadily increased**.

Practice Questions

Q1 Describe the difference between short run and long run economic growth.

Q2 Give three examples of ways that a government could encourage long run economic growth.

Exam Question

Q1 Explain how economic growth might contribute to an improvement in the standard of living in a country. [8 marks]

Slumps usually follow long periods of revision...

Right, there's a lot of stuff here that you might remember from AS, but it's covered again because it's bloomin' important to learn it. Also, make sure you know the UK's recent macroeconomic performance so you can slip some useful points into your answers.

Unemployment

These pages are for AQA Unit 4, Edexcel Unit 4 and OCR Unit 5 (The Global Economy).
Again, a lot of what's covered on these pages will be familiar to you, but you need to make sure it's all clear in your head so that you can understand the trickier stuff that's coming up in a bit.

There are **Two** ways of **Measuring Unemployment** in the UK

1) In the UK there are **two ways** of **measuring unemployment** — the **claimant count** and the **labour force survey** (**LFS**).
2) The **claimant count** is the number of people **claiming unemployment-related benefits** from the government, known as **Jobseeker's Allowance** (**JSA**). It's **easy** to measure — you just **count** the number of people **claiming JSA**.
3) The **LFS** is conducted by the **International Labour Organisation** (**ILO**). The ILO asks people who **aren't working** if they're **actively seeking work** and uses the number of people who answer **yes** to produce the **unemployment count**.
4) The LFS count is **usually higher** than the claimant count because it **measures people** who are **unemployed**, but who **don't claim benefits**. The LFS is usually used for **international comparisons** of **unemployment**.

Governments want **Full Employment**

1) Governments aim for **full employment**, which is where everybody of working age (excluding students, retirees, etc.), who wants to work, can find employment at the **current** wage rates.
2) Full employment **doesn't mean** everyone has a job — in most economies there will **always** be people **between jobs**.
3) Governments **want** full employment because this will **maximise production** and **raise standards of living** in a country.
4) If there's **unemployment** in an economy then it **won't** be operating at **full capacity**, so it'll be represented by a point **within** the **PPF curve** (e.g. point A). At **full employment** the economy can **operate** at **full capacity**, so it can be represented by a point **on** the **PPF curve** (e.g. point B).

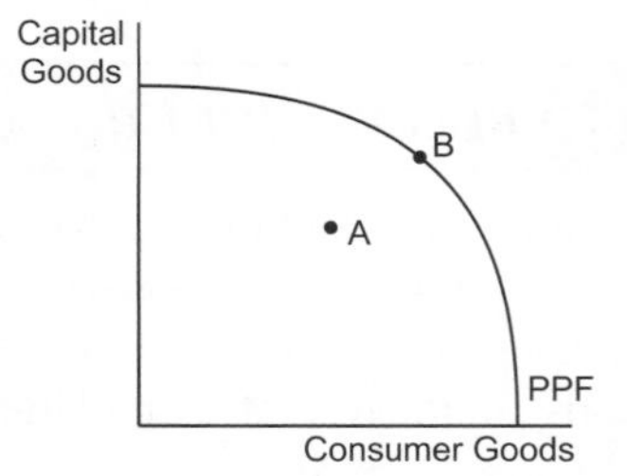

Economic Growth affects **Unemployment**

1) Labour is a **derived** demand — an employer's demand for labour is derived from **consumers'** demand for goods/services. So when demand in the economy is **low** (e.g. when there's negative economic growth), unemployment will **rise** — but when demand is **high**, unemployment will **fall** (e.g. when there's positive economic growth).
2) **Cyclical** unemployment (or demand-deficient unemployment) usually happens when the economy is in a **recession** — when aggregate demand falls, employment will **fall** too. A country suffering from a **negative output gap** (see p.97) is likely to have cyclical unemployment too.

Recessions don't bother Clive — he has cyclical employment.

Structural Unemployment is made worse by **Labour Immobility**

1) Structural unemployment is caused by a **decline** in a certain **industry** or **occupation** — usually due to a **change** in **consumer preferences**, **technological advances** or **cheaper alternatives**. It often affects **regions** where there's a decline in **traditional manufacturing** (e.g. shipbuilding or the steel industry) and it's made worse by **labour immobility**:
   - **Occupational** immobility occurs when some occupations may decline over time, but the workers in these occupations **don't** have the skills required to be able to do the jobs that are available.
   - **Geographical** immobility is where workers are unable to **leave** a region which has high unemployment to go to another region where there are jobs. This might be because they can't **afford** to move to a different region, or they have **family ties**.
2) If a **region** is affected by structural unemployment then it could also suffer from the **negative multiplier effect** — unemployment will lead to less **spending**, and so cause **more** unemployment in the region.
3) The **problem** of structural unemployment may become **more common** in the future:
   - **Technological change** in both products and production methods is **accelerating quickly**. This will **speed up** the **decline** of out-of-date industries and **reduce** the number of workers needed to make products.
   - Consumer spending is **more likely** to change as consumers are better **informed** (through the internet and social media) than ever before — making them more likely to **switch** to **lower priced** or **higher quality** goods.

Unemployment

Frictional Unemployment is caused by the *Time* it takes to find a *New Job*

1) **Frictional** unemployment is the unemployment experienced by workers **between** leaving one job and starting another. This **includes** those who have finished education and are looking for a job.
2) Even if an economy is at **full employment**, there will be **some** frictional unemployment. There will always be some employees who are **changing jobs** — maybe because their contract has run out or because they want to earn higher wages.
3) The **length** of time that employees spend looking for a **new** job (the 'time lag' between jobs) will depend on several things:
   - In a **boom** the number of job vacancies is much **higher**. So frictional unemployment is likely to be **short term**.
   - In a **slump** frictional unemployment could be much **higher** as there will be a **shortage** of jobs.
   - **Generous welfare benefits** will give people **less incentive** to look for a new job, or they can enable people to afford to **take their time** to look for a good job — so the time spent between jobs **may** increase.
   - The **quality** of **information** provided to people looking for jobs is important too. If people **don't know** what jobs are available or what skills they need to get the job they want, then they're likely to **remain unemployed** for **longer**.
   - Labour and geographical immobility will also affect the length of time between jobs. If a region is suffering from **structural** unemployment (see previous page) then this length of time can increase.

Real Wage Unemployment is caused by wage increases *Above* the equilibrium

1) **Real wage unemployment** is caused by **real wages** being pushed **above** the **equilibrium level** of employment (where labour demand **equals** labour supply). It's usually caused by **trade unions** negotiating for **higher wages** or by the **introduction** of a **national minimum wage**.
2) For example, introducing a **national minimum wage** (**NMW**) **above** the **equilibrium wage rate** (**W_e**) would cause the **supply** of labour to **increase** from **Q_e** to **Q_s**. This would then cause **unemployment** of **Q_s** to **Q_d** because there's an **excess supply** of **labour**.
3) However, a **rise** in **productivity** or in **consumer spending** would increase the **demand** for **labour** (causing the **labour demand curve** to **shift** to the **right**) and this would **reduce** the **size** of the **increase** in **unemployment**.

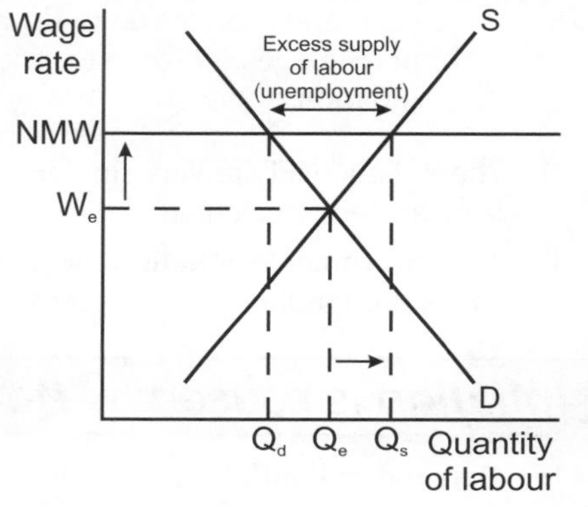

There are several *Costs* and *Consequences* of *Unemployment*

1) Unemployment means there's a **waste** of **labour**, which is a **scarce resource**. This means that the economy isn't operating at full capacity and some resources will be unused or underused, e.g. **empty** offices and factories, **unexploited** natural resources, or **unused** machinery.
2) The unemployed will have **lower incomes**, which means that they'll spend less and this could **reduce** firms' **profits**.
3) Unemployment will mean **less** income tax revenue for governments, and **less** consumer spending will reduce their indirect tax revenue. The government will also have to **spend** more on unemployment **benefits**.
4) Areas with high unemployment can have high **crime** rates, and reduced incomes can cause people to have **health problems**.
5) Workers who are unemployed a **long** time may find that their skills and training become **outdated**. This will **reduce** their **employability** and make it **more** likely that they'll stay unemployed.

Practice Questions

Q1 Briefly explain why unemployment will rise during a recession.

Q2 What might cause a region to be affected by structural unemployment?

Q3 Give three examples of things that could increase frictional unemployment.

Exam Question

Q1 Explain how high unemployment may affect a country's economic growth. [8 marks]

Structural unemployment — when buildings have no work to do...

There are a few types of unemployment you need to learn here — make sure you can define them and explain what causes them.

Inflation

These pages are for AQA Unit 4, Edexcel Unit 4 and OCR Unit 5 (The Global Economy).
Oh boy, you're in for a treat here. Quantity theory of money is just as exciting as it sounds and you get to learn all about it right here, right now. There's some other stuff on inflation too, but it doesn't have such an exciting name.

There are Two Ways of Measuring Inflation in the UK

1) Inflation is the **sustained rise** in **average prices** over time. It can also be seen as a **fall** in the **value of money**.
2) In the UK inflation is measured using the **Retail Price Index** (**RPI**) and the **Consumer Price Index** (**CPI**). These are measures of the changes in the average prices of goods and services in the UK. So, at AS-level you learnt that:
   - **Two** surveys are carried out to **calculate** the RPI.
   - The first survey is a survey of around 6000 households, called the **Living Costs and Food Survey**. It's used to find out **what** the 'average family' spends its money on and it shows the **proportion** of income spent on various items by calculating their relative weighting (e.g. if **20%** is spent on transport, then a 20% **weighting** is given to transport).
   - The second survey is based on **prices** — it measures the **changes** in price of around **700** of the most **commonly** used **goods** and **services** (these goods and services are often referred to as the 'basket of goods').
   - The items in the basket are chosen **based on** the Living Costs and Food Survey. The items change over time as technology, trends and tastes change, so it always **reflects** what the **average household** spends its money on.
   - The price **changes** in the second survey are **multiplied** by the **weightings** from the first survey. These are then converted to an **index number**. The first recorded year is the base year (and the index is usually set at 100 in this year) and changes up or down are shown as numbers above and below the base number. So **inflation** is just the **percentage change** to the index number over one year — e.g. if the index number **rises** from 100 to 102, then **inflation** is 2%.
3) The RPI and CPI are **very similar**, but CPI tends to be **lower** than RPI. A **larger sample** of the **population** is measured to calculate the CPI, and **mortgage rates** and **council tax** are **excluded** from the CPI.
4) The **government's inflation target** is **2%** and this is based on the **CPI** measure rather than the RPI. CPI is used more often for **international comparisons** of inflation.

Inflation is caused by Demand-Pull Factors

1) **Demand-pull inflation** is inflation caused by **excessive growth** in **aggregate demand** compared to supply. This growth in demand **shifts** the **aggregate demand curve** to the **right** (from AD to AD_1), which allows sellers to **raise prices**.

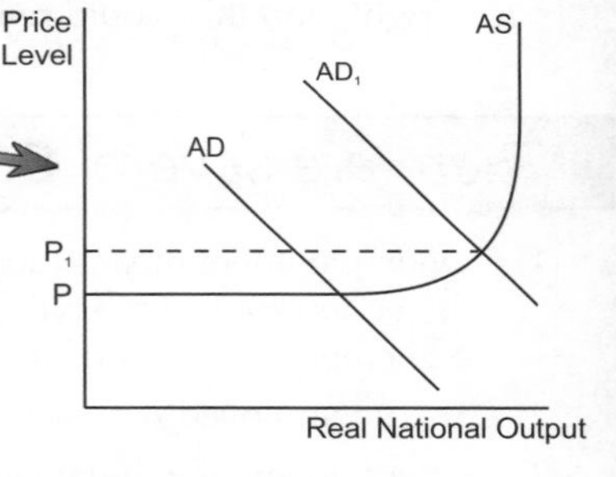

2) **Keynesian economists** argue that demand-pull inflation is usually caused by **high consumer** or **government spending**, which causes aggregate demand to **increase**.
3) As aggregate demand grows, and the AD curve reaches the vertical part of the AS curve, the economy is likely to experience **shortages** because labour and resources are being **fully utilised**. Shortages will cause firms' **costs** to **increase** and **prices** to **rise** more sharply.
4) **Monetarist economists** believe that **increases** in the **money supply** are the **main cause** of **inflation**. If interest rates are low and borrowing increases then this could mean there's **more money** in the economy than can be matched by the output of goods/services (sometimes termed 'too much money chasing too few goods'), and this leads to a **rise** in **prices**. This is known as the **quantity theory of money**.

Quantity Theory of Money

1) The quantity theory of money is based on **Fisher's equation of exchange**:

money supply × velocity of money = price level × aggregate transactions

MV = PT

2) On the **left-hand side** of the equation is **M**, which is the **total amount** of **money** in the economy, and **V**, which is the **speed** at which money is spent. On the **right-hand side** is **P**, the **price level**, and **T**, which is the **total** amount of **transactions** (the buying and selling of stuff) in the economy.
3) Monetarists argue that, in the **short run**, **V** and **T** are **unlikely** to change, so any **increases** in **P**, the **price level**, will be **directly** caused by an **increase** to **M**, the **money supply**. Both sides of the equation are assumed to be **equal** to each other, so any **increase** in the **money supply** (**M**) will create the **same percentage increase** in the **price level** (**P**).
4) To **avoid inflation**, monetarists believe that the **money supply** needs to be **strictly controlled**.

Inflation

Inflation can be caused by Cost-Push Factors

1) **Cost-push inflation** is inflation which is caused by the **rising cost** of **inputs** to production. It's an idea that's popular with **Keynesian economists**.
2) Rising costs of inputs to production force firms to **pass on** the **higher costs** to **consumers** in the form of **higher prices**, which causes the **aggregate supply curve** to shift to the left (from AS to AS_1).

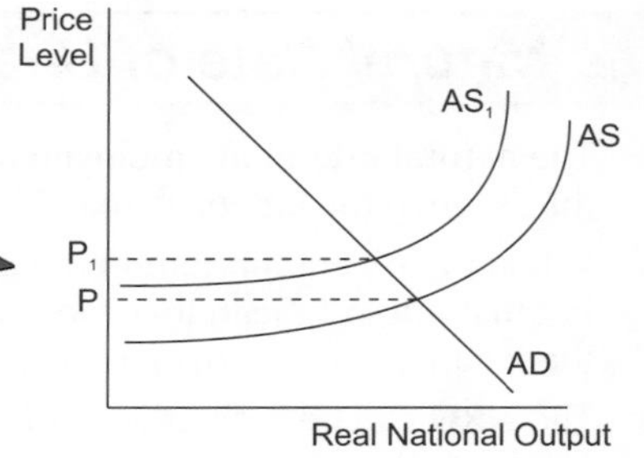

3) Here are some **examples** of causes of cost-push inflation:
   - Wage increases above any rise in productivity (possibly due to trade union pressure, see p.62) will increase a firm's **total costs** and lead to **price rises**. Price rises could lead to **further** wage demands and a **wage-price spiral**.
   - A **rise** in the **costs** of **imported raw materials** would increase producers' costs — so they'll set **higher prices**. This is an example of a **supply-side shock**.
   - If a government **raised indirect taxes**, this would **increase costs** and so **prices** would be higher. If a good is **price inelastic** then **more** of the cost of the tax will be **passed on** to the **consumer**.

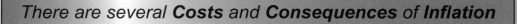

There are several Costs and Consequences of Inflation

1) Inflation will cause the **standard of living** of those on **fixed**, or **near-fixed**, **incomes** to **fall**. This will have the **biggest impact** on those in **low-income employment** or on **welfare benefits**.
2) As prices rise, so will **demand** for **higher wages** — leading to a **wage-price spiral**.
3) A country's competitiveness will be **reduced** by **inflation** as exports will cost **more** to buy and imports will be **cheaper**. If **exports fall** and **imports rise**, then this could create a **deficit** in the **balance of payments** and **increase unemployment**.
4) Inflation **discourages saving** because the value of savings falls. This makes it **more attractive** to spend (creating demand-pull inflation) **before** prices rise further.
5) Inflation creates **uncertainty** for firms as rising costs will **reduce investment** — harming future growth. Furthermore, a **rise** in **interest rates** to curb inflation will also **reduce investment** by firms.
6) Inflation can cause **shoe leather costs**, which are the costs of the **extra time** and **effort** taken by consumers to search for **up-to-date** price information on the goods and services they're using, and **menu costs**, which are the **extra costs** to firms of **altering** the **price information** they provide to consumers.

Deflation suggests an economy is In Trouble

1) Deflation is when the **rate of inflation** falls **below 0%**. It's usually a sign that an economy is **doing badly**.
2) If **aggregate demand** is falling at such a rate as to cause deflation then the economy will be suffering from **reduced output** and **increased unemployment** — the economy is likely to be in a **recession**.
3) Deflation can also worsen a **recession**. For example, if there's deflation because aggregate demand is falling, consumers may believe that prices will fall further and choose **not** to spend until they do — **reducing aggregate demand** even more.
4) However, deflation can be a sign that the economy is **doing well**. If, for example, **improvements** in **labour productivity** or **innovations** in **production methods** lead to increases in aggregate supply then **deflation** may occur. Increases in aggregate supply will lead to increased output and employment, so the presence of deflation can be a **positive sign**.
5) Governments will try to **avoid deflation** because it **usually** means there's a **fall** in **aggregate demand**.

Practice Questions

Q1 Briefly explain what monetarist economists believe to be the main cause of inflation.

Q2 Why might a government be keen to avoid deflation?

Exam Question

Q1 Discuss the main causes of inflation in an economy. [15 marks]

Fisher's equation — (hook + bait) × fish = dinner...

As with many of the pages so far, there will be some familiar things here and some new things. The quantity theory of money sounds scary, but the key thing to remember is that changes in the money supply are likely to lead to changes in the price level.

Tackling Unemployment and Inflation

These pages are for AQA Unit 4, Edexcel Unit 4 and OCR Unit 5 (The Global Economy).
You've got to know how governments deal with unemployment and inflation.

The *Natural Rate of Unemployment* occurs at *Labour Market Equilibrium*

1) The **natural rate of unemployment** (NRU) is the rate of unemployment when the **labour market** is in **equilibrium** — this is when the **labour demand** is **equal** to **labour supply**.
2) When there's equilibrium in the labour market that means there's **enough jobs** for **every worker** in the **labour force**, but that **doesn't** mean that every worker will be **in a job** (because of **frictional** and **structural unemployment**). So, there can be unemployment when the labour market is in equilibrium, and that unemployment is the **NRU**.
3) The **NRU** can be seen as being **full employment**, as it's **not possible** for **every** person in the workforce to have a job. No matter how much aggregate demand is increased, frictional and structural unemployment will **always exist**.

The *Phillips Curve* shows the *Trade-off* between *Inflation* and *Unemployment*

1) At AS-level you learnt about the **Phillips curve**, which at A2-level is known as the **short run Phillips curve**.
2) The Phillips curve shows that as **inflation falls, unemployment rises**, and vice versa. So, the Phillips curve shows the **trade-off** between inflation and unemployment. If the government wants to **reduce unemployment**, then it must **increase aggregate demand** and **accept higher inflation**.
3) However, the Phillips curve only takes into account the **current rate** of inflation — it **doesn't** take into account the influence of the **expected rate** of inflation. That's where the **long run Phillips curve** comes in.

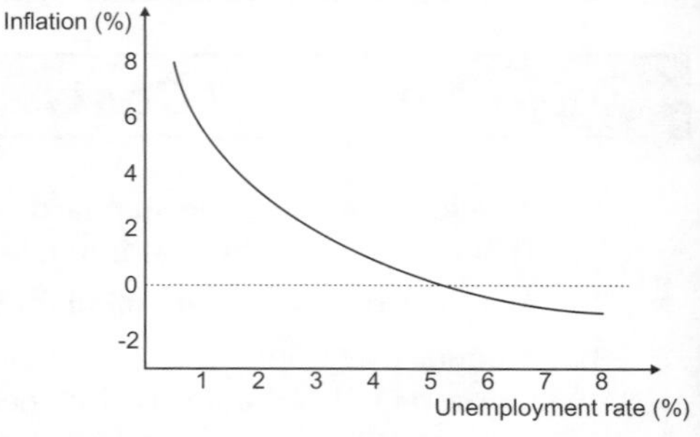

Expectations about *Inflation* can cause *Inflation Rises* to become *Embedded*

1) **Assume** that an economy that's at **point A** on the diagram has **unemployment** at its **natural rate** (U_N) — that's the **NRU**.
2) At point A **inflation** is **0%**, so the **economic agents** (workers, firms, etc.) in the economy will **expect** that inflation will **stay** at **0%** and this will influence things like **workers' wage negotiations**.
3) However, if **aggregate demand increases** and this **forces** unemployment **below** the **NRU** (to U_1), then this will cause **wage demands** to **go up** and **inflation** will **increase** (to **3%**).
4) At **point B** economic agents will now **expect inflation** to **stay** at 3%. As a result, future **wage negotiations** will be **based on** inflation being at 3%.

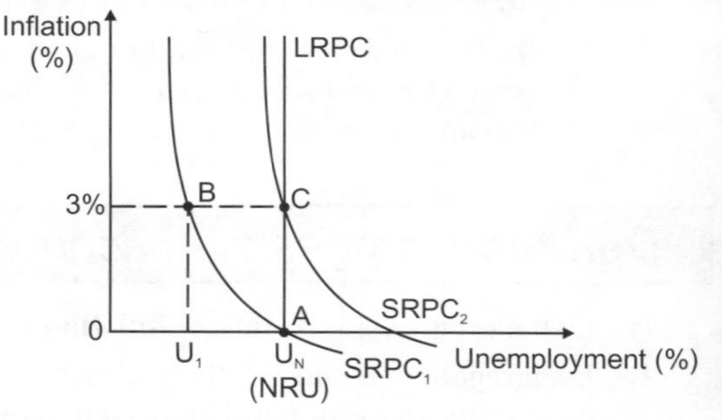

5) **Higher wage demands** will mean firms are **less willing** to take on workers, so **unemployment** will **rise back** to the NRU (to U_N). So the **short run Phillips curve** (**SRPC**$_1$) will **shift right** to **SRPC**$_2$. (No matter how the SRPC curve shifts, it will always return to the NRU, so the **long run Phillips curve**, **LRPC**, will always be a **vertical curve** coming up from U_N.)
6) When the $SRPC_1$ curve **shifts right** to **SRPC**$_2$ (and the economy is at **point C**), you can see that, **despite** unemployment returning to the **NRU**, an **inflation rate** of **3%** has become **'embedded'** in the economy. Further **increases** in **aggregate demand** will mean that **higher inflation rates** can become embedded in the economy.
7) This shows how important it is for governments to use policies that **stop** inflation **rising continuously**. In the UK, the Bank of England is tasked with keeping inflation **close** to the target rate of **2%** so that the **expectations** of economic agents are based on 2% inflation. On top of this, governments will use policies to **lower unemployment** and even **lower** the **NRU**.

Demand-side Policies can reduce *Cyclical Unemployment*

1) To **reduce unemployment**, governments need to understand what **type** of unemployment they're trying to tackle.
2) During a **recession** an economy is likely to have **cyclical unemployment**, so a government would need to introduce policies that **boost aggregate demand**. For example, the government could use **reflationary fiscal policies**, such as decreasing taxes or increasing welfare payments, or **expansionary monetary policies**, such as a lowering of interest rates.
3) However, there are **problems** with these kinds of demand-side policies.
   - A **lack of information** about the **size** of an economy's **output gap** may mean that the government **overspends** when it tries to **boost aggregate demand** and causes the economy to **'overshoot'** (i.e. grow too quickly) — leading to **inflation**. Alternatively, the government might **under-spend** and **prolong** a **recession**.

Tackling Unemployment and Inflation

- A **lack of information** about the size of the **multiplier** can cause problems too. For example, if the multiplier in a country is **bigger** than the government **expects**, then an increase in government spending could cause **inflation**.

4) It's **hard** for a government to use demand-side policies to **fine-tune** the economy — they can be quite **clumsy** and **cause more problems**. **Time lags** can also mean that improvements are **slow** to develop — governments may think that their policies aren't working, so they **increase spending further** and create inflation.

Supply-side Policies reduce the Natural Rate of Unemployment

1) To **reduce** the **NRU** governments need to use **supply-side policies** that make the labour market more **flexible**, and **reduce frictional** and **structural unemployment**.
2) The **flexibility of labour** is determined by **three important factors**:

- **Labour mobility** — the ability of workers to **switch jobs easily**. The more **transferable skills** workers have, the more easily they can switch jobs — so labour mobility will depend on **how skilled workers are**. On top of that, labour mobility will also depend on the **willingness** of workers to **move** to where there are jobs.
- **Wage flexibility** — the ability of **wages** to **change** with changes to the labour market (i.e. respond to supply and demand). For example, during a **recession**, employers can **lower wages** to avoid having to **lay workers** off.
- **Flexibility of working arrangements** — the ability of **employers** to **hire workers** in a way that **suits them**. Things such as **part-time work**, **short-term contracts** (or **zero-hour contracts**) and **shift employment** make it **easier** and **cheaper** for firms to **hire** or **fire** workers and **respond** to **changes** in the **market**.

3) So, policies that **improve labour market flexibility** will focus on **improving** these **three factors**. For example:
   - Labour mobility can be tackled by the **same policies** that are used to **reduce structural unemployment** (see below).
   - Governments can improve wage flexibility by **scrapping** the **NMW** and **limiting trade union power**.
   - The flexibility of working arrangements could be improved if the government **passed laws** that made it **easier** for firms to **hire workers** on **short-term** or **zero-hour contracts**.
4) **Frictional unemployment** will be reduced by policies which **encourage** people to find a job and **speed up** this process:
   - **Reducing benefits** will give unemployed workers a greater **incentive** to find a job and it will help the government **avoid** the **unemployment trap** (where unemployed workers are better off than those working on low wages).
   - **Income tax cuts** will **increase** the **incentive** for workers to find a job, or encourage them to **work longer hours**.
   - **Increased information** about jobs will help workers find the **right job** for themselves **more quickly**.
5) **Structural unemployment** will be reduced by policies which tackle **geographical** and **occupational immobility**:
   - Governments can improve **occupational mobility** by **investing** in **training schemes** that help workers to **improve** their **skills**, or by **encouraging firms** to **set up** their **own training schemes**.
   - **Geographical immobility** can be tackled by giving workers **subsidies** to move to different areas or by building **affordable houses** in areas that need workers. However, workers will still often be **reluctant** to leave their homes and families.
   - Governments can **bring jobs** to areas with **high unemployment** by providing benefits to firms that locate in certain areas. This might be **combined** with **training schemes** to give local workers the skills required for the jobs provided.

Monetary Policy is usually used to tackle Demand-pull Inflation

1) Governments also need to use policies that deal with **demand-pull** and **cost-push inflation**.
2) **Monetary policy** is usually used to **tackle demand-pull inflation** — you'll find out how monetary policy works on p.112.
3) The **supply-side policies** described **above** to **tackle frictional** and **structural unemployment** are the kinds of policies often used to **tackle cost-push inflation**. For more supply-side policies see p.116.

Practice Questions

Q1 Briefly explain how rises in inflation can become embedded in an economy.

Exam Question

Q1 Explain how a government could reduce the natural rate of unemployment in a country. [8 marks]

I'm going to be embedded under a duvet if I hear any more about inflation...

Phew... there's a lot to learn here. That Phillips curve stuff is tricky, but it'll make sense if you stick at it. Cover. Scribble. Repeat.

Macroeconomic Policy

These pages are for AQA Unit 4, Edexcel Unit 4 and OCR Unit 5 (The Global Economy).
Here's a bit about what governments want to do and the problems they face in doing it.

Governments have **Four Main Macroeconomic Objectives**

Look back at your AS notes for more about government objectives.

1) Most governments have **four main macroeconomic objectives**:
   - Strong economic growth,
   - Keeping inflation low,
   - Reducing unemployment,
   - Maintaining an equilibrium in the balance of payments.
2) Governments will also have **other objectives**, such as:
   - A more equal distribution of income and wealth,
   - Maintaining economic stability,
   - Protecting the environment,
   - Improving productivity and international competitiveness.
3) Unfortunately, it's very unlikely a government will achieve **all** that it wants to achieve without its objectives **conflicting**.

Changes in **Aggregate Demand** are likely to cause **Conflict** between objectives

1) **Short run economic growth** is caused by the AD curve shifting to the **right**. This could be due to an **increase** in any of the **components** of **aggregate demand** (C + I + G + (X – M)).
2) For example, if the AD curve shifts to right from AD to AD_1 then there will be an **increase** in **output** (i.e. economic growth) from Y to Y_1 and, as a result, there will be a **decrease** in **unemployment** (because of the derived demand for labour).
3) However, a shift to the right of the AD curve will also result in an **increase** in the **price level** from P to P_1. Higher prices may also lead to a **lack** of **competitiveness** internationally, meaning a **decrease** in exports, a **rise** in imports and therefore a **worsening** in the current account of the **balance of payments**.
4) So, in this case, an increase in aggregate demand will only help the government to achieve **two** of its macroeconomic objectives.

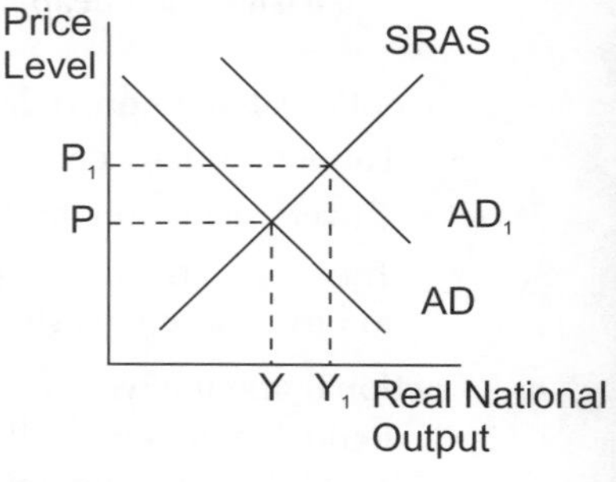

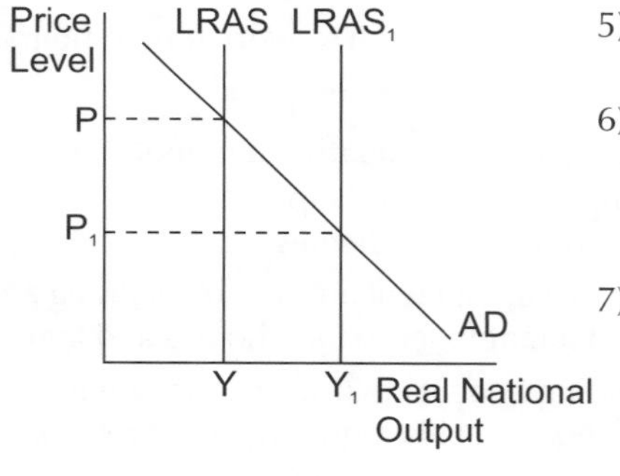

5) However, a shift in the LRAS (or AS) curve will enable a government to achieve **all four** of the main macroeconomic objectives at the **same time**.
6) For example, if the LRAS curve shifts to the right to $LRAS_1$ then this will lead to an **increase** in **output** (from Y to Y_1) and **reduce unemployment**. The **price level** will also **fall** (from P to P_1) and this will **improve** the country's **competitiveness** — **improving** the **balance of payments**.
7) This suggests that if the government **only** used **demand-side policies** to achieve its macroeconomic objectives then this would lead to **conflict** between the objectives. However, **supply-side policies** (see p.116) are more likely to help a government achieve their four main macroeconomic objectives in the **long run**.

Learn the **Main Causes** of **Conflict** between the **Macroeconomic Objectives**

Make sure you understand the **cause** of these **key conflicts** between **government objectives**. Remember, these objectives are likely to conflict in the **short run**, but in the **long run** these conflicts may **not** occur if **aggregate supply increases**.

Inflation and Unemployment

1) When unemployment is **reduced** and the economy begins to **approach** full capacity, there are **fewer** spare workers, so **demand** for workers increases — especially for **skilled** workers. This will lead to an **increase** in wages and the **extra cost** of this may be passed on by producers to consumers in the form of **higher prices** — causing **cost-push** inflation.
2) Low unemployment may cause consumers to **spend** more because they feel more **confident** in their **long-term** job prospects. This may cause **prices** to **rise** due to **demand-pull** inflation.
3) So reducing unemployment makes it more **difficult** to keep inflation at the **preferred low rate**.

Macroeconomic Policy

Economic Growth and Environmental Protection

Economic growth can put a **strain** on the **environment**. For example:

1) New factories and increases in production can raise levels of air and water **pollution**, as well as increase the amount of **waste** that needs **disposing** of.
2) Economic growth will tend to increase the use of **natural resources** — this can be a major problem if these resources are **non-renewable**.
3) Ecosystems might be **damaged** or even **destroyed** by the **construction** of new factories, housing, etc. — in the most **extreme** cases, this can lead to the **extinction** of certain animals or plants.

Economic Growth and Inflation

1) A rapidly **growing** economy can cause large **increases** in **prices**, due to an increase in **demand**. This will cause a **higher** than desirable level of **inflation**.
2) Similarly, attempts to keep **inflation low** can **restrict** growth. For example, if **interest rates** are kept **high** to reduce inflation by **discouraging** spending (and encouraging saving), this can **restrict economic growth**.

In moments of quiet reflection, Stephen often worried about the seeming incompatibility between economic growth and low inflation.

Inflation and Equilibrium in the Balance of Payments

1) **Sometimes** the government's objectives for low inflation and equilibrium in the balance of payments will be **compatible**, but at other times they'll **conflict**.
2) For example, if **inflation** is **low**, this implies that prices are **rising slowly**. If prices rise **more slowly** than those in other countries, then **exports** to other countries will **increase** and **imports** will **decrease**. This would **increase** a **surplus** on the balance of payments, but **reduce** a balance of payments **deficit**.
3) Similarly, low inflation is often **maintained** by **high interest rates**. High interest rates **encourage** foreign investment, which **increases demand** for the domestic currency — **increasing** its **value**. This will make exports **more expensive** and imports **cheaper**, so **exports** will **decrease** and **imports** will **increase**. This would **reduce** a **surplus** on the balance of payments, but make a **deficit worse**.

*In the **Short Run** governments make **Trade-offs** between their objectives*

1) In the short run, governments decide which objectives they think are **most important** and **accept** that these decisions may have an adverse effect on their other objectives — i.e. they must make **trade-offs** between their objectives.
2) Governments may have to use **short-term policies** to correct **sudden problems**, such as major unemployment caused by a severe recession. In a scenario like this the government may **accept** that inflation will result from a policy designed to reduce unemployment quickly because it's more important to get people back to work.
3) Governments have different **tools** at their disposal to achieve their objectives — these are their **fiscal**, **monetary** and **supply-side policies** (see p.108-117).

Practice Questions

Q1 Name the four main macroeconomic policy objectives of most governments.

Q2 Briefly explain how a government's objectives for economic growth and inflation might conflict.

Exam Question

Q1 Explain, using a diagram, how a government could improve all four of its main macroeconomic objectives at the same time. [12 marks]

My macaroni-economic policy involves eating lots of pasta and cheese...

Before you go on to look at the macroeconomic policy tools, it's important that you've got an idea of what governments are trying to achieve. You should also notice that supply-side policies are the best way for governments to achieve their goals in the long run.

Fiscal Policy

These pages are for AQA Unit 4, Edexcel Unit 4 and OCR Unit 5 (The Global Economy). *The next few pages are about the macroeconomic policy tools that governments can use to achieve their macroeconomic objectives. As has been mentioned a few times, it's important that you look back at your AS notes when you revise these topics. Anyway, fiscal policy...*

You've got to learn the **Key Features** of **Fiscal Policy**

1) **Fiscal policy** (or budgetary policy) involves **government spending** (public expenditure) and **taxation**. It can be used to **influence** the **economy as a whole** (macroeconomic effects) or **individual firms** and **people** (microeconomic effects).
2) Fiscal policy can be used to **stimulate aggregate demand**:
   - **Reflationary fiscal policy** (sometimes called 'expansionary' or 'loose' fiscal policy) involves **boosting** aggregate demand (causing the AD curve to shift to the right) by **increasing** government spending or **lowering** taxes. It's likely to involve a government having a **budget deficit** (government spending > revenue).
   - **Deflationary fiscal policy** (sometimes called 'contractionary' or 'tight' fiscal policy) involves **reducing** aggregate demand (causing the AD curve to shift to the left) by **reducing** government spending or **increasing** taxes. It's likely to involve a government having a **budget surplus** (government spending < revenue).
3) A reflationary fiscal policy is likely to be used during a **recession** or when there's a **negative output gap**. It'll **increase economic growth** and **reduce unemployment**, but it'll also **increase inflation** and **worsen** the **current account** of the **balance of payments** because as incomes increase, more is spent on imports.

> Reflationary and deflationary fiscal policy is known as demand-side fiscal policy — it affects aggregate demand.

4) A deflationary fiscal policy is likely to be used during a **boom** or when there's a **positive output gap**. It'll **reduce economic growth** and **increase unemployment**, but it'll also **reduce price levels** and **improve** the **current account** of the **balance of payments** because as incomes fall, less is spent on imports.
5) There are **two important features** of fiscal policy that you need to be aware of:
   - **Automatic stabilisers** — Some of the government's fiscal policy may **automatically** react to changes in the economic cycle. During a **recession**, **government spending** will **increase** because the government will pay out more benefits, e.g. JSA. The government will also receive **less tax revenue**, e.g. due to unemployment. These automatic stabilisers **reduce** the problems a recession causes, but at the expense of creating a **budget deficit**. During a **boom**, the automatic stabilisers create a budget surplus as **tax revenue increases** and **government spending** on benefits **falls**.
   - **Discretionary policy** — This is where governments **deliberately** change their level of spending and tax. At **any given point** a government might choose to spend on improving the country's infrastructure or services, and increase taxes to pay for it. On other occasions the government might take action because of the **economic situation**, e.g. during a recession the government might spend more and cut taxes to stimulate aggregate demand.

Government spending creates a **Multiplier Effect**

1) An **increase** in government spending will create a **multiplier effect** — this is where an **injection** into the **circular flow of income** creates a **change** in the **size** of **national income** that's **greater** than the **size** of the **injection**.
2) The **size** of the **multiplier effect** and the **effectiveness** of an **injection** into the circular flow of income will depend on the size of the **leakages** (such as spending on imports and taxes) from the circular flow and the **marginal propensity to consume** (MPC) in that country.

> The MPC is the proportion of an increase in income that people will spend instead of saving.

3) **Demand-side fiscal policy** (also known as '**Keynesian**' fiscal policy) was a **popular** way of creating **economic growth** in the early part of the 20th century. However, it's become **less popular** in the **UK** since the **1970s** and **1980s**. One of the main reasons for this is that the government spending **multiplier effect** is **small** — partly because government spending is **paid for** by **taxes**, so **increases** in **government spending** may be **matched** by **increases** in **taxes** (a withdrawal from the circular flow).
4) There are a **few other reasons** why demand-side fiscal policy has become **less popular**:
   - Government spending '**crowds out**' spending by the **private sector**, **discouraging enterprise**.
   - **Continuous** government spending, paid for by **borrowing**, will lead to **inflation**, a **budget deficit** and an **increase** in **national debt** (see p.110).
   - It's **difficult** to **control** the effects of fiscal policy. To be successful it requires **very accurate information**, and getting it wrong can lead to '**stop-go cycles**'.
   - Policies that **only** affect aggregate demand will lead to **conflicts** between the **four main macroeconomic objectives** (see p.106-107).

> A reflationary fiscal policy may cause an economy to 'overshoot' (i.e. grow too quickly), causing high inflation. A government may then 'apply the brakes' with a deflationary fiscal policy, which might cause a recession.

5) An **exception** to this trend came during the **recession** of **2008-2010** when the government **increased spending** to **stimulate aggregate demand**. However, increased government spending made the UK's **national debt much larger** and this policy was replaced by '**austerity measures**' (see p.110) to **cut public sector spending** and **reduce** the **national debt**.

Fiscal Policy

The government's approach to fiscal policy has Changed

Nowadays, governments use fiscal policy **differently** to the traditional 'Keynesian' approach. For example:

1. Supply-side fiscal policy is used to increase **aggregate supply**, which will help a government to achieve all four of its main economic objectives (unlike demand-side fiscal policy). For example, **tax cuts** could be offered to entrepreneurs to encourage them to start up new businesses that will increase the **productive potential** of the economy.

2. Fiscal policy is used on a **microeconomic** level to influence the behaviour of **consumers** and **firms**. For example, **demerit goods** are **taxed** to decrease consumption, and **merit goods** can be provided by the state or **subsidised** to increase their consumption. Fiscal policy can also be used to help governments achieve their **environmental policy objectives**. For example, the government could introduce '**green taxes**' that discourage the use of coal or oil, or provide **subsidies** to firms that use renewable energy (e.g. solar or wind power).

3. **Government spending** can be directed at **specific regions** that need extra help. For example, if a region loses a big employer and is suffering from **structural unemployment**, then the government could **invest** in that region to **create jobs**, or encourage **firms** to move there with **subsidies** and **tax breaks**.

4. **Progressive taxation** allows the government to **redistribute** wealth from those who are **better off** to those who are **less well off** (for more see below).

Taxation is an Important Tool for governments

1) Taxes should be **cheap to collect**, **easy to pay** and **hard to avoid**, and they **shouldn't** create any **undesirable disincentives**, e.g. discouraging people from working or from saving.

2) On top of this, governments may want taxes to achieve **horizontal** and **vertical equity** (for more on equity see p.50).
   - **Horizontal equity** will mean that people who have **similar incomes** and **ability** to **pay taxes** should pay the **same amount** of tax.
   - **Vertical equity** will mean that people who have **higher** incomes and **greater ability** to **pay taxes** should pay **more** than those on **lower incomes** with **less ability** to **pay** taxes.

3) Governments may also want taxes that **promote equality** in an economy. This might involve using taxes to **reduce major differences** in people's **disposable income**, or to **raise revenue** to pay for **benefits** and the **state provision** of **services**.

4) Governments **raise tax revenue** through **direct taxation** (e.g. income tax) and **indirect taxation** (e.g. VAT or excise duty). They also use **different tax systems** to achieve different economic objectives — the ones you need to know are **progressive taxation**, **regressive taxation** and **proportional taxation**.

5) **Progressive taxation** is where an **individual's taxes rise** (as a percentage of their income) as their **income rises**, and it's often used to **redistribute income** and **reduce poverty**. A government can use the tax revenue from those on high incomes and **redistribute** it to those on low incomes in the form of benefits or state-provided merit goods (e.g. health care or education) — **increasing equality**. Progressive taxation follows the '**ability to pay**' **principle** (the tax achieves **vertical equity**).

6) **Regressive taxation** is where an **individual's taxes fall** (as a percentage of their income) as their **income rises**, and they're used by governments to **encourage supply-side growth**. By **reducing** the taxes of the **rich** the government will hope that the economy will **benefit** from the **trickle-down effect** (see p.50). A regressive tax system gives people more of an **incentive** to **work harder** and **earn more income**, but it may **increase inequality**.

- **Supply-side economists** argue that increasing direct taxes creates a **disincentive** to work and will **reduce** a government's **tax revenue**. This is shown on the **Laffer curve**.
- The Laffer curve shows that **as taxes increase**, eventually this will lead to a **decline** in **tax revenue** because people will have **less incentive to work**. At the most extreme level, a 100% tax rate will result in no tax revenue because **no one** would work.

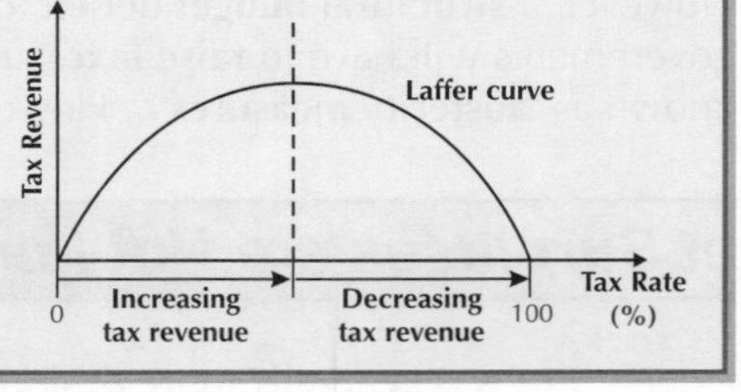

7) **Proportional taxation** is where everyone pays the **same** proportion of tax **regardless** of their **income** level. This tax system can achieve **horizontal equity**, but setting a fair tax rate to apply to all members of society is **difficult**. For example, a 25% tax on income might be too high for those on lower incomes to afford, and it might not raise enough revenue from those on higher incomes for the government to be able to pay for all of the public goods and services it provides.

Fiscal Policy

Here's a bit more on fiscal policy, yay...

You'll need to know some information about **Taxes** in the **UK**

1) In the UK there's a **sales tax** on most products known as **VAT** (value-added tax). VAT is a **proportional tax** — it's a **fixed percentage** regardless of the selling price of a product. However, it can also be seen as a **regressive tax**. This is because the **percentage** of **total income** that the **rich** spend is **less** than that of the **poor** (e.g. because the rich can afford to save more of their income), so that means the percentage of total income that the rich spend on VAT will be **less** than it is for the **poor**.
2) A more **progressive system** of **VAT** might be to tax **luxury goods** at a **higher tax rate** so that the **rich** pay a **higher rate** of **tax** for some of the more expensive products that they buy.
3) It's argued that the UK has a **progressive income tax system**. There's a **tax-free allowance** of about £10 000, and then individuals on **low income** above £10 000 have their income taxed at **20%** and, over a certain threshold, those on **middle-to-high income** are taxed at **40%**.
4) However, it's also argued that the UK tax system is **regressive**. People making this claim say that, if you consider **direct** and **indirect** taxes **together**, the **lowest earners** in the UK economy have to pay a **higher proportion** of their household income as tax than the **highest earners** do.

Large Budget Deficits can cause **Big Problems**

1) A **budget deficit** (also known as **public sector net borrowing** — **PSNB**) must be **paid for** by **public sector borrowing**, so that the government can spend **more money** than it **receives** in **revenue**.
2) In the UK, the government can borrow the money it needs from **UK banks**, which will create **deposits** that the government can spend. It can also **borrow money** from the private sector by selling **Treasury bills**, which the government will **pay off over a period of time** (e.g. 3 months), or it can borrow money from foreign **financial markets**.
3) This kind of borrowing is **fine** in the **short run**, especially if the borrowed money is used to **stimulate demand** in a country. But there will be **problems** if there's **excessive borrowing**:
   - Excessive borrowing could cause **demand-pull inflation** (see p.102), partly due to the fact that government borrowing **increases** the **money supply**, so there's **more money** in the economy than can be **matched** by **output**.
   - As borrowing may cause inflation, it can also lead to a **rise** in **interest rates** to curb that inflation (see p.112). **Higher** interest rates will **discourage investment** by firms and make a country's **currency rise in value**, meaning that its **exports** are **less price competitive**.
4) **Continued government borrowing** will **increase** a country's **national debt** (also known as **public sector net debt** — **PSND**). A **large** and **long-term** national debt can cause **several problems** too:
   - If a country's debt becomes very large then it may cause **firms** and **foreign countries** to **stop lending** money to that country's government. This will **constrain** the country's ability to **grow** in future.
   - **Future taxpayers** will be left with **large interest payments** on **debt** to pay off. Debt repayments have an **opportunity cost** as future governments may have to **cut spending** to pay off a debt, which may **harm economic growth**.
   - A **large national debt** suggests that there's been **excessive borrowing**, which **causes inflation** and **interest rates** to **rise** (see above). It also suggests that public sector spending is very large, which may '**crowd out**' private sector spending.
   - A country with large debt is **less attractive** to **foreign direct investment** (**FDI** — see p.119), as foreign countries will be **uncertain** how the debtor nation's economy will do in future and whether it will be a good bet for investment.
5) Methods to **correct** a **budget deficit** will depend on what kind of budget deficit it is.
   - A **cyclical budget deficit** is caused by **recessions** and comes about due to a government's **automatic stabilisers** (when government spending on benefits increases and tax revenue falls). This kind of deficit will be **corrected** when the economy **recovers** again — the deficit will be replaced by a surplus.
   - However, a **structural budget deficit**, caused by **excessive borrowing**, is much harder to solve. To cure this problem, governments will have to **raise taxes** and **reduce public spending** so that they can pay off their debt (these are known as '**austerity measures**'). However, these actions could **harm economic growth** and cause other problems.

Budget Surpluses are **Not Ideal** either

1) A budget surplus is **generally more desirable** than a budget deficit — however, it's **not** always a good thing either.
2) A budget surplus might suggest that **taxes** are **too high** or that governments **aren't spending** enough on the economy. Both of these things could **harm** or **constrain economic growth**.
3) **Lowering taxes** or **increasing government spending** would **correct** a budget surplus.

Fiscal Policy

Governments follow **Fiscal Rules** to **Avoid Overspending** on their economies

1) The **European Union** (EU) has created fiscal rules, known as the **Stability and Growth Pact** (**SGP**), that **member states** of the EU **agree** to **follow**. These rules are more **strictly enforced** in the Eurozone (see p.137), to help keep the euro **stable**.
2) The rules require EU countries to:
   - **Not** have a **budget deficit** that **exceeds 3%** of **GDP**.
   - **Not** have a **national debt** that **exceeds 60%** of **GDP**.
3) Following these rules should help to **prevent** a government from **continuously borrowing** and **overspending** to promote growth, which increases national debt and inflation, and it'll help governments to achieve **economic stability** as they'll **avoid** uncertainty and fluctuating inflation.
4) However, many EU countries have **ignored** these rules and the EU has been **unwilling** to **impose punishments** on these countries (such as fines). This means that they've had **very limited** success.
5) In 2010 the UK government created the **Office for Budget Responsibility** (**OBR**) — an independent body that publishes reports **analysing** UK **public spending**. By doing this, the OBR **helps** the government to keep its fiscal policy **under control**.

Governments use fiscal policy to **Tackle Poverty**

For more information on poverty and ways to tackle it, turn to pages 50-53.

1) Fiscal policy can be used to **reduce poverty** in a country. **Three** key ways a government can do this is through **benefits**, **provision** of **certain goods** and **services**, and **progressive taxation**.
2) Government spending on **benefits**, e.g. JSA, pensions and disability benefits, is a way of **helping** those who are **unemployed** or **unable** to work, and reducing **absolute poverty**.
3) A government can also spend its tax revenue to **provide** goods and services, such as free health care or education, to enable those who are suffering from poverty to have **access** to these things.
4) Furthermore, by **providing** some **goods** and **services** to poorer members of society, a government will be **investing** in the **improvement** of its country's **human capital** — i.e. this spending may make **labour** (one of the factors of production) **much more productive**.
5) **Progressive taxation** may **reduce relative poverty** by **narrowing** the **gaps** between people's **disposable income**, and the revenue raised can pay for benefits and the state provision of goods and services. On top of this, governments could **provide tax cuts** and **discounts** for the **poor**.
6) Finally, if fiscal policy creates **growth**, then this may reduce both **relative** and **absolute poverty**. Greater economic growth will mean **more jobs**, **higher incomes** and a **better standard of living**.

The government's physical policy was a big hit with Claude and Sue.

The **Size** of **Government Spending** can be affected by several things

1) The **size** and **structure** of a **country's population** will affect levels of government spending. For example, a country with a **large population** may require greater levels of government spending than a country with a **small population**, and a country with an **ageing population** will have **greater demand** for **state-funded health care**.
2) Government policies on **inequality**, **poverty** and the **redistribution of income** will alter the amount of government spending — this might vary from government to government depending on their **political views**. For example, a government that wants to redistribute income may **spend more** on **benefits**.
3) The **fiscal policies** governments use to tackle **certain problems** in a country will also have an effect. During a **recession** a government may increase public spending to **encourage growth** and **reduce unemployment**, but if these policies lead to a **large national debt** then the government may introduce '**austerity measures**' and **severely reduce** their spending.

Practice Questions

Q1 Briefly explain the difference between automatic stabilisers and discretionary fiscal policy.

Q2 What does the Laffer curve show?

Q3 Give three examples of problems caused by large, long-term national debt.

Exam Question

Q1 Discuss how taxation can be used to help a government reduce inequality in a country. [10 marks]

People laugh, but I love the automatic stabilisers on my bike...

Hmm, there's a lot to take in here, so go through it all carefully. Demand-side fiscal policy has gone out of fashion now — it's a bit clunky, leads to overspending for little reward, and demand-side tinkering can cause conflicts between macroeconomic objectives.

Monetary Policy

These pages are for AQA Unit 4, Edexcel Unit 4 and OCR Unit 5 (The Global Economy).
Monetary policy is largely about setting interest rates. But there's a lot of things to take into account as you do it.

Monetary Policy is about Controlling Money

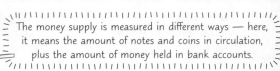

The money supply is measured in different ways — here, it means the amount of notes and coins in circulation, plus the amount of money held in bank accounts.

1) **Monetary policy** involves making decisions about **interest rates**, the **money supply** and **exchange rates**.
2) Monetary policy has a huge effect on **aggregate demand** — it's a **demand-side** policy.
3) The most important tool of monetary policy is the ability to set **interest rates**. Changes to interest rates affect **borrowing**, **saving**, **spending** and **investment**.
4) Interest rates also affect the other components of monetary policy — the **money supply** and **exchange rates**. For example, a **high** interest rate can **restrict** the money supply as there'll be **less demand** for loans.

See page 113 for more about exchange rates.

5) Monetary policy can either be **contractionary** ('tight') or **expansionary** ('loose'):
   - **Contractionary monetary policy** — this involves **reducing** aggregate demand (AD) using high interest rates, restrictions on the money supply, and a strong exchange rate.
   - **Expansionary monetary policy** — this involves **increasing** aggregate demand using low interest rates, fewer restrictions on the money supply, and a weak exchange rate.
6) As with **demand-side fiscal policy** (see p.108), monetary policy **can't** help achieve **all** of a government's macroeconomic objectives simultaneously — there's a **trade-off**. For example, using monetary policy to **increase economic growth** and **reduce unemployment** may mean **increasing inflation** and **worsening the current account** of the balance of payments.
7) In the UK, the main aim of monetary policy is to ensure **price stability** — i.e. **low inflation**. But it also has the aims of **promoting economic growth** and **reducing unemployment**.

Interest Rates are set by the Monetary Policy Committee (MPC)

1) The **Monetary Policy Committee** (**MPC**) of the **Bank of England** sets interest rates in order to meet the inflation target that's set by the government — this target is currently **2% inflation**, as measured by the **Consumer Price Index** (CPI).
2) If the MPC believed that inflation was likely to get **too high** with current interest rates, it would **increase** the official rate of interest (sometimes called the **Bank Rate** or **Base Rate**) to **reduce** aggregate demand and keep inflation close to 2%.
3) A low rate of inflation that's **stable** and **credible** (i.e. trustworthy and accurate) stops higher rates of inflation becoming **embedded** in the economy (see p.104). It also helps a government achieve **macroeconomic stability** — a high or rapidly changing rate of inflation creates **uncertainty**, prevents **investment**, and makes it difficult to **plan** for the future.
4) To achieve this **stability** and **credibility**, the Bank of England is **independent** and **accountable**:
   - The Bank of England's **independence** means that interest rates **can't** be set by the government at a level that will win votes, but which might not be right for the economic circumstances at the time.
   - The Bank of England is **accountable** — if the inflation rate is **more than 1%** away from the **target rate** (either above or below), then the Bank's Governor must write to the Chancellor to explain **why** the target has been missed.
5) Although price stability is the **main objective** of monetary policy, the Bank of England must pursue this in a way that **doesn't harm** the government's other macroeconomic policy objectives (e.g. economic growth or low unemployment).
6) When the MPC is making a decision on interest rates it will look at important **economic data**, such as:
   - house prices,
   - the size of any output gaps,
   - the pound's exchange rate,
   - the rate of any increases or decreases in average earnings.
7) The MPC has to consider interest-rate changes very carefully, since these changes can have a **huge** effect (see next page).

Monetary Policy

A Rise in Interest Rates causes a Ripple Effect

Even very small changes in interest rates can create a '**ripple effect**' through the whole economy.
Here are some likely effects of an **increase** in interest rates:

- less **borrowing**,
- less **consumer spending** (i.e. less **consumption**),
- less **investment** by firms,
- less **confidence** among consumers and firms,
- more **saving**,
- a decrease in **exports**,
- an increase in **imports**.

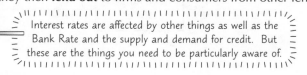

All these 'ripple effects' are explained by the transmission mechanism — see p114.

A **decrease** in interest rates will have the **opposite effects**.

Markets affect Interest Rates too

1) The **Bank Rate** is the lowest rate at which the Bank of England will lend to financial institutions (e.g. banks). But it **isn't** the rate of interest that you'd pay if you applied to a high-street bank for a **mortgage** or took out a **bank loan**.
2) However, these various types of interest rates are **linked** — if the Bank Rate goes **up**, then that will usually lead to interest rates charged on mortgages and bank loans also **increasing**. The same happens in reverse if the Bank Rate **falls** — i.e. other interest rates in the economy will also **fall**.
3) But the Bank Rate is **not** the **only** thing that affects these 'market' interest rates.
4) For example, banks often need to **borrow** the money that they then **lend out** to firms and consumers from other lenders. If lots of banks are trying to borrow money at the same time, then they'll have to pay a **higher rate** of interest themselves, which will affect the cost of mortgages and loans they offer to **consumers**.

Interest rates are affected by other things as well as the Bank Rate and the supply and demand for credit. But these are the things you need to be particularly aware of.

Interest Rates affect Exchange Rates

1) When interest rates are **high** in the UK, big financial institutions (such as large banks or insurance companies) want to **buy the pound**. They do this so that they can put their money into UK banks and take advantage of the **high rewards** for savers brought about by the high interest rates. This is likely to be a short-term movement of money and it's called '**hot money**'.
2) An **increased demand** for the pound means its **price goes up** — i.e. the pound's exchange rate **rises**.
3) Unfortunately, a **high exchange rate** makes UK exports **more expensive**.

- Suppose the **exchange rate** of the pound against the dollar is **£1 = $2**. And suppose a British firm makes pens that cost, say, £1.
- To buy one of these British pens, someone in the USA would first have to buy the pound. This would mean that the price of one of these pens in the USA is effectively **$2**, since it costs them **$2** to buy **£1**, and then they can spend this £1 on buying a pen.
- Now suppose the exchange rate **changed** to **£1 = $4** (i.e. the pound's exchange rate goes up, or the pound becomes **stronger**).
- Someone in the USA would now have to spend **$4** to pay for the same £1 pen. Remember, the pen's price in the UK **hasn't changed** at all — this **extra cost** to the person in the USA is **all** to do with the **cost** of **buying pounds**.

4) When this happens **exports go down**, **worsening** the current account on the **balance of payments**.
5) For the same reason (but in reverse), **high** UK interest rates mean **imports** from abroad become **cheaper**. Again, this **worsens** the current account.
6) And remember... imports are a **leakage** in the circular flow of income, and so more spending on imports means a **reduction** in AD.
7) When UK interest rates **fall**, the opposite happens:

- The **exchange rate** of the pound **falls**.
- UK **exports increase** (as UK goods become cheaper) and **imports decrease** (as foreign goods become more expensive).
- The **balance of payments improves**.

Remember though, this depends on the price elasticity of demand of exports and imports.

Jimmy always got excited when the decisions of the Monetary Policy Committee were about to be announced.

Monetary Policy

The diagram on this page looks fairly intimidating, but it's only describing things you've already read about. So don't panic.

*The **Transmission Mechanism** shows the effect of **Interest-Rate Changes***

The **knock-on effects** that a change to the official Bank Rate can have are best shown by the **transmission mechanism** — this is shown in the diagram below. The **end result** of any **change** in the **official Bank Rate** will be a **change** to the level of **inflation**.

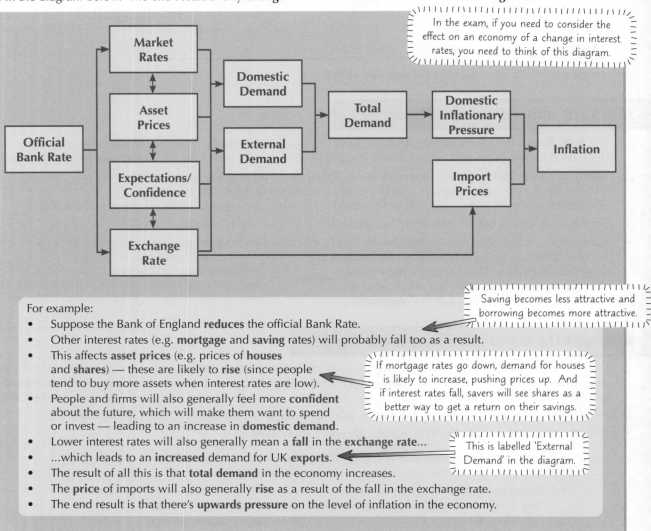

In the exam, if you need to consider the effect on an economy of a change in interest rates, you need to think of this diagram.

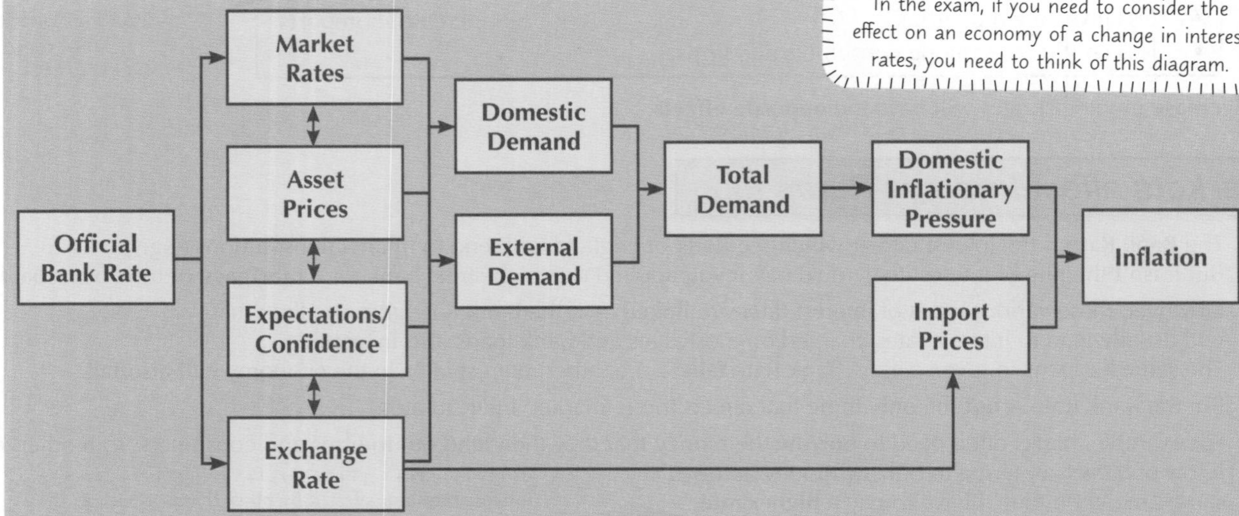

For example:

- Suppose the Bank of England **reduces** the official Bank Rate.
- Other interest rates (e.g. **mortgage** and **saving** rates) will probably fall too as a result.
- This affects **asset prices** (e.g. prices of **houses** and **shares**) — these are likely to **rise** (since people tend to buy more assets when interest rates are low).
- People and firms will also generally feel more **confident** about the future, which will make them want to spend or invest — leading to an increase in **domestic demand**.
- Lower interest rates will also generally mean a **fall** in the **exchange rate**...
- ...which leads to an **increased** demand for UK **exports**.
- The result of all this is that **total demand** in the economy increases.
- The **price** of imports will also generally **rise** as a result of the fall in the exchange rate.
- The end result is that there's **upwards pressure** on the level of inflation in the economy.

Saving becomes less attractive and borrowing becomes more attractive.

If mortgage rates go down, demand for houses is likely to increase, pushing prices up. And if interest rates fall, savers will see shares as a better way to get a return on their savings.

This is labelled 'External Demand' in the diagram.

*Monetary policy needs to look about **Two Years** into the **Future***

1) The effect of changing interest rates is **not** felt straight away — it takes time for the effects to feed through the transmission mechanism shown in the diagram above.
2) For example, reducing interest rates **won't** usually cause a **sudden surge** in investment or house buying.
   - Firms **plan** investment projects **very carefully** — it can take months or years before they increase their spending.
   - **House buying** can also take a long time — people first need to **find** a suitable home, and then the actual purchase can take a long time too. **Fixed-rate mortgage** holders won't even notice the effect of an interest rate change until their fixed-rate period ends.
3) In fact, the **time lags** between changes in the Bank Rate and its effect on the economy can be very long indeed.
   - The maximum effect on **firms** is usually felt after about **one year**.
   - The maximum effect on **consumers** is usually felt after about **two years**.
4) So the Bank of England has to look up to **two years** into the future when it's making a decision about interest rates.

These are 'typical' time lags — actual time lags can be very different.

Monetary Policy

Quantitative Easing injects New Money into the Economy

1) **Quantitative easing** (QE) is used when it's necessary to adopt a 'loose' monetary policy to **stimulate aggregate demand** (or create upwards pressure on **inflation**) at a time when interest rates are already very **low** (or **negative**).
2) QE **increases** the **money supply**, which will enable individuals and firms to spend more.
3) It involves the Bank of England 'creating new money' and using it to **buy assets** owned by **financial institutions** and other firms. The hope is that these will then either **spend** the money or **lend** it to other people to spend.

Aggregate demand was low because the 2007 'credit crunch' (when banks suddenly cut back the amount they were willing to lend) had reduced aggregate demand.

4) QE was introduced in the UK in 2009. **Aggregate demand** needed to be stimulated after the **2008 recession**, but **interest rates** were already at a very **low** rate (0.5%).

Treasury bills are a form of government debt.

- The Bank of England **bought assets** (e.g. government Treasury bills) from firms such as insurance companies and commercial banks.
- However, QE was **slow to work** at first because the banks were still reluctant to lend money after the credit crunch. Instead they used it just to increase their reserves of money.
- Eventually these banks did begin to **lend** money to other firms and individuals — who used the money to, for example, invest in new machinery, start new businesses or buy houses.
- All of this spending boosted **aggregate demand** and led to an increase in the rate of **inflation** (see below).

5) Using QE to bring up the rate of inflation (rather than decreasing interest rates) has the added benefit that it will keep a **currency weak** (i.e. its exchange rate will remain low). This can increase the **competitiveness** of an economy and **boost exports**.
6) QE also provides a boost to overall **confidence** in an economy (especially during a recession), as consumers and firms see the central bank taking action.
7) One **danger** of using QE is that financial institutions may initially use this 'new money' to increase their reserves, and only **lend** it out when the **economy improves**. This **extra lending** at a time when **inflation** may already be **increasing** can lead to demand-pull inflation becoming harder to control.

Although the Bank of England could use QE 'in reverse' — i.e. sell assets to institutions to decrease the amount of money in circulation.

The Bank of England also has to consider the Wider Economy

1) The **main aim** of monetary policy in the UK is to ensure **price stability** — i.e. keep **inflation** close to its **target rate**. Under normal circumstances, this would mean that during a period of **high inflation**, interest rates would **increase**.
2) But between January 2010 and March 2012, inflation was **3%** or **higher** (and so was outside the 1% limit above the 2% target), but the Bank of England **kept** interest rates at 0.5% during this entire period and **continued** its use of QE.
3) The reason is that the UK economy had suffered some '**economic shocks**', and there were concerns about the possibility of entering the second dip of a '**double dip**' recession.
4) The Bank of England reasoned that raising interest rates was **unnecessary** — it said inflation would fall **naturally** even without an interest rate rise, and that if it did increase interest rates, then a double dip recession was **more likely**.
5) Remember... as long as inflation is under control, the Bank has a duty to support the government's economic objectives. The Bank therefore continued with its very **loose monetary policy** in order not to further harm the economy.

Practice Questions

Q1 What are the Monetary Policy Committee's objectives when setting the UK's official interest rate?

Q2 Use the transmission mechanism to show why an increase in the official Bank Rate can put downward pressure on inflation.

Exam Question

Q1 Explain the use of quantitative easing and analyse the effects it can have on an economy. [10 marks]

I use quantitative easing to squeeze into my favourite jeans...

Yeah, that diagram's not at all scary or complicated. Piece of cake. Nothing could be simpler. Okay... you saw through me. It looks a nightmare, I agree. But don't get too down about it... just write down the steps involved for both an increase and decrease in interest rates a couple of times, and you'll get a feel for how it all hangs together. I mean it. Do it. You'll regret it if you don't.

Supply-side Policies

These pages are for AQA Unit 4, Edexcel Unit 4 and OCR Unit 5 (The Global Economy).
Supply-side policies are very popular at the moment among economists. That goes for Economics examiners too.

Supply-side Policies aim to Increase the economy's Trend Growth Rate

1) The aim of supply-side policies is to **expand** the **productive potential** (i.e. long run aggregate supply) of an economy, or to increase the **trend rate** of growth, as shown in these diagrams.

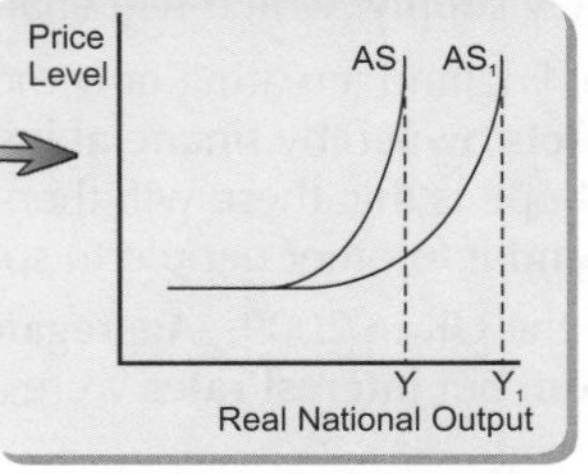

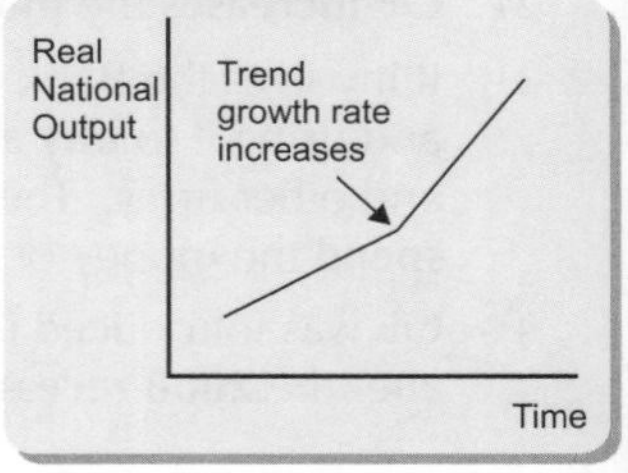

2) Supply-side policies are about the government creating the **right conditions** to allow **market forces** to create **growth**, as opposed to the government creating growth **directly** by, for example, increasing its spending or subsidising industries.
3) Supply-side policies involve making **structural changes** to the economy to allow its 'individual parts' to work **more efficiently** and **more productively**.
   - For example, some supply-side policies aim to help **markets** function more efficiently.
   - Other supply-side policies might involve creating **incentives** for **firms** or **individuals** to become more **productive** (or more **entrepreneurial**).
4) The effects of supply-side policies are generally **microeconomic** — i.e. their direct effects are usually on **individual** workers, firms or markets. However, these changes can have a powerful **macroeconomic** effect.
5) Supply-side policies can make an economy more **robust** and **flexible**.

High taxes can create unhelpful disincentives to work — supply-side policies may aim to correct these.

Supply-side policies can Increase the Efficiency of various Markets

Supply-side policies can be used to make markets function **more efficiently** or to correct a **market failure**.
Here are some examples of supply-side policies that might be used in different kinds of markets:

There are more examples of supply-side policies on pages 105 and 109.

The Product Market

- **Create incentives** for firms to **invest**, for example:
  - Offer firms **tax breaks** (i.e. reductions in the amount of tax they need to pay) if they **invest** profits back into the business **instead** of paying **dividends** to shareholders.
- **Trade liberalisation** — this means removing or reducing **trade barriers**, and allowing goods and capital to flow more freely between countries.
- **Encourage competition**, for example:
  - **Deregulation** (see p.45) can lead to improved **efficiency** in a market.
  - **Privatisation** (see p.44) may be effective if **nationalised** industries are **inefficient**.
  - **Contract services out** — this means the government asks private firms to bid to carry out services on its behalf (though the government retains responsibility for the service).
  - Provide extra support for **new** and **small firms**, or make it easier to set up a **new company**.

The Capital Market

Deregulation of financial markets — e.g. The 'Big Bang' of 1986 removed a lot of the traditional **'restrictive practices'** that were felt to have made British financial markets (e.g. banks and stockbrokers) inefficient.

The Labour Market

- **Reduce unemployment benefits** — to create **incentives** for people to take a job (even a low-paid one) rather than live on benefits. Making it easier for people to **find out** about what jobs are **available** can also help.
- **Reduce (or reform) income tax** — introducing **progressive taxation** with the aim of creating more **incentives** for people to work (e.g. by ensuring that people **don't** become **worse off** if they take a job or earn a pay rise).
- Improve **education and training**:
  - E.g. apprenticeships allow people to learn **practical skills** while gaining relevant **qualifications**.
  - Improvements in education will not only allow employees to become more **productive**, but can also lead to greater **occupational mobility** (see p.67).
- Improve **labour market flexibility** — e.g. through **trade union reforms**, or by making it easier for firms to make workers **redundant** when times are tough.
- **Reduce regulations on firms** — this would **reduce** firms' **non-wage costs** and may **encourage** them to **employ more workers**.

Progressive taxation is on p.109.

See p.105 for more about labour market supply-side policies.

Supply-side Policies

Suitable Demand-side policies are needed alongside supply-side policies

1) Supply-side policies aim to make an economy more able to **supply** products. But for maximum benefit there needs to be a **demand** for those products — this means appropriate **demand-side policies** are also necessary.
2) Nowadays, supply-side and demand-side policies are often used together, but to achieve different aims:
   - **Supply-side** policies create **long-term growth**,
   - **Demand-side** policies **stabilise** the economy in the **short term**.

It also means that during a global recession, supply-side policies might not have their full impact until other countries' economies start to recover as well.

Example — Tackling unemployment

- Using an expansionary fiscal policy to boost **aggregate demand** might reduce unemployment. However, a supply-side economist would say that reducing unemployment in this way **doesn't change** the natural rate of unemployment (**NRU** — see p.104). So when the effects of your expansionary fiscal policy end, unemployment is likely to **return** to its **'pre-boost equilibrium'**.

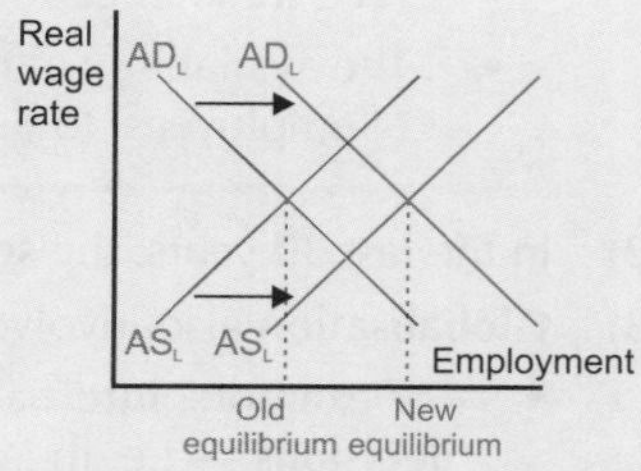

- A supply-side approach to this problem might be to try to **reduce the NRU** itself, i.e. create a **new equilibrium position** in the labour market. The hope is that this effect is likely to be more **long-lasting**. In the diagram, for example:
  - **Tax breaks** encouraging firms to **invest** have created **greater demand** for **labour** (i.e. the AD_L curve shifts right).
  - **Increased incentives** to work have created a **greater supply** of **labour** (i.e. the AS_L curve shifts right too).
  - The overall effect is that the equilibrium position in the labour market has moved to the **right** (meaning employment has risen, and that the **NRU** should **fall**).
- However, demand-side policies can still be useful in tackling **short-term** surges in unemployment.

There are huge potential Benefits of supply-side policies

Increasing the economy's **trend growth rate** makes it easier for a government to achieve its **macroeconomic objectives**, with fewer **conflicts** between **objectives** (such as those described on p.106-107) — which isn't the case with demand-side policies.

- For example, **unemployment** should fall as the **economy grows** and output expands.
- And **cost-push inflation** should be reduced, as greater efficiencies (and lower costs) are achieved.
- The **current account** of the **balance of payments** should also improve because of increased international **competitiveness**.

Supply-side policies are Not Perfect in every way

1) It can take a **long time** to see the results of supply-side policies, so they **can't** be used to fix the economy **quickly**. For example, it'll take **many years** to see the effects on an economy's labour supply that occur from **improvements** in **education**.
2) There can be **unintended consequences** — e.g. the deregulation of financial markets (starting with the 'Big Bang' in 1986) led to excessive **risk-taking** in financial markets, which contributed towards the recent recession.
3) Supply-side policies can be **unpopular**, and there are also concerns about whether some are **inequitable** (i.e. **unfair**).
   - For example, **benefit cuts** can lead to the poorest people in society worrying about their ability to cope financially.
   - **Greater flexibility** in the labour market and **trade-union reforms** could lead to some people having **less job security**.
4) So while a government may hope that improved economic performance will lead to **greater prosperity** overall in the **long term**, it can be very difficult in the short term to introduce some of these policies.

Practice Questions

Q1 Why are suitable demand-side policies important if supply-side policies are to be effective?

Q2 Explain some of the possible criticisms of supply-side economic policies.

Exam Question

Q1 To what extent should government macroeconomic policy focus on supply-side policies rather than demand-side policies? [25 marks]

Supply-side policies aren't perfect — they're useless for making a lasagne...

In practice it's actually quite difficult to create increases in trend growth rate using supply-side policies. But at the moment, supply-side policies are economists' and governments' favourite tool for trying. So they're probably just going to have to try quite hard and for quite a long time, given that there are few alternatives around that are clearly better. Okay... see what you remember.

Globalisation

These pages are for AQA Unit 4, Edexcel Unit 4 and OCR Unit 5 (The Global Economy).
There are many aspects to globalisation — it's all about the world's economies increasingly becoming more like one economy, through things such as increased trade and the movement of labour and capital.

Globalisation is about the world becoming more like a Single Economy

1) **Globalisation** is the **increasing integration** of economies **internationally**. The **main characteristics** of **globalisation** are:
   - The **free movement** of **capital** and **labour** across international boundaries.
   - **Free trade** in **goods** and **services** between different countries.
   - The availability of **technology** and **intellectual capital** (e.g. the knowledge of employees) to be used (and patented) on an **international scale**.
2) In the last 30 years, the **scale** and **pace** of globalisation has dramatically **increased**.
3) **Globalisation** also involves **political** and **cultural** factors:
   - For example, **international bodies** such as the United Nations (UN) tend to lead to a **convergence** of **political decisions** — i.e. there are more joint decisions made between countries, and more international cooperation.
   - Examples of **cultural globalisation** include the spread of things such as **McDonald's** and **yoga** across the world.
4) Some of the other **characteristics** of globalisation include:
   - **International** trade becoming a greater **proportion** of **all** trade.
   - An increase in **financial capital flows** between countries.
   - Increased **integration** of **production** — e.g. different parts of a product being produced in different countries.
   - A **greater number** of countries becoming **involved** in **international trade**.
   - An **increase** in **foreign ownership** of firms.
   - **Deindustrialisation** of developed countries, and the **industrialisation** of developing countries.
   - More international **division** and **movement** of labour — i.e. the labour used to produce products is **divided** between **more countries** or **moves** from developed to less developed countries. For example:
     - Developing countries are increasingly obtaining the levels of **skills** and **technology** needed to produce goods for **more developed** countries. Furthermore, labour is also **relatively cheap** in developing countries compared to developed countries.
     - These factors have led to foreign companies starting to **produce goods** in developing countries, especially if there are other appealing factors for foreign companies, such as a **good transport network** in the developing country.
     - For example, **India** provides **software development** for many **European** companies.

Many firms Operate in More Than One Country

1) A **key** feature of globalisation is the growth of **multinational corporations (MNCs)**.
2) MNCs are firms which function in **at least** one other country aside from their country of origin — e.g. Nissan and KFC®.
3) Factors which **attract** MNCs to **invest** in a country are:
   - The **availability** of **cheap labour** and **raw materials**.
   - Good **transport** links.
   - **Access** to different markets.
   - **Pro-foreign investment** government policies.
4) MNCs may choose to **divide** their operations and **locate** each part in the country with the **lowest costs**.
5) For example, this can be done by **offshoring** (setting up a company abroad) and by **outsourcing** (subcontracting work to another organisation).

Multinational corporations are sometimes referred to as multinational companies or transnational corporations or companies (TNCs).

Globalisation

There are many **Causes** contributing to **Globalisation**

Trade liberalisation — this is the **reduction** or **removal** of **tariffs** and other **restrictions** on international trade (i.e. reducing protectionism). Countries might **negotiate** these trade agreements using the **World Trade Organisation (WTO)**.

See p.127-129 for more on the WTO and protectionism.

A reduction in the **real cost** and **time needed** for the transportation of goods means that it's **cheaper** to export and import. For example, due to the development of **larger cargo ships**.

Improvements in **communications** technology — for example, the internet is making the communication needed for international trade **easier** and **cheaper**.

Firms, especially MNCs, wishing to **increase profits** — for example, this means they might **invest** in setting up a factory in a developing country where labour is **cheaper**.

Globalisation had allowed Barney to fulfil his life-long dream of performing on the West End.

An increased **number** of MNCs and the growth of their **significance** and **influence** — for example, as MNCs have a greater influence, there's likely to be more **international trade** of goods and services, and more **international investment**.

Governments wishing to obtain the **benefits** of increased trade (see p.122) — so, for example, a government might provide **incentives** for foreign firms to **encourage** them to invest in their country.

The **opening** of new (or more) markets to **trade** and **investment** — for example, following the **collapse** of the Soviet Union after the Cold War, many communist Eastern European countries (including Russia) previously had **closed economies**. Also, China **opening** its economy to trade and then **joining** the WTO in 2001 has had a **big** impact on globalisation.

Increasing amounts of **foreign direct investment (FDI)** by MNCs. Foreign direct investment just means a firm **based** in **one country** making an investment in a **different country**. For example, there have been large amounts of **capital invested** in China from **overseas**.

Increasing investment by sovereign states — e.g. Norway **invests** some of its **oil revenues** in **foreign companies**.

More international **specialisation** (see p.122) — if countries specialise in making the products they're **best** at making, this will **encourage international trade**.

Practice Questions

Q1 Briefly define what is meant by globalisation.

Q2 Give three characteristics of globalisation.

Q3 Give three causes of globalisation.

Exam Question

Q1 Over the past two decades, developing countries, such as India, have seen increased investment from multinational corporations (MNCs). Explain why an MNC might invest in a country like India. [6 marks]

Globalisation has many more characteristics — it's optimistic, adventurous...

So globalisation is about all the world's economies integrating to become more like one, single, big economy. Globalisation can't happen unless economies are open to trade and investment, so a key part of globalisation is the reduction or removal of any barriers. Don't forget that as well as trade between economies, globalisation involves other factors, such as the existence of MNCs.

Costs and Benefits of Globalisation

These pages are for AQA Unit 4, Edexcel Unit 4 and OCR Unit 5 (The Global Economy).
Globalisation has various consequences, costs and benefits. Although many people see globalisation as a positive thing, there are certain elements which might need controlling, e.g. so that workers aren't exploited or to reduce environmental damage.

Globalisation has brought many **Benefits** to economies

1) Trade encourages countries to **specialise** in the goods and services they're best at producing/providing, which **increases output**.
2) **Producers** can benefit from **economies of scale** and **lower** production costs because markets become **bigger** when countries trade. Global sourcing (i.e. countries buying things, such as raw materials, from anywhere in the world) has also led to **lower** raw material **costs**.
3) Globalisation can allow countries to produce the things where they have a **comparative advantage** (see p.123), leading to an improvement in **efficiency** and the **allocation of resources**.
4) **Lower production costs** are also sometimes passed on to **consumers** in the form of **lower prices**.
5) Globalisation provides consumers with a greater **choice** of goods and services to purchase.
6) **World GDP** has risen as a result of globalisation due to many factors — for example, increased **efficiency** means firms can **increase output**. Countries which **aren't** open to trade have seen a **reduction** in their growth rates.
7) Globalisation has also helped to **reduce** the levels of **absolute poverty** in the world because levels of world **employment** have **increased** — e.g. as increased output has meant the creation of **more jobs**.
8) Increases in **competition** brought about by globalisation can lead to lower prices for consumers.
9) There has been an **increased awareness** of, and quicker response to, **foreign disasters** (e.g. earthquakes) and **global issues** (e.g. **deforestation**) and their consequences.

Globalisation also has **Drawbacks** for economies

1) Globalisation is causing the **price** of **some** goods and services to **rise** — **increasing world incomes** lead to **increasing demand** for goods and services, so when **supply** is **unable** to meet this demand, **prices rise**.
2) Globalisation can lead to **economic dependency** (i.e. countries' economies being dependent on each other), so this can lead to **instability** in economies — for example, if the US economy goes into a **recession** and **reduces** its imports, this may cause **European** economies to go into a recession too.
3) Increasing **world trade** has led to global **imbalances** in balance of payment accounts. Some countries, e.g. the USA, have large **deficits** and others, e.g. China, have large **surpluses**. These balances are **unsustainable** (see p.110), leading to calls for increased protectionism.
4) **Specialisation** can lead to **overreliance** on a few industries by an economy, which is risky (see p.122).

MNCs have both **Positive** and **Negative Effects**

Positive Effects

- Foreign direct investment (FDI) by MNCs creates **new jobs**, and brings **new skills** and **wealth** to an economy. MNCs also **buy** local goods and services, leading to **inflows** of foreign currency.
- MNCs can benefit from **economies of scale**, helping them to be **more efficient**, i.e. they can produce products more cheaply.
- Some people believe MNCs **raise living standards** by providing **employment**.

FDI also occurs in developed countries, for example, the UK is the recipient of very high levels of FDI.

Negative Effects

- Some people argue MNCs **exploit** workers in developing countries by paying them **lower wages** than in **developed** countries.
- MNCs can force local firms **out of business** — for example, because local firms might be **unable** to obtain similar **economies of scale**, they'll be **less competitive**.
- MNCs can relocate rapidly and cause **mass unemployment**.
- They can **withdraw profits** from one country and place them in another with **low tax rates** — so the former country **won't** be able to gain **tax revenue** from those profits.
- They can use their economic power to **reduce choice** and **increase prices**.
- MNCs can **influence** government policies in other countries to their advantage, which can be **unfair** to local people or **unhelpful** to the domestic economy.
- Governments may be forced to **reduce corporate tax levels** to attract or keep MNCs in their country.

Costs and Benefits of Globalisation

Globalisation has a Big Impact on the Environment

1) Environmental **degradation** has resulted from globalisation. For example, international trade leads to an increase in the **international transportation** of goods — this means **more** fossil fuels are used, contributing to **climate change** and causing **resource depletion** (see p.41).
2) Carbon emissions are also increased by, for example, **rising production levels** of manufactured goods to meet rising **global demand**.
3) Other threats to the environment that are **linked** to globalisation include:
   - **Deforestation** — from logging for wood and the clearing of forests for factories or farmland.
   - Increasing depletion of other **non-renewable** resources, e.g. metal ores.
4) Some people argue that international trade is **not sustainable** at current levels if its **environmental impact** is considered.

Globalisation Consequences differ for Developing and Developed countries

1) Globalisation may have contributed to **increasing** levels of **inequality** between countries and within countries.
2) There are **large differences** in income between **more economically developed** countries, e.g. the USA, and **less economically developed** countries, e.g. Cambodia.
3) In some **developing countries**, such as India and Brazil, there are **big** income gaps between their **wealthiest** and **poorest** citizens.

Consequences of globalisation for developing countries

- **Health and safety laws** are generally **less strict** in **developing** countries and MNCs may take advantage of this.
- MNCs may **exploit** workers by offering very **low wages**.
- **Skilled workers** often **leave** developing countries to work in more developed countries. This **reduces** the developing country's **potential** for **economic growth**.
- However, globalisation **creates** jobs, **reducing** unemployment.
- MNCs often bring **more efficient** production methods and **technology** to developing countries.

There are varying opinions on whether globalisation is a good thing for developing countries — you need to weigh up the costs against the benefits.

Consequences of globalisation for developed countries

1) **Cheap** overseas production of goods has led to a severe **reduction** in some industries in **developed** countries, causing **structural unemployment** (see p.100). For example, cheap clothes from countries such as Bangladesh have **contributed** to the **collapse** of the **textile industry** in the UK.
2) Such collapses lead to **deindustrialisation**, which has **further impacts** on economies — such as a **fall** in exports.
3) **Increased** levels of **imports** result from increased trade and have a **negative effect** on a country's balance of payments.
4) Globalisation gives countries **greater access** to cheap raw materials and semi-manufactured goods from other countries, which can be used in the **production** of domestic goods. These goods can then be exported or sold domestically.
5) MNCs gain access to **cheap labour**, which leads to **lower production costs** and **lower prices** for consumers.

Practice Questions

Q1 Give two environmental costs of globalisation.

Exam Question

Q1 Evaluate the likely advantages and disadvantages of globalisation for a developing country. [15 marks]

FDI — Federal Desk of Investigation...

For some globalisation questions, you'll have to consider the different effects on the various parties involved — make sure you remember that globalisation can have both positive and negative effects in developing and developed countries.

Trade

***These pages are for** AQA Unit 4, Edexcel Unit 4 **and** OCR Unit 5 (The Global Economy).*
When countries trade internationally, they tend to start to specialise in the products they're best at producing.
The law of comparative advantage can be used to help judge the amount of output that countries should produce.

There are many **Advantages** to **International Trade**

1) Countries **can't** produce all the things they **want** or **need** because resources are **unevenly distributed.**
2) **International trade**, which is the **exchange** of goods and services **between** countries (i.e. imports and exports), can give countries **access** to resources and products they otherwise **wouldn't** be able to use — countries can **export** goods in order to **import** the things they can't **produce** themselves. For example, the UK exports goods so that it can import things such as tea, rice and diamonds.
3) By trading internationally, not only do a country's consumers enjoy a **larger variety** of goods and services, but increased **competition** resulting from international trade can lead to **lower** prices and **more** product innovation — so people's **standards of living** are raised by having more **choice**, and **better quality** and **cheaper** products.
4) **Additional markets** (i.e. markets abroad) allow firms to exploit more **economies of scale** — if the additional markets mean there's an **increase** in **demand** for their products.
5) International trade can also expose firms to **new ideas** and **skills** — for example, a MNC might bring **new manufacturing skills** to a **developing** country.

International Trade allows countries to **Specialise**

1) International trade allows countries to **specialise** in the goods and services they're **best** at **producing**.
2) Countries specialise because:
   - They have the **resources** to produce the good or service **efficiently**.
   - They're **better** than other countries at producing the good or service.
3) Specialisation has its **advantages**:
   - **Costs** are **reduced**, which can be passed on to **consumers** in the form of **lower prices**.
   - The world's resources are used **more efficiently**.
   - Global output is **increased** and living standards are **raised**.

International Trade and **Specialisation** also have their **Disadvantages**

International Trade

1) Trading internationally usually involves **higher transport costs.**
2) **Currency exchanges** when trading abroad can carry costs, potentially resulting in **financial losses.**
3) There are other **costs** to firms that trade internationally, such as **complying** with other countries' legal and technical requirements, **translating** legal documents and advertising material, and **performing market research** for overseas markets.
4) International trade increases **globalisation**, which has its own **disadvantages** — see p.120.

Toby specialised in cuteness.

Specialisation

1) National industries may be forced to **shut down** because **foreign firms** are **better** at producing the goods or services provided by that industry.
2) Specialisation can lead to **overreliance** on **one** industry — if something happened to **negatively** affect that industry, it would have a **severe impact** on the **whole** economy.
3) Countries are **vulnerable** to cuts in the supply of goods that they don't produce themselves.
4) Specialisation can have **negative impacts** on a country's exchange rates, balance of payments and unemployment levels — for example, the loss of a national industry is likely to result in **increased** unemployment.

Trade

It's useful to consider **Absolute Advantage** when looking at **Trade**

1) A country will have an **absolute advantage** when its output of a product is **greater per unit of resource used** than any other country.
2) To explain absolute advantage economists make a number of **simplifying assumptions**.

Example 1 — absolute advantage

Assume:
- There are only **two countries** in the world, A and **B**, who each have the **same amount** of resources.
- They both produce **only crisps** and **chocolate**.
- If each country splits its resources **equally** to produce the **two** goods, then output would be:

	Units of crisps output per year	Units of chocolate output per year
Country A	1000	5000
Country B	2000	3000

Before specialisation, world production of crisps is 1000 + 2000 = 3000 units, and of chocolate is 5000 + 3000 = 8000 units.

- Country A has the **absolute advantage** in producing chocolate and country B has the **absolute advantage** in producing crisps.
- So if the countries **specialised** in the products they have an absolute advantage in, then **world production** of crisps would rise to 4000 units (all produced by country B) and of chocolate to 10 000 units (all produced by country A). (Remember — each country **splits** its resources **equally** between the two products, so if country A **only** made chocolate, then the **half** of its resources that **were** used to make **crisps** would be used for **chocolate** instead, and chocolate production would **double**.)
- Through specialisation, **more output** is produced using the **same amount** of resources — so the **cost per unit is reduced**.

Comparative Advantage uses **Opportunity Costs**

1) **Comparative advantage** uses the concept of **opportunity cost** — the opportunity cost is the **benefit** that's **given up** in order to do something else. In this case, it's the number of units of one good not made in order to produce one unit of the other good.
2) A country has a comparative advantage if the opportunity cost of it producing a good is **lower** than the opportunity cost for other countries.

Example 2 — comparative advantage

Make the same **assumptions** as above, but this time country A and country B produce **only wheat** and **coffee**. If they each split their resources **equally**, they can produce the following quantities:

	Units of wheat output per year	Units of coffee output per year	Opportunity cost of wheat	Opportunity cost of coffee
Country A	3000	3000	1 unit of coffee	1 unit of wheat
Country B	2000	1000	½ unit of coffee	2 units of wheat
Total output before specialisation	5000	4000	–	–

- Country A has the **absolute advantage** in producing **both** wheat and coffee.
- Country A has the **lower opportunity cost** in producing **coffee**, and therefore the comparative advantage — i.e. if country A makes **one extra unit of coffee**, it must give up **one unit of wheat**, but if country B makes **one extra unit of coffee**, it must give up **two units of wheat**.
- Country B has the **lower opportunity cost** in producing **wheat**, and therefore the comparative advantage — i.e. if country B makes **one extra unit of wheat**, it must give up **half of a unit of coffee**, but if country A makes **one extra unit of wheat**, it must give up **one unit of coffee**.

Flip to the next page to see what happens when the countries specialise.

Trade

Specialising Fully often Won't increase output

Example 3

- Using **example 2** from the previous page, if the countries specialise **fully** in the goods they have a comparative advantage in, allocating **all** of their resources to **one product**, total output of **coffee** will **increase** from 4000 to 6000 units, but total output of **wheat** will **decrease** from 5000 to 4000 units (see the table below).
- However, it's possible to increase the output of **both** goods by only reallocating **some** resources. Countries can **split** production and then **trade**. For example, in the bottom row of the table below, ¼ of country A's resources are allocated to wheat and ¾ to coffee, while country B just specialises in wheat. By using **partial** specialisation, wheat and coffee output are **both** greater than they were **before** specialisation.

	Units of wheat output per year	Units of coffee output per year	Opportunity cost of 1 unit of wheat (1W)	Opportunity cost of 1 unit of coffee (1C)
Country A	3000	3000	1 unit of coffee (**1C**)	1 unit of wheat (**1W**)
Country B	2000	1000	½ unit of coffee (**½C**)	2 units of wheat (**2W**)
Total output before specialisation	5000	4000		
Total output after specialisation	4000	6000		
E.g. of total output with partial specialisation	1500 (country A) 4000 (country B)	4500 (country A)	–	–

If country B specialises in wheat and stops making coffee, it can only double its wheat output to 4000 units with the resources it has.

- Countries are **unlikely** to specialise 100% — instead they produce at a level where their combined production of **both** goods is **greater** than without specialisation.
- For trade to **benefit** both countries, the **terms of trade** must be set at the right level (see below).
- If the **opportunity cost** of production is the **same** in both nations, there would be **no benefit** from trade.

Trade should be Beneficial to All countries involved

1) Usually, for trade to occur between two countries, **both** countries must **benefit** from trading, or at least not be any **worse off** than if they **hadn't** traded. So, **neither** country will **pay more** for a good than it would **cost** for them to **produce** it themselves, and **neither** will **accept less** for a good than it **costs** for them to **produce** it.
2) Whether trade is beneficial or not depends on the **opportunity cost ratios** for each country.
   - For Country A above, the opportunity cost ratio of wheat to coffee is **1C : 1W**.
   - For Country B, the opportunity cost ratio of wheat to coffee is **1C : 2W**.

   These ratios come from either of the last two columns in the table.
3) As long as the **rate of exchange** lies between **"1C for every 1W"** (i.e. 1C : 1W) and **"1C for every 2W"** (i.e. 1C : 2W), trade will benefit at least one of the two countries, while neither will be worse off.
4) For example, suppose the countries agree to trade at a rate of exchange of **"1C for every 1.5W"** (i.e. 1C : 1.5W). Then the cost to country A of **importing** 1.5W is 1C — this is **less** than the **opportunity cost** of producing 1.5W **itself** (= 1.5C). And by **exporting** 1.5W, country B receives 1C, which is **more** than it'd be able to produce **itself** — country B would have to give up **2W** to produce **1C** itself.

If a country's Terms of Trade Rises then it's Better Off — if it Falls then it's Worse Off

1) A country's **terms of trade** is the **relative** price of its **exports** compared to its **imports**.
2) In the real world, a country's **terms of trade** is often described using an index number. It's **calculated** using the formula:

$$\text{terms of trade index} = \frac{\text{index of average price of exports}}{\text{index of average price of imports}} \times 100$$

Think of a country's terms of trade as the 'rate of exchange' used between it and the rest of the world — i.e. the amount of imports it can buy per unit of exports.

3) If the price of a country's **exports rises**, but the price of its **imports stays the same**, its **terms of trade index** will **increase** — e.g. if a country exports lots of tea and the price of tea **rises**, its terms of trade index is likely to **rise** (e.g. from 102 to 120). This increase will mean it'll effectively become **'better off'**, as it'll be able to afford more imports.
4) And if a country's terms of trade index **falls** (e.g. from 110 to 105), it'll effectively be **worse off**.
5) For example, during the recession in 2008-2010, the UK's terms of trade index fell — this was because the price of its imports rose more quickly than the price of its exports.

Trade

Comparative Advantages may be Difficult to Assess in the Real World

1) Comparative advantages **fluctuate**, e.g. because costs of production **vary** — so it's hard to keep track of **how much** of each good countries should be producing.
2) The law of comparative advantage is based on several **assumptions**, which make it hard to apply it to the **real world**:
   - There are **no economies** or **diseconomies** of scale.
   - There are **no transport costs** or **barriers to trade**.
   - Factors of production are **mobile**.
   - There's **perfect** knowledge.
   - Externalities are **ignored**.

EDEXCEL ONLY

Comparative Advantage can be seen using Production Possibility Frontiers

1) Remember, a production possibility frontier (PPF) shows the **maximum amounts** of two goods/services that an economy can produce with a **fixed** level of resources.
2) The diagram shows the **PPF curves** for the two countries in example 3 on the previous page — e.g. if country A produces **only wheat**, it can produce **6000** units.
3) The **gradient** indicates which country has the **comparative advantage** in each good. The **steeper** gradient of **country B's PPF** shows it has the comparative advantage in **wheat**, whereas the **gentler** gradient of **country A's PPF** shows it has the comparative advantage in **coffee**.
4) By using **specialisation** and **trade**, countries can consume **outside** of their PPF.
5) For example, using example 3 from the previous page, country A splits production, so it produces 1500 wheat and 4500 coffee, and country B produces 4000 wheat and no coffee. If country B **exports 2000 wheat** to country A, and country A **exports 1500 coffee** to country B, then country A will consume at **point P** and country B will consume at **point Q** — which are both **beyond** their respective PPFs.

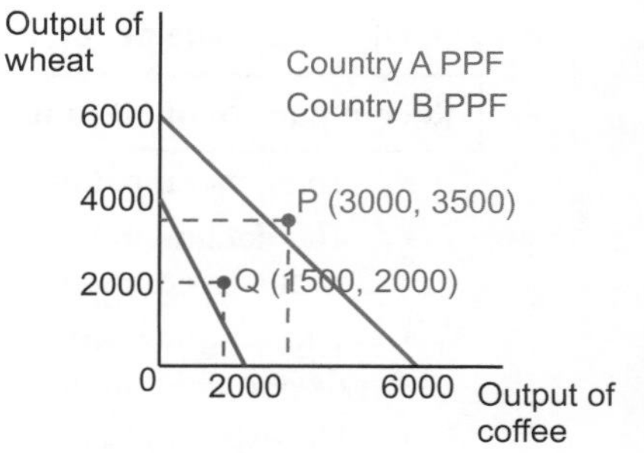

The country with the gentler PPF gradient has the comparative advantage in the good on the x-axis, and the country with the steeper PPF gradient has the comparative advantage in the good on the y-axis.

Trade is Important for Developing and Developed countries

1) You also need to think about how the benefits of trade **vary** for **developed** and **developing** countries. For example:

For developed countries

- Imports are **crucial** to **maintaining high standards of living** in developed countries.
- Products will often be **cheaper** when bought from abroad — e.g. due to **increased competition** and **cheaper labour** in developing countries.

For developing countries

- Developing countries can **import** goods they don't have the technology to produce themselves, which results in a **higher** standard of living.
- Trade also gives these countries access to **new materials**, meaning **new industries** will be **created** because they can produce **new products**. This will help to **improve** the economies of developing countries.

2) Look back at the **benefits** of **globalisation** (see p.120) and of **trade** (see p.122) — these benefits will apply to **both** developed and developing countries.

Practice Questions

Q1 What is international trade?

Q2 What is the difference between absolute and comparative advantage?

Q3 List three assumptions of comparative advantage which limit its application in the real world.

Exam Question

Q1 Explain two possible benefits of international trade for developing countries. [6 marks]

The opportunity cost of not learning these pages is X marks in your exam...

Although there are disadvantages to international trade and specialisation, most countries choose to trade because the benefits seem to outweigh the costs. However, for trade to be beneficial, things such as comparative advantage need to be considered.

Patterns of Trade

This page is for AQA Unit 4, Edexcel Unit 4 and OCR Unit 5 (The Global Economy).
Trade is an important factor affecting the development of countries. The pattern of trade has changed dramatically over the last century — developing countries such as China are now playing a major role in international trade.

UK trade has seen a Rise in Imports and a Fall in Exports

1) The UK has **high levels** of imports and exports. It's the **second** largest **exporter** of **services** in the world.
2) The UK's main **exported goods** are things such as **cars**, **fuels** and **pharmaceuticals**.
3) The **biggest** single market for **UK exports** is the **USA** — but just under **half** of the UK's exports go to countries in the **European Union (EU)**.
4) Like many other countries, the UK often **imports** and **exports** the **same types** of goods — the UK's main **imported goods** are **cars**, **fuels** and **pharmaceuticals**.
5) Most UK **imports** come from the **EU**, **China** and the **USA**.
6) The UK has a **trade deficit** in **goods** and a **trade surplus** in **services**.

Recent pattern of UK trade

- The **general** pattern in UK trade since 2000 has seen exports **fall** and imports **rise**.
- The **decline** in UK exports is similar to that seen in most other **major industrialised** countries, and is due to **competition** from **emerging** and **newly industrialised** economies, such as China.
- UK imports have tended to **rise** for similar reasons — goods are often **cheaper** to buy from **less developed** countries. However, the country the UK imports the **most** from is **Germany**.
- UK exports to countries such as **China**, whose economies are **growing** extremely quickly, are **rising**.
- However, the level of the **exports** going to **China** and **India** are both **less than 5%** of the UK's total exports.

World Patterns of trade are Changing

1) A hundred years ago, **developed** countries, such as the **UK**, had a **comparative advantage** in **manufactured** goods, whereas **developing** countries had a **comparative advantage** in **primary** goods, such as commodities.
2) Most trade took place **between developed** and **developing** countries.
3) Now, **developed** countries tend to have a comparative advantage in **high** value, **technologically advanced**, **capital-intensive** products, and **developing** countries tend to have a comparative advantage in **low** value, **labour-intensive** products.
4) **Developed** countries do most of their trade with **other developed** countries.
5) **Developing** countries also tend to do **most** of their trade with **developed** countries.
6) **China** and **India** have had a big impact on the recent pattern of world trade. They're both now important **global** traders.
7) China is the **largest exporter** and the **second largest importer** of goods in the world. Its **main** exports are **electronic equipment** and **machinery**.
8) China's **high-tech industry** has seen **rapid growth** in recent years — it's now the **largest** exporter of **high-tech** goods.
9) India's **main** goods exports are **fuels** and **materials**, e.g. **glass**. It's also a big exporter of **services**, such as **IT services**.

Megan had the pattern part sorted — it was just the trade that wasn't going so well.

Practice Questions

Q1 List three changes in the pattern of trade in the UK since 2000.

Q2 List four changes in the pattern of world trade that have taken place over the last 100 years.

Exam Question

Q1 Discuss how the growth of China and India's economies may affect the UK. [8 marks]

CGP imports 83% of its jokes from Vanuatu...

Economies such as China are having a big impact on the patterns of international trade — China is now the biggest exporter of goods in the world. However, most trade still occurs between developed countries — e.g. the UK imports the most from Germany.

Free Trade, Protectionism and the WTO

These pages are for AQA Unit 4, Edexcel Unit 4 and OCR Unit 5 (The Global Economy).
The World Trade Organisation (WTO) wants to promote free trade, but countries often impose policies to protect their domestic industries. Sometimes countries form trading blocs, which have both positive and negative effects on free trade.

***Free Trade** means **Unrestricted** international trade*

1) **Free trade** is international trade **without restrictions** such as tariffs or quotas (see below). Free trade provides **benefits** from specialisation, increased competition and the ability to transfer resources (see p.122 for more trade benefits).
2) Trade restrictions have been **reduced** in recent years — mainly amongst members of **trading blocs** (see next page).
3) The **World Trade Organisation (WTO)** aims to help trade to be as **free** as possible. It's an international organisation which provides a forum for its **member governments** to **discuss trade agreements** and **settle disputes**, using a set of **trade rules**.
4) The WTO currently has **over 150 members**, including the countries with the biggest economies.
5) The WTO has **many agreements** its members must follow — some examples of the principles behind them are:
   - Countries must treat **all** their **trading partners**, and **foreign** and **domestic** goods, **equally**.
   - The WTO wants to **encourage** competitiveness and **discourage** trade barriers, such as subsidies.
6) The WTO has played a big part in the **movement towards free trade** in recent years.

Governments** might want to use **Protectionist Policies

1) Governments might want to impose certain **trade barriers** to tackle the **disadvantages** of **free trade**:
   - **To protect jobs** — there might be a risk of too many **job losses** if domestic firms are **outcompeted** by foreign firms.
   - **To protect infant industries** — industries that are just starting out, particularly in developing countries, struggle to compete with **international** companies. Governments might choose to impose trade barriers until the companies **are** big enough to compete. However, there's a **risk** that the industry may never become **truly** competitive, and in the meantime, **domestic consumers** are stuck with **higher** prices or **lower quality** goods.
   - **To ban certain goods** — the government may simply want to **ban** certain goods altogether because they consider them to be **bad** for **society**, e.g. firearms or drugs.
   - **To avoid overdependence** — specialisation could lead to **overdependence** on **one** industry (see p.122).
   - **To protect against dumping** — when companies sell goods abroad at a price that's **below** the production cost to try to **force** other countries' domestic producers **out of business**.
   - **To correct imbalances in the balance of payments** — see p.131.
2) There are various tariff and non-tariff **policies** governments can use to **protect** domestic industries:
   - **Tariffs** can be imposed in the form of a tax on selected imports. This makes imports more expensive, which helps **domestic** manufacturers to compete and raises **tax revenue** for the government.
   - **Quotas** can be fixed, which limit the **quantity** of a certain good that can be imported — any demand for the good **above** the quota will be **diverted** to **domestic products**.
   - **Embargoes** (bans) can be imposed on certain products — these are usually restricted to **extreme** cases, e.g. drugs or elephant ivory, but may also be for **political** reasons, e.g. if two countries are having a **disagreement**, they might impose embargoes on imports from **each other**. Embargoes tend to be **less** about protecting **domestic industries** and **more** about politics or enforcing laws.
   - The value of the currency can be **reduced** — this **raises** the price of **foreign** imports and **lowers** the price of **domestic** exports.
   - Tight **product standard regulations** can be imposed — foreign products which don't comply with the requirements **cannot** be imported. Product standard regulations could include things such as **high safety** standards, or **low emissions** requirements. These might be used for **environmental** or **consumer protection**, or to help to protect **domestic** industries that **can comply** with the **regulations**.
   - **Subsidies** can be given to domestic producers — this **reduces** the cost of production of domestic products, making them cheaper to buy, but subsidies can be **costly** to a government.

Non-tariff policies are just any barriers which don't involve actual tariffs.

3) **Trade disputes** occur when one country or trading bloc (see p.128) is seen to be acting **unfairly** when trading internationally. Trade disputes might be caused by the use of **protectionist policies** — for example, one country may see the subsidies paid by **another country's government** to one of its **domestic industries** as **unfair**.

EDEXCEL ONLY

Free Trade, Protectionism and the WTO

Tariffs (or Customs Duties) are a Tax imposed on certain Imports

1) Tariffs are a common form of **protectionism**. They're a tax that can be a **fixed amount** per unit or ***ad valorem*** (i.e. a percentage of the value of a good).
2) In this example, a **fixed** tariff per unit is imposed on imports — this **increases** the price for **domestic consumers** from P_e to P_1. The tariff is P_1 minus P_e:
   - Domestic demand **reduces** from D to C.
   - The **consumer surplus** reduces from P_e**LH** to P_1**LK**.
   - Domestic supply **increases** from A to B.
   - The level of **imports falls** from AD to BC.
   - The **producer surplus** increases from **M**P_e**E** to **M**P_1**J**.
   - The level of **tax revenue** raised by the government is **JKGF**.
   - There's a **net welfare loss** of **EFJ** and **GHK**.

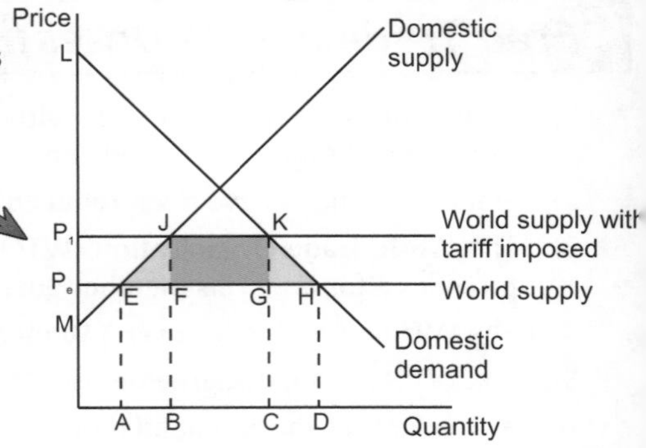

Some people don't think Protectionism is a good thing

1) Restricting imports **reduces** specialisation, **diverting** resources away from their **most efficient** use — this reduces **allocative** and **productive efficiency**.
2) Protectionism will mean **prices** tend to be **higher**, as there's a **lack** of **specialisation** and **competition**.
3) Once trade barriers are in place, it can be **difficult** to **remove** them — industries may **depend** on them to **survive**, so removing them could **destroy** domestic industries.
4) If **demand** for imports is **high**, this could be due to **poor domestic efficiency** — a **lack** of competition **doesn't** encourage firms to **improve** their efficiency, so there'll continue to be a **misallocation of resources**.
5) Trade barriers imposed by one country may lead to **retaliation** by other countries — this is often referred to as a **'trade war'**. It **reduces** world trade, worsening other problems — e.g. there'll be a further **misallocation** of resources caused by **inefficiency** and a **lack** of **specialisation**.

Trading Blocs are Agreements between governments about Trade

1) **Trading blocs** are associations between different governments that **promote** and **manage** trade.
2) This tends to mean that **members** make agreements to **remove** or **reduce** protectionist barriers between them.
3) **Bilateral** agreements are between **two** countries or trading blocs, e.g. between the EU and one other country.
4) **Multilateral** agreements are between **more than two** countries or trading blocs.
5) There are **different types** of trading blocs:

- **Free trade areas** — all barriers to trade are **removed** between members, but **individual** members can still **impose barriers** on outside countries. For example, the North American Free Trade Agreement (NAFTA).
- **Customs unions** — these are **free trade areas** where there are also **standard tariffs** imposed on **non-members**. For example, the EU or Mercosur (made up of some South American countries).
- **Common markets** (sometimes referred to as **single markets**) — these are **customs unions** with the addition of the **free movement** of factors of production between members. For example, the Single European Market (SEM) (see p.136).
- **Economic unions** — trading blocs might be referred to as economic unions when their economies become **more integrated**, e.g. member states adopt the **same**, or **similar**, economic policies, regulations and rules.
- **Monetary unions** — members implement a **single**, **common currency**, and therefore have a common **monetary policy**, usually controlled by a **central bank**. For example, the Eurozone.
- **Economic and monetary union** — a monetary union will usually **also** be an economic union, so it might be referred to as an economic and monetary union.

> You might see slightly different definitions of each type of union, especially for economic unions and monetary unions — but just make sure you're aware of the key features of each.

Free Trade, Protectionism and the WTO

Trading Blocs can sometimes Conflict with the WTO

1) Trading blocs can lead to **trade creation** — this is when patterns of trade change after barriers are removed, as a result of products being bought from the cheapest source. Removing barriers also allows countries within the trading bloc to **specialise** in the products where they have a **comparative advantage**. This **helps** with **WTO** objectives, as it **opens** up trade, **encouraging** competitiveness and therefore **improving** efficiency.
2) Trading blocs can also lead to **trade diversion** — if **trade barriers** are imposed on non-members, trade will be **diverted** away from any **cheaper non-members**. It means countries outside the trading bloc **aren't** able to fully use their **comparative advantage** by specialising, as trade is **restricted**. This **conflicts** with WTO objectives, as it **interferes** with competition, **preventing** the lowest-cost, most efficient products from being traded, e.g. by raising their prices through tariffs.
3) Trading blocs between **developed** countries can **limit** the development of developing countries if they **aren't** members and **cannot** trade on equal terms.
4) Trading blocs can help to **reduce protectionism** on a **global** scale by **reducing** the number of parties that have to **negotiate** a trade agreement. However, they can **limit** progress towards **free trade** if there's **excessive** trade diversion.

EXAMPLE

- The EU's **Common Agricultural Policy (CAP)** has caused **disputes** between the EU and other countries.
- The CAP uses measures such as **subsidies** and **buffer stocks**, along with **import restrictions** on goods from outside the EU, to guarantee a **minimum price** for many agricultural products. For example, **tariffs** are placed on **imported goods** to allow the guaranteed minimum price level to be maintained.
- When stocks build up, governments **sell** these excess stocks at a **low price** outside of the EU — this **harms** farmers outside the EU who **cannot compete** with such **low prices**.
- After disputes with other countries, in recent years the EU has reformed its CAP. As a result, prices have **moved closer** to the **market price** — but there are still problems with the policy.

The WTO has a Varying impact on Developing economies

1) Developing countries might be **prevented** from **protecting** infant industries by WTO policies — stopping them from **diversifying** away from agriculture. Not only will this harm **individual** economies, but it might **hold back** worldwide improvements in efficiency, e.g. through **specialisation**.
2) However, **free trade** has been a **major** factor in the rapid economic development of nations such as **China** and **India**.
3) The WTO played a part in the **reduction** of the level of subsidies on the EU's agricultural goods — this reduction has led to developing nations' agricultural products becoming **more competitive**.

Kevin's infant industry involved selling pumpkins.

Practice Questions

Q1 What is the WTO?

Q2 Give two arguments for protectionism.

Q3 List three non-tariff forms of protectionism.

Q4 What is a tariff?

Q5 Give three arguments against protectionism.

Q6 How might a trading bloc conflict with the WTO?

Exam Questions

Q1 How might a government use protectionist policies to protect infant industries? [10 marks]

Q2 Define what is meant by a 'customs union'. [2 marks]

think these pages are just tariff-ic...

he WTO aims to promote free trade, but countries are often reluctant to trade freely, as they want to protect their own industries. lany countries are members of trading blocs, who'll trade freely between themselves, but impose restrictions on non-members.

The Balance of Payments

These pages are for AQA Unit 4, Edexcel Unit 4 and OCR Unit 5 (The Global Economy).
Make sure you look back at everything you learnt on the balance of payments at AS.

The BOP records All Financial Transactions of a country with Other countries

1) The **balance of payments (BOP)** records **all** flows of money **into** and **out of** a country.
2) The UK BOP is made up of the **current** account, the **capital** account and the **financial** account. You should know about the current account from AS. It's made up of trade in **goods** (visible trade), trade in **services** (invisible trade), **investment income** and **transfers**.
3) The **capital** account includes **transfers** of **non-monetary** and **fixed** assets — the most important part of this is the flow of non-monetary and fixed assets of **immigrants** and **emigrants**, e.g. when an immigrant comes to the UK, **their assets** become part of the UK's **total assets**.
4) The **financial** account involves the movement of financial assets. It includes:
   - **Foreign direct investment** (FDI) (see p.119).
   - **Portfolio investment** — investment in **financial** assets, such as **shares** in overseas companies.
   - **Financial derivatives** — these are **contracts** whose value is based on the **value** of an asset, e.g. a **foreign currency**.
   - **Reserve assets** — these are **financial assets** held by the **Bank of England**. They're there to be used **as and when** they're needed.
5) **Income** from the **financial** account, e.g. in the form of **interest**, is **recorded** in the **current** account.
6) The current account **should balance** the capital and financial accounts, e.g. a deficit of £5bn on the current account should be offset by a surplus of £5bn on the capital and financial accounts. However, due to **errors** and **omissions**, the current account and capital and financial accounts often **don't** balance, so a **balancing figure** is needed.

You don't need to know about the capital and financial accounts in great detail — just make sure you understand the difference between them.

There are both Short-term and Long-term capital and financial flows

1) **Long-term** flows are due to things such as FDI and portfolio investment. They're usually quite **predictable** as, for example, FDI is often made when a country gains a **comparative advantage** in producing something, which tends to happen over a **long** period of time.
2) **Short-term** flows (sometimes called '**hot money**' — see p.113 for more) are based on **speculation** and people/firms trying to **quickly** make money — e.g. by **moving** money from one currency to another expecting to make a profit through **changes** in **exchange rates**.

For OCR, you need to be aware that private financial flows come from individuals and firms, and official financial flows go to and from governments and other official organisations (e.g. the EU).

There are usually Many Causes of a BOP Surplus or Deficit

1) A country might experience a **current account deficit** if:
   - Its domestic currency has a **high value** — this will make exports **more expensive** and imports **cheaper**.
   - It's a developed country which is experiencing a **reduction** in **manufacturing** — this is likely to lead to an **increase** in imports and a **fall** in exports.
   - It has **structural problems**, e.g. labour immobility, which are making domestic products and exports **more expensive**.
2) A country might experience a **current account surplus** if:
   - It's been experiencing a **recession** — sometimes domestic producers will **struggle** to sell products domestically, so they'll focus their efforts on competing in **international** markets instead. There may be a **fall** in imports too as a result of an **overall reduction** in spending.
   - Its domestic currency has a **low value** — this will make exports **cheaper** and imports **more expensive**.
   - **High interest rates** are causing **more** saving and **less** spending.

The UK has a deficit on its current account
- In recent years, the UK has had a **deficit** on its balance of payments. Although the UK has usually had a **surplus** in **invisible trade**, it has also had a **large deficit** in **visible trade**.
- One of the reasons for the UK's **surplus** in **invisible trade** is the fact that the **City of London** provides **large** amounts of **international financial services**, e.g. option traders and insurance brokers.
- The **large deficit** in **visible trade** is caused by **many** factors — for example, there's been a **decline** in UK **manufacturing**, largely due to a **lack of competitiveness**.

The Balance of Payments

There can be Consequences of a BOP Surplus or Deficit

BOP deficit

1) A balance of payments **deficit** could indicate that an economy is **uncompetitive**.
2) A deficit **isn't always** a bad thing — it might mean that people in that country are **wealthy** enough to be able to afford **lots of imports**. A deficit may also allow people to enjoy a **higher** standard of living, as they're importing the things they want and need. But, a **long-term deficit** is likely to cause problems.
3) The consequences of a deficit include a **fall** in the value of a currency, leading to **higher import prices** — at least in the **short run**. Take a look back at your **AS notes** for more consequences of a BOP deficit.

BOP surplus

1) **Surpluses** can show that an economy is **competitive**.
2) However, if a country has a **surplus** for a **prolonged** period of time, e.g. Japan, they may experience **stagnation**. This means that, for example, due to **low domestic demand**, they'll experience **low**, or even **negative**, **economic growth** — which also has the potential to lead to **other** problems, such as **high unemployment**.
3) A large surplus on a current account may also be a result of an economy's **overreliance** on **exports**.
4) If a surplus is created by a country having an **undervalued currency**, this will create **inflationary pressures** — the price of **imported components** for use in **production** will **rise**, meaning a **rise** in the **costs of production** and therefore a **rise** in the **price level**.

Governments often try to Correct Imbalances in the BOP

1) Governments might try to correct a **BOP deficit**:
   - They might use **policies** to **reduce** the price of **domestic** goods — this should **increase** exports and **reduce** imports. For example, a government might use **supply-side policies** to remove **structural** problems (see p.116 for more).
   - Governments might impose **restrictions** on **imports** — for example, a government might impose **tariffs** on **imports** to make them **relatively** more expensive (compared to domestic goods) for **domestic consumers**. This might cause **inflation** if demand for imports is too **price inelastic**.
   - They may **devalue** (fixed exchange rate systems) or **depreciate** (floating exchange rate systems) the **currency** (see p.132) — this will make exports **cheaper** and imports more **expensive**. For this to be **successful**, the Marshall-Lerner condition must hold (see p.134).
   - Governments might use **fiscal** or **monetary policy** to reduce spending in the economy (see p.108-112 for more) — however, as well as **reducing imports**, it's likely to also **reduce domestic demand** and harm economic growth.
2) Governments might try to correct a **BOP surplus** — for example, they might **raise** the value of their currency. This will **reduce** the demand for **exports** and **increase** the demand for **imports**. However, this is likely to result in a **reduction** in output and has the potential to cause a **rise** in unemployment.
3) When the governments of **major economies** try to correct imbalances in their BOP, it can have **global impacts**:
   - **Supply-side policies** to correct deficits may lead to an **increase** in **world trade** and **growth**.
   - **Restrictions** on imports can lead to **trade wars**, **reducing** international trade and leading to **lower** global efficiency. Restrictions might also break **WTO rules** (see p.127).
   - If a government's attempts to reduce its BOP deficit lead to a **fall** in exports from **developing** countries, this may have many **negative** consequences. For example, **economic growth** in those developing countries will be **limited**, leading to a **rise** in **unemployment**. **Reduced** economic growth in developing countries has the potential to **hold back** global improvements in **efficiency**.

Practice Questions

Q1 Briefly explain the difference between the current, capital and financial accounts of the balance of payments.

Q2 List four methods a government might adopt to remove a persistent trade deficit.

Exam Question

Q1 The US has a current account deficit on its balance of payments, and it imports a lot of goods from China. Evaluate the possible benefits to the US balance of payments current account of a rise in the value of the Chinese renminbi. [15 marks]

Stag Nation — the world's #1 destination for deer...

Phew — there's quite a lot to learn on the balance of payments, but don't let it overwhelm you. Make sure you can see how it links to other aspects of the economy, e.g. exchange rates and economic growth... and don't forget what you learnt at AS.

Exchange Rates

These pages are for AQA Unit 4, Edexcel Unit 4 and OCR Unit 5 (The Global Economy).
Exchange rates have an impact on many aspects of the economy, such as economic growth, inflation and the balance of payments. Some countries set a fixed exchange rate, whilst others mainly leave a floating exchange rate to market forces.

There are **Two** main types of **Exchange Rate**

1) A **fixed** exchange rate is where the **government** or its **central bank**, such as the Bank of England, sets the exchange rate. This often involves **maintaining** the exchange rate at a **target rate** (see below).
2) A **floating** exchange rate is free to **move** with changing supply of and demand for a currency.
3) However, exchange rates can also be **semi-fixed** exchange rates or **managed floating** exchange rates:
   - **Semi-fixed** means the exchange rate is allowed to **fluctuate** within a **set band** of exchange rates.
   - **Managed floating** means the government plays some part in **influencing** the exchange rate, but it's mainly left to **market forces**.

Market Forces or **Government Intervention** can cause exchange rates to **Rise** or **Fall**

1) The **devaluation** of a **fixed** exchange rate occurs when the exchange rate (i.e. the value of the currency) is **lowered** formally by the government. They can achieve this by **selling** the currency.
2) The **opposite** of exchange rate **devaluation** is exchange rate **revaluation** (achieved by **buying** the currency).
3) The **depreciation** of a **floating** exchange rate is when the exchange rate (i.e. the value of the currency) **falls**. This might occur naturally by **market forces**, or the government might **influence** it, e.g. by either **selling** the currency or **lowering** interest rates.
4) The **opposite** of exchange rate **depreciation** is exchange rate **appreciation**.

This crowd **really** appreciated the exchange rate.

Fixed exchange rates have to stay at a **Target Rate**

1) **Fixed** exchange rates have a **target** rate. However, they'll often be allowed to **fluctuate** slightly from this rate, so they'll actually be **semi-fixed** exchange rates.
2) Fixed exchange rates **won't** be completely free to change with changing **supply** and **demand** for the currency. Instead, a **government** or **central bank** will use **interest rates** and **foreign currency reserves** to maintain the exchange rate at the target rate, by **preventing** large changes in supply of or demand for the currency.
3) This will be achieved by **controlling** interest rates so they're at a level which **keeps** supply of and demand for a currency **steady**, and by **buying** and **selling** the currency (using foreign currency reserves) to also keep supply and demand **stable**.
4) Sometimes an exchange rate will be '**pegged**' to another country's exchange rate. This means the government **adjusts** the exchange rate so that the **value** of its currency **rises** and **falls** by the **same amount** as the currency it's pegged to.

OCR ONLY

Exchange Rates don't always reflect the **True Worth** of two currencies

1) To **overcome** the problem that exchange rates don't always reflect the **true worth** of two currencies, the principle of **purchasing power parity (PPP)** can be used.
2) **Purchasing power** is the **real** value of an amount of money in terms of what you can **actually** buy with it. This can **vary** between countries — for example, in a **less developed** country, e.g. Malawi, $1 will buy **more** goods than in a **more developed** country, e.g. Canada. **Relative** inflation rates and differences in the **cost of living** will influence the purchasing power of a currency.
3) So PPP can be used to find the **true relative value** of two different currencies by taking into account the **identical** goods and services each currency will buy in the two countries. It's often **better** to use PPP than exchange rates to make comparisons between different nations' currencies because it takes into account the **differences** in their economies.

Exchange Rates

Floating and Fixed exchange rates both have Advantages and Disadvantages

	Advantages	Disadvantages
Floating	Under **fixed** exchange rate systems, central banks require **foreign currency reserves** so that they can intervene to maintain their exchange rate target — a **floating** exchange rate will **reduce** the need for currency reserves.	Floating exchange rates can **fluctuate** widely, which makes business planning **difficult**.
Floating	A floating exchange rate can help to **reduce** a BOP current account **deficit** — a BOP deficit will lead to a **fall** in the value of the currency, so if demand for exports and imports is moderately **price elastic**, exports will **increase** and imports will **decrease**, reducing the BOP deficit.	Speculation can **artificially strengthen** an exchange rate — this would cause a country to **lose competitiveness**, as domestic goods will become **over-priced**.
Floating	A floating exchange rate means that a government **doesn't** need to use monetary policy, e.g. interest rates, to help to maintain the exchange rate — it can use it for **other objectives**.	**Falls** in exchange rates can lead to inflationary pressures — for example, if demand for imports tends to be **price inelastic**.
Fixed	Fixed exchange rates create **certainty** which is likely to **encourage** investment.	The country effectively **loses control** of interest rates, as they need to be used to keep the **exchange rate** at the desired level.
Fixed	**Speculation** may be **reduced** — unless dealers feel that the exchange rate is no longer **sustainable**.	If speculators feel a fixed exchange rate **isn't sustainable**, they might take advantage of this by **selling** the currency.
Fixed	**Competitive pressures** are placed on firms — they need to keep costs **down**, **invest** and **increase productivity** to remain competitive.	Fixed exchange rates are **difficult** to maintain.

Supply and Demand determine Floating exchange rates

1) Floating exchange rates are determined by **changes** in **supply** and **demand** for a currency.
2) For example, an **increase** in the **supply** of pounds to S_1 will cause a **decrease** in the **value** of the pound to P_1. This increase in supply may be due to things such as an **increase** in **imports** to the UK and **increased selling** of the pound.

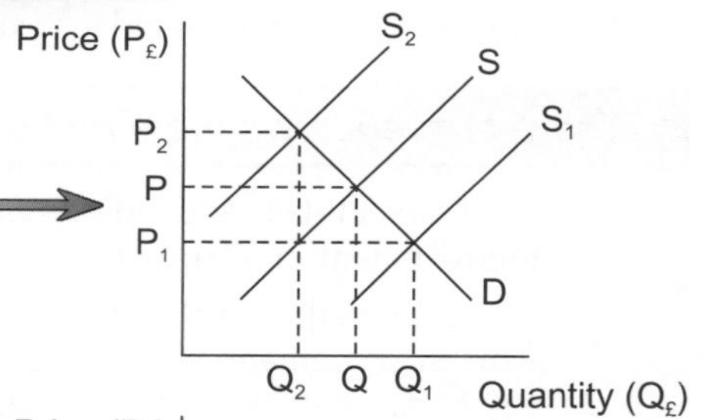

3) A **decrease** in the **demand** for pounds to D_1 will cause a **decrease** in the **value** of the pound to P_1. This decrease in demand may be due to, for example, a **decrease** in **exports** from the UK and **decreased buying** of the pound.

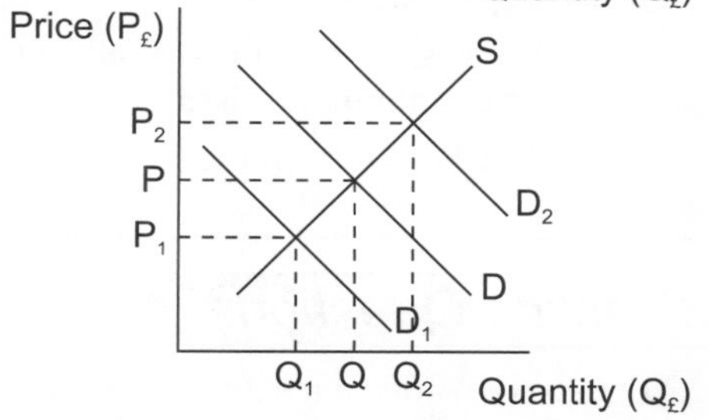

4) Supply and demand **fluctuations** are caused by many factors, for example:

- **Changes** in the **levels** of imports and exports (see above).
- **Speculation** — where people **buy** and **sell** currency because of changes they **expect** are going to happen in the future.
- The **official** buying and selling of the currency by the **government** or **central bank**.
- **Relative inflation rates** — if a country's inflation rate is **higher** than its **competitors'**, then the **value** of its currency is likely to **fall**. **Prices** in the country will become **less competitive**, leading to **reduced exports** and **increased imports**, so **demand** for the currency **decreases** and **supply increases**.
- **Relative interest rates** — **high** interest rates **increase demand** for a currency because there's an **inflow** of '**hot money**' (see p.113 and 130).
- **Confidence** in the state of the economy — there'll be **greater demand** for a currency if people feel confident in, for example, a country's **growth** and **stability** (this will include a country's **economic** and **political** stability — investors are **unlikely** to have confidence in **unstable** governments).
- The balance on the **current account** of the balance of payments has a **small** effect on the exchange rate — for example, a current account **deficit** will mean there's a **high supply** of the currency due to the **purchase** of **imports**.

Exchange Rates

Fluctuations in the Exchange Rate have Impacts on the economy

1) If the value of a currency **falls**:
   - **Exports** will become **cheaper**, so domestic goods will become **more competitive**.
   - This means that **demand** for **exports** will **increase**.
   - **Imports** will become **more expensive**, so **demand** for **imports** will **fall**.
   - A current account **deficit** should therefore be **reduced**, but a surplus should **increase**.
2) The current account deficit will only reduce if the **Marshall-Lerner** condition holds — see below.
3) The **J-curve** shows how the current account may actually **worsen** in the **short run**, but **improve** in the **long run** — see below.
4) A **fall** in the value of a currency can also mean:
   - If exports increase and imports decrease, there'll be **economic growth** caused by an **increase** in aggregate demand.
   - **Unemployment** may also be **reduced** through the **creation** of more jobs from economic growth.
   - **Inflation** may **rise** if demand for imports is **price inelastic**.
   - **Increased** import prices can also cause **cost-push** inflation.
5) A **rise** in the value of a currency will tend to have the **opposite** effects on an economy.
6) For example, **exports** will become **more expensive** and **imports** will become **cheaper**. This will potentially mean:
   - An **increase** in the size of a current account **deficit**, or a **reduction** in a current account **surplus**.
   - A **fall** in aggregate demand, which is likely to lead to a **fall** in output.
   - **Unemployment** may **rise**.
   - The impact on inflation will depend on the **price elasticity of demand** for imports and for domestic goods.

A Fall in the Value of a currency Might Not improve a current account Deficit

1) A fall in the value of a currency will only reduce a current account **deficit** if the **Marshall-Lerner condition** holds.
2) The Marshall-Lerner condition says that for a **fall** in the value of a currency to lead to an **improvement** in the balance of payments, the price elasticity of demand for **imports plus** the price elasticity of demand for **exports** must be **greater than one**, i.e. $PED_M + PED_X > 1$.

The J-curve shows the effect of Inelastic Demand for imports and exports in the Short Run

1) The Marshall-Lerner condition might hold in the **long run**, so there'll be an **improvement** in a current account deficit if the value of a currency **falls**.
2) However, in the **short run** a current account deficit is likely to **worsen**, as demand for imports and exports will be **inelastic** — e.g. because it takes time for people to switch to a cheaper substitute.
3) In the short run, the **overall** value of **exports falls** and the **overall** value of **imports rises**, so the current account deficit worsens.
4) This is shown on the **J-curve**.

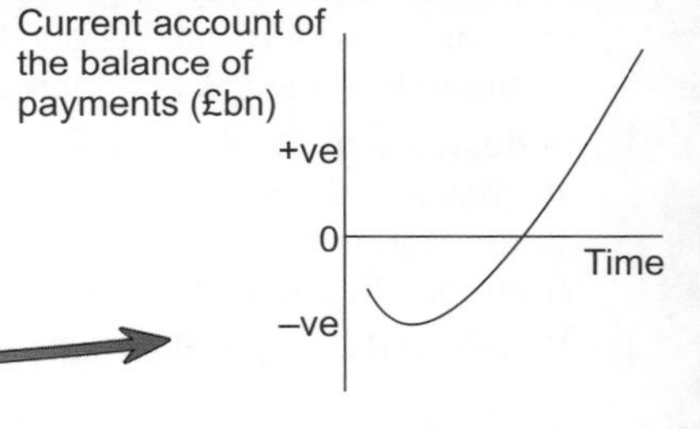

Practice Questions

Q1 Give one advantage and one disadvantage of floating exchange rates.

Q2 Give one advantage and one disadvantage of fixed exchange rates.

Q3 What impact might a fall in the value of a country's currency have on a current account deficit?

Exam Question

Q1 Discuss the likely impact of hosting a major sporting event on a country's currency. [4 marks]

I lost £7 learning that floating exchange rates are nothing to do with water...

Exchange rates play an important part in every economy — they directly affect exports and imports, which then have knock-on effects on other aspects of the economy, such as economic growth, unemployment, inflation and the balance of payments. As well as understanding the exchange rate's impact on the economy, make sure you know the factors which can affect the exchange rate.

Economic Integration

This page is for AQA Unit 4, Edexcel Unit 4 and OCR Unit 5 (The Global Economy). *Different trading blocs (see p.128) are at different stages of economic integration. Some are happy with little integration — others work towards fuller integration.*

There are Several Stages of Economic Integration

1) **Economic integration** is the process by which the economies of different countries become **more closely linked**, e.g. through free trade agreements or common currencies.
2) The types of **trading bloc** listed on p.128 show the **stages** of **economic integration** — free trade areas, customs unions, common (single) markets, economic unions and monetary unions. The list goes from **least** integrated to **most** integrated.
3) For example, the North American Free Trade Agreement (NAFTA) is a free trade area — it's made up of the **USA**, **Canada** and **Mexico**. The Association of South-East Asian Nations (ASEAN) is also a free trade area with **ten** members. These are at the **first** stage of economic integration.
4) The **EU** is a **customs union**, whilst the **Eurozone** (or **euro area**) is a **monetary union** (or **economic and monetary union**).

Economic Integration can have Positive and Negative impacts

1) There's the possibility of **trade creation** within a trading bloc — e.g. when **tariffs** are **removed**, consumers may switch from **high-cost** domestic producers to **lower-cost** trading partners.
2) So if there's **more trade** within the bloc, this can lead to **greater efficiency** — e.g. as a result of increased **competition**, **specialisation** and **economies of scale**.
3) **Non-members** may **gain** from things such as **improvements** in **efficiency** and **infrastructure** within the bloc.
4) The **removal** of **tariffs** will **increase** consumer surplus, but producer surplus and government revenue from tariffs will both be **reduced**.
5) **Trade diversion** can occur when **trade barriers** (imposed on non-members) divert trade **away** from **cheaper**, **more efficient** non-members.
6) Not only might this mean there's **no overall increase** in trade, but there may be a **reduction** in **efficiency** as trade is diverted to **less efficient** producers, and non-members **aren't** able to fully exploit their **comparative advantage**.

Trade creation and diversion are short run impacts of economic integration. Changes in efficiency are long run impacts.

Monetary Unions have Costs and Benefits for Domestic economies

1) By adopting a **single currency**, countries **don't** need to consider **costs** related to buying **another currency** when they buy goods and services from countries within the monetary union, and it makes **price comparisons** very simple.
2) There are also no **exchange rate risks** when trading within the monetary union.
3) The **policies** countries need to adopt in a monetary union, e.g. fiscal and monetary policies, **might** be **beneficial** to their economies, especially in the **long run**. For example, there might be **fiscal rules** (see p.111) to stop countries from having **long-term budget deficits**.
4) However, the policies which must be adopted to **suit** the **whole** union may **not** be helpful for **individual** countries' economies. For example, a member state might be in a **recession**, but if the central bank, e.g. the European Central Bank (ECB), **raises interest rates** to restrain the inflation of other member states, then the recession may **worsen**.
5) Countries **lose** a certain amount of **sovereignty** (i.e. their ability to make decisions on and control their own economies) in a monetary union as they'll **lose control** of their **monetary** policy — they can **no longer** change interest rates and exchange rates to help with their **macroeconomic objectives**. **Only** the central bank can change interest rates and exchange rates.

Practice Questions

Q1 Briefly explain the stages of economic integration.

Exam Question

Q1 Discuss the possible costs and benefits of economic integration to a country. [10 marks]

Trade diversion — redirecting all the chocolate-carrying lorries to my house...

It's really important that you understand the different stages of economic integration, and the positive and negative effects it can have on economies. A lot of the downsides relate to the amount of control a government has over its own economy.

The European Union

These pages are for AQA Unit 4, but may be useful for Edexcel Unit 4 and OCR Unit 5 (The Global Economy) too.
You've seen bits about the European Union — but here's a whole double page dedicated to everything European.

The **European Union** currently has **28 Member** countries

1) The EU has 28 members, with several others waiting as **candidates** to join.
2) The EU is made up of **various** bodies and institutions. Four of the **main** ones are:

- The **European Council** — made up of the **heads of state or government** of all the member states and the **presidents** of the Council and the Commission (see below). In general, they meet a few times a year to decide on the **main priorities** of the EU, and to discuss any **major** issues.
- The **European Parliament** — consists of **directly elected MEPs** who are there to represent EU citizens. The European Parliament's roles include **passing laws** with the Council and checking that **other** EU institutions are working properly.
- The **European Commission** — has **one Commissioner** from **each** member country. Amongst other things, it **allocates** EU funding, **manages** budgets, and **proposes** laws and helps to **enforce** them.
- The **European Central Bank (ECB)** — **manages** the euro and tries to keep prices **stable**. It sets **interest rates** to help control inflation, **issues** euro banknotes and manages **foreign currency reserves** to maintain the euro's exchange rate.

The **EU** is a **Customs Union**

1) In the EU, there's **free trade** between members and **common external tariffs** are imposed — so the EU is a **customs union**.
2) The **Single European Market (SEM)** was created in 1993. It meant that the EU became much more like a **common** (single) **market**. As well as free trade of **goods** and **services**, the SEM allows:

- Free mobility of **labour** — **people** are allowed to **move freely** between countries to **live** and **work**.
- Free mobility of **capital** and **currency** between countries.

While Tony was distracted by his book, Edna liked to check out the singles market.

There are **Several** countries **Waiting** as candidates to **Join** the **EU**

1) **Enlargement** of the EU by the **addition** of **new members** will have impacts on **existing** members, such as the UK.
2) For example, the impacts of **previous** enlargements and the **potential** impacts of **future** enlargements include:

Advantages

- **Increased** economies of scale and price competition, which should lead to **higher efficiency** and **lower prices**.
- **Migration** from **new** member states to **old** member states will increase **aggregate supply** for the old member states, e.g. the UK, helping with their **economic growth**.
- Migrants tend to be employed at **lower** hourly rates than domestic workers — this can **reduce** production costs and **increase** productive capacity.
- Migration might also bring **skilled workers** to existing members.

Disadvantages

- The **migration** from **new** member states to **old** member states might lead to **overcrowding** in cities, and it's likely there'll be an **increase** in **demand** for **services, housing** and **benefits**.
- Migrants might contribute to **domestic unemployment**.
- If **new** member states are **poorer** than **existing** member states, there might be **increased inequality** as people **migrate** from the **new** to **existing** member states.
- **Increased competition** from new members may drive **domestic** firms out of business.

The European Union

The EMU is a further step in European Economic Integration

1) The European **Economic and Monetary Union (EMU)** involves:
   - A **common monetary** policy — this is dealt with by the ECB.
   - Member states **coordinating fiscal** and **economic** policies.
   - Member states using a **common currency** — the **euro**.
2) **Not all** members of the EU are part of the EMU. If members want to **join** the EMU, they need to meet **convergence criteria** — this means keeping budget deficit, inflation, exchange rate and interest rate levels all close to **specified** levels.
3) The EMU represents a further step towards an **economic and monetary union** between the Eurozone member states of the EU.

There are many arguments For and Against the UK Joining the Euro

1) The UK is a **member** of the **EU**, but **isn't** a member of the **single currency area** (the Eurozone).
2) Monetary unions have many **costs** and **benefits** — see p.135.
3) There are further arguments on **either side** of the debate of whether the UK should join the Eurozone:

Reasons for the UK to join the euro

- **FDI** into Eurozone countries may be **increased** because if the UK joins the Eurozone, this will create a **bigger** market. **Not** joining the euro may mean that the UK **loses** some inward FDI.
- There's the potential that with **reduced transaction costs**, there may be **increased trade**, which could lead to **higher** growth and employment. It could also **improve** living standards and the balance of payments.
- UK firms may benefit from **economies of scale**.
- There would still be **fiscal policy** tools available for the UK government to use to manage the UK economy, though these would have to be in line with **EU policies** on, for example, budget deficits.

Reasons against the UK joining the euro

- **Price stability** is a major aim of the ECB — **Eurozone inflation targets** are **less flexible** than UK ones. **Slower** growth may result from having to meet these targets.
- Various problems have been encountered within the Eurozone recently as a result of the **global financial crisis**. For example, **falls** in real GDP, **weak** consumer spending and capital investment, and **high** unemployment. The crisis led to **rising national debt** in some countries, e.g. Spain, resulting in the need for **bailout** packages from other countries in the Eurozone and the setting up of the **European Stability Mechanism (ESM)**.
- There's a large amount of **structural unemployment** within the Eurozone. This, along with the **widening divergence** in trade balances within the Eurozone, indicates problems with **competitiveness** within it — for example, **Germany** has a large current account **surplus**, and **Cyprus** has a current account **deficit**.
- The UK would **no longer** be able to use **monetary policy** to help with its **own** economy.

The European Stability Mechanism provides emergency loans to Eurozone countries experiencing financial difficulties.

Practice Questions

Q1 What are the main roles of the European Commission?

Q2 Give one advantage and one disadvantage to the UK of the addition of new members to the EU.

Exam Question

Q1 Evaluate the costs and benefits of the UK joining the Eurozone. [15 marks]

EMU — that's bound to ruffle some feathers...

You don't need to know loads of details about the various EU bodies — just make sure you know the main objectives of the ones given on the previous page. If you need to write about the pros and cons of the UK joining the euro, then as well as the arguments for and against given here, you can use the monetary union costs and benefits from p.135.

Measuring a Country's Competitiveness

These pages are for Edexcel Unit 4 and OCR Unit 5 (The Global Economy). *Competitiveness is all about making sure that, as a country, you're making things that people want to buy and selling them at prices that they're happy to pay.*

Competitiveness involves a lot of **Price Factors**

1) International **competitiveness** is a complex thing to try to **measure** — it involves trying to measure a country's **ability** to provide better-value goods and services than its rivals.
2) This will, to a large extent, depend on the **price** at which a country can produce and sell those goods and services. Various measures give an indication of this — such as **relative unit labour costs**, **relative productivity** and **relative export prices**.

The 'relative' part of these terms means 'in comparison with competing countries'.

- The cost of **labour** will have a significant effect on **relative export prices**, especially in **labour-intensive** industries, such as many manufacturing industries. (In **capital-intensive** industries, it's **less useful** as a guide to overall competitiveness.)
- **Unit labour costs** measure the cost of the **labour** needed to generate output. If one country has **lower** unit labour costs than another country, then (all other things being equal) that country will be **more competitive** — i.e. better able to sell its products.
- To **compare** unit labour costs in different countries, you need to convert each country's unit labour costs to the **same currency**. In fact, comparisons are usually carried out by converting the costs to an **index number** that tries to allow for differences between countries, to make comparisons more valid.
- **Increasing productivity** (e.g. the output per worker per hour) will have a similar effect on competitiveness to reducing unit labour costs — i.e. all other things being equal, **higher** productivity means **greater competitiveness.**

Exchange rates are also important — see p.134.

3) There are also many **other factors** that affect a country's overall competitiveness.
4) The **Global Competitiveness Index** is an attempt by the World Economic Forum (WEF) to determine **how productive** and **how wealthy** various countries have the **potential** to be, based on assessing what it calls "The 12 Pillars of Competitiveness":

The World Economic Forum is a not-for-profit institution that tries to find solutions to pressing international problems.

i) **Institutions** — e.g. the strength of a country's **legal system**, levels of **corruption** and **accounting standards**.
ii) **Infrastructure** — e.g. the efficiency of **transport** links and **communication** networks.
iii) **Macroeconomic environment** — e.g. general economic **stability** and soundness of the **public finances**.
iv) **Health and primary education** — the absolute essentials for a **productive** workforce.
v) **Higher education and training** — a more **highly qualified** workforce leads to a more **advanced** economy.
vi) **Goods market efficiency** — this means the ability for firms to provide goods and services efficiently, and takes into account things like a 'business-friendly' **tax system**.
vii) **Labour market efficiency** — i.e. an efficient and flexible market to make best use of a country's **workers**. This includes the ease with which firms can 'hire and fire' workers when it needs to (see p.68).
viii) **Financial market development** — i.e. sound **financial institutions** that can make capital available for businesses that want to invest.
ix) **Technological readiness** — the ability of an economy to **adopt** new technologies **quickly**, so firms can improve productivity by benefiting from modern information and communication technology, for example.
x) **Market size** — this includes **export markets** that a country has access to and the market **within** the country itself. The more markets a country can sell into, the more products it's likely to sell.
xi) **Business sophistication** — including the extent of **business networks** (e.g. firms and suppliers located in '**clusters**' to improve efficiency and spark greater innovation) and **sophistication** of individual firms (e.g. how well they can develop, produce, market and distribute their goods).
xii) **Innovation** — leading to **new products** and **new ways** to produce existing products.

You don't need to memorise all of these, but it's handy to learn some of them.

Competitiveness also includes **Non-Price Factors**

Competitiveness is **not** just about price — it also involves **non-price factors**. For example:

- **Design** — are a country's products what people want to buy?
- **Quality** — are products well made, and do they work properly?
- **Reliability** — do a country's products keep working?
- **Availability** — is it easy to buy a country's products?

Strong management and investment in technology can play a big part in improving some of these factors.

Measuring a Country's Competitiveness

Competitiveness depends on **Innovation**, **Efficiency** and **Flexibility**

Some of the following factors are included in the WEF's global competitiveness index, but there's a bit **more detail** on these things below. Others **aren't** included directly in the global competitiveness index.

Real Exchange Rates and Relative Inflation Rates

- **Real exchange rates** affect the **relative export prices** of different countries, impacting on a country's competitiveness — e.g. if the **pound** was **strong** compared to the **dollar**, then other countries would be more likely to buy **US exports**.
- The **real exchange rate** is the **nominal exchange rate** (the exchange rate determined by the foreign exchange rate markets), but it's **adjusted** to take into account the **price levels** within the countries being compared (i.e. the **purchasing power** of a currency — see p.132).
- It's worked out using the following **formula**:

$$\text{real exchange rate} = \text{nominal exchange rate} \times \frac{\text{price level in a country}}{\text{price level abroad}}$$

- So, the real exchange rate will be **affected** by changes to the **nominal exchange rate** and the **rate of inflation** in a country or abroad. This means, for example, the real exchange rate will **fall** if the nominal exchange rate **falls** or if the price levels abroad **rise** relative to domestic prices.

Productivity

- Productivity will be affected by the level of **human capital** in workers...
- ...which is affected by the levels of **education** and **training** of the population.
- The amount and sophistication of **capital equipment** used by workers will also be a factor here.

Wage Costs and Non-Wage Costs

- As well as **wage costs** (what a firm spends on wages), **non-wage costs** will affect the competitiveness of a country's firms.
- Non-wage costs will include things like:
  - employers' **national insurance** contributions and **pension** contributions,
  - costs incurred as a result of **environmental protection** or **anti-discrimination** laws, or **health-and-safety** regulations.

Labour Market Flexibility

As well as the things mentioned in the WEF's '7th pillar', this will include:

- the strength of **trade unions**,
- the willingness of workers to work **part-time** or on **flexible contracts**.

See p.57 for more about unit labour costs and productivity.

Research and Development

A country that's able to **innovate** and create **new products** (and perhaps even whole **new markets** as a result) or new, more efficient **methods of production** is likely to have an advantage when it comes to competing internationally.

Regulation

Regulations often **increase costs** for firms, forcing them to **raise** prices and become **less competitive** internationally.

Practice Questions

Q1 Give four examples of non-price factors that could affect a country's competitiveness.

Q2 How can non-wage costs affect a country's international competitiveness?

Exam Question

Q1 Between 2011 and 2012, the UK rose on the Global Competitiveness Index from 10th to 8th. Discuss the factors which may have led to this improvement in the UK's competitiveness. [20 marks]

My competitiveness peaks during family games of charades...

Productivity and unit labour costs are pretty vital here — if your productivity falls, your international competitiveness will also fall, unless other costs can be reduced to compensate, of course. Okay, time to soak up all the above into your overloaded brain.

Policies to Improve Competitiveness

These pages are for** Edexcel Unit 4 **and** OCR Unit 5 **(The Global Economy). *Competitiveness is a good thing, so it should be no surprise that there are various things that governments and firms might do to try to improve it.*

Firms can try to improve their Own competitiveness

1) If firms want to **thrive** (or even **survive**), then they need to remain **competitive**.
2) There are various things a **firm** can do to improve its competitiveness. Basically, anything that helps a firm provide **something people want** at a **price they're willing to pay** will improve competitiveness. For example:

- **Research and Development (R&D)** — a firm that invests in R&D is likely to be **innovative**. It'll be able to take advantage of new products (see p.19) and new, more efficient **production methods**.
- **Investment in capital equipment** — e.g. to improve **productivity** (see p.7) or to achieve **economies of scale** (see p.8).
- **Competitive pricing** — this might also include 'aggressive' pricing tactics, such as **limit pricing** (see p.24).
- Improve some aspect of their products **other than price** — e.g. provide better **customer service** or products that are **easier to use** (see p.23 for more suggestions).

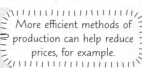

More efficient methods of production can help reduce prices, for example.

Governments can try to improve the Economy's competitiveness

1) To improve **firms' competitiveness** and the competitiveness of the economy **as a whole**, governments can introduce a range of **supply-side** policies — see p.116 for more information.
2) These policies will often aim to improve one or more of the '**pillars**' mentioned on p.138. For example:

- Improve **education and training**
  - E.g. apprenticeships allow people to learn **practical skills** while gaining relevant **qualifications**.
  - Improvements in education will not only allow employees to become more **productive**, but can also lead to greater **occupational mobility** (see p.67).
- Improve **labour market flexibility**
  - E.g. in the past, policies have been introduced that weakened some of the powers of **trade unions** — firms are now able to make workers **redundant** more easily when times are tough.
- **Create incentives** for firms to **invest**
  - E.g. offer firms **tax breaks** (i.e. reductions in the amount of tax they need to pay) if they **invest** profits **instead** of paying **dividends** to shareholders.
- **Improve infrastructure**
  - E.g. build faster transport links or improve communication links.
- **"Cut red tape"**
  - This means **removing** any **regulations** that no longer seem necessary and which may be increasing firms' costs unnecessarily — e.g. outdated **environmental** or **health-and-safety** regulations.
  - Making it easier to set up a company can lead to more **entrepreneurship** and **innovation**.
- **Encourage competition**
  - E.g. **deregulation** (see p.45) can lead to improved **efficiency** in a market.
  - **Privatisation** (see p.44) may be effective if **nationalised** industries are **inefficient**.
- **Encourage immigration**
  - Foreign workers may have the **skills** that businesses need.
  - This can be a very quick way to obtain the **human capital** needed in an economy.
- **Maintain economic stability**
  - E.g. by keeping **inflation** low, **exchange rates** steady, and the **balance of payments** under control.

3) It may **not** be **simple** to introduce these policies though, and it may take a **long time** to feel their full effect.
   - For example, it takes a long time to plan and build extra schools and colleges to improve **education** and **training**.
   - Some policies may be **controversial** — e.g. trade union reforms can be unpopular with some people.
   - There may also be difficulties in **affording** these policies — e.g. the government may not be able to spend money on **improving infrastructure**, or firms may not be able to **invest** at the most appropriate time.

Policies to Improve Competitiveness

Devaluing the Currency is an option if **Exchange Rates** are **Fixed**

1) Governments in some countries are able to **devalue** their currency — i.e. **reduce** its **value** against other currencies. However, this is not an option in a country with **floating** exchange rates (see p.132), such as the UK.
2) Devaluing a country's currency can lead to **increased demand** from abroad for that country's **exports**. But it also means **imports** become more expensive, so people in that country are more likely to buy **domestically** produced goods (i.e. those made in that country).
3) The overall effect is that the country should become **more competitive**. It should also lead to improvements in the **balance of payments**.
4) But devaluation can lead to **cost-push inflation** (see p.103) if imports are used in the production of other goods. It may also mean that firms aren't under as much pressure to **reduce their costs**, something that will be necessary in the long run if they're hoping to compete with foreign firms.

Decreasing interest rates would usually lead to a fall in the exchange rate — so you might think a government could devalue the currency that way. But in the UK, interest rates are set by the Bank of England rather than the government.

Tariffs and **Subsidies** may be impossible due to **International Agreements**

1) It may be possible for a government to **increase** the competitiveness (at least within the country) of domestic firms by imposing **tariffs** on imported goods. This will make foreign goods more expensive.
2) Similarly, a government may be able to offer **subsidies** to **domestic** producers, enabling them to supply their goods more cheaply than similar ones produced abroad. This should make those firms appear more competitive, although subsidies can be very **expensive** for a government.
3) Both tariffs and subsidies have the **disadvantage** that, like devaluation, producers may not seek the **efficiency improvements** that are necessary for them to **genuinely** compete internationally.
4) **International agreements** may also prevent governments from taking these kinds of actions. For example, EU rules would **prevent** any member state imposing tariffs on any other member state. There are also strict EU rules governing **state subsidies** to industries.

Falling competitiveness can have **Serious Consequences**

1) If a country becomes **less competitive**, it can lead to **serious problems**.
2) A country that's less able to sell its products is likely to experience a worsening in its **balance of payments**. This is because **exports** will **fall** while **imports increase**.
3) In addition, as economic activity generally decreases, **unemployment** will probably **increase**.
4) Remaining competitive is particularly important for countries whose industries rely on **international trade** to achieve **economies of scale**.

As the 'Enhancing Productivity' company bonding day neared its climax, Sandy was sure it wasn't falling competitiveness that was uppermost in her mind.

Practice Questions

Q1 How might a devaluation of a currency help a country regain its competitiveness? Explain why devaluation might not be an option for certain countries.

Q2 Describe some of the consequences for a country of a loss of competitiveness.

Exam Question

Q1 Discuss some of the approaches that may be used by a government to help improve its country's overall competitiveness. [20 marks]

Changing devalue of the currency isn't always an option...

A loss of competitiveness can be painful for a country and for the people living in it. And while some things can be done quickly to help improve competitiveness, a lot of these measures take time before the country will see any real benefit. It's a bit like revision — a bit of cramming the night before can help, but it's a long slow effort over many months that really works in the end.

Measuring Economic Development

These pages are for AQA Unit 4, Edexcel Unit 4 and OCR Unit 5 (The Global Economy).
This section is all about economic development — this is related to economic growth, but is not the same thing.

Economic Development is Not just about economic growth

1) **Economic growth** is relatively easy to define — it's an **increase** in the size of a country's **GDP**.
2) **Economic development** is more complicated to define and measure, because it's a **normative** concept. It involves making **value judgements** about what would make up a '**more developed**' country.
3) But the aim is to somehow measure how **living standards** and people's **general welfare** in a country **change** over time.
4) The size of a country's **economy** is important when measuring its development, but so are things such as the **size** and **health** of the **population**, and the **quality of life** they have.
5) To some extent, measuring **development** means assessing not just the amount of **economic growth** that has occurred, but also its '**quality**' — e.g. the effect it has on **people's lives** or the **uses** extra income resulting from that growth is put to.

Examples

- Economic growth that causes **vast** amounts of **pollution** would be considered **less beneficial** than the same amount of economic growth but with much **less** pollution.
- Economic growth that directly **improves** the lives of a **large part** of the population (e.g. by improving access to clean drinking water) would be considered **more positive** than growth that brings financial benefits to just a **small** number of **already wealthy** people.

National Income Figures like GNI Per Capita don't tell the whole story

1) One important measure of economic development is **national income data**, such as **real GDP per capita** or **real GNI (gross national income) per capita**.
   - **Real** GDP and **real** GNI have the effects of inflation **removed**. (Nominal GDP and nominal GNI will increase as a result of inflation, even if no genuine growth has occurred.)
   - Using GDP or GNI **per capita** (i.e. **per person**) will give a better indication of people's **standards of living**. This will be very important if the size of a country's population is **changing**. Using 'per capita' figures also means you can **compare** figures **between countries** whose populations are different sizes.

GDP measures economic output produced within a country. A country's GNI measures economic output too, but also includes various forms of income earned abroad by residents of that country.

2) Comparisons between different countries based on national income data make use of the principle of **purchasing power parity, PPP** (see p.132). This is important as $1 will buy **more** in a **less developed** country than in a **developed** one.
3) Generally speaking, countries with a **higher** GDP or GNI per capita have **higher standards of living**, but national income data **doesn't** tell you about lots of '**quality-of-life**' factors, such as the amount of **leisure time** people have or their **health**.
4) National income data also **ignores** economic welfare brought about by 'informal' economic activity — i.e. economic activity that's **not recorded** by government statistics (which is a **large** chunk of some developing countries' economies).

Higher national income figures could mean people are working longer hours, with less leisure time and poorer health as a result.

The Human Development Index considers a Wider Range of indicators

1) The United Nations **Human Development Index** (**HDI**) is an attempt to describe people's welfare and a country's economic development in a way that goes beyond just looking at national income figures. It takes into account people's:
   - **Health** (as measured by life expectancy at birth).
   - **Education** (as measured by the expected number of years a child will spend in school).
   - **Income** (as measured by real GNI per capita, adjusted for purchasing power parity).
2) It **doesn't** capture all the information that's relevant to people's welfare or economic development, but it does place a **greater emphasis** on the **quality of life** of a country's people instead of just considering **economic growth**.
3) Countries' HDI figures can be used to **rank** those countries from **most developed** to **least developed**. Or a country's HDI figure (a number between 0 and 1) can be used to assess its **general** level of development — e.g. a figure **above 0.8** signifies a **high** level of human development, while a figure **below 0.5** shows a **low** level of human development.

The Human Development conference was interesting, but not really what Susan had expected.

Two countries that have a similar HDI can achieve it in very different ways — e.g. one country might have a high life expectancy but a poorly developed education system, while another may have a low life expectancy but a much more successful education system.

Measuring Economic Development

Extreme Inequality is usually seen as a *Problem*

1) Even when a country's national income grows, **inequality** within that country can still cause problems.
2) In **developing** countries, those with very low wealth and incomes can suffer **hardship** if circumstances change (e.g. if harvests fail or demand for their goods decreases).
3) In **developed** countries, those with the lowest wealth and incomes may not be in **absolute poverty**, but they may still be in **relative poverty** (see p.51), or at risk of **social exclusion** (i.e. they may not have access to all the opportunities or resources needed to **fully participate** in society, such as employment opportunities and decent health care).
4) Some people say that inequality is an **inevitable consequence** of economic development (i.e. some people will always do better than others). Others say that some inequality is actually **necessary** for capitalism to function effectively, since inequality gives people an **incentive** to work hard and succeed.
5) However, it can also be argued that inequality can **slow down** economic development, for various reasons:
   - The **poorest** within a country may find it difficult to **start businesses**. They may not have the resources to **invest**, will find it difficult to **save**, and their lack of **assets** (for use as **collateral**) may make it difficult for them to get **loans**.
   - People on higher incomes may well spend a lot on **imports**, or invest their money **abroad** (see p.144) — so this money will **leave** the economy.
6) Inequality and social exclusion may also be linked to **social problems** in a country, such as higher levels of **crime** or **health problems**.

If the benefits of development go to those who are already wealthy, extreme poverty can exist alongside genuine affluence.

Collateral means goods that you promise to give to a lender if you aren't able to repay a loan.

Inequality can be measured using the *Lorenz Curve* or *Gini Coefficient*

1) Causes of inequality will **vary** between countries, but the following are important factors:
   - **wage** and **tax** levels
   - **unemployment** levels
   - **education** levels
   - **property ownership** and **inheritance laws**
   - level of government **benefits**
2) The amount of **inequality** in a country can be shown using a **Lorenz curve** or a **Gini coefficient**.

The Lorenz curve
- The Lorenz curve for a country is shown in **red** in this diagram.
- Remember... **perfect equality** would be shown by a **straight line**.
- A 'saggier' curve means a **greater share** of the country's overall income goes to a relatively **small number** of people.

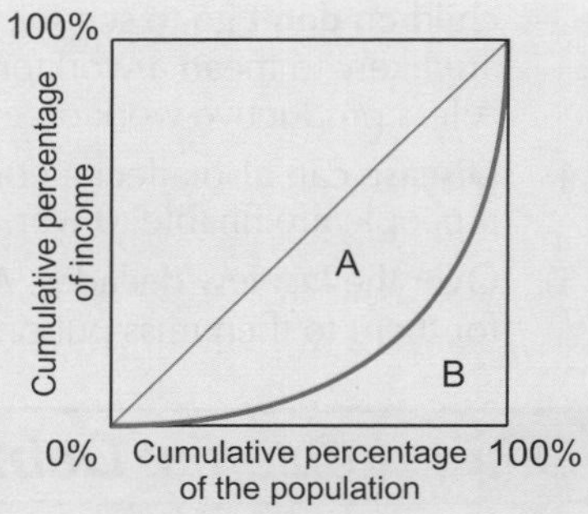

The Gini coefficient
- Remember... the Gini coefficient (G) is always a value **between 0** (everyone earns the same) **and 1** (one person gets all the country's income).
- $G = \frac{A}{A + B}$

See p.51 for more about the Lorenz curve and Gini coefficient.

Practice Questions

Q1 Describe why national income figures don't give a true indication of economic welfare in a country.

Q2 What is the HDI? What three factors are assessed in order to work out a country's HDI?

Exam Question

Q1 Explain two causes and two consequences of inequality in a country. [15 marks]

The Genie coefficient — how many wishes you get after rubbing a magic lantern...

conomic development is tricky — it sounds like a similar kind of thing to economic growth, but it's actually quite different. conomic development is a lot more general, and involves people's overall quality of life rather than just their income. Inequality is mportant here too — some degree of inequality is probably inevitable, but extreme inequality can lead to all sorts of problems.

Limits to Growth and Development

***These pages are for** Edexcel Unit 4.*
All countries are different, but there are some common obstacles that developing nations frequently face.

Poor Infrastructure makes it difficult for an economy to grow

1) The **infrastructure** of a country means the **basic facilities** and **services** needed for the country and its economy to function.
2) For example, a country's infrastructure includes:
   - roads
   - railways
   - water supplies
   - telephone services
   - schools
   - hospitals
   - electricity supplies
   - sewerage
   - internet services
3) Poor infrastructure makes it **difficult** for a country's economy to grow or be internationally competitive. For example:
   - If **energy supplies** are unreliable, then firms and factories won't be able to operate efficiently.
   - If **transport links** are poor, it can be difficult to **move** goods **around** or **out of** the country.
   - If **telephone** and **internet services** are scarce, then businesses will find it difficult to coordinate their operations and communicate with customers.
4) Poor infrastructure also makes it very difficult to attract **foreign direct investment** (FDI).
5) **Foreign aid** (see p.146) is often used to **improve** or **maintain** infrastructure, but developing nations can sometimes persuade foreign investors to help **improve** their infrastructure — perhaps because these nations have important **raw materials** or because they would become attractive **new markets** for foreign firms.

For example, Chile has large reserves of **minerals** and has attracted large amounts of **FDI** in various parts of its economy, such as in its **energy** and **communications** industries.

The natural resources available in a country can also affect how it develops.

Disease and lack of **Education** can cause **Human Capital Inadequacies**

1) If a country's **population** grows **faster** than its **economy**, then this will lead to a fall in **GNI per capita** (and probably also a fall in people's **standards of living**). Developing nations, such as those in certain parts of Africa, have some of the fastest growing populations in the world.
2) A fast growing population means there'll be lots of **children**, which can put pressure on a country's **education system**.
3) However, household poverty is a major factor in keeping children **out** of school, and if children **don't** go to school, this can lead to further problems. **Low educational standards** are likely to mean a workforce that's **less productive**, as they have less **human capital**. A less productive workforce will make it difficult to attract **FDI**.
4) **Disease** can also affect a country's economy — e.g. it can result in **lower productivity** if people are unable to work, and put a strain on the country's **health care system**.
5) Over the last few decades, **AIDS** has also led to a huge number of children being **orphaned** — it's common for them to then miss out on going to **school**, with long-term consequences both for them and the economy.

See p.142 for more about development and a country's population.

Other problems: **Debt**, **Savings Gap**, **Capital Flight**, **Foreign Exchange Gap**

1) The '**savings gap**' can be a problem when incomes are low — it's the **gap** between the **level of domestic savings** in an economy and the **investment** needed to grow that economy. This lack of investment in **capital** means incomes are likely to remain **low**, as shown in the diagram.

See p.146 for the importance of savings in the Harrod-Domar model.

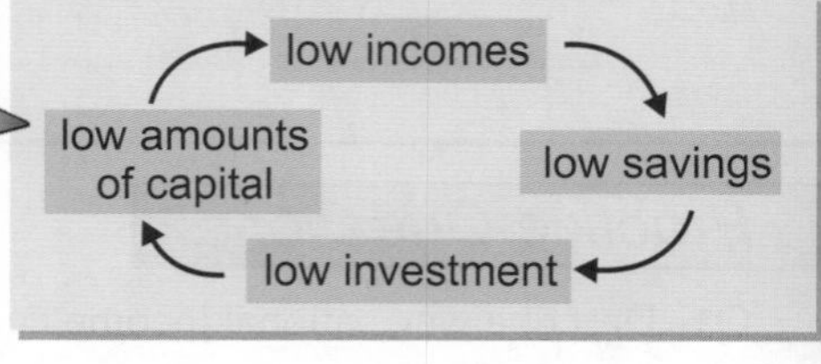

2) **Capital flight** is when people start holding their savings **abroad** (often as a result of high tax rates or political instability). This lack of domestic investment makes economic growth more difficult to achieve. It also means that **less tax** is collected (since the government won't receive taxes due on those savings).
3) Many developing countries borrowed heavily in the past. Just **servicing** (i.e. paying the **interest** on) these debts can be vastly expensive, leaving **less** money available for **health** and **education**, for example, or investment in **capital**.
4) A **foreign exchange gap** means capital outflows from a country are greater than capital inflows. This is more likely when a country:
   a) is dependent on **exports** of **primary products**, or **imports** of **manufactured goods** (see p.145),
   b) has to spend a lot of money **servicing debt**.

Limits to Growth and Development

Primary Product Dependency has many potential Disadvantages

1) Many countries depend on **primary products** — i.e. products taken directly from the earth. These might include **minerals** like copper and iron ores, or **plants** like rice, wheat or fruits, where the 'value added' is low.

'Value added' describes how much a firm increases what a product is worth. Many primary products are 'low value added' — this means they won't generate huge profits (see p.147).

2) **Demand** for primary products is usually **price inelastic** — this means that a change in **demand** will have a **large** effect on the **price**.
3) **Supply** of some primary products (e.g. agricultural products) will be **price inelastic** in the short term, since supplies can't quickly increase or decrease (e.g. because it takes time for plants to grow). **Agricultural** products are also easily damaged by **natural disasters** and **extreme weather events**.
4) These factors mean that producers' **incomes** and earnings from **exports** can **change quickly**. If supply and demand are both price inelastic then **slight changes** in either will cause **big fluctuations** in price. The **uncertainty** this creates makes it very difficult to **plan**, and attract **investment**.
5) **Developed** countries may use **protectionist policies** to protect their own primary industries — e.g. EU policies such as the Common Agricultural Policy (CAP) make it difficult for farmers in **developing** nations to compete on equal terms.
6) The **Prebisch-Singer hypothesis** describes how countries that rely on **exporting** primary products and **importing** manufactured goods may become steadily **worse off** over time, as there'll be a decline in the **terms of trade** (see p.124).

The Prebisch-Singer hypothesis says that:

- Demand for **primary products** is income inelastic — as incomes rise, demand changes very little.
- However, demand for **manufactured products** is more income elastic — as incomes rise, demand for these goods rises quickly. This will usually then lead to **large** increases in **price**.
- As the price of manufactured goods increases, countries **exporting** mainly **primary products** will find they're able to **import fewer** manufactured goods for a **given level** of exports.

7) The Prebisch-Singer hypothesis suggests that overreliance on, say, **cash crops** (i.e. crops grown for profit) is **not** an effective long-term development strategy. However, there are criticisms of this hypothesis:
   - As the world's **population** grows, greater demand for agricultural products to eat may push prices **up**.
   - Demand for some primary products (e.g. gold or oil) is **income elastic** — as incomes rise, demand rises **even quicker**.
   - If a country has a **comparative advantage** in producing primary products, then it makes sense to use that country's resources for this purpose.

Corruption and Civil Wars stop an economy functioning efficiently

1) **Corruption** occurs when power is abused for **personal gain** (e.g. by government officials accepting **bribes**). The result is often that the country's resources are **diverted away** from their most productive use, so governments and private firms become **less efficient**.

E.g. some African firms export goods using much longer routes than necessary to avoid having to pay bribes.

2) The effects of corruption can be even worse. For example, if the police expect to be paid the same **bribe** by people whether or not they've broken the law, there's little incentive for people to act honestly. The effect is that the **legal system**, and eventually even the **government**, stop functioning properly.
3) Even if there's little corruption, an **unreliable bureaucracy** in a country (e.g. a tax office that's unable to collect the taxes that are due) can also make development difficult to achieve.
4) **Civil wars** are also a disaster for a country's economy, and are **more likely** in less developed nations. Large numbers of people are **killed** or become **refugees**, **absolute poverty** generally increases and **infrastructure** is damaged. Even after the war ends, **capital flight** and **military spending** usually remain high.
5) All these effects make it very difficult to **compete internationally** and attract **foreign direct investment** (FDI).

Practice Questions

Q1 List three factors that can limit a country's economic development.

Exam Question

Q1 Explain how primary product dependency can limit a country's economic development. [8 marks]

Capital flight — in economics, this doesn't mean a trip to Paris or Rome...

The factors on these pages are bad enough and can hugely hamper a country's development. But they aren't the only problems to face developing countries. For example, landlocked countries (i.e. those with no coastline) tend to be less economically successful than those on the coast. Although you can't shift a country and give it a coastline, development policies can help.

Ways of Promoting Growth and Development

***These pages are for** Edexcel Unit 4 **and** OCR Unit 5 (The Global Economy).*
There are lots of policies to help improve economic development, but each has its pros and cons.

Different Strategies are used in international development

1) The **policies** on the next few pages are mostly based on one of the following **strategies** for helping countries develop:
   - **Aid** and **debt relief** (see below).
   - **Structural change** — e.g. development of the **agricultural**, **industrial** or **tourism** sectors (see p.147).
   - Policies favouring either an **interventionist** approach or a **market-oriented** approach — see page 148.
2) Since all developing countries are **different**, each will need a particular **mix** of **strategies** and **policies**, probably involving both **markets** and the **state**. But there's **no guarantee** that what's worked in one country will be successful in another.

Aid means Transferring Resources from one country to another

1) In economics, **aid** means the **transfer of resources** from one country to another. There are various types:
   - **Bilateral aid** — when a donor country (i.e. the country sending the aid) sends aid **directly** to the recipient country.
   - **Multilateral aid** — when donor countries pass the aid to an **intermediate agency** (e.g. the World Bank — see p.149), which then distributes the aid to recipient countries.
   - **Tied aid** — aid sent **on condition** that the money is spent in a particular way (e.g. on imports from the donor country).
2) There are arguments for and against using aid to assist in **development**:

But offering emergency aid after natural or man-made disasters is uncontroversial.

Arguments in favour of development aid:
- It reduces **absolute poverty**.
- If it leads to improvements in **health** and **education**, this will improve a country's **human capital**.
- It helps to fill the **savings gap** (see the Harrod-Domar model below) and the **foreign exchange gap**.
- There can be '**multiplier effects**'. For example, if aid is used to improve a country's **infrastructure**, there will be a **direct** increase in aggregate demand. An increase in aggregate demand will mean more people will have **jobs** (and **money** to spend), and this will lead to further increases in aggregate demand.

Harrod-Domar model

The **Harrod-Domar model** says that the growth rate of an economy is directly linked to:
- the level of **saving** in the economy,
- the efficiency with which the **capital** in the economy can be used.

If either of these factors can be **increased**, then economic growth should be **faster**.

Arguments against development aid:
- Some people claim that aid leads to a **dependency culture**, meaning that countries start to count on receiving aid **indefinitely**, instead of **developing** their own economies.
- Aid can be **misused** by **corrupt** governments, meaning the money doesn't help the people it was meant to help.
- Some say aid is aimed more at securing 'favours' for the **donor country** than helping the **recipient countries**.

Debt Relief means Not expecting Existing debts to be repaid

1) A country with **large debts** has to spend a large amount of its income on **servicing** that debt (i.e. paying the **interest**).
2) For **low-income** countries, debt servicing can use up a **large proportion** of their total income.
   This leaves **less** money available for other services, such as **health care** or **education**.
3) **Debt relief** means **cancelling** some of the debts owed by developing countries. Again, there are **pros** and **cons**:

Arguments in favour of debt relief:
- It frees up money for **public services**, such as **health care** and **education**.
- The money saved by the developing country can be invested in **capital goods** to help grow its economy.

Arguments against debt relief:
- Some people claim that cancelling debt creates a risk of **moral hazard** and a **dependency culture**.
  For example, countries may feel that **future** debts will also be cancelled, so they may just **borrow** more.
- Cancelling the debt of countries run by **corrupt** governments may mean more money is **misused** — e.g. for **personal gain** or to buy **weapons** for internal repression (i.e. using force to control the country's people).
- Debt cancellation can be used by a donor country as a way to secure **influence** in the recipient country.

Ways of Promoting Growth and Development

The policies on this page can be thought of as part of a structural-change strategy.

Developing the **Agricultural Sector** can help

1) The agricultural sector is often seen as a **low-productivity** sector (i.e. the **output** is low compared to the **inputs** required) where it's difficult to **add value**.
2) Although there are potential problems for a country if it depends too much on **primary products** (see p.145), it can be worth a country developing its agricultural sector if that's where it has a **comparative advantage**.
3) Developments in the agricultural sector can be seen as a **stepping stone** to developing other sectors. For example, if improvements in the agricultural sector lead to increases in national income, **other** sectors can then be **invested** in.

The **Lewis Model** describes the development of the **Industrial Sector**

1) The **Lewis model** has been used to argue that increasing an economy's **industrial sector** is the key to development. It says growth in industry and manufacturing can be achieved **without** reducing agricultural output or increasing inflation.

Lewis model

- The **Lewis model** assumes that there's **excess labour** in the **agricultural** sector (i.e. the same amount of agricultural output could be produced by fewer people). This means that there's **no opportunity cost** if agricultural workers transfer to **industry** to take advantage of the **higher wages** available.
- So industry develops **without** reducing agricultural output. And while there's excess labour (i.e. 'spare workers') in agriculture, wages in industry **don't rise** — i.e. a country can industrialise **without** causing **inflation**.
- **Profits** from industry can be reinvested in **capital goods**, leading to greater **productivity gains**.
- The reduction in excess labour in agriculture will also mean **agricultural productivity** increases.
- Eventually, an equilibrium will be reached where everyone is **better off** than they were, and **profits** (and savings) are increased, leading to even more **investment** and **growth**.

2) Like all models, the Lewis model involves a lot of **simplifications**. In practice, things often work out **differently**.
3) It may not be easy to **transfer labour** to industry — workers (often young males) **migrating** from the countryside will leave fewer people to do physically demanding agricultural labour, while at **harvest times** there may be **no** 'spare workers' at all. **Investment** in **education** and **training** is also needed to develop the **human capital** needed to expand industrial output.
4) Also, profits **aren't** always reinvested locally — they may be invested **abroad** or used for **consumption**.
5) And if industrial production is **capital intensive** and involves little **human labour**, economic growth may not provide many additional **jobs**.

This is especially likely if a firm is owned by a foreign company.

Developing the **Tourism Industry** involves some **Risks**

1) Developing a country's **tourism industry** can improve a country's economy, though it's not without problems.
2) Increasing tourism will mean that a country earns **foreign currency** from tourists. It also means it's likely to attract **foreign investment** (e.g. from multinational hotel chains).
3) **Employment** should also increase. However, employment in the tourism industry may be **seasonal**, and multinational companies may want to bring in their own **management**, meaning that the **local** jobs created will be **low-skilled**.
4) An increase in tourism is likely to mean that more goods are **imported** (either **capital** goods to build facilities or goods demanded by **tourists** on holiday). This will be **bad** for the country's **balance of payments**.
5) Extra tourism may lead to **environmental damage** or **inconvenience** for the locals, as **tourists'** needs are prioritised.
6) Also, demand in the tourism industry is likely to be **income elastic** — it will increase quickly as people's incomes increase. The disadvantage is that during **economic downturns**, demand is likely to **fall quickly** too. And tourist destinations **aren't** guaranteed to remain popular forever — tourists' **tastes** can **change** quickly.

Practice Questions

Q1 Explain some of the advantages and disadvantages of using aid to help a country develop its economy.

Q2 What is meant by the phrase 'debt relief'? Explain some of the arguments for and against it.

Exam Question

Q1 Discuss how expanding the industrial and tourism sectors might affect the development of a country's economy. [12 marks]

The Lewis model — not that system for deciding results of cricket matches...

Development is difficult, and each country will be difficult in its own particular way. Just because a way has been found to promote development in one country, that doesn't mean the same method will work in a different country.

Ways of Promoting Growth and Development

The first section on this page describes policies that make use of either an interventionist approach, or a market-oriented one.

Protectionism is **Inward-Looking** — Free Trade is **Outward-Looking**

1) **Inward-looking** strategies seek to '**protect**' domestic industries until they're ready to **compete** internationally.
   - The main policy adopted is one of **import substitution**. Goods that were previously **imported** are replaced by **domestically made** goods. This is achieved by imposing **tariffs** and **quotas** on imported goods (see p.127-8).
   - **Subsidies** might be provided:
     - **either** to domestic producers to allow them to sell their goods at competitive prices
     - **or** on certain necessary products that everyone will need (even if they're imported from abroad), allowing them to spend more of their own income on domestically produced goods.
   - A currency might be maintained at an artificially **high exchange rate**, allowing the country to **import** selected goods from abroad cheaply — e.g. **raw materials** in order to reduce **production costs** for domestic firms.
2) The aim in the short term is to **create jobs**, **reduce poverty** and improve the country's **balance of payments**.
3) In the long term, the idea is that domestic industries will **grow**, benefit from **economies of scale**, and gain the necessary **knowledge** to compete on equal terms with firms from other countries.
4) However, being **protected** from international competition can result in **inefficiency**. And it can lead to a country's **resources** being misallocated — a country's **comparative advantage** may not be exploited as fully as it could be.
5) **Outward-looking** strategies, on the other hand, emphasise **free trade**, **deregulation** and the promotion of **foreign investment**.
6) Firms are encouraged to **invest** and seek new **export markets**.
7) The benefits and costs of outward-looking strategies are what you might expect from greater **free trade** — **increased efficiency** and **competitiveness**, but more **economic dependence** between countries. See Section 8 for more information.

Countries like India and China have used outward-looking policies to great effect in recent decades.

Interventionist strategies used to be popular, but now Free-Market strategies are more common

- **Interventionist strategies** are similar to **inward-looking** strategies — e.g. they often involve import substitution, subsidies and high exchange rates. They may also involve industries being **nationalised** (i.e. taken into government ownership), and policies forcing producers to sell their goods to government-run distributors to keep prices low.
- They were popular in the past and were based on '**dependency theory**', a theory that claims developing countries are still held back economically because of the way they were previously **exploited** by richer ones — e.g. by being **forced** to specialise in primary products. In practice these interventionist strategies were associated with **low rates** of economic growth, **balance of payments** problems, **government deficits**, **corruption** and general **inefficiency**.
- From about the 1980s, **free-market strategies** have been more popular. These are very similar to the **outward-looking** strategies described above. Free-market strategies recommend **less government intervention**, and place a much greater emphasis on **free trade**. There's a lot more information on pages 127-9.

Microfinance involves making **Small Loans** to **Businesses** and **Individuals**

1) **Microfinance** means providing loans to **small businesses** and low-income **individuals** who may not be able to get loans from traditional banks.
2) The aim is for people in developing countries to use the loans to become more **financially independent** — either by developing **businesses** or investing in **education**.
3) **Interest** is charged, but this may be at a **lower rate** than would be charged by normal banks.
4) Although microfinance works for **some people**, it's not clear that microfinance can reduce poverty on a **large scale**.

One aim is to avoid people needing to go to informal lenders charging very high rates of interest ('loan sharks').

Fair Trade schemes guarantee producers a **Minimum Price**

1) **Fair trade** schemes aim to offer **individual farmers** (or **groups** of small producers) in developing countries a **guaranteed minimum** ('fair') price for their goods. In return, the producers usually have to accept certain **conditions** (e.g. they must agree to **inspections**, use **approved** farming techniques, and treat employees **fairly**).
2) The guaranteed minimum price makes **long-term planning** easier for producers — they're not subject to the large fluctuations in price that are often associated with primary products (see p.145).
3) However, the **distortion** of the **market price** can lead to **overproduction** — farmers may not realise that a **low price** is a sign that they should grow a **different** crop. So when prices are low, farmers may flood the market and drive the price down **further** — affecting producers who **don't** belong to the fair trade scheme.

These schemes ultimately rely on buyers being willing to pay above the market price — this may not always be the case.

Ways of Promoting Growth and Development

International Institutions and Non-government Organisations also offer help

International Monetary Fund (IMF)

- The IMF was set up in 1945 to "ensure the stability of the international monetary system".
- Most countries in the world are members of the IMF. Each member has a '**quota**', based on the size of its economy. A country's quota determines the amount of **financial resources** it has to make available to the IMF.
- The IMF uses these resources to offer **loans** (as well as **technical advice**) to developing countries in order to **fight poverty** and to help countries facing **economic difficulties** (e.g. problems with their balance of payments).
- If necessary, the IMF can **borrow** further funds from member countries under two schemes — the General Arrangements to Borrow (GAB) and the New Arrangements to Borrow (NAB).
- Nowadays, the IMF offers policy advice to countries so they can maintain **economic stability** and **raise living standards**. It also carries out economic **research**, making the data available to **member countries**.

The International Bank for Reconstruction and Development (IBRD) — part of The World Bank

- The IBRD aims to **reduce poverty** in middle- and low-income countries, and promote **sustainable development** (see p.150) that helps to improve employment prospects.
- It offers **loans**, **grants** and **advice** to its member countries.
- It raises most of its funds from **commercial financial institutions**, where it can borrow at **favourable rates** as a result of it being backed by most of the world's **governments**.

The International Development Association (IDA) — another part of The World Bank

- The IDA aims to **reduce poverty** in the world's **poorest** countries.
- It offers **loans** (called **credits**), **grants**, **debt relief** and **advice** to the world's poorest countries.
- It concentrates on funding schemes that relate to:
  - **health care** (especially in reducing the impact of AIDS, malaria and TB),
  - **education**,
  - **clean-water** provision,
  - **infrastructure** improvements — e.g. after civil war or natural disaster,
  - **institutional reforms** — i.e. reform of state institutions (such as government departments or the police) to reduce corruption or improve opportunities for businesses.

Loans are either interest-free, or interest is charged at very low rates.

Non-government organisations (NGOs)

- These include **private organisations** and **charities**.
- They may be large institutions, but the work they do is often on a **small scale**.
- For example, they may offer **microfinance**, **training** in business skills, **technical** or **medical** assistance, or **advice** on environmental sustainability.

Different countries will need different Development Policies

1) The policies adopted to help any particular country will depend on what it's thought has **caused** that country's problems. Various **economic theories** are used to justify different approaches (e.g. 'dependency theory' on p.148).
2) But all developing countries are **different**, so each country will require its own particular **mix** of **policies**. What worked well in one country may not have the same effect in another — it's important to find out what works **in practice**.

Practice Questions

Q1 Describe the differences between inward-looking and outward-looking development strategies.

Q2 What is microfinance?

Exam Question

Q1 Comment on the effectiveness of fair trade schemes for promoting growth and development in developing countries. [12 marks]

Stop staring out the window — that outward-looking strategy won't help...

There's no 'magic development wand' that can be waved to make everything better. Economies are (very) complex things, and trying to steer an economy towards a particular outcome is tricky. So be ready to recognise the pros and cons of any approach.

Sustainable Development

***These pages are for** OCR Unit 5 (The Global Economy).*
Sustainability is a fairly easy thing to understand, but it's often quite difficult to achieve in practice.

Sustainability** is about not being **Unfair** to **Future Generations

1) **Sustainability** is quite a simple idea:

> **Sustainability** is about meeting the needs of people **now**, without making it more difficult for people **in the future** to meet their own needs.

2) For example, a country may be able to **boost** its economic development, but if it uses up its **natural resources** in the process, this may lead to problems **maintaining** this economic progress in the future.
3) It's feared that the world's production and consumption are **unsustainable** in the long run — i.e. we won't be able to carry on producing and consuming **forever** in the way we currently are.

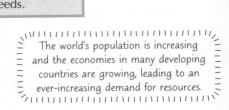

> The world's population is increasing and the economies in many developing countries are growing, leading to an ever-increasing demand for resources.

Sustainable Development** means looking after the **Environment

Some of the biggest issues concerning sustainability are to do with **climate change** and **environmental damage**. For example:

Deforestation

- In South America and Africa, large areas of **rainforest** have been **cleared**, both for the **timber** that can be harvested, and to turn the land over to **agriculture** (e.g. to graze cattle).
- Although there were **economic benefits**, such as the creation of extra **jobs** and increased **foreign income**, the effect was **short-lived**. **Farming** the land often proved to be **less profitable** than was hoped. And the **fertile soil** that made the land attractive for farming was sometimes **washed away** after the trees holding it in place had been removed.
- The removal of the forest also meant the **loss** of an important source of **fuel**, **food** and **medicines** for many of the poorest people in those regions.
- There's a more widespread impact too. As forest is lost, **biodiversity** (i.e. the number of species of animals and plants in that area) **falls**, and large amounts of **carbon dioxide** (see below) are emitted if trees are **burned** or left to **rot**. The risk of **flooding** also **increases**.

Carbon dioxide emissions

- Carbon dioxide is a **'greenhouse gas'**, and it contributes to **climate change**.
- As some countries (e.g. China) have developed their economies over recent decades, the amount of **carbon dioxide** they emit has **increased dramatically**.

> Developed countries still emit far more carbon dioxide than most developing nations though.

Demographic Changes** affect **Sustainability

1) Changes in a country's **demographics** (i.e. the size of different **groups** within the country's **population** — e.g. men, women, children under 16, people over 60) can have a large effect on the **sustainability** of its **economic development**.
2) Some developing countries have **fast-growing populations**. This isn't necessarily a bad thing, but it can create difficulties — although people are an **economic resource**, they also **drain** other resources (which causes problems for sustainability).
3) The problem is especially bad if there's a high **dependency ratio** (a dependency ratio shows the number of people who are either **too young** or **too old** to work compared to the number of people of **working age**).
4) For example, if there are lots of **children** in a population, the country's **education** system can struggle to cope. Similarly, an **ageing population** can place a huge demand on a country's **health care** system.

> A high dependency ratio means there are relatively few people who can pay the taxes needed to support those who can't work. High dependency ratios can also be a problem in developed countries.

5) So development strategies have to take into account the likely effects on a country's demographics. These can be significant, because as a country develops, its **mortality** and **fertility** rates tend to decrease.
6) This can be a good thing, since it could eventually result in an **increase** in the **working-age population**, which can create economic benefits, such as more **saving** and **investment**. This can then lead to even **more** improvements in the economy.
7) But unless there's been proper **planning** for when these workers **retire** (e.g. suitable **pension** arrangements and improvements in **health care**), there can be difficulties looking after them in their old age. This may mean any economic development **may not** turn out to be sustainable.

> The overall effects of changes in population and demographics depend on the policies adopted by governments over a large number of years.

Sustainable Development

There's **No Agreed** way to measure **Sustainability**

1) There **isn't** an **internationally agreed** way to measure **how sustainable** a country's economic growth is. However, this is what the **Index of Sustainable Economic Welfare (ISEW)** tries to do.
2) **ISEW** is an **adjusted** version of GDP — it measures improvements in **standards of living**, while taking into account the **environmental damage** and **resource depletion** caused as a result. Other adjustments allow for factors that affect people's **economic welfare** (either for the better or for the worse), but which **aren't included** in the 'normal' GDP figure.
3) For example, if an activity leads to a lot of **pollution**, **resource depletion** or increased **inequality**, then the GDP figures are adjusted **downwards**. However, activities like **unpaid household labour** (such as child care or washing-up) which **improve** people's welfare will result in the GDP figures being adjusted **upwards**.
4) ISEW also excludes **'defensive' spending** — i.e. spending needed to **repair** the **damage** caused by other spending. For example, the cost of treating smoking-related illnesses isn't included in the ISEW figures.
5) Although ISEW is an attempt to produce a **more comprehensive** measure of welfare, it's criticised for having certain **value judgements** built into the way it's calculated. For example, the value of unpaid household labour or the cost that should be attached to the burning of each tonne of fossil fuels is difficult to measure **objectively**.

   Although any measure will include some value judgements — e.g. GDP assumes that the value or cost of these things is zero.
6) This is one of the major problems with measurements of this kind — it's hard to work out what needs to be **included**, what can be **ignored**, and what **monetary value** should be attached to each benefit or cost.
7) But measures that help governments understand the **'true cost'** (i.e. including economic, social and environmental costs) of economic activities are useful. For example, if economic activities have large **negative externalities**, then a government can introduce policies to internalise those negative externalities.

Introducing **Policies** to achieve **Sustainable** growth **Isn't Easy**

1) Governments will usually want to create **economic growth** and bring people out of **poverty**, but this can often involve a **trade-off** with **environmental sustainability** (see p.107). For example, economic growth may depend on there being supplies of cheap **energy** (e.g. for factories to operate efficiently). But if, as in China, this comes from lots of coal-fired power stations, then **pollution** can be high.
2) This isn't an easy problem to solve. Deciding whether to remove people from poverty **now** or develop environmentally friendly technologies to maintain the environment for **future generations** is not an easy choice for a government to make.
3) It's especially difficult for governments in **politically unstable** countries to take measures whose benefits will only be felt in the **long term**. They may prefer instead to introduce popular policies with much greater benefits in the **short term**.
4) **International agreements** are often vital when it comes to ensuring sustainability. For example, if one government introduces measures to reduce the amount of **pollution** emitted by vehicles (e.g. a new tax on carbon dioxide emissions), then that might put its transport industry at a disadvantage compared to **other countries**. This means it's important for groups of countries to **work together**, as there's often **no incentive** for any **single country** to take measures on its own.
5) Governments also need to be careful that growth is reasonably evenly spread throughout a country. **Regional policies** (i.e. policies aimed at helping particular areas) can offer **incentives** to create growth in **disadvantaged** regions, and can help make the best use of local **resources**, and ensure **uneven development** doesn't lead to **social problems**.

Everyone at the International Development summit was agreed — growth in a country should be as evenly spread as the butter on their morning crumpets.

Practice Questions

Q1 What is meant by the term 'sustainability'?

Q2 Describe some difficulties often encountered when trying to achieve sustainable economic development.

Exam Question

Q1 Discuss how useful adjusted economic indicators, such as the Index of Sustainable Economic Welfare (ISEW), are for measuring sustainable economic development. [15 marks]

There are no diagrams in this topic — I didn't need any demographics...

I've said it once, I've said it a thousand times... sustainable development is not an easy nut to crack. But it's not all doom and gloom. Some people argue that with economic growth and greater prosperity, cleaner technologies can be afforded. So perhaps the trade-off between economic growth and environmental sustainability isn't as great as it initially seems. We shall see.

Get Marks in Your Exam

These pages explain how you'll get marks in the exams. To do well you need to satisfy four different Assessment Objectives (AO1, AO2, AO3 and AO4), each of which requires different skills. Prove you've got the skills and you'll get the marks.

Make Sure You Read the Question Properly

It's easy to **misread** a question and spend 10 minutes writing about the **wrong thing**. A few simple tips can help you avoid this:

1) **Underline** the **command words** in the question (the ones that tell you **what to do**). Here are some common ones:

Command words	Means write about...
Define	the **meaning** of the word
Explain	**why** it's like that (i.e. give reasons)
Analyse	something's **causes** and/or **effects**, and consider any **links** between them
Assess / **Evaluate** / **Comment on** / **Discuss**	the **advantages** and **disadvantages OR** the **arguments for** and **against**

When you explain you need to **apply** your **economic knowledge** to the **context** you're given. The context could be a **specific market** or some **data**. E.g. *Explain why the price of beef changed in 2011.*

If you need to **define** a word, you need to give its **meaning**. E.g. *Define the term 'merit good'.*

Analysing requires you to **apply** your **own ideas** and your **economic knowledge** to show **why** you think something has happened or will happen. E.g. *Analyse the effect of higher interest rates on the economy.*

'Assess', 'Evaluate', 'Comment on' and 'Discuss' all mean roughly the **same thing**. They're about **weighing something up**. E.g. *Evaluate the success of reducing government spending to lower inflation.* You need to give a **balanced** answer — talk about all the **different viewpoints** on the subject.

2) **Underline** the **key words** (the ones that tell you **what it's about**), e.g. productivity, sustainability, market failure.
3) **Re-read** the question and your answer **when you've finished** to check that your answer addresses **all parts** of the question. A **common mistake** is to **miss a bit out** — like when questions say 'refer to the data from...' or 'illustrate your answer with...'.

You get marks for AO1 (showing knowledge) and AO2 (applying knowledge)

AO1 and **AO2** questions usually start with words like "**Define**", "**State**", "**Give**", "**Explain**" or "**Calculate**".

1) **AO1** marks are for **content** and **knowledge**.
2) This means things like knowing the **proper definitions** for **economics terms**.

1) **AO2** marks are for **application** — applying your knowledge to a situation.
2) Numerical **calculations** are also marked as **application**.

To make sure you'll get marks for content, always give definitions of key terms you're using, or formulas if you're doing a calculation.

You'll get more marks when you Analyse (AO3) and Evaluate (AO4)

AO3 marks are for **analysis** — thinking about benefits, costs, causes, effects and constraints. Analysis questions usually start with words like "**Analyse**", "**Examine**" or "**Explain why**".

1) Use your knowledge to **explain** your answer and give **reasons**. Consider **both sides** of the **argument** — you can only get **limited** analysis marks by looking at **one side**.
2) If there's data, say what the figures **mean**, talk about what might have **caused** them and say what **effect** you think they will have on the economy in the **future**.

AO4 marks are for **evaluation** — using your **judgement**. Evaluation questions usually start with words like "**Evaluate**", "**Assess**", "**Discuss**", "**Comment on**" or "**To what extent**".

1) **Weigh up** both sides of the argument — consider the **advantages** and **disadvantages** and say which **side** of the argument you think is **strongest**.
2) You **don't** need to give a **definite** answer. You can point out that it **depends** on various factors — as long as you say **what those factors** are, and say **why** the issue depends on them. Use your judgement to say what the **most important factors** are. The main thing is to **justify** why you're saying what you're saying.

Get Marks in Your Exam

There are marks for the **Quality** of your **Writing**

1) For **all three** exam boards the **quality** of your **written communication** (QWC) will be assessed. Examiners will mark **specific questions** for QWC — in the **Edexcel** exams these questions will be **labelled** with an **asterisk** (*) and in the **AQA** exams these questions will be the ones worth **25 marks**. If you're doing **OCR** QWC is assessed in the **Section B** question in **Units 3 and 4** and the **final essay question** in **Unit 5**.
2) Your QWC is **very important** because the examiner will decide whether to give your answer **more** or **fewer** marks depending on your QWC.
3) You have to write **formally** and **arrange relevant information clearly** — write a **well-structured essay**, not a list of bullet points. You need to use **specialist vocabulary** when it's appropriate, so it's well worth **learning** some of the **technical terms** used in this book.
4) You have to write **neatly** enough for the examiner to be able to read your answer. You also need to use good **spelling**, **grammar** and **punctuation** to make your meaning **crystal clear**. If your handwriting, grammar, spelling and punctuation are **so** far up the spout that the examiner **can't understand** what you've written, **expect problems**.

Impressive... but it won't get you any marks.

Jotting down a quick essay plan will help you to structure your essay.

Use the **Data** for **Data-response Questions**

That sounds **pretty obvious**, but there are some things you need to bear in mind:

1) If a question asks you to **refer** to a table of data, a graph, or some text, make sure you **use** it in your answer.
2) **Don't** just copy out loads of data — any data you use in your answer must be **relevant** to the specific point you're making.
3) If a question asks you to 'analyse' or 'explain why', you'll need to use the data as well as your **economic knowledge** to **back up** the points you make.
4) If you need to draw a diagram, do it in **pencil** so you can rub it out if you make a mistake. However, label your diagrams in **pen** so they're nice and clear.
5) Sometimes you might need to do a **calculation**. You can use a calculator to find the answer, but **write down** your **working out**. If you get the answer **wrong** you can still **pick up marks** for using the correct method.

Don't forget to include **All** the **Skills** in **Extended Answer Questions**

1) Essay questions need a bit of **planning**. Jot down a **rough outline** of what you want to say — remember, you need to make your answer **balanced**, so make a list of the **advantages** and **disadvantages**, or the arguments **for** and **against**.
2) **Diagrams** are a quick and easy way of explaining quite difficult concepts in your answers, but make sure you **explain** what your diagrams show and **always** refer to them in your answers. **Label** your diagrams properly so they're clear.
3) In an essay answer you need to show **all** the skills — **don't jump** straight to the **evaluation** part. So, if you're asked to evaluate the extent to which lowering the price of exports can bring about the recovery of the UK economy, you need to:

- **Define** what is meant by exports and recovery (this will get you your **AO1** marks).
- Explain how an increase in exports is **relevant** to the recovery of the UK economy (for **AO2** marks).
- Give the **advantages** and **disadvantages** of lowering the price of exports (for **AO3** marks).
- Finally, for the **AO4** marks, **weigh up** both sides of the argument and **decide** how successful, in your opinion, lowering the price of exports would be in helping the UK economy to recover.

Learn this stuff for some inflation of marks...

Of course, to do well in the exam you've got to know all that economics stuff inside out, but these pages will give you an idea of how you can put that knowledge to best use in the exam. Keep in mind that you don't just need to learn the facts for economics — you've got to prove to the examiner that you understand them and can apply them to various scenarios. So all very simple, really...

Do Well in Your AQA Exam

*These pages are most useful for students taking the **AQA** exam. But the sample exam questions are worth a read no matter what exam board you're doing.*

A2 Economics is divided into *Two Examined Units*

1) Both of the units in A2 are **synoptic** — this means you are expected to use the knowledge you gained at AS to support your understanding of the topics you'll be covering at A2.
2) Unit 3 is called **Business Economics and the Distribution of Income** and builds upon knowledge gained in Unit 1 — it introduces you to more complex microeconomic models, and gives you an insight into how firms make decisions and how the labour market works.
3) Unit 4 is called **The National and International Economy** and builds upon knowledge gained in Unit 2 — in this unit you are expected to carry out more advanced analysis and evaluation of the causes of changes to macroeconomic indicators (and the results of those changes).
4) The exam papers for Unit 3 and Unit 4 have the **same format**:

> 1) You have **2 hours** for each exam.
> 2) **Section A** contains **extracts** of information about two different scenarios (one scenario will have a **global** context and the other one will be in the context of **the EU**) — you have to choose **one** of these scenarios to answer questions about. Each scenario is followed by **three** compulsory **data-response** questions, worth **40 marks** in total. You have to show that you **understand** the information and can **analyse** and **evaluate** it.
> 3) **Section B** contains three essay-style questions — you have to choose **one** to answer. This section is worth **40 marks** in total.
> 4) There are **80 marks** available overall, so you should aim to get a mark **every one and a half minutes** — this will give you a guide as to how long to spend on each question.

Here's an Example Question and Answer

This question is like the data-response ones you'll get in Section A of the exams.

Extract A: Average hourly wage for full-time employees in the UK in 1986 and 2011 and the % change in this period (1986-2011).

Full-time employees		Hourly wage (£)* 1986	Hourly wage (£)* 2011	Percentage change (%)
Lowest earners	Bottom 1% earn less than	3.48	5.93	+ 70
	Bottom 10% earn less than	4.80	7.01	+ 46
Average		7.78	12.62	?
Highest earners	Top 10% earn more than	14.78	26.75	+ 81
	Top 1% earn more than	28.18	61.10	+ 117

*1986 wages converted to 2011 prices

Q1) Using **Extract A**, calculate to the nearest whole number the percentage change in the average wage of a full-time employee between 1986 and 2011 **and** identify **one** significant feature of the hourly wage data.

5 marks

Answer:

$$\text{Percentage change} = \frac{12.62 - 7.78}{7.78} = \frac{4.84}{7.78} \times 100 = 60\%$$

This answer is incorrect, but the correct working out would achieve 1 mark.

One significant feature of the data is that the percentage change in wage for the top 1% of earners was considerably higher than for the bottom 1% of earners (117% and 70% respectively).

You need to refer to data from the extract to get all of the available marks.

This answer would get 3 marks. Even though the percentage change is wrong, 1 mark is given for correct working. A further mark would be given if the answer had been between 62 and 63%. The correct answer (62%) would get 3 marks, even without working. For the significant feature of the data there are lots of different answers you could give — 1 mark is given for identifying a feature and then a second mark is awarded if you back it up with some data from the table. Some other valid points include: 'The percentage change in hourly wage is highest in the top 1% of earners' and 'The average hourly rate in 1986 (£7.78) was considerably lower than the average wage in 2011 (£12.62)'.

Do Well in Your AQA Exam

An **Example Essay-Style Question** and **Answer** to give you some tips

Extract B: Wage rates and the introduction of the National Minimum Wage.

The National Minimum Wage (NMW) sets a legal minimum hourly wage rate for employees of different ages. It was introduced by the Labour government in 1999 to help prevent workers from being exploited by being paid such a low wage that they would not be able to afford a decent standard of living. A key aim of the NMW was to increase the earnings of the poorest workers in society and create a more equitable distribution of income. For example, if a worker was in a low-paid job the introduction of the NMW may have increased their hourly wage and therefore increased their earnings.

From looking at data collected about full-time UK workers between 1986 and 2011, the introduction of the NMW seems to have had the desired effect of increasing earnings of workers on the lowest wages. Between 1986 and 1998 (before the NMW was introduced) the bottom 1% of earners experienced a 15% increase in real wages. However, after the introduction of the NMW (1998-2011) the bottom 1% of earners experienced a larger increase in real earnings of 51%.

When the NMW was being introduced it had some strong opponents who suggested that it would have negative impacts for the UK labour market and economy as a whole. However, on reflection the introduction of the National Minimum Wage has been considered one of the most successful government policies of recent times.

Q3) **Extract B** (lines 12-15) suggests that the National Minimum Wage in the UK was not universally popular before its introduction but that it's now considered to have had an overall positive impact.

Using the data and your economic knowledge, discuss the positive and negative impacts for the UK labour market associated with the introduction of a National Minimum Wage. 25 marks

The National Minimum Wage is a pay floor. This means that employers can't pay a wage less than the NMW.

Introducing a NMW can have several positive impacts on the labour market. One impact that it can have is to increase the wages of the poorest workers in society and help reduce poverty. For example, if you are on a low wage and the NMW means that your hourly wage rate increases, then this can make a real difference to the amount you earn. The NMW having an impact on the wages of low earners is demonstrated in the data in Extract B because it shows that after the NMW was introduced, the bottom 1% of earners experienced a higher increase in real wages than during a similar period before its introduction. This boost in earnings might also act as a morale boost, resulting in happier workers who might be more productive.

There is some good evaluation here. It's important to use the data as this is asked for in the question.

Also, the NMW helps to encourage people to seek work. For example, having a minimum wage might act as an incentive to unemployed people to take jobs that would previously have paid less than the NMW. In addition, increasing the number of people in work is good for the economy. An increased number of people willing to work means that the supply of workers in the labour market increases.

Having a NMW can have some negative impacts though. It might lead to a decreased level of employment in a labour market. This is because an increased wage rate could result in reduced demand for labour due to increased wage costs for firms, although the impact on firms might vary depending on the staff they employ. If a firm has lots of staff below the NMW then the introduction could considerably increase their wage costs, but if they only employ a small number of staff below the NMW then it might not have much of an impact.

You could use diagrams to support this answer — e.g. a diagram showing the excess supply of labour when wages rise. This is a good way of picking up marks.

A NMW may not actually decrease poverty. This is because many of the poorest people in society, such as the elderly and disabled, are not in work, so aren't able to benefit from the increased earnings that a NMW could bring.

The last sentence isn't specifically about the labour market, so wouldn't get any marks.

A NMW might also decrease the competitiveness of UK firms compared to firms in other countries that have lower wage costs. UK firms may pass on their increased costs to consumers by increasing their prices, and this could contribute to inflation.

There's no conclusion to this essay, but it's always best to put one in.

This essay is a good effort. There's quite a lot of analysis and there's definite discussion of the pros and cons of introducing a NMW. However, there's a bit of discussion that isn't directly relevant to the question and there's no conclusion. A diagram or two might really help your discussion too. This answer would get about 19 marks.

Do Well in Your Edexcel Exam

*These pages are most useful for students taking the **Edexcel** exam. But the sample exam questions are worth a read no matter what exam board you're doing.*

A2 Economics is divided into Two Examined Units

1) Both of the units in A2 are **synoptic** — this means you are expected to use the knowledge you gained at AS to support your understanding of the topics you'll be covering at A2.
2) Unit 3 is called **Business Economics and Economic Efficiency**. This unit develops the knowledge you learnt in Unit 1 and looks into competition between firms and how this is influenced by the number and size of firms in a market.
3) Unit 4 is called **The Global Economy**. This unit develops the knowledge you learnt in Unit 2 and applies it to a wider global context. It covers different economic models and how policies are used to deal with certain economic problems.

Unit 3 Exam — 1 hour 30 minutes

1) **Section A** is made up of two-part questions — the first part is a **multiple-choice** question, and in the second part you have to **explain** why the answer you've chosen is correct. This section is worth a total of **32 marks**.
2) **Section B** contains two **data-response** questions — but you only have to answer **one**. You have to show that you **understand** the information and can **analyse** and **evaluate** it. This section is worth a total of **40 marks**.
3) There are **72 marks** in total, so you should aim to pick up a mark roughly **every minute.**

Unit 4 Exam — 2 hours

1) **Section A** is made up of three essay-style questions — you have to choose **one** to answer. This section is worth a total of **50 marks**.
2) **Section B** contains two **data-response** questions — but you only have to answer **one**. You have to show that you **understand** the information and can **analyse** and **evaluate** it. This section is worth a total of **50 marks**.
3) There are **100 marks** in total, so once again you should aim to pick up a mark roughly **every minute**.

Here's an Example Question and Answer

This question is like the multiple-choice ones you'll get in Section A of the Unit 3 exam.

1

The diagram shows a firm operating under conditions of perfect competition. Which one of the following is true?

A The market has high barriers to entry.

B The area PXQO represents the firm's total costs.

C In the short run the firm experiences supernormal profits.

D In the long run the level of supply in the market would increase and this would cause the market price to rise.

E The lack of profit available acts as a disincentive to firms entering the market.

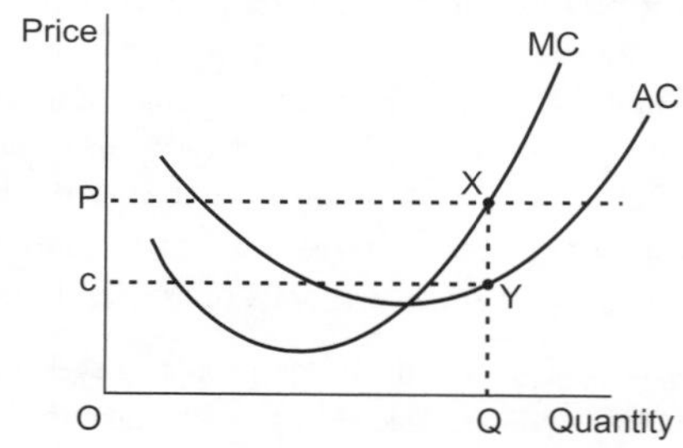

Answer ☐ 1 mark

Explanation 3 marks

Answer: C ← You'd get 1 mark for giving the correct answer.

Explanation:

In perfect competition, consumers and producers in a market have perfect knowledge. When perfect competition exists a firm can experience supernormal profits in the short run, so C is the correct answer. These profits act as an incentive for firms to enter the market, so E is incorrect, and this is possible because there are no barriers to entry in a perfectly competitive market, so A is also incorrect.

Giving a characteristic (or definition) of perfect competition would get you 1 mark.

An explanation of why option C is correct gets you 1 mark.

You can get 1 mark for an appropriate explanation of why a particular option is incorrect.

This answer gets full marks. Even if you get the answer wrong, you can still earn explanation marks, e.g. you can be awarded 1 mark for a correct definition, or 1 mark for correctly rejecting an option. If you are unsure which option is correct, start by explaining as fully as you can which options are incorrect.

Do Well in Your Edexcel Exam

Here's another **Example Question and Answer**

This question is like the essay-style ones you'll get in Section A of the Unit 4 exam.

***1** (b) To increase the welfare of its population, a government could act to reduce levels of poverty. Discuss the different ways that a government in a developing country could intervene to alleviate poverty.

30 marks

People experience poverty when they have a very low standard of living. There are two types of poverty: relative and absolute. Relative poverty is when a person's income is below a certain fraction of the average income in society, and absolute poverty is when a person can't meet their own basic needs, such as housing, with the amount they earn.

> A clear definition is a good way to start your answer.

Unemployed people are some of the most likely to be poor (e.g. those that can't find work or aren't able to work due to sickness), and people on very low wages (which are paid to many people in developing countries) may also live in poverty.

> This shows an understanding of who is likely to be affected by poverty in society.

There are a number of different policies that can be used to address poverty in developing countries and distribute wealth more evenly in society.

A developing country could introduce a system to pay benefits to people on low incomes to increase their standard of living. This could be brought in alongside a progressive tax system, which taxes people on higher incomes more than those on a lower income and could help fund the benefits system. This would redistribute money from high earners to people in poverty. However, benefits and a progressive tax system might not reduce poverty due to the poverty trap. The poverty trap happens when poorer people earn higher wages but then get a reduced level of benefits. This can act as a disincentive to finding work, working more hours or going for a promotion to earn more — overall their income and wealth might not increase much even though they are earning more money. In addition a progressive tax system could contribute to high earners leaving the country to avoid taxes, which in turn could reduce tax revenue and reduce the government's ability to pay benefits to poorer members of society (possibly increasing poverty).

> Here is a thorough explanation and discussion of two policies. This is the sort of detail you need to get the higher marks.

> It's important to talk about pros **and** cons in a question that asks you to 'discuss'.

A developing country could also introduce (or increase) a national minimum wage. This can reduce poverty for low earners by increasing their earnings, although it has the downside that it may reduce labour demand due to increased wage costs for firms — this can be seen in the diagram on the right.

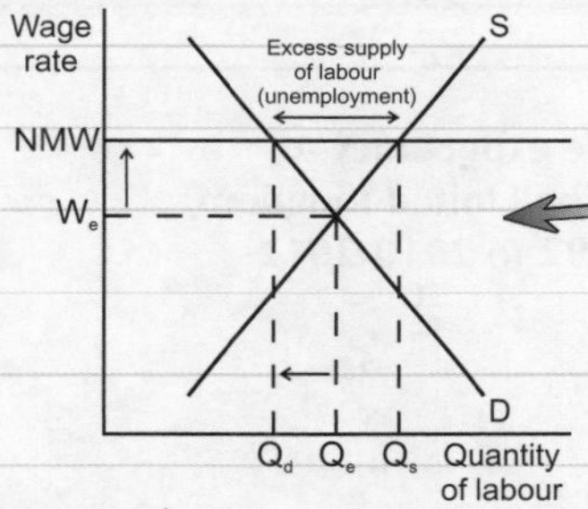

> An accurate, relevant diagram is always worth putting in. It's a good way of picking up marks.

Introducing a minimum wage would raise the wage rate from W_e to NMW. This would cause the supply of labour to increase from Q_e to Q_s and demand to fall from Q_e to Q_d. This could cause unemployment of Q_s to Q_d because there's an excess supply of labour, which could lead to increased poverty.

Another possible policy would be the state provision of some services, such as health care and education. These could be paid for by tax revenues. Providing these services could reduce inequalities caused by income differences (e.g. the poor not being able to afford health treatments).

> These are valid policy ideas but there's no evaluation so they don't attract the top marks.

A government could also act to reduce the geographical immobility of labour. For example, by making sure there is affordable housing (or other accommodation) available near where jobs are available, they can make it possible for people to move and fill the jobs. This policy could avoid people having to live in poor quality accommodation (e.g. in shanty towns on the outskirts of some cities in developing countries) because they can't afford suitable housing.

> As usual, it's a good plan to include a conclusion in an essay-style answer like this.

For developing countries some of these policies may be more feasible than others. These policies seem likely to involve considerable government spending (e.g. a benefits system, or reducing geographical immobility), which a government in a developing country may simply not be able to afford. Also, as discussed earlier, there is a possibility that some of these policies (in addition to being hugely expensive) may not have the desired effect of reducing poverty and may, in fact, make it worse.

> This shows that you've thought about how these policies may not always have the desired effects.

This is a high-scoring answer. It shows evidence of real understanding of how a developing country could implement policies that could contribute to reducing poverty. There could be a little more evaluation of a couple of the policies, but apart from that there's not much wrong here. This answer shows again how it's worthwhile to put in a diagram if it's relevant and correct. This answer could get around 24 marks.

Do Well in Your OCR Exam

*These pages are most useful for students taking the **OCR** exam. But the sample exam questions are worth a read no matter what exam board you're doing.*

A2 Economics is divided into Three Units, but you only study Two of them

1) You will study Unit 5 along with **either** Unit 3 or Unit 4.
2) All of the units in A2 are **synoptic** — this means you are expected to use the knowledge you gained at AS to support your understanding of the topics you'll be covering at A2.
3) Unit 3 is called **Economics of Work and Leisure** — it covers what work and leisure are and looks in depth at the labour and leisure markets. It also covers how government failure can affect the labour market, and the role of trade unions.
4) Unit 4 is called **Transport Economics** — it introduces you to trends in transport and transport markets, and looks at how government intervention and policy impacts transport markets.
5) Unit 5 is called **The Global Economy** — it looks in depth at macroeconomic indicators, trade, sustainability of development, and globalisation.

Unit 3/4 Exam — 2 hours

1) **Section A** contains one **data-response** question — you must answer all parts of the question. You have to show that you **understand** the information and can **analyse** and **evaluate** it. This section is worth a total of **25 marks**.
2) **Section B** is made up of three **essay-style** questions — you have to choose **one** to answer. This section is worth a total of **35 marks**.
3) There are **60 marks** in total, so you should aim to pick up a mark roughly **every two minutes**.

Unit 5 Exam — 2 hours

1) In this paper you're asked questions based on **'stimulus material'** which will be given to you before the date of the exam.
2) Some questions may be **data-response** questions and most will be **essay-style**, requiring answers of differing lengths.
3) There are **60 marks** in total, so once again you should aim to pick up a mark roughly **every two minutes**.

Here's an Example Figure with an accompanying Question and Answer

Fig. 1 Life expectancy at birth in the United Kingdom, 1990-1992 to 2010-2012

Year	Males	Females
1990-1992	73.16	78.70
1991-1993	73.36	78.78
1992-1994	73.67	79.02
1993-1995	73.83	79.11
1994-1996	74.08	79.31
1995-1997	74.24	79.38
1996-1998	74.49	79.55
1997-1999	74.73	79.70
1998-2000	75.01	79.91
1999-2001	75.32	80.12
2000-2002	75.61	80.36
2001-2003	75.85	80.47
2002-2004	76.15	80.68
2003-2005	76.50	80.91
2004-2006	76.87	81.24
2005-2007	77.14	81.44
2006-2008	77.38	81.61
2007-2009	77.68	81.84
2008-2010	78.01	82.08
2009-2011	78.41	82.42
2010-2012	78.71	82.58

Do Well in Your OCR Exam

This question is like a data-response one that you could be asked in Section A of the Unit 3, 4 or 5 exam.

1 (b) With reference to Fig. 1, comment on the possible implications of changes in life expectancy for government spending in the UK. 6 marks

The data in Fig. 1 shows that the life expectancy for both men and women in the UK has increased continuously between 1990 and 2012. This means that there will be an increasing number of older people in the UK population. This has an impact on the UK economy and in particular the level of government spending on state pensions and health care delivered by the NHS.

It's important to talk about what the data in Fig. 1 shows. This can get you up to 2 marks.

Generally, older people make more use of the NHS than younger people, so having an ageing population means that the NHS will require more resources to deliver sufficient health care. Similarly for pensions — as people live longer, there will be a larger number of people claiming a state pension from the government.

There is a worry that as the population ages the tax revenue that the government receives from people in work (e.g. via income tax) will not be enough to cover the increasing costs of pensions and health care. In order to address this problem, the UK government is reforming pensions. For example, it is raising the state pension age to try to reduce the demands put on the state pension budget.

A good explanation of what an ageing population means for the government can earn you up to 4 marks.

An increased number of older people may also reduce some government spending. For example, more retired people could mean that there are a larger number of people willing to volunteer for roles that the government would otherwise have to pay people to do.

Relevant information about what the UK government is planning will impress the examiners.

This answer gets 5 marks. There's some good analysis of the situation, but there's no data quoted from the figure and you need this to get the final mark available.

An *Example Extended Answer* to give you some tips:

2 (a) Analyse, using a diagram, the negative externalities linked to increasing levels of travel via road transport. 15 marks

Travelling by road (e.g. by car or lorry) generates negative externalities, so increasing use of road transport means that the impact of these negative externalities will be increasing. The negative externalities of production can be seen on the diagram.

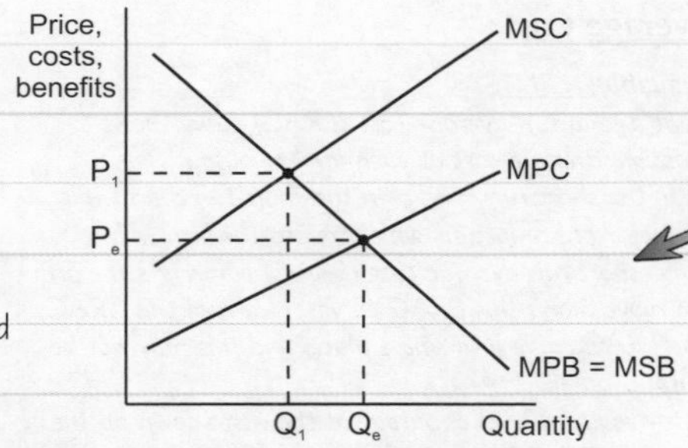

A perfect diagram like this can earn lots of marks, so it's a good idea to take time to check it over.

In this diagram the socially optimal output level of this service (where MSC = MSB) is Q_1 and the optimal price is P_1. However, in the free market only private costs are considered, so output would be Q_e and the price would be P_e. This would cause overproduction and underpricing of this service — more is produced and sold at a lower price than is desirable for society. This means that for each unit of road transport produced between Q_1 and Q_e the marginal social cost is greater than the marginal social benefit.

This is a really complete explanation of the diagram.

Increased road transport will result in increased levels of pollution, which will be damaging to the environment. Road transport can also have negative impacts for local residents. For example, their health may be affected by emissions from vehicles, which could result in increased costs for the NHS. Also, people who live next to roads may lose out financially — if they live next to an increasingly busy road, the value of their house could fall. More road transport could also increase pressure on the NHS and emergency services, as it may mean there is an increase in road accidents.

A thorough explanation of some externalities generated by road transport like this will get you higher marks.

There are many negative externalities linked to increased road transport that can increase costs to society. Increasing the cost of travelling by road may help reduce the overuse of road transport.

It's always a good idea to round off an essay-style question with a brief conclusion.

This answer could get 11 marks. It's a good answer but it's missing a definition of negative externalities (e.g. that MSC are greater than MPC). You can get 9 marks here for a perfectly labelled diagram (as shown in this answer). You need to give a couple of examples of negative externalities that can be generated (e.g. pollution due to increased emissions) and then explain their effects (e.g. could cause increased NHS costs).

Answers

Section One — Business Economics

Page 5 — The Costs of a Firm

1 Maximum of 4 marks available. HINTS:
- *The correct answer is C.*
- *The marginal cost is the additional cost of producing one more unit of output, so it only depends on variable costs. Because Firm X and Firm Y have the same variable costs, they must also have the same marginal cost.*
- *If you're not sure, you can rule out the other options one by one (and you'll get marks for doing this correctly, even if you get the final answer wrong). The firms have the same variable costs but different fixed costs, so they must also have different total costs and average costs. This lets you rule out options A, B, D and E.*

Page 7 — The Law of Diminishing Returns

1 a) Maximum of 3 marks available. HINTS:
- *Start by describing the shape of the marginal cost curve between A and B — i.e. that it decreases as output rises.*
- *Explain that as the levels of factor inputs that are variable in the short run are increased, the firm is getting more additional output from each unit of input, so the cost per unit of that additional output is decreasing.*

b) Maximum of 3 marks available. HINTS:
- *Start by describing the shape of the marginal cost curve between B and C — i.e. that it increases from its minimum value as output rises.*
- *Explain that this is the result of the law of diminishing returns — as the levels of factor inputs that are variable in the short run are increased, the firm is getting less additional output from each unit of input, so the cost per unit of that output will be greater.*

Page 9 — Economies and Diseconomies of Scale

1 Maximum of 5 marks available. HINTS:
- *State that what's being described in the question is a firm encountering 'diseconomies of scale' — this is where the average cost per unit increases as the firm's output rises.*
- *Give examples of how diseconomies of scale can arise, e.g. 'Larger firms whose output has grown can suffer from increases in wastage and loss, as materials may seem in plentiful supply', or 'As a firm grows and its output increases, communication between workers may become less efficient.'*

Page 10 — Long Run Average Cost

1 Maximum of 6 marks available. HINTS:
- *Start by explaining what a long run average cost (LRAC) curve shows — i.e. the minimum possible average cost at each level of output.*
- *Explain what happens in the short run — e.g. 'In the short run a firm will have at least one fixed factor of production, which means the firm will be operating on a particular short run average cost (SRAC) curve. As the firm varies its output, it can move along this SRAC curve. However, this SRAC curve will only meet the LRAC curve in a single place, and this may not be the required level of output.'*
- *State that to produce the required level of output at the cost shown on the LRAC curve, it may be necessary to move to a different SRAC curve, and this will involve varying the levels of all factors of production — this is something that can only be done in the long run.*

Page 11 — Returns to Scale

1 Maximum of 6 marks available. HINTS:
- *Start by defining returns to scale — e.g. 'Returns to scale describe the effect on output of increasing all factor inputs by the same proportion. For example, increasing returns to scale describe the situation when doubling the levels of all factor inputs, say, leads to output more than doubling. Similarly, decreasing returns to scale describe a situation when doubling the levels of all factor inputs leads to output less than doubling. And constant returns to scale describe a situation when doubling the levels of all factor inputs leads to output also doubling.'*
- *Explain when a firm might experience increasing, constant and decreasing returns to scale and how each of these affects average costs — e.g. 'As a business grows over the long run, it will often find it can initially achieve increasing returns to scale — i.e. more output is being produced per unit of input, so the average cost of output falls.'*

Page 13 — The Revenue of a Firm

1 Maximum of 15 marks available. HINTS:
- *Start by defining a price-making firm — i.e. it's a firm that has enough market power to set the price they sell their goods at.*
- *Then explain that even for a price-making firm, the higher it sets the price, the lower demand will be — its demand curve will slope downwards.*
- *But the firm's demand curve will also be its average revenue (AR) curve (since a demand curve and an average revenue curve both show what quantity of a product the firm will be able to sell at a particular price). This means the firm's average revenue curve will also slope downwards.*
- *The firm's marginal revenue (MR) curve must also slope downwards, because to increase sales, the firm has to reduce the price. In fact, the firm's MR curve will be twice as steep as its AR curve.*
- *Then define a price-taking firm — i.e. it's a firm that has no market power and so has to sell its goods at the price determined by the market. If it increases prices, it won't sell anything, and there's no need to decrease prices.*
- *Explain that for a price-taking firm, average revenue will be the same, no matter what quantity of goods it sells — i.e. its average revenue curve will be horizontal.*
- *Finish by explaining why the MR curve is horizontal, e.g. 'Marginal revenue = average revenue, because each extra unit sold brings in the same revenue as all the others — so the MR curve is also horizontal.'*

Page 15 — Profit

1 Maximum of 4 marks available. HINTS:
- *Explain that there are two options available for a company whose average costs exceed its average revenue in the long run, and that which option a firm chooses will depend on whether its average revenue is greater than or less than its average variable costs — e.g. 'If the firm's average revenue is greater than its average variable costs, the firm will continue to trade in the short run, but if the firm's average revenue is less than its average variable costs, the firm will shut down immediately.'*
- *In the long run, the firm will have to close down, since it will be making less than normal profit.*

2 Maximum of 4 marks available. HINTS:
- *The correct answer is D.*
- *Explain that if marginal revenue (MR) is greater than marginal cost (MC) at a particular level of output, the firm would increase its profit by increasing output, because the revenue gained by doing so will be bigger than the cost. This rules out options A, B and C.*
- *Then explain that if MR is less than MC, the firm would increase its profit by reducing output, because it cost the firm more to produce the last unit of output than it received for it in revenue. This rules out option E.*
- *Therefore, since it's a profit-maximising firm, it'll output at a level where MC = MR.*

Page 17 — The Objectives of Firms

1 Maximum of 25 marks available. HINTS:
- *Start by explaining that the traditional theory of the firm assumes that firms aim to maximise profit, but state that there are also other objectives that many firms try to achieve.*
- *You'll need to then describe some other objectives that are commonly pursued by firms and give possible reasons why — e.g. 'Firms may choose to maximise sales or revenue rather than profit, perhaps to increase their market share or to make it easier to obtain finance. However, pursuing any of these objectives will reduce profit, at least in the short term.'*
- *Explain that even if a firm is prioritising an objective other than profit maximisation in the short term, this may in fact be a way to maximise profit in the long term — e.g. 'A new firm may be aiming to increase output as quickly as possible in the short run in the hope of achieving its minimum efficient scale of production (MES). Although this means sacrificing profit in the short run, this may allow the firm to maximise profits in the longer term.'*
- *You should also discuss who decides what objectives a firm should pursue — e.g. 'The divorce of ownership from control means that it may not be a firm's owners who set the objectives but the directors and managers, and these may have priorities other than profit maximisation, such as enjoying the prestige of running a large firm.'*
- *For this question, you'll need to evaluate all your points and come to some kind of balanced conclusion — e.g. 'While long run profit maximisation is an objective pursued by many firms, there are good reasons to believe that other firms will have different objectives, even if only in the short run. It may even be that some of these firms' owners would like to pursue profit maximisation, but that those in day-to-day control are actually prioritising something else without their knowledge.'*

Answers

Page 19 — Why Firms Grow

1 Maximum of 10 marks available. HINTS:
- Start by defining horizontal integration — e.g. 'Horizontal integration is when firms at the same stage of the production process for similar products are combined to form a single company.'
- Then explain some of the benefits this might bring — e.g. 'The new, larger firm may be able to achieve economies of scale that weren't available to the smaller firms. These could be of various types, including marketing economies of scale, financial economies of scale, and technical economies of scale.'
- Explain that the integration would result in less competition in the market, so the new firm would possibly be able to further increase its market share.
- 'Discuss' means your answer needs to include some kind of 'weighing up', and so you should also mention that there are risks when firms merge to create a new, larger firm — e.g. 'Large firms can become complacent and less efficient, or they might not be able to react as fast as a smaller firm to changing circumstances. There are also other diseconomies of scale that the new firm might face — for example, communication might become more difficult, and it might be harder to coordinate all the actions of the larger firm.'

Section Two — Market Structures

Page 21 — Perfect Competition

1 Maximum of 15 marks available. HINTS:
- Draw some diagrams to show how the long run equilibrium position will be reached. You should include diagrams similar to those shown below.

Diagram 1 — Industry

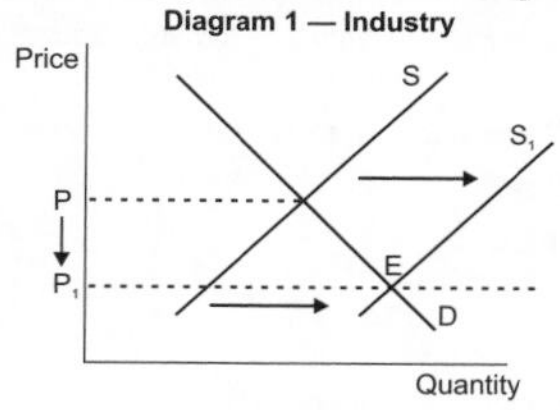

Diagram 2 — Firm

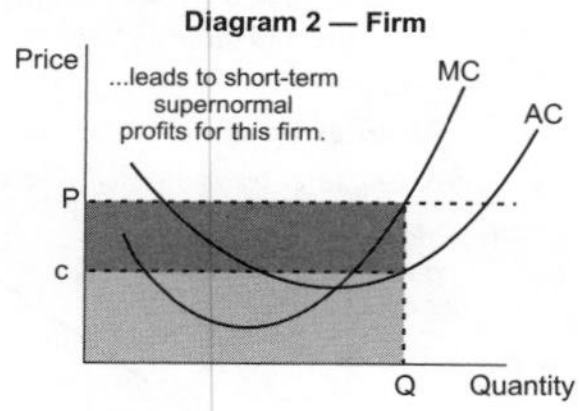

Diagram 3 — Firm

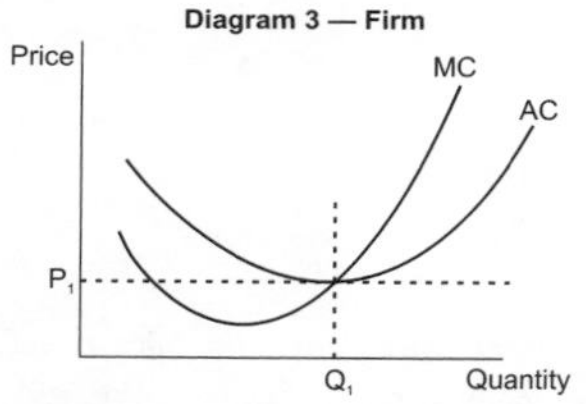

- Explain that diagram 1 shows initial supply (S) and demand (D). A firm will produce quantity Q at price P (shown on diagram 2).
- Describe how diagram 2 shows the supernormal profit a firm will make (the dark grey area), and explain how this will attract new firms to the market.
- State that this will shift the industry supply curve from S to S_1 (see diagram 1), and firms will undercut each other until they all make normal profit — so the long-term industry equilibrium is at E.
- Finish by explaining that — as the price falls from P to P_1 — the firm will reduce its output from Q to Q_1. So, in the long term, the equilibrium for this firm is at price P_1 and quantity Q_1 (shown on diagram 3).

Page 23 — Perfect Competition

Maximum of 5 marks available. HINTS:
- Briefly define dynamic efficiency — e.g. the ability to improve efficiency or products over time.
- Explain that the strategies to achieve dynamic efficiency involve investment and risk, and therefore if they are to take place, they need adequate reward.
- Explain that this means dynamic efficiency won't be achieved in a perfectly competitive market, e.g. 'Firms in a perfectly competitive market make normal profit, so there's no incentive to take risks as there's no reward — so dynamic efficiency won't be achieved in a perfectly competitive market.'
- State that, however, even in the most competitive real-life markets, some dynamic efficiency can usually be achieved.

Page 25 — Barriers to Entry

1 Maximum of 5 marks available. HINTS:
- Define barriers to entry, e.g. 'A barrier to entry is any potential difficulty or expense a firm might face if it wants to enter a market.'
- Explain why branding can be a barrier to entry — it creates familiarity, so it often makes a product the first choice for consumers.
- Finish by giving the possible ways in which an incumbent firm can create this barrier to entry — for example, the incumbent firm might create a strong brand by producing a product which is genuinely better than the competition, or it might create a strong brand using effective advertising.

2 Maximum of 15 marks available. HINTS:
- Define barriers to entry.
- Give examples of various barriers to entry — those which come from anticompetitive behaviour, e.g. 'Incumbent firms might lower prices to a level that new entrants can't match, therefore driving new entrants out of business.', and those which don't, e.g. 'Economies of scale exist in some industries, so there will naturally be a cost advantage for large incumbent firms.'
- You'll need to weigh up the various barriers to entry and use this reasoning to give a conclusion on the extent to which they result from anticompetitive behaviour.

Page 27 — Monopolies

1 Maximum of 10 marks available. HINTS:
- Define supernormal profit — e.g. 'Supernormal profit occurs when a firm's total revenue exceeds its total costs.'
- You need to include a diagram similar to the one below.

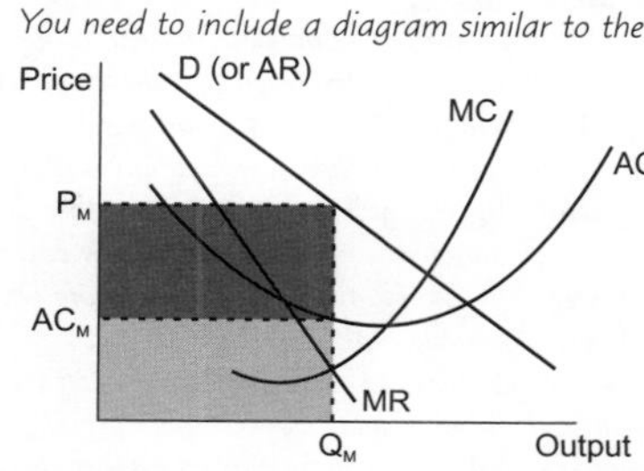

- Explain that a firm will aim to maximise profits, so it'll output where MC = MR.
- Go on to explain how this means that the firm will make a supernormal profit shown by the dark grey area.
- Finish by using barriers to entry to explain why the firm will continue to make this supernormal profit in the long run. E.g. 'Barriers to entry in a monopoly market are total — so no new firms can enter the market, and the supernormal profit won't be competed away. This means that, in the long run, nothing will change, so the firm will continue to make the same supernormal profit.'

Page 29 — Price Discrimination

1 Maximum of 10 marks available. HINTS:
- Define price discrimination, e.g. 'Price discrimination occurs when a seller charges different prices to different customers for exactly the same product.'
- Explain how price discrimination will lead to the transfer of some, or all, of the consumer surplus to the producer — so producers' revenues increase, which is a good thing for producers, but not consumers. Use diagrams to demonstrate this.
- Go on to give the possible benefits to consumers of price discrimination — explain that the extra revenue might be used, for example, to improve products, or that those who can afford higher prices might effectively be subsidising the lower prices paid by other consumers.
- Conclude your answer, e.g. 'So price discrimination is good for producers, but it can have both positive and negative effects for consumers.'

Page 31 — Oligopolies

1 Maximum of 10 marks available. HINTS:
- Briefly define an oligopoly, e.g. 'An oligopoly is a market which is dominated by just a few firms. There may be high barriers to entry, differentiated products, interdependency and the use of competitive or collusive strategies.'
- Mention the anticompetitive behaviour that might exist in an oligopoly — for example, collusion on prices might result in higher prices for consumers. This means firms would be making supernormal profits at the expense of consumers.

Answers

- Explain that there are possible benefits to consumers too — e.g. 'Firms might try to differentiate their products from those made by firms they're colluding with, which can lead to improved products.'
- The word 'extent' in the question is key — make sure you emphasise the importance of each argument you make to the interests of consumers. For example, explain that even with price collusion, prices are unlikely to be very high as this would probably attract new firms to the market — even if there are high barriers to entry. This may limit the negative effects on consumers.

Page 33 — Interdependence in Oligopolistic Markets

1 Maximum of 15 marks available. HINTS:
- Include a diagram of the kinked demand curve to back up your answer.
- Give the two assumptions of this model — e.g. 'This model assumes that if one firm raises its prices, then other firms will not raise their prices, but if one firm lowers its prices, then other firms will also lower theirs.'
- Explain what these assumptions will lead to — i.e. that when price is increased, demand is price elastic, and when price is decreased, demand is price inelastic.
- Give the consequences of firms raising or lowering prices — i.e. that any firm that either raises or lowers its prices will lose out as a result.
- Conclude by explaining, for example, 'Firms have no incentive to change prices, because they'll lose out either way — therefore there is price stability.'

Page 35 — Monopolistic Competition

1 Maximum of 12 marks available. HINTS:
- Start by explaining that in the short run, monopolistic competition resembles a monopoly market because of barriers to entry (even though they'll usually be quite low) and/or product differentiation — use a diagram.
- Explain that the long run position of monopolistic competition is more like perfect competition, and explain why — e.g. 'Barriers to entry either don't exist or are very low in markets with monopolistic competition, so new entrants will join the market, and therefore in the long run it'll behave more like there's perfect competition than like a monopoly market.'
- Explain that this is because a firm's demand curve shifts to the left as new firms join the market (because demand is split between more firms). State that this continues until only normal profit can be earned — include a diagram like the one at the bottom of p.34.
- Mention that firms aren't productively or allocatively efficient — and explain why. But state that if there's monopolistic competition, it's likely to be more efficient than a monopoly market, and that prices will generally be lower.

Page 37 — Contestability

1 Maximum of 10 marks available. HINTS:
- Start by giving a definition of high contestability — e.g. 'A market is highly contestable if barriers to entry and exit are low, and supernormal profits can potentially be made by new firms.'
- Explain that if incumbent firms were to achieve large supernormal profits, this would attract new firms to the market, so incumbent firms are likely to set relatively low prices to avoid attracting new entrants — because they don't want increased competition.
- Give some further effects of high contestability on incumbent firms, e.g. 'High contestability is more likely to encourage firms to create high barriers to entry.'
- Explain the long run effect — that firms in highly contestable markets will move towards productive and allocative efficiency.

Section Three — Government Intervention in the Market

Page 40 — Market Failure and Government Failure

1 Maximum of 10 marks available. HINTS:
- Define what public goods are and explain how they might lead to market failure — e.g. due to the free rider problem.
- Give a possible method of government intervention, e.g. 'The most common way of reducing this market failure is state provision of a public good. This means the state provides the good that the free market underprovides or won't provide.'
- You should include some examples — e.g. 'For example, governments often provide things such as education and street lighting.'
- Explain that, although this means that the public good is provided, there are problems with state provision. For example, you could mention the opportunity cost of providing a public good — other services won't be provided, or you could say that because the price mechanism won't work in a market for a public good, it's easy to under- or overprovide public goods.

Page 43 — Environmental Market Failure

1 Maximum of 10 marks available. HINTS:
- Start by defining what 'extending property rights' means, e.g. 'Extending property rights over a resource means giving someone, or a firm, ownership of the resource so that they will take responsibility for it.'
- Give examples of the possible ways that extending property rights can reduce negative externalities. For example, you could explain that if someone has control over a resource, they can charge (or refuse permission) for others to use or pollute that resource.
- Explain how the market mechanism should ensure that a resource isn't overused because its use will be determined by the forces of supply and demand, so any negative externalities are internalised. You could also mention that revenue from charging people to use the resource can be used to clear up or counteract any damage or pollution caused.
- Give examples of why extending property rights won't always successfully protect natural resources, e.g. 'Suing an individual or firm that infringes property rights can be expensive, so people can be put off from taking legal action to uphold their property rights.'

2 Maximum of 25 marks available. HINTS:
- Define market failure, e.g. 'Market failure (including environmental) occurs when there's an inefficient or inequitable allocation of resources.'
- Give some examples of environmental market failure, such as resource depletion.
- Use an externalities diagram like the one below to explain how externalities can cause environmental market failure.

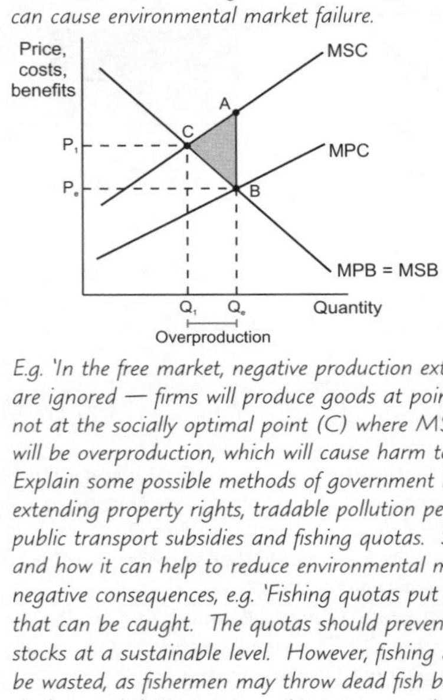

E.g. 'In the free market, negative production externalities, such as pollution, are ignored — firms will produce goods at point B where MPC = MPB, and not at the socially optimal point (C) where MSC = MSB. This means there will be overproduction, which will cause harm to the environment.'
- Explain some possible methods of government intervention — for example, extending property rights, tradable pollution permits, road congestion schemes, public transport subsidies and fishing quotas. State what each method is and how it can help to reduce environmental market failure, and consider any negative consequences, e.g. 'Fishing quotas put limits on the amount of fish that can be caught. The quotas should prevent overfishing and help to keep stocks at a sustainable level. However, fishing quotas can cause resources to be wasted, as fishermen may throw dead fish back into the water so that they don't exceed their quotas — this is an example of government failure.'
- You could go on to say how the free market could reduce environmental market failure if everything was treated as a scarce resource that people had to pay to use — however, this is put into practice with property rights, which often require government intervention to set up and then uphold the rights.
- Conclude your answer, taking into account the likely success of the various methods of government intervention you have written about.

Page 45 — Privatisation, Regulation and Deregulation

1 Maximum of 15 marks available. HINTS:
- Give a brief definition of what a public monopoly is.
- Explain that the lack of competition for a public monopoly tends to mean it'll be inefficient.
- Governments can use privatisation, i.e. a government can sell a publicly owned firm, to introduce competition to a market. You'll need to explain why private firms have incentives to be more efficient, e.g. 'Private firms tend to be open to free market competition, so they have an incentive to keep prices down, and therefore keep costs down by being more efficient.'

- Discuss the various advantages and disadvantages of privatisation, e.g. 'Privatisation should improve resource allocation, as privatised firms have to react to market signals of supply and demand.'
- You could argue that, in this case, privatisation alone is likely to result in a private monopoly, so there may be the need for deregulation and/or regulation to increase competition and, therefore, efficiency.
- Give the creation of internal markets as an alternative to privatisation — make sure you give examples, e.g. 'If hospitals were given more funding for each patient they treated, they'd need to compete with each other to get more patients to use, or be referred to, their hospital. This would increase competition and efficiency.' Explain some advantages and disadvantages of the creation of internal markets.

Page 47 — Competition Policy

1 Maximum of 10 marks available. HINTS:
- Explain that the Competition and Markets Authority (CMA), and similar bodies, monitor competition to look out for unfair behaviour by firms towards consumers or other firms — you should go on to explain that this is part of the UK government's competition policy, which aims to increase competition, improve fairness to consumers and reduce monopoly power.
- Give some specific examples of what the CMA monitors, such as mergers, agreements between firms (they're looking for anti-competitive agreements) and the opening of markets to competition — e.g. 'The CMA monitors mergers and takeovers so they can prevent those that aren't beneficial to the efficiency of the market or to consumers. They may choose to stop a merger that would give a firm too high a market share (e.g. over 25%) and make it a monopoly, or that would give a firm too much monopoly power.'

Page 49 — Cost Benefit Analysis

1 Maximum of 25 marks available. HINTS:
- Begin your answer by explaining what a cost benefit analysis (CBA) involves.
- Explain that the private and external costs and benefits are identified and assigned monetary values — give some examples of what would be considered in this case, e.g. the external benefit of increased tourism and the private cost of building new facilities, such as stadiums.
- State that the net social benefit = social benefit – social cost, and that the bid should go ahead if there's a net social benefit, and it shouldn't go ahead if there's a net social cost.
- Discuss the various advantages and disadvantages of carrying out the CBA. For example, you could explain that an advantage is that the various consequences of hosting the event are thoroughly assessed, so a government should be able to make a well-informed decision on whether or not to make the bid. A disadvantage is that it can be difficult to put a value on some costs/benefits, so the final decision might be incorrect.
- Make sure you weigh up the importance of the advantages and disadvantages, and finish with a concluding point, e.g. 'Despite the cost of carrying out the CBA, and the difficulties of assigning monetary values to some costs and benefits, it's better that a government uses a CBA so that it can make the most well-informed decision possible.'

Page 51 — Equity and Poverty

1 Maximum of 8 marks available. HINTS:
- Start by defining income and wealth, e.g. 'An individual's income is the amount of money they receive over a set period of time, e.g. per year. Income comes from a number of places, such as wages and interest on bank accounts. An individual's wealth is the total value of all of their assets. Assets can include money, property and shares.'
- Give some reasons for differences in income in the UK — you could say that people earn different wages, e.g. because there are different levels of demand for labour in different markets, and some people only earn state benefits as their income, which tend to be quite low.
- You could explain that wealth is more unevenly distributed than income — partly because income can be redistributed, e.g. through progressive taxation and benefits, but wealth isn't taxed, so it can't be.
- Another reason why wealth is unequally distributed is because those with high wealth can easily generate more wealth. Assets tend to increase in value more quickly than rises in income, and income created by assets can be used to buy more assets (i.e. more wealth).

Page 53 — Government Policies to Tackle Poverty

1 Maximum of 10 marks available. HINTS:
- Give brief definitions of absolute and relative poverty.
- Discuss the various positive and negative effects on absolute and relative poverty of the introduction of a national minimum wage (NMW), and of means-tested state benefits — you'll need to explain each point. For example, 'A NMW, if it's set at the right level, will reduce poverty amongst the lowest paid workers and increase the incentive to work.' and 'Means-tested benefits can be expensive — they're paid for by tax, so the introduction of means-tested benefits might mean that those on low incomes are taxed more.'
- You can mention how one policy can help in an area that the other can't, e.g. 'A NMW won't help anyone who's in absolute poverty if they're unemployed — especially if they're unable to work. However, means-tested benefits would provide these people with some form of income, reducing their relative poverty and potentially lifting them out of absolute poverty.'
- Make sure you include conflicts between the two policies, such as 'Means-tested benefits and a NMW might be set at a level where the combination worsens the poverty trap — if the NMW isn't high enough, the incomes of the unemployed who are receiving means-tested benefits might actually fall if they start earning minimum wage, e.g. because of the fall in their means-tested benefits and the increase in their taxes, so there would be no incentive for them to work.'
- Finish by saying how effective you think these policies might be overall.

Section Four — The Labour Market

Page 55 — The Structure of Employment in the UK

1 Maximum of 2 marks available. HINTS:
- E.g. 'The participation rate is the proportion of people of working age that are in work or actively seeking work in an economy (i.e. are economically active).'
- To get full marks you need to say that it's a proportion/percentage.

2 Maximum of 4 marks available. HINTS:
- Explain that an average increase in wages could be caused by all workers getting a pay rise — however, this isn't necessarily the case.
- There are several possible reasons why every person in the economy might not be getting a higher wage per hour, e.g. 'An increase in the average wage could be caused by some workers receiving very large increases in wages whilst the wages of other workers don't increase, or actually fall.' Another potential reason is regional pay differences — even though the average wage may have increased across the country, this may not be the case for all of the different regions.

Page 57 — Labour Demand

1 Maximum of 6 marks available. HINTS:
- There are several factors that can lead to the demand for labour increasing — you need to give two possibilities and explain them fully.
- For example, you could explain how increased demand for the goods/services that labour produces and increased labour productivity can result in increased labour demand, e.g. 'If a firm trains its staff and this increases their productivity, this would decrease the firm's unit labour cost, which would increase its demand for labour.'

Page 59 — Labour Supply

1 Maximum of 15 marks available. HINTS:
- Start off by explaining that the amount of labour that an individual supplies depends on the number of hours they are willing to work at a particular wage rate — individuals have to make a decision about how much time they spend on work and how much they spend on leisure.
- Explain that when wages rise from a low level, individuals are more willing to work because earning a higher wage can increase their standard of living.
- Explain how this is affected by the substitution effect and the income effect — e.g. 'The substitution effect means that higher wages should, in the short run, encourage people to work more, but when people reach a target income, the income effect will mean they want to start working less.' You should also mention opportunity cost here.
- You can go on to state that the substitution and income effects mean that the supply of labour can be shown with a backwards bending supply curve (see p.58). It'd be a good idea to include a diagram showing this curve to support your answer — if it's drawn correctly and explained well this will be worth lots of marks and it'll make it easier to explain the substitution and income effects.

Answers

Page 61 — Wages

1 Maximum of 15 marks available. HINTS:

- *Start off by explaining what transfer earnings and economic rent mean in relation to the labour market, e.g. 'Transfer earnings are the minimum payment that's required to keep labour in its current occupation. They can be thought of as the minimum wage that keeps a worker from switching to a different job. The wage that a worker is paid in excess of their transfer earnings is known as economic rent.'*
- *Then present a diagram that shows both transfer earnings and economic rent — see below (this diagram was shown on p.60).*

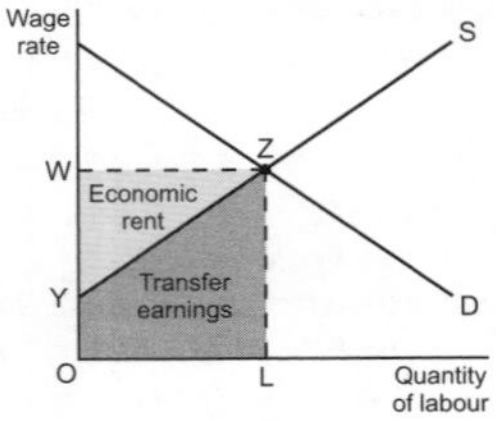

- *Explain fully what is shown by the diagram, e.g. 'In this labour market the equilibrium wage rate is W. A worker who's paid this wage supplies their labour at the margin because if the wage decreased, the worker would leave this market and look for alternative employment. For the marginal worker the wage rate is equal to their transfer earnings. The total of the transfer earnings of workers in this market is represented by the area under the supply curve below the equilibrium point (OYZL). The total of the wages of all workers in the market is equal to OWZL. This means that the economic rent is equal to the part of this area which doesn't represent transfer earnings — the triangle above the supply curve (YWZ).'*
- *You could also mention the effect that the elasticity of the supply curve has on the proportion of total earnings that are made up of economic rent and transfer earnings, e.g. 'As the supply curve becomes more elastic, the proportion of total earnings that's made up of economic rent decreases and therefore the proportion that's transfer earnings increases.' You could include a diagram to show this too.*

Page 63 — Labour Market Failure: Trade Unions

1 Maximum of 20 marks available. HINTS:

- *Start your answer with a definition of market failure — e.g. 'Market failure is the failure of the market mechanism to allocate resources efficiently.'*
- *Explain how trade unions can cause market failure, e.g. 'Trade unions (TUs) can cause market failure by negotiating higher wages that are above the market equilibrium wage, which can result in a surplus of labour and therefore unemployment.' You could use a diagram like the one on p.62 to explain how this can occur in a perfectly competitive labour market.*
- *However, it's important to also give some reasons why these increased wages might not lead to unemployment (and therefore market failure) — e.g. if workers agree to become more productive when receiving a higher wage.*
- *Explain what happens in a monopsonistic labour market — e.g. 'The presence of a trade union in a monopsonistic labour market can lead to an increase in the wage rate and level of employment.' This could also be explained with the help of a diagram (see p.63).*
- *Remember, in questions like this you need to give reasons to justify the points you're making (in this case, for and against the idea that trade unions cause market failure).*
- *Round off your answer with a brief conclusion — you could give your opinion about the extent to which trade unions cause market failure based on the points you've discussed.*

Page 65 — Labour Market Failure: Discrimination

1 Maximum of 10 marks available. HINTS:

- *Start by explaining what labour market discrimination is, e.g. 'Labour market discrimination is where employers treat a specific group of workers differently to other workers in the same job.'*
- *Explain some different types of discrimination (e.g. racial and age) and how they can impact the wages that are paid to any workers being discriminated against — in general these workers earn less than those that aren't suffering from discrimination. You can also go on to give other impacts on the wages of these workers, e.g. 'Workers being discriminated against may accept a job paying a low wage that they are overqualified for because they haven't been able to find a more suitable job.'*
- *You need to also explain how discrimination can impact worker productivity. For example, a worker being discriminated against might not be able to get a job that would make the most of their skills and maximise their productivity.*

2 Maximum of 8 marks available. HINTS:

- *You could draw a diagram similar to the one below (see p.65).*

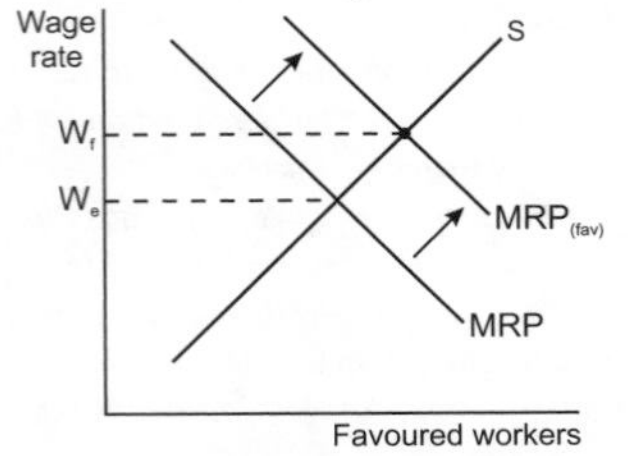

- *Using your diagram, explain that firms who discriminate believe that the MRP of their favoured workers (the workers the firm doesn't discriminate against) is higher than it really is, e.g. 'Employers believe the MRP of their favoured workers to be greater than it really is. This means they demand more of these workers, so the MRP curve shifts to the right, increasing the wage rate for these workers from W_e to W_f.'*
- *Make sure you explain how costs for firms that discriminate can be higher than firms that don't discriminate, e.g. 'This discrimination means that these firms have fewer workers to choose from and have to pay higher wages to the workers they choose to employ — this is shown on the diagram as the MRP curve for favoured workers is shifted to the right, meaning that favoured workers are paid wages above the market equilibrium wage level. By ignoring workers who may have been more suited to a job and more efficient, they increase their costs of production.'*

Page 67 — Labour Market Failure: Imperfections

1 Maximum of 8 marks available. HINTS:

- *In your answer you should explain what labour market segmentation means — e.g. 'A segmented labour market is one that consists of many individual labour markets.'*
- *Explain how the labour market would operate in the absence of barriers to entry and exit, e.g. 'If there were no barriers to entry and exit, workers would move from low wage jobs to high wage jobs until everyone had the same wage. However, in reality there would still be some wage differentials because not everyone has the motivation and talent to do a high-paying job.'*
- *Explain that the presence of barriers to entry and exit in reality means that segmented labour markets exist. This is because these barriers prevent the free movement of workers between all of the different jobs that are available, so many distinct labour markets exist.*
- *You could give an example of one of these barriers to entry, e.g. 'A barrier to entry for some jobs is a particular qualification — for example, to get a job as a pharmacist you need a particular university qualification.'*

Page 69 — Government Intervention: Taxes and Benefits

1 Maximum of 8 marks available. HINTS:

- *You could start your answer by defining what a flexible workforce is, e.g. 'A flexible labour force is one where workers can transfer between activities quickly in response to changes in the economy.'*
- *You need to mention different methods that governments can use to increase labour force flexibility and discuss the likely effectiveness of each method, e.g. 'The government could provide or subsidise training schemes for workers to increase their flexibility. The skills and knowledge the workers gain from such training will make them more attractive to employers and are likely to allow them to transfer between jobs more easily.'*
- *Other examples of methods include making it less costly for firms to hire and fire workers, and reducing the power of trade unions.*

Page 71 — European Union Intervention and Migration

1 Maximum of 15 marks available. HINTS:

- *Start by briefly describing what a national minimum wage (NMW) is.*
- *Describe and explain some advantages that the introduction of a NMW would bring — for example, reducing poverty for some of the poorest members of society, boosting morale of low-wage workers and increasing their productivity, and increasing tax revenue to allow greater government spending e.g. 'Introducing a NMW may increase the earnings of people on very low incomes and reduce the number of people living in poverty in a country.'*

Answers

- Describe and explain some disadvantages surrounding the introduction of a NMW — for example, increasing wage costs for firms leading to them reducing the number of staff they employ, decreasing competitiveness compared to countries with lower wage costs, and increasing prices of goods due to increased wage bills for firms being passed on to consumers, e.g. 'The increased wage costs brought about by the introduction of a NMW might mean that firms pass on these costs to consumers by increasing their prices, which could also contribute to inflation in the economy.'
- Make a conclusion about the impact of introducing a NMW — here you can give your opinion of whether you think introducing a NMW will have a positive or negative impact given the advantages and disadvantages you've discussed.

Section Five — The Leisure Market

Page 73 — Leisure

1 Maximum of 2 marks available. HINTS:
- E.g. 'Leisure is free time that people can spend how they choose. It doesn't include time used for necessary activities like chores, sleeping and travel.'
- You could give some examples of activities that people might consider leisure — for example, watching TV or going to the beach.

Page 75 — The Cinema Admissions Market

1 Maximum of 15 marks available. HINTS:
- Start by describing the structure of the market for live Premier League broadcasting rights — you need to explain that the Premier League is the monopsony seller of these broadcasting rights, and that the rights are sold in bundles to broadcasters. The fact that there's a monopsony means there's no competition amongst sellers.
- 'Discuss' means you need to cover both sides of the argument, so you need to explain aspects of the market that are competitive as well as those that aren't, e.g. 'The market has become more competitive after the European Commission ruled that the rights had to be sold in bundles rather than in a single exclusive package. This lowered a barrier to entry for broadcasters because the amount they had to pay to enter the market was reduced. As a result, the market became more contestable and other firms could enter the market (introducing competition).'
- You can develop this further by explaining how other broadcasters needed to buy a large number of very expensive rights to successfully compete with BSkyB, so there was no real competition in the market until BT managed to win a significant proportion of the rights.
- Explain that the market has been changed from a monopoly to a duopoly, as BT now also has a dominant position in the market.
- You can then talk about the degree of competition in a duopoly — this is an oligopolistic market dominated by a very small number of firms (just two), e.g. 'It will be difficult for new firms to enter the market, but if the two large firms in the market are offering similar products then there might be a great deal of competition between them (reducing supernormal profits), unless the firms are colluding rather than competing.'

2 Maximum of 8 marks available. HINTS:
- First you could define economies of scale, e.g. 'Economies of scale occur when the average cost of producing a unit of output decreases as a firm's output rises.'
- Then explain two specific economies of scale that might occur, and say how they're relevant to the cinema industry.
- To get all the marks you'll need to explain how each economy of scale will result in lower average costs, e.g. 'If a firm has a cinema with a large capacity then they will be able to sell more seats for the same showing than a firm with a smaller cinema. This will result in a technical economy of scale because some costs will be fixed (e.g. electricity and maintenance for the screen), and these will be spread across more customers — so the average cost of providing the service will be lower.'

Page 77 — The Holiday Market

Maximum of 20 marks available. HINTS:
- First describe the characteristics of monopolistic competition, i.e. lots of firms in the market, low barriers to entry, some product differentiation, and so on.
- Then analyse how well the holiday market matches these characteristics — come up with some ways in which it matches the model, e.g. 'There are many firms in the holiday market, and their products are differentiated — holidays differ on destination and length, for example. Products are particularly differentiated in the specialist holiday market, which offers holidays for particular activities or to unusual destinations, and this market is made up of a large number of small firms. The specialist holiday market therefore appears to have some of the characteristics of a monopolistically competitive market'.
- To get all the marks you need to balance your answer by coming up with ways that the market doesn't match the model, or ways that it displays characteristics of other models, e.g. 'However, the package holiday market displays characteristics of an oligopoly — this part of the market has high concentration ratios, as it's dominated by a few large firms. This is due to high barriers to entry and large economies of scale which mean mergers are common in the package holiday market.'
- Once you've thoroughly covered how well the market fits the model, you need to come to a conclusion. Refer back to your earlier arguments so it's clear you've weighed them up to justify your conclusion, e.g. 'The extent to which the holiday market is monopolistically competitive depends on which area of the market you are looking at. The specialist holiday market appears to be monopolistically competitive, whereas the package holiday market does not — it displays characteristics of an oligopoly.'

Page 79 — The Television Broadcasting Market

1 Maximum of 8 marks available. HINTS:
- Start by giving the characteristics of an oligopoly, i.e. it's a market dominated by a few firms offering differentiated products, where barriers to entry are high, and so on.
- Then describe how the air travel market fits this model, e.g. 'The market is dominated by a few large firms, such as British Airways, and barriers to entry are very high because of limited capacity at airports, and the high cost of buying or leasing planes.'
- To get all the marks you also need to come up with ways in which the market doesn't fit the model, e.g. 'Deregulation, such as open skies policies, has made the market more contestable, and there is now increased competition from low-cost airlines whose products are less differentiated. As a result, the market for some routes could be considered to be monopolistically competitive.'

2 Maximum of 8 marks available. HINTS:
- First explain what's meant by a contestable market, e.g. 'A contestable market is a market that's open to new competitors because the barriers to entry and exit are low.'
- Then discuss how well the television broadcasting market matches this description — you need to come up with arguments on both sides to get all the marks.
- Explain aspects of the market which are contestable, e.g. 'The switch to digital broadcasting and the availability of cheap programming has made the market more contestable. Small broadcasters can enter and leave the market easily, for example, because their sunk costs are reduced by buying cheap programmes — so barriers to entry and exit are low.'
- Then give ways in which the market isn't contestable, e.g. 'However, the subscription television market has extremely high barriers to entry because existing firms are vertically integrated — they make their own programmes and transmit them over their own network. This makes it very difficult for new entrants to compete because they can't access these programmes or networks, and the costs of making their own programmes and setting up their own network are extremely high. These high sunk costs form a barrier to exit too.'

Section Six — The Transport Market

Page 81 — Transport

1 Maximum of 5 marks available. HINTS:
- Start by giving a definition of derived demand — e.g. 'Demand for something is derived if it only exists as a consequence of demand for something else.'
- Explain how demand for transport is usually a result of other demands — the question doesn't specify freight or passenger transport, so you need to cover both, e.g. 'The demand for passenger transport comes from demand to get to places, such as work. Demand for freight transport results from demand from firms to bring raw materials together for production, and to bring their finished products to the market.'
- You could then expand your answer by explaining why demand may not always be derived, e.g. 'People don't usually travel just to consume transport. However, occasionally transport is consumed as a leisure activity — for example, a scenic train journey.'

Answers

Page 83 — Trends in Transport

1 Maximum of 4 marks available. HINTS:
- Give a couple of changes in the last 20 years that have increased demand for air travel — for example, the falling price of air travel, and rising incomes.
- Explain how each change has resulted in increased demand, e.g. 'Real incomes have risen in the UK in the last 20 years, and this has increased demand for air travel because demand for passenger air travel is income elastic to some extent. For example, people may choose to take more foreign holidays as their incomes rise, and these often involve air travel.'

Page 85 — Privatisation

1 Maximum of 8 marks available. HINTS:
- You could start with a brief explanation of what privatisation means, e.g. 'Privatisation is the transfer of the ownership of a firm from the public sector to the private sector.'
- You then need to explain why privatisation of transport industries should improve efficiency, e.g. 'Privatisation should reduce x-inefficiency and improve dynamic efficiency because firms are motivated by the incentive of profit to reduce costs and invest in improving their products. Private provision should also improve allocative efficiency because firms can respond to market forces, which should improve the allocation of resources.'
- The question says 'discuss', so you need to cover both sides of the argument — give some reasons why privatisation may not improve efficiency. For example, because market prices ignore the externalities of transport, allocative efficiency may actually be worse in a privatised transport industry.
- Finally, to get all the marks, you need to come up with a conclusion, e.g. 'Whether or not privatisation improves efficiency will depend to some extent on whether privatisation brings competition to the market. Without competition there will be less incentive for firms to improve efficiency, as they won't be forced to do so in order to remain competitive.'

Page 87 — Deregulation and Market Structure

1 Maximum of 20 marks available. HINTS:
- Start by giving some characteristics of a competitive market. For example, explain that competitive markets contain a large number of firms offering products which are good substitutes for one another.
- Then explain how the bus market has been deregulated, e.g. 'Local Authorities previously controlled the market for local bus services — they had to give approval for operators to run these services, and imposed price controls. Outside of London, these restrictions on routes and prices were removed when the bus market was privatised.'
- Give ways in which deregulation of bus transport has encouraged competition in the market, e.g. 'Deregulation has removed legal barriers to entry to the market for bus transport outside London. This has made the market more contestable, so firms can now enter the market more easily. If more firms enter a market this should result in greater competition.'
- Then explain why in practice there isn't much competition in the market, e.g. 'Though the bus transport market became highly competitive soon after deregulation, it has since become more concentrated, and is now oligopolistic. Large economies of scale mean that mergers are common in the market, and large firms also have an advantage in being able to link a larger network of services together conveniently. There have also been suggestions that larger firms have engaged in predatory pricing, forcing smaller firms out of the market, and creating a barrier to entry.'
- You could also explain that in some areas there's no competition — local monopolies often exist because firms tend to focus on a specific area rather than competing nationally.
- To get all the marks you need to offer a conclusion — refer back to the points you've made on either side of the argument to show that your conclusion is backed up, e.g. 'Although deregulation initially brought competition to the bus transport market by lowering barriers to entry, in the long term it hasn't been successful in doing this. This is in part because of the advantages that large firms have in the bus transport market, which mean that the market has become more concentrated and less competitive over time.'

Page 89 — Transport Market Failure

1 Maximum of 4 marks available. HINTS:
- Begin by defining negative externalities, e.g. 'Negative externalities are costs of production and consumption which are imposed on third parties (i.e. people other than the producer and consumer).'
- Then explain how the existence of negative externalities of transport results in market failure, e.g. 'Transport has negative externalities, so the marginal social cost of transport use is higher than the marginal private cost. This causes market failure because it results in overconsumption of transport — the external cost is not included in the price of transport use, so the market equilibrium occurs at a lower price and a higher level of consumption than is socially optimal.'
- You could use a diagram like the one on p.88 to answer this question, but make sure you label it properly so it's clear what you're showing. You'll still need to explain that the market failure is overconsumption, and refer to the diagram to make it clear why negative externalities cause this.

Page 91 — Government Intervention in Transport

1 Maximum of 8 marks available. HINTS:
- Explain how subsidies work, and how they might reduce congestion, e.g. 'Governments can offer subsidies to firms providing public transport. This will reduce costs for public transport providers, so supply will increase and prices will fall. Lower prices will encourage more people to use public transport, which may mean they switch away from car use, and so congestion would be reduced.' You could also use a diagram to help explain your answer, like the one on p.91.
- Once you've covered how subsidies might reduce congestion, balance your answer by giving some reasons why this method might not be effective, e.g. 'The effect of subsidies may be limited if demand for public transport is price inelastic, which it may be on some routes. Subsidies are only likely to reduce congestion on routes where public transport and car travel are suitable substitutes for one another — people will only switch away from car travel if public transport is available for the journey they're making.'
- You could also mention that subsidies may not actually result in lower prices if firms simply use them to increase profits.
- Then come to a conclusion — make it clear why the points you've made so far lead to this conclusion, e.g. 'Subsidies are likely to lower the price of public transport, making it more attractive. However, public transport isn't always a suitable alternative to travelling by car, so this may not actually result in reduced car use in general, or in congested areas in particular.'

Page 93 — Resource Allocation

1 Maximum of 15 marks available. HINTS:
- Start by explaining what CBA is, e.g. 'CBA (cost benefit analysis) is a method of judging whether to go ahead with a proposed project. CBA involves giving monetary values to the expected costs and benefits of the project, in order to come up with the net social cost or net social benefit.'
- Then you could give some examples of factors that might be included in a cost benefit analysis of a new transport infrastructure project, e.g. 'A cost benefit analysis of a new transport infrastructure project can include external costs and benefits. For example, a CBA of a project to build a new road might include the cost of blight in communities close to the new infrastructure and the benefit of reduced congestion.'
- You can then explain why including external costs and benefits could make CBA more effective than other methods at assessing the overall worth of infrastructure projects, e.g. 'By putting monetary values on externalities, CBA can include them in a calculation of the worth of a transport infrastructure project. This should mean that a CBA gives a more accurate estimate of the worth of a project than assessments that only consider private costs and benefits.'
- Balance this by explaining at least one reason why it might not be effective, e.g. 'However, the effectiveness of CBA may be limited by the fact that putting monetary values on non-money costs and benefits (such as accidents or saved time) is extremely difficult, and may be inaccurate. So the net social cost or benefit that a CBA arrives at may not be a true reflection of the overall worth of an infrastructure project.'
- Finally, you need to make a judgement of whether it's effective overall, e.g. 'CBA should be effective at measuring the overall worth of transport infrastructure projects — despite problems with accurately putting values on external costs and benefits, it does at least attempt to include externalities. This means that CBA is likely to be more effective than the approach that private firms take, which typically only considers financial costs and benefits.'

Page 95 — Transport Policy

1 Maximum of 15 marks available. HINTS:
- Start with a definition of a sustainable transport policy, e.g. 'A sustainable transport policy aims to provide for current transport needs, without impeding the ability of future generations to meet their needs.'

Answers

- Then discuss types of policy which may be seen as sustainable. For example, policies which encourage people to restrict their use of modes of transport that have high external costs, or policies which encourage people to switch their travel to modes of transport with fewer negative externalities, by increasing the availability and attractiveness of these modes.
- Explain why each type of policy can be seen as sustainable, and give specific examples of each type of policy, e.g. 'Policies that aim to encourage less use of modes of transport with higher negative externalities may be seen as sustainable, because they reduce the external cost of transport use for current and future generations. These include policies such as fuel taxes and road pricing.'

Section Seven — The National Economy

Page 99 — Economic Growth

1 Maximum of 8 marks available. HINTS:
- You could start by explaining what's meant by an improvement in the standard of living, e.g. 'The standard of living in a country includes many things, such as the level of wealth and access to necessary goods and services. An improvement in the standard of living will occur when there's an improvement in people's economic welfare. This might be the result of increased wages, or improvements in the services that people use.'
- Then you should give at least two reasons why economic growth might improve standards of living, e.g. 'Economic growth means that output is rising, which will lead to an increase in jobs, causing a fall in unemployment, and a rise in wages. If more people are employed and have higher wages, then their standard of living will improve.' You could go on, for example, to mention how economic growth might lead to investment in cleaner, more efficient production processes — this will reduce pollution that harms the environment, and therefore improve living standards, e.g. if the air is cleaner, this may improve people's health.
- Balance your answer by considering how economic growth might not improve the standard of living, e.g. 'Short run economic growth can lead to inflation, and higher prices may mean that some people's standard of living will decrease, even when there's economic growth.'

Page 101 — Unemployment

1 Maximum of 8 marks available. HINTS:
- First state what unemployment may mean for an economy, e.g. 'Unemployment means that an economy isn't operating at its full capacity, as there's wasted labour that isn't being used. As a result, there may also be other resources that are not being exploited, such as offices and machines.'
- Then explain how this will impact upon economic growth, e.g. 'A country's economic growth may be harmed if there's high unemployment because fewer people will have income to spend, which may mean that firms' profits and output will fall. However, a government might respond by increasing its spending on unemployment benefits, so spending might not decrease by a large amount.' You could go on to talk about how it's hard for people who are unemployed for long periods of time to get a job (because their skills become outdated), and how this might affect economic growth.

Page 103 — Inflation

1 Maximum of 15 marks available. HINTS:
- You could start off by defining inflation, e.g. 'Inflation is a sustained rise in average prices over time. It's measured in the UK using the Retail Price Index (RPI) and the Consumer Price Index (CPI).'
- Demand-pull factors and cost-push factors are the main causes of inflation, so you need to explain each in turn.
- Start by explaining demand-pull factors and their effect on inflation, e.g. 'Demand-pull inflation is caused by excessive growth in aggregate demand compared to aggregate supply. Keynesian economists argue that this is caused by high consumer and/or government spending, which leads to an increase in aggregate demand. Rises in inflation are likely to be sharper when the economy reaches full capacity, as there will be shortages of labour and resources that will cause prices to rise.' You could go on to say that monetarists believe demand-pull inflation is caused by increases in the money supply, and briefly explain the quantity theory of money.
- Then you can talk about cost-push factors, e.g. 'Cost-push inflation is caused by rising costs of inputs to production, which firms are forced to pass on to consumers in the form of higher prices. For example, a wage increase above a rise in productivity will increase firms' total costs and lead to price rises. Price rises could then lead to further wage demands and a wage-price spiral.'
- You could include diagrams of demand-pull and cost-push inflation in your answer like the ones on p.102-103.
- Make sure you finish your answer with a conclusion.

Page 105 — Tackling Unemployment and Inflation

1 Maximum of 8 marks available. HINTS:
- You could start by defining the natural rate of unemployment, e.g. 'The natural rate of unemployment (NRU) is the rate of unemployment when the labour market is in equilibrium.'
- Then give at least two ways that the NRU could be reduced by a government — for example, you could mention some supply-side policies that are used to make the labour market more flexible, or to reduce frictional or structural unemployment, e.g. 'A government could improve occupational mobility by investing in training schemes that help workers to improve their skills.'

Page 107 — Macroeconomic Policy

1 Maximum of 12 marks available. HINTS:
- Start by explaining what the four main macroeconomic objectives are, i.e. strong economic growth, reducing unemployment, low inflation and equilibrium in the balance of payments.
- Then describe how these four objectives can be achieved by an increase in a country's aggregate supply (or long run aggregate supply) — use a diagram to show this:

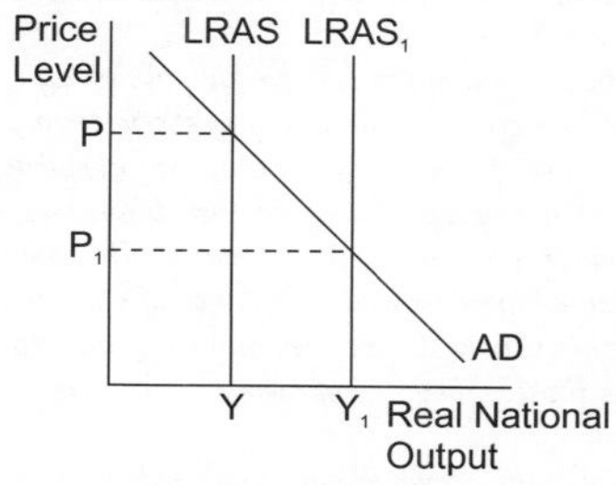

- You must explain what the diagram shows, e.g. 'If aggregate supply is increased so that the LRAS curve shifts to the right (from LRAS to $LRAS_1$) then this will achieve an increase in output (from Y to Y_1). This increase in output is economic growth, which will lead to a reduction in unemployment. In addition, the price level will fall (from P to P_1), so inflation will be controlled. This will also improve the country's competitiveness — so the balance of payments will improve.'
- You should give some examples of how a government could achieve this kind of increase in aggregate supply (i.e. long run economic growth), e.g. 'To shift the LRAS curve to the right a government would need to stimulate an increase in the quantity and quality of the factors of production. For example, it could encourage immigration in order to increase the country's workforce.'

Page 111 — Fiscal Policy

1 Maximum of 10 marks available. HINTS:
- It's likely that a government would use a progressive tax to reduce inequality, so you could start by explaining how progressive taxation could achieve this, e.g. 'A government might use a progressive taxation system to redistribute income. A progressive tax system is one where an individual's taxes rise as a percentage of their income as their income rises. This means that the rich will pay higher taxes, reducing income inequality. Revenue raised in this way can be used to provide benefits and state-provided services for the poor, which will also help to reduce inequality.'
- You could go on to mention how the government could also reduce inequality by providing tax relief for the poor.
- You should balance your answer by considering why taxation may not be effective at reducing inequality, e.g. 'If a progressive tax is set too high for the rich it might create a disincentive to work and lead to a fall in revenue received by the government. This would mean that the government would have less to spend on benefits and services, which may increase inequality.'

Page 115 — Monetary Policy

1 Maximum of 10 marks available. HINTS:
- Start by explaining what quantitative easing involves, i.e. the creation of 'new money' to increase the money supply and help boost aggregate demand in an economy.

Answers

- You then need to explain how this 'new money' might be created and what positive effects this can have, e.g. 'The central bank of a country (e.g. the Bank of England) will buy assets, such as government Treasury bills, from private firms. This will provide these firms with money to spend or lend to other firms and individuals — boosting aggregate demand.' Make sure you fully explain what positive effects a boost in aggregate demand will create for an economy.
- Balance your answer by thinking about any drawbacks of a policy of quantitative easing, e.g. 'Quantitative easing has been used during recessions to boost demand — however, its effectiveness has been limited by the reluctance of banks and insurance companies to lend the money that they've received from the central bank. As a result, quantitative easing can be slow to take effect if confidence in the economy is low, and firms and individuals are reluctant to spend.' You could also mention the problem that quantitative easing can lead to demand-pull inflation that's difficult to control.

Page 117 — Supply-side Policies

1 *Maximum of 25 marks available. HINTS:*
- *For this question you'll need to look at the advantages and disadvantages of supply-side policies, and also think about what role demand-side policies should play in an economy. You could start by briefly describing the role of demand-side and supply-side policies, e.g. 'Demand-side policies are most useful for managing an economy in the short run, as they can be used to make small adjustments to its performance. Supply-side policies will increase an economy's productive capacity and improve efficiency, which will lead to long run improvements in the economy.'*
- *You could then talk about the advantages of supply-side policies, e.g. 'Successful supply-side policies are crucial to an economy's long-term growth. For example, policies that improve efficiency in the product market, such as tax breaks for firms that invest their profits back into their businesses, will help a country's firms to produce more and better products. This will improve the country's international competitiveness and its balance of payments.' You could go on to talk about other supply-side policies and their importance to a country's economy, such as those aimed at improving the efficiency of the capital and labour markets.*
- *It's important to also talk about the drawbacks of supply-side policies. For example, too much deregulation can cause unintended negative effects, such as excessive financial risk-taking.*
- *You should then discuss when demand-side policies might be more appropriate than supply-side policies, e.g. 'Demand-side policies are more appropriate for short-term management of the economy. For example, sharp rises in inflation can be tackled more effectively by using monetary policies, like raising interest rates, than with long-term supply-side approaches to improve efficiency. Demand-side policies are especially important during a recession when aggregate demand needs to be stimulated quickly in order to create economic growth and jobs. It might cause too much harm to an economy, in the short run, if a government uses supply-side policies to tackle the effects of a recession.'*
- *To develop this further you could consider how supply-side policies and demand-side policies could be used together for the benefit of an economy, e.g. 'Supply-side policies will create more supply in an economy, but to bring the maximum benefits to an economy, demand will also need to be stimulated to match that supply. For example, if supply-side policies were introduced to make the labour market more efficient, then this might lead to lower real wages for workers, unless aggregate demand was also increased (e.g. by providing tax breaks for firms that employ more workers).'*
- *Make sure you conclude your answer with a judgement that sums up your arguments, e.g. 'Supply-side policies are very important for a country's economy and a government should try to increase aggregate supply in order to help it achieve its macroeconomic objectives. However, demand-side policies shouldn't be ignored as they're useful for managing an economy, e.g. controlling inflation, and are an important tool during a recession. In addition, for supply-side policies to be more successful they need to be combined with demand-side policies to create demand for the new supply that's produced.'*
- *You'll get marks for any relevant diagrams you include — as long as they're correctly drawn and explained.*

Section Eight — The Global Economy

Page 119 — Globalisation

1 *Maximum of 6 marks available. HINTS:*
- *Give a definition of a multinational corporation (MNC) — e.g. 'A multinational corporation (MNC) is a firm which functions in at least one other country aside from its country of origin.'*
- *Explain what factors might encourage investment from MNCs in developing countries and why — e.g. 'MNCs look for ways to increase profits and lower costs. The availability of cheaper labour in a developing country, such as India, may encourage an MNC to set up a factory there.' You should go on to discuss at least one other factor that might encourage investment from MNCs, such as the availability of raw materials, or the existence of good transport links in the developing country.*

Page 121 — Costs and Benefits of Globalisation

1 *Maximum of 15 marks available. HINTS:*
- *Start by defining globalisation — e.g. 'Globalisation is the increasing integration of economies internationally.'*
- *Discuss the advantages of globalisation for developing economies — make sure you assess the relative importance of each point you make, e.g. 'Globalisation can lead to the creation of jobs in developing countries — for example, MNCs may build factories in a developing country and employ local workers, which will reduce unemployment. This is important for developing countries for a number of reasons — for example, if more people are employed, more people will be earning a wage, and demand for domestic products might increase because people have more money to spend. This will create economic growth in that country.'*
- *Discuss the disadvantages of globalisation for developing economies — again, you'll need to assess the relative importance of each of your points, e.g. 'Skilled workers often end up leaving developing countries to work in more developed countries. This can massively limit economic growth in those developing countries because they're losing their brightest and most productive workers.'*
- *Give a conclusion at the end of your answer, summing up whether or not you think that the advantages of globalisation are likely to outweigh the disadvantages.*

Page 125 — Trade

1 *Maximum of 6 marks available. HINTS:*
- *You could start by defining international trade, e.g. 'International trade is the exchange of goods and services between countries.'*
- *The question asks for two benefits — make sure you explain both of them, e.g. 'International trade allows developing countries to import goods they don't have the technology to produce themselves. This raises the standard of living in those developing countries.'*

Page 126 — Patterns of Trade

1 *Maximum of 8 marks available. HINTS:*
- *You should start by explaining that the growth of China and India's economies has led to them producing more and cheaper products — including high-tech goods. You can go on to say that both countries are becoming more important trading partners of the UK.*
- *Give some examples of how the growth of China and India may affect the UK, e.g. 'UK exports, especially of manufactured goods, have declined and will continue to decline because of competition from newly industrialised economies like China. This will mean that there'll be fewer and fewer manufacturing jobs in the UK.'*
- *Try to balance the points that you make, e.g. 'The UK may be able to increase exports of services to India and China as their economies grow, which will improve the UK's balance of payments. However, less than 5% of UK exports go to each country, so this may mean the UK's balance of payments won't improve greatly — at least in the short run.'*

Page 129 — Free Trade, Protectionism and the WTO

1 *Maximum of 10 marks available. HINTS:*
- *Give a definition of protectionist policies — e.g. 'Protectionist policies are trade barriers imposed by governments to protect domestic industries from the disadvantages of free trade.'*
- *Explain why governments might want or need to protect infant industries — for example, when infant industries are just starting out, they might find it hard to compete internationally, so their government may choose to protect them until they are big enough to compete.*

Answers

- *Briefly describe at least two protectionist policies a government might use to protect infant industries, such as tariffs on imports, quotas, reducing the value of its currency, and subsidies. Make sure you explain how each of your examples could be used to protect infant industries, and not just domestic industries in general, e.g. 'To protect an infant industry, a government could impose a tariff on some specific foreign imports. This would make the products produced by the infant industry more competitive domestically, and give it time to become big enough to compete internationally without the help of tariffs.'*

2 *Maximum of 2 marks available. HINTS:*
- *E.g. 'A customs union is a group of countries who have removed all barriers to trade between themselves, and impose standard tariffs on non-member countries.'*

Page 131 — The Balance of Payments

1 *Maximum of 15 marks available. HINTS:*
- *You should start by explaining the possible negative effects of a rise in the value of the Chinese renminbi, e.g. 'A significant rise in the value of the Chinese renminbi is likely to cause a very large increase in the US's current account deficit on its balance of payments, at least in the short term, because it imports a lot of goods from China.' You could go on to mention how a rise in the value of the renminbi may also cause prices to rise in the US because it imports a lot of goods from China.*
- *You should then explain how the rise in the value of the Chinese renminbi might have a positive effect. For example, if demand was price elastic, then US consumers might stop buying so many Chinese imports and they may switch to buying domestic products. This would improve the US's current account deficit.*
- *Conclude your answer by stating what you think is most likely to happen — e.g. 'A rise in the value of the Chinese renminbi may not benefit the US balance of payments current account deficit if domestic products aren't suitable substitutes for Chinese imports or if domestic products are still more expensive than imports from China. Both of these factors would mean that the US current account deficit would worsen.'*

Page 134 — Exchange Rates

1 *Maximum of 4 marks available. HINTS:*
- *Describe the likely effect on demand for a currency of a country hosting a major sporting event — e.g. 'A major sporting event, such as the Olympics, can attract tens, or even hundreds, of thousands of visitors to a country. These visitors will require the domestic currency, e.g. to pay for tickets, hotels and transport, so demand for the currency will increase.'*
- *Explain what effect this will have on the exchange rate — e.g. 'An increase in demand for a currency will cause its value to rise.' You can use a diagram like the one below to show how the value of the currency (e.g. the pound) rises as demand increases — make sure you refer to your diagram in your answer.*

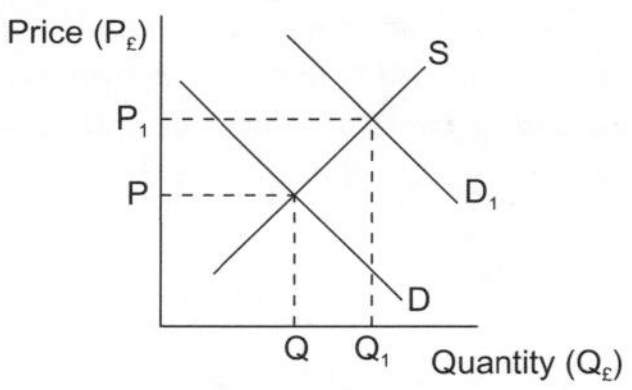

Page 135 — Economic Integration

1 *Maximum of 10 marks available. HINTS:*
- *Start by defining economic integration, e.g. 'Economic integration is the process by which the economies of different countries become more closely linked, e.g. through free trade agreements and the harmonisation of economic policies.'*
- *You can then discuss the possible benefits of economic integration, e.g. 'The removal of tariffs within a trading bloc can lead to trade creation — consumers might switch from high-cost domestic products to lower-cost products from a trading partner.' Give any further benefits this may bring, such as greater efficiency as a result of increased competition.*
- *You'll need to include the possible costs of economic integration too — for example, you could discuss trade diversion and its possible consequences, e.g. 'Economic integration can lead to trade diversion — trade barriers divert trade away from cheaper, more efficient non-members and prevent them from fully exploiting their comparative advantage.'*
- *Explain why the overall impact of economic integration depends on the specific countries who are involved, e.g. 'The impact of economic integration can vary between trading blocs and between countries — for example, trade may lower prices in one country in a trading bloc if it enables them to buy from another cheaper member. However, for another country in that bloc, it may raise prices by diverting trade away from a cheaper non-member.'*

Page 137 — The European Union

1 *Maximum of 15 marks available. HINTS:*
- *You need to discuss the possible benefits to the UK of joining the Eurozone, assessing how important each of these benefits is likely to be, e.g. 'FDI into the Eurozone may increase because the market will become bigger if the UK joins — so the UK could see an increase in FDI. However, as the UK already receives high levels of FDI, this might not be a strong reason to encourage the UK to join the Eurozone.' Make sure you mention at least one other benefit of the UK joining the Eurozone, such as increased economies of scale or the reduction in the cost of converting currencies during trade due to the UK having the same currency as many of its main trading partners.*
- *Discuss the potential costs to the UK, and their likely importance. For example, the UK would lose control over its own monetary policy and it may experience restraints on its economic growth if it had to meet Eurozone inflation targets.*
- *Conclude your answer by stating whether, given your arguments and their relative importance, joining the Eurozone is more likely to be beneficial or harmful to the UK, e.g. 'Joining the Eurozone is likely to be more beneficial than harmful to the UK. The potential benefits of the Eurozone and a single currency, such as increased FDI and economies of scale, and reduced costs of trade, are likely to outweigh the potential costs, such as possible restraints on growth and the loss of control over monetary policy.'*

Page 139 — Measuring a Country's Competitiveness

1 *Maximum of 20 marks available. HINTS:*
- *Discuss at least three factors which could have contributed to the UK's rise in competitiveness. For each point, you should evaluate its likely significance, and whether it's a short or long run effect, e.g. 'A fall in the UK's real exchange rate, i.e. a fall in the value of the pound, could lead to increased competitiveness of UK goods. If the relative export prices of UK goods compared to other countries' goods fall, then demand for exports from the UK is likely to increase. However, this is only likely to be a short run effect, because an increase in demand for UK exports will cause an increase in demand for the pound, so its value will rise.'*
- *Other factors you could discuss include a fall in the rate of inflation in the UK compared to other countries, an improvement in non-price factors of exports, such as reliability, an increase in the UK's relative productivity, e.g. due to improvements in training, and research and development.*
- *You could conclude your answer by saying which factor you think is the most significant and why.*

Page 141 — Policies to Improve Competitiveness

1 *Maximum of 20 marks available. HINTS:*
- *Explain that a government can use supply-side policies to improve its country's overall competitiveness. Give at least three examples of supply-side policies a government could use and explain how they can help to improve competitiveness. Make sure you evaluate the points that you make, e.g. 'A government could improve the productiveness of workers by improving education in the country or providing apprenticeships to help people to learn practical skills and get qualifications. However, policies like this take a long time to have an effect and aren't appropriate if competitiveness needs to be improved in the short run.'*
- *Other approaches you could discuss include improving labour market flexibility, improving infrastructure, privatisation, deregulation and maintaining macroeconomic stability.*
- *You could conclude your answer by saying which approach you think is the most effective and why, e.g. 'Improvements in education are crucial to improve a country's competitiveness. If a country's workforce has greater skills then it's likely that it'll be more productive, and that will lead to significant improvements in competitiveness.'*

Answers

Section Nine — Development and Sustainability

Page 143 — Measuring Economic Development

1 Maximum of 15 marks available. HINTS:

- *Describe two causes of inequality — for example, differences in access to education, and insufficiently progressive taxation.*
- *You need to explain why each cause leads to inequality, e.g. 'Differences in the level and type of education that people are able to receive result in individuals getting different qualifications, and having access to different opportunities. This may lead to income inequality if some people are excluded from accessing higher paying jobs.'*
- *Then describe two consequences of inequality — these can be consequences for individuals, or for the economy. For example, relative poverty within a country, and increased overseas spending limiting growth and development.*
- *Explain why these consequences come about, e.g. 'Inequality means that some people in a country will be very wealthy compared to others. These people will only need to spend a very small amount of their income on necessities, so are likely to spend larger amounts on imported goods or travel abroad. This will result in more money leaving the country's economy. This will limit growth and development because this leakage from the circular flow of income will reduce the amount of money being spent and invested.'*

Page 145 — Limits to Growth and Development

1 Maximum of 8 marks available. HINTS:

- *You could start by giving a definition of primary products, e.g. 'Primary products are products extracted from the earth, like coal or wheat.'*
- *Give at least two reasons that economic development might be limited in a country dependent on primary products. Examples include: the fact that firms can't add much value to primary products, the Prebisch-Singer effect, and the uncertainty of income from agricultural products because of the possibility of damage from natural disasters or extreme weather.*
- *For each reason you list, explain exactly how this may limit economic development, e.g. 'Because the value that firms can add to primary products is very low, firms selling these products won't generate large profits. This means there is likely to be little investment in a country which is dependent on primary products, and this will limit economic development.'*

Page 147 — Ways of Promoting Growth and Development

1 Maximum of 12 marks available. HINTS:

- *Explain how expanding the industrial sector can help an economy develop, e.g. 'The Lewis model argues that there is excess labour in the agricultural sector, so productivity can increase by moving agricultural workers to industry, without wages rising. This means inflation is avoided. The increased profit from the higher output of industry can be invested in equipment which will increase productivity further. Therefore everyone will be better off as savings, investment, and growth all increase.'*
- *To balance this you also need to evaluate whether this approach is likely to be effective in practice — give some downsides to the approach, e.g. 'However, profits from industry may be invested abroad, especially when firms have foreign owners, so industrialisation may not contribute as much to the economy as the Lewis model suggests.'*
- *Now do the same for the tourism sector — first explain how it should contribute to economic development, e.g. 'Expanding the tourism industry should bring in foreign currency from tourists, and foreign investment from firms catering to tourists. As well as increasing investment, employment should increase as jobs are created in the industry.'*
- *To fully evaluate this approach, counter your explanation of the benefits of developing tourism with some reasons why this might not be successful, e.g. 'However, employment in the tourist industry is often seasonal, and jobs may not be secure as demand for holidays is income elastic, so the industry could be badly affected by an economic downturn.'*
- *Finally, come to a conclusion, commenting on the relative significance of the points you've made, e.g. 'Expansion of these sectors should create economic growth, by increasing output and productivity. However, this growth may not contribute significantly to development if it doesn't provide quality local jobs. If firms bring in foreign workers or develop industries which don't require much labour, then there may not be much of a positive effect on development, because the benefits of growth will not be spread very widely.'*

Page 149 — Ways of Promoting Growth and Development

1 Maximum of 12 marks available. HINTS:

- *First explain what fair trade schemes are and how they work, e.g. 'Fair trade schemes involve offering farmers in developing countries who are members of the scheme a guaranteed minimum price for their goods. In order to be part of a scheme farmers are required to meet certain conditions, such as agreed farming practices and fair treatment of employees.'*
- *Then give a few ways in which these schemes might help promote growth and development, for example by raising wages for agricultural workers, by reducing environmental damage by changing farming methods, or by encouraging farmers to invest in capital by giving them more income security.*
- *Explain exactly how each factor could contribute to growth and development, e.g. 'Farmers in fair trade schemes don't have to deal with large fluctuations in the price they can get for their product, so they're much more able to plan for the long term than they otherwise would be. This means they're more likely to invest in equipment or staff training, which will contribute to development, and may lead to more growth in the future as productivity is likely to increase.'*
- *Then offer some drawbacks of fair trade schemes to balance your answer, e.g. 'Fair trade schemes distort the market price of the products that farmers produce. This means that farmers in these schemes won't react to the signal that low prices give to limit production. So when prices are low there may be overproduction, which will flood the market with goods, driving the price even lower. This will be detrimental to farmers who aren't part of the fair trade scheme, because they have to accept the market price for their goods.'*

Page 151 — Sustainable Development

1 Maximum of 15 marks available. HINTS:

- *Start by explaining how the ISEW works, e.g. 'The ISEW (Index of Sustainable Economic Welfare) is an adjusted version of GDP. Adjustments are made to try to factor in things that contribute to people's welfare but which aren't included in GDP — for example, the positive contribution of unpaid work. The negative effects of things like pollution are also taken into account. And any spending that was needed to repair damage caused by other spending (such as cleaning up a river polluted by a road-building project) is removed from the figures.'*
- *Then discuss what's useful about indicators like this. Make sure you explain exactly why each benefit comes about — don't just state how they're used. E.g. 'Indicators like the ISEW attempt to assess how sustainable economic growth is, by giving a fuller picture of economic activity than GDP. Understanding the true costs and benefits of spending can help governments to make decisions aimed at growing the economy in a way that doesn't have large social or environmental costs. Putting these kinds of costs and benefits into a standardised measure like ISEW also allows comparison of sustainable economic development between countries.'*
- *You also need to explain some of the reasons why these indicators may not be useful, e.g. 'Adjusted indicators are criticised because trying to factor in social and environmental costs and benefits involves making judgements about what to include, and how much value to give each cost or benefit. These judgements are subjective, which may mean they're not an accurate measure of the value of economic activity, and therefore aren't actually useful for decision making or international comparisons of development.'*

Glossary

abnormal profit See supernormal profit.
absolute advantage A country will have an absolute advantage when its output of a product is greater per unit of resource used than any other country.
absolute poverty This is when someone doesn't have the income or wealth to meet their basic needs, such as food, shelter and water.
accelerator process This is where any change in demand for goods/services beyond current capacity will lead to a greater percentage increase in the demand for the capital goods that firms need to produce those goods/services.
active leisure Leisure activities that involve mental or physical effort. (As opposed to passive leisure.)
actual economic growth A measure of economic growth which is adjusted for inflation.
aggregate demand The total demand, or total spending, in an economy at a given price level over a given period of time. It's made up of consumption, investment, government spending and net exports.
Aggregate Demand = C + I + G + (X – M)
aggregate supply The total amount of goods and services which can be supplied in an economy at a given price level over a given period of time.
allocative efficiency This is when the price of a good is equal to the price that consumers are happy to pay for it. This will happen when all resources are allocated efficiently.
asymmetric information This is when buyers have more information than sellers (or the opposite) in a market.
automatic stabilisers These are parts of fiscal policies that will automatically react to changes in the economic cycle. For example, during a recession, government spending is likely to increase because the government will automatically pay out more unemployment benefits, which may reduce the problems the recession causes.
average cost The cost of production per unit of output — i.e. a firm's total cost for a given period of time, divided by the quantity produced.
average revenue The revenue per unit sold — i.e. a firm's total revenue for a given period of time, divided by the quantity sold.
backward vertical integration See vertical integration.
balance of payments A record of a country's international transactions, i.e. flows of money into and out of a country.
bank rate The official rate of interest set by the Monetary Policy Committee of the Bank of England.
barriers to entry Barriers to entry are any potential difficulties that make it hard for a firm to enter a market.
barriers to exit Barriers to exit are any potential difficulties that make it hard for a firm to leave a market.
budget deficit When government spending is greater than its revenue.
budget surplus When government spending is less than its revenue.
capital account on the balance of payments A part of the record of a country's international flows of money. This includes transfers of non-monetary and fixed assets, such as through emigration and immigration.
cartel A group of producers that agree to limit production in order to keep the price of goods or services high.
circular flow of income The flow of national output, income and expenditure between households and firms.
national output = national income = national expenditure
comparative advantage A country has a comparative advantage if the opportunity cost of it producing a good is lower than the opportunity cost for other countries.
competition policy Government policy aimed at reducing monopoly power in order to increase efficiency and ensure fairness for consumers.
concentration ratio This shows how dominant firms are in a market, e.g. if three firms in a market have 90% market share then the three-firm concentration ratio is 90%.
conglomerate integration Mergers or takeovers between firms which operate in completely different markets.
constant returns to scale See returns to scale.
consumer surplus When a consumer pays less for a good than they were prepared to, this difference is the consumer surplus.
contestability A market is contestable if it's easy for new firms to enter the market, i.e. if barriers to entry are low.
cost benefit analysis (CBA) This involves adding up the total private and external costs and benefits of a major project in order to decide if the project should go ahead.
cost-push inflation Inflation caused by the rising cost of inputs to production.
cross elasticity of demand (XED) This is a measure of how the quantity demanded of one good/service responds to a change in the price of another good/service.
cross-subsidy (transport) Using profit from profitable routes or services to subsidise unprofitable routes or services.
current account on the balance of payments A part of the record of a country's international flows of money. It consists of: trade in goods, trade in services, international flows of income (salaries, interest, profit and dividends), and transfers.
cyclical unemployment Unemployment caused by a shortage of demand in an economy, e.g. when there's a slump.
decreasing returns to scale See returns to scale.
demand-pull inflation Inflation caused by excessive growth in aggregate demand compared to aggregate supply.
demand-side policy Government policy that aims to increase aggregate demand in an economy. For example, a policy to increase consumer spending in an economy.
demerger A firm selling off part(s) of its business to create a separate firm, or firms.
demerit good A good or service which has greater social costs when it's consumed than private costs. Demerit goods tend to be overconsumed.
deregulation Removing rules imposed by a government that can restrict the level of competition in a market.
derived demand The demand for a good or factor of production due to its use in making another good or providing a service.
diminishing returns See law of diminishing returns.
diseconomies of scale A firm is experiencing diseconomies of scale when the average cost of production is rising as output rises.
divorce of ownership from control This occurs when a firm's owners are no longer in control of the day-to-day running of the firm (e.g. because it's run by directors). Also known as the principal-agent problem.
duopoly An oligopolistic market dominated by two firms.
dynamic efficiency This is about firms improving efficiency in the long term by carrying out research and development into new or improved products, or investing in new technology and training to improve the production process.
economic cycle The economic cycle (also known as the business or trade cycle) is the fluctuations in actual growth over a period of time (several years or decades).

Glossary

economic growth An increase in an economy's productive potential. Usually measured as the rate of change of the gross domestic product (GDP), or the GDP per capita.
economic integration The process by which the economies of different countries become more closely linked, e.g. through free trade agreements.
economic rent The excess a worker is paid above the minimum required to keep them in their current occupation (this minimum payment is their transfer earnings).
economies of scale A firm is experiencing economies of scale when the average cost of production is falling as output rises.
equilibrium A market for a product is in equilibrium when the quantity supplied is equal to the quantity demanded.
equity This means fairness.
exchange rate The price at which one currency buys another.
extending property rights When property rights over a resource are given to an individual or firm. This gives them control over the usage of that resource.
external growth A firm growing through mergers/takeovers.
externalities The external costs or benefits to a third party that is not involved in the making, buying/selling and consumption of a specific good/service.
factors of production These are the four inputs needed to make the things that people want. They are: land, labour, capital and enterprise.
financial account on the balance of payments A part of the record of a country's international flows of money. This involves the movement of financial assets (e.g. through foreign direct investment).
fiscal policy Government policy that determines the levels of government spending and taxation. Often used to increase or decrease aggregate demand in an economy.
Fisher's equation of exchange See quantity theory of money.
fixed costs Costs that don't vary with the level of output of a firm in the short run.
foreign direct investment (FDI) This is when a firm based in one country makes an investment in a different country.
forward vertical integration See vertical integration.
franchise (rail) An agreement where the government allows a train operating company to run a certain set of passenger rail services, under a set of agreed conditions.
free market A market where there is no government intervention. Competition between different suppliers affects supply and demand, and as a result determines prices.
free rider problem This means that once a public good is provided it's impossible to stop someone from benefiting from it, even if they haven't paid towards it.
free trade International trade without any restrictions from things such as trade barriers.
frictional unemployment The unemployment experienced by workers between leaving one job and starting another.
globalisation The increasing integration of economies internationally, which is making the world more like a single economy.
government failure This occurs when government intervention into a market causes a misallocation of resources.
gross domestic product (GDP) The total value of all the goods and services produced in a country in a year.
hit and run tactics This is when firms enter a market while supernormal profits can be made and then leave the market once prices have been driven down to normal-profit levels.
horizontal equity This means that people in identical circumstances are treated fairly (i.e. equally).
horizontal integration Mergers or takeovers between firms that are at the same stage of the production process of similar products.
'hot money' Money that's moved to take advantage of high interest rates in a country. It's likely to be a short-term movement of money.
Human Development Index (HDI) A measure of a country's economic development, used by the UN, that combines measures of health (life expectancy), education (average and expected years in school), and the standard of living (real GNI per capita).
imperfect information A situation where buyers and/or sellers don't have full knowledge regarding price, costs, benefits and availability of a good or service.
income elasticity of demand (YED) This is a measure of how the demand for a good/service responds to a change in real income.
increasing returns to scale See returns to scale.
inflation The sustained rise in the average price of goods and services over a period of time.
infrastructure The basic facilities and services needed for a country and its economy to function.
inorganic growth See external growth.
integrated transport policy Policy that considers the transport network as a whole rather than just focusing on a single transport mode or project. (This includes policy to create an integrated transport system.)
integrated transport system A transport network where freight and passengers can easily move from one mode of transport to another.
interest The money paid to the lender by someone who borrows capital. This will often be a fixed percentage rate — known as an interest rate.
internal growth A firm growing as a result of increasing the levels of the factors of production it uses, rather than through mergers or takeovers.
labour immobility This occurs when labour can't easily move around to find jobs (geographical immobility) or easily switch between different occupations (occupational immobility).
law of diminishing returns The idea that if a firm increases one variable factor of production while other factors stay fixed, then the marginal returns the firm gets from the variable factor will always eventually begin to decrease.
leisure The time that people have left to spend how they like, after work, chores and travel are done.
long run A time period in which all the factors of production are variable, so a firm can expand its capacity.
long run aggregate supply (LRAS) In the long run it is assumed that, because factors and costs of production can change, an economy will run at full capacity — so LRAS is the productive potential of an economy.
long run Phillips curve See Phillips curve (long run).
marginal cost The cost to a firm of producing the final unit of output.
marginal product The extra output that's produced when a firm adds one more unit of one of the factors of production they're using.
marginal propensity to consume The proportion of an increase in income that people will spend (and not save).
marginal returns See marginal product.
marginal revenue The extra revenue received as a result of selling one more unit of output.

Glossary

market failure This is where the price mechanism fails to allocate resources efficiently.
merger Two firms uniting to form a new company.
merit good A good or service which provides greater social benefits when it's consumed than private benefits. Merit goods tend to be underconsumed.
minimum efficient scale of production (MES) The lowest level of output at which a firm can achieve the lowest possible average cost of production.
mode of transport A means of moving passengers or freight, for example train, motorbike or container ship.
monetary policy Government policy that involves controlling the total amount of 'money' in an economy (the money supply), and how expensive it is to borrow that money. It involves manipulating interest rates, exchange rates and restrictions on the supply of money.
monopoly A pure monopoly is a market with only one supplier. Some markets will be referred to as a monopoly if there's more than one supplier, but one supplier dominates the market.
monopoly power The ability of a firm to be a 'price maker' and influence the price of a particular good in a market.
monopsony A market with a single buyer.
multinational corporations (MNCs) Firms which function in at least one other country, aside from their country of origin.
multiplier effect The process by which an injection into the circular flow of income creates a change in the size of national income that's greater than the injection's size.
National Minimum Wage (NMW) A legal minimum hourly rate of pay, set for different age groups. There's a national minimum wage in the UK.
nationalised industry An industry owned by the government.
natural monopoly An industry where economies of scale are so great that the lowest long run average cost can only be achieved if the market is made up of a single provider.
natural rate of unemployment (NRU) The rate of unemployment when the labour market is in equilibrium (i.e. when labour demand is equal to labour supply).
non-pure public good See quasi-public good.
normal profit A firm is making normal profit when its total revenue is equal to its total costs.
oligopoly A market dominated by a few large firms that offer differentiated products, with high barriers to entry. The firms are interdependent and may use competitive or collusive strategies.
open skies agreement An agreement between governments that allows airlines to fly between (and sometimes within) the countries involved, with few restrictions.
opportunity cost The benefit that's given up in order to do something else — it's the cost of the choice that's made.
organic growth See internal growth.
output gap The gap between the trend rate of economic growth and actual economic growth. Output gaps can be positive or negative.
participation rate The proportion of working age people in an economy that are either in work or actively seeking work.
passive leisure Leisure activities that don't involve much mental or physical effort. (As opposed to active leisure.)
perfect information This is when buyers and sellers have full knowledge of prices, costs, benefits and availability of products.
Phillips curve (long run) A curve that shows the relationship between inflation and unemployment in the long run — it's always a vertical line positioned at the natural rate of unemployment (NRU).
Phillips curve (short run) A curve that shows the relationship between inflation and unemployment in the short run — as the level of one falls, the level of the other rises.
predatory pricing An aggressive pricing tactic which involves incumbent firms in a market lowering their prices to a level that a new entrant to the market can't match, in order to force them out of the market.
price cap A limit on price rises that makes a market fairer to consumers. A price cap also provides an incentive for firms to increase efficiency. Two common price caps are: RPI – X, and RPI – X + K.
price discrimination This occurs when a seller charges different prices to different customers for exactly the same product.
price elasticity of demand (PED) This is a measure of how the quantity demanded of a good/service responds to a change in its price.
price elasticity of supply (PES) This is a measure of how the quantity supplied of a good/service responds to a change in its price.
price maker A firm that has some power to control the price it sells at.
price mechanism This is when changes in the demand or supply of a good/service lead to changes in its price and the quantity bought/sold.
price taker A firm that has no power to control the price it sells at — it has to accept the market price.
price war A situation where one firm in a market lowers their prices, and other firms follow suit, possibly triggering a series of price cuts as firms try to undercut one another.
principal-agent problem See divorce of ownership from control.
private finance initiatives (PFIs) These are schemes where a private firm provides public infrastructure, which the government then pays for by leasing it from that firm for a long period of time.
privatisation When a firm or a whole industry changes from being run by the public sector to the private sector.
producer surplus When a producer receives more for a good than they were prepared to accept, this difference is the producer surplus.
production possibility frontier (PPF) A curve which shows the maximum possible outputs of two goods or services using a fixed amount of inputs.
productive efficiency This occurs when products are produced at a level of output where the average cost is lowest.
productivity The average output produced per unit of a factor of production — for example, labour productivity would be the average output per worker (or per worker-hour).
profit A firm's total revenue minus its total costs.
progressive taxation A tax system where an individual's tax rises (as a percentage of their income) as their income rises.
proportional taxation A tax system where everyone pays the same proportion of tax regardless of their income level.
protectionism When a government uses policies to control the level of international trade and protect its own economy, industries and firms.
public good A good which people can't be stopped from consuming, even if they've not paid for it, and the consumption of which doesn't prevent others from benefiting from it (e.g. national defence).
purchasing power parity (PPP) An adjustment of an exchange rate to reflect the real purchasing power of the two currencies.

Glossary

quantitative easing (QE) This involves a central bank (e.g. the Bank of England) 'creating new money' and using it to buy assets owned by financial institutions and other firms. It increases the money supply, which will enable individuals and firms to spend more, or lend it to other people to spend.

quantity theory of money This theory is based on the idea that changes in the money supply will cause changes to the price level. It uses the formula: MV = PT, which is known as Fisher's equation of exchange.

quasi-public good A good which appears to have the characteristics of a public good, but doesn't exhibit them fully.

real income A measure of the amount of goods/services that a consumer can afford to purchase with their income, adjusted for inflation.

real wage unemployment Unemployment caused by real wages being pushed above the equilibrium level of employment. It can be caused by trade unions negotiating for higher wages, or the introduction of a national minimum wage.

recession This occurs when there's negative economic growth for at least two consecutive quarters. Typically there's falling demand, low levels of investment and rising unemployment during a recession.

regressive taxation A tax system where an individual's tax falls (as a percentage of their income) as their income rises.

relative poverty This is when someone has a low income relative to other incomes in their country.

returns to scale How much a firm's output changes as they increase input (i.e. increase all factors of production). Returns to scale are increasing if output increases more than proportionally with input, constant if output increases proportionally with input, and decreasing if output increases less than proportionally with input.

revenue The total value of sales within a time period. It can be calculated using the formula: price per unit × quantity sold.

satisficing Running a firm in a way that does just enough to satisfy important stakeholders in the firm, rather than trying to maximise something (e.g. profit or revenue).

shadow price A price given to something (e.g. an accident) that has no market price (estimated using the opportunity cost).

short run A time period in which at least one of a firm's factors of production is fixed.

short run aggregate supply (SRAS) This is aggregate supply when the factors of production are fixed.

short run Phillips curve See Phillips curve (short run).

static efficiency This occurs when allocative and productive efficiency are both achieved at a particular time.

structural unemployment Unemployment (usually) caused by the decline of a major industry, which is made worse by labour immobility (geographical or occupational).

subsidy An amount of money paid by a government to the producer of a good/service to lower the price and increase demand for the good/service.

sunk cost This is an unrecoverable cost of entering a market, e.g. advertising. It can act as a barrier to exit.

supernormal profit A firm is making supernormal profit when its total revenue exceeds its total costs.

supply-side policy Government policy that aims to increase aggregate supply in an economy. For example, a policy to increase the productive capacity of the economy.

sustainability This is about meeting the needs of people now, without making it more difficult for people in the future to meet their own needs.

takeover One firm buying another firm, which then becomes part of the first firm.

tariff A form of tax placed on certain imports to make them more expensive and discourage their consumption.

tax An amount of money paid to a government. It's paid directly, e.g. income tax, or indirectly, e.g. excise duty.

terms of trade A measure of the relative price of a country's exports compared to its imports.

total cost All the costs for a firm involved in producing a particular amount of output.

total revenue The total amount of money a firm receives from its sales, in a particular time period.

trade creation The removal of trade barriers within a trading bloc, allowing members to buy from the cheapest source.

trade diversion When trade barriers are imposed on non-members of a trading bloc, so trade is diverted away from any cheaper non-members.

trade liberalisation The reduction or removal of tariffs and other restrictions on international trade (i.e. reducing protectionism).

trade union An organisation of workers that acts to represent their interests, e.g. to improve their pay.

trading blocs These are associations between the governments of different countries that promote and manage trade between those countries.

transfer earnings The minimum pay that will stop a worker from switching to their next best paid occupation.

transport infrastructure Structures that need to be in place for transport to operate, for example roads and railways.

transport mode See mode of transport.

unemployment The level of unemployment is the number of people who are looking for a job but cannot find one. The rate of unemployment is the number of people out of work (but looking for a job) as a percentage of the labour force.

variable costs Costs that vary with the level of output of a firm.

vertical equity This means people with different circumstances are treated differently, but fairly.

vertical integration Mergers or takeovers between firms at different stages of the production process of the same product. If a firm takes over another firm that's further forward in the production process it's forward vertical integration, and if a firm takes over another firm that's further back in the production process it's backward vertical integration.

wage differentials The differences that exist in wages between different groups of workers, or between workers in the same occupation.

wage rate The price of labour, i.e. the rate of pay to employ a worker.

World Trade Organisation (WTO) The WTO is an international organisation which provides a forum for its member governments to discuss trade agreements and settle disputes, using a set of trade rules. It aims to help trade to be as free as possible.

x-inefficiency Inefficiency caused by unnecessary costs and waste (i.e. organisational slack).

Index

Index